Millard Merz, Jr.

F R Kent

Hamilton Owens

THE SUNPAPERS OF BALTIMORE

FROM A DAGUERREOTYPE, 1836

THE FOUNDER AND HIS PARTNERS

WILLIAM M. SWAIN *ARUNAH S. ABELL* *AZARIAH H. SIMMONS*

1837–1937

THE SUNPAPERS OF BALTIMORE

BY
GERALD W. JOHNSON
FRANK R. KENT
H. L. MENCKEN
HAMILTON OWENS

Alfred A. Knopf : New York
MCMXXXVII

FIRST EDITION

Manufactured in the United States of America

TO THE MEMORY OF

ALL OLD SUN MEN

PREFACE

Of the four authors whose names appear upon the title page of this volume, Mr. Johnson wrote the first six chapters, bringing the narrative down to the death of A. S. Abell, the Founder; Mr. Kent wrote Chapters VII to X, inclusive, dealing with The Sun's political battles in the 80s and 90s of the last century; Mr. Mencken wrote Chapters XI to XVIII, inclusive, and Mr. Owens wrote the section beginning with Chapter XIX and running to the end. But there was much overlapping, and each part owes something to the other authors. Thus Mr. Johnson, Mr. Kent and Mr. Mencken made numerous exchanges of material, and the last-named, who served as general editor, supplied a part of that used by Mr. Owens. Many other members of the staffs of the *Sunpapers* had important hands in the book, notably Mr. James W. Dove, who has, for his own amusement, kept a record of salient events in office history for many years; Mr. Edgar Ellis, librarian of the *Sunpapers;* Mr. J. Fred Essary, chief of the Washington bureau of The Sun, and Mr. Harold E. West, who, though he is no longer on the staff, is still ardently interested in the history of the paper with which he was so long connected. Mr. Ellis and his assistants were indefatigable in their researches, and are largely responsible for whatever historical accuracy the story shows. Valuable aid was also received from Dr. L. H. Dielman and his staff at the Peabody Library, Baltimore; from the staff of the Enoch Pratt Free Library, Baltimore (especially the staff of the Department of Economics); from Dr. R. D. W. Connor, archivist of the United States; from the staff of the Library of Congress, and from Dr. E. K. Marshall and Dr. Sanford V. Larkey, of the Johns Hopkins University. Others whose friendly help is hereby acknowledged with gratitude are Mrs. James Dudley Morgan, a granddaughter of the Founder; Mrs. Edward A. Robinson, Miss Gertrude Knipp, and Messrs. Walter W. and Charles S. Abell, Edwin G. Baetjer, David Rankin Barbee, McKee Barclay, Maurice Bendann, Harry C. Black, E. H. Bouton, Hervey Brackbill, George W. Combs, George C. Cutler, James C. Fenhagen, William L. Fitzell, E. Paul Flaherty, Fabian Franklin, Louis Fries, John W. and Robert Garrett, Frank Gould, Charles Morris Howard, Charles McHenry Howard, Joseph Katz, E. P. Kavanaugh, Joel Lewis of *Printer's Ink*, William E. Moore, Edwin F. A. Morgan, J. Edwin Murphy, Sidney L. Nyburg, Stuart Olivier, John W. Owens, Paul Patterson, Walter A. Poole, Blanchard Randall, C. M. Purdy, Lawrason Riggs, William F. Schmick, Karl A. M. Scholtz, John E. Semmes, Richard D. Steuart, Neil H. Swanson, Raymond S. Tompkins and Mark S. Watson. Thanks are due, too, to the gentlemen of the *Sunpapers'* composing room, who set and reset this history many times in its early stages, and especially to the proofreaders, whose professional skill and alertness purged the first drafts of numerous errors.

The title of the volume will seem natural (and indeed inevitable) to every Marylander, but other readers may wonder why *Sunpaper* appears in it instead of SUN. *Sunpaper* is used simply because THE SUN has been the *Sunpaper* in Maryland for many, many years. How the form originated no one knows, but it goes back to the earliest days of the paper, and it is cherished today as a trade mark hallowed by a long tradition, and mirroring a flattering popular pride and affection.

TABLE OF CONTENTS

LIST OF ILLUSTRATIONS

PLATES

THE SUNPAPERS OF BALTIMORE

CHAPTER I

THE BEGINNINGS OF THE SUNPAPER

ARUNAH SHEPHERDSON ABELL published the first issue of THE SUN in Baltimore on the morning of May 17, 1837.

Baltimore was not impressed. The town of 90,000 people had already six daily newspapers, and since the turn of the century at least a dozen others had been established, lived feebly and briefly, and died. In the first half of the Nineteenth Century tradition held that all the equipment needed to establish a newspaper was "a Washington hand-press and a shirt-tail full of type." Papers were set up as prodigally as filling-stations and grocery-stores were in the first decades of the Twentieth Century; and their establishment and subsequent collapse had as little effect on the life of the community.

So the new establishment at 21 Light street, "two doors from Mercer street," received no great attention from the citizens. Yet in the very first issue of this little four-page sheet, printed in what would now be called tabloid form, was evidence of the quality which was to leave THE SUN, after a hundred years, the sole survivor of the Baltimore daily newspapers of 1837 and an institution known, whether favorably or unfavorably, to every inhabitant of a city ten times the size of the one in which it began. This evidence was very slight, and probably made no impression even on newspaper men of that distant day; but viewed in the perspective of history it takes on immense significance.

It is simply the fact that the right-hand column of the front page on that day was occupied by an account of the previous day's meeting of the City Council, at which it had been determined to issue $100,000 in scrip to serve the town as fractional currency in the absence of real coin. In itself, the item is of no great importance. But turn, now, to the issue of the same date of the paper that was to Baltimore in 1837 what the *Times* is to modern New York, the newspaper Bible of the business community. This paper bore the formidable title of the *American and Commercial Daily Advertiser;* it was a journal of impeccable respectability and high antiquity, having lasted for thirty-eight years, and it specialized in news that would appeal to the commercial and other business interests.[1] The longest single item in its issue of May 17, 1837, was a letter, occupying nineteen inches of space, written by Nicholas Biddle in defense of the Bank of the United States. The paper carried not a line about the meeting of the City Council.

The attitude toward news exemplified by this incident unques-

[1] The *American* was first published on May 14, 1799. In later years efforts were made to connect it with the *Maryland Journal and Baltimore Advertiser,* which went back to August 20, 1773, but J. Thomas Scharf says in his History of Baltimore City and County; Baltimore, 1881, that the *Journal* suspended publication from December 4, 1796, to January 2, 1797, again from February, 1797, to March 21, 1797, and "finally expired" on June 30, 1797, nearly two years before the first issue of the *American* appeared. The *American* survived until March 31, 1928, when its week-day issue was suspended. Its Sunday issue is still published in connection with the Baltimore *News-Post.*

tionably accounts for the fact that Mr. Abell succeeded brilliantly from the beginning in a field overcrowded with newspapers and none too friendly toward his ideas and beliefs. The prevailing opinion of newspaper men at the time was that the journalist was in some sense a moral and intellectual preceptor; his business was to instruct and edify his customers. If, as a matter of cold fact, he frequently filled his columns with misinformation and vituperation, nevertheless the principle remained — he was the instructor, rather than the servant of his constituency.

But a new ideal was percolating into American journalism, boldly advanced by young Ben Day and old James Gordon Bennett in New York, with the *Sun* and the *Herald* respectively; to it Abell himself had adhered with success in Philadelphia, where he had joined in establishing the *Public Ledger* a year earlier. This was the idea that the first business of a newspaper is to furnish its readers with the news in which they are interested, whether or not it conforms to the editor's prejudices.

In 1837 a letter by Nicholas Biddle unquestionably seemed important. The country was still ringing with echoes of the terrific battle over the Bank of the United States; and although the fight was actually over, and the Bank whipped, few as yet realized it. Even the enemies of the Bank were not quite sure of their victory; and this very letter stirred the wrath of Old Bullion Benton so deeply that many years later, in his great history of the time, he described it as "one of those complaçent epistles, models of quiet impudence and cool mendacity, with which Mr. Biddle was accustomed to regale the public in seasons of moneyed distress."[1] A letter that could spur the Administration leader in the United States Senate to such an explosion of fury unquestionably was a good newspaper story. Yet at that only the

[1] Thomas H. Benton: Thirty Years' View; New York, 1856, Vol. II, p. 21.

small group composing the city's commercial leaders had any really vivid interest in what happened to the Bank of the United States; while there was not a housewife in Baltimore who wasn't interested in the problem of getting enough pennies, nickels, dimes and quarters to make change for the butcher's boy. So while the *American*, with the Biddle letter, may have published the more important news, THE SUN, with its announcement of the forthcoming shinplasters, published the more interesting news.

This was the continuing policy of the paper.[1] It was frankly a commoners' sheet. It appealed to the non-intellectuals. It printed a great deal of "elegant" matter, including poems, moral essays and extracts from books, but its conspicuous difference from its rivals was its vigorous effort to inform Baltimoreans of what was going on in their own town. The rich and well-educated might be interested more in what President Van Buren was thinking, or what was going on at the Court of St. James's, than in what was happening in Gay street; but not so the masses. THE SUN sold for one cent, and so was within the means of the masses. The result — looking back on it, one is inclined to say the inevitable result, although it filled Editor Abell with delighted surprise — was that the circulation of the new paper swiftly outran that of any other Baltimore daily. Before its first birthday it was claiming 12,000 subscribers.[2]

[1] For instance, in the first issue 13% of all the reading matter consisted of local news; in the *American* of the same date there was no local news at all. Three months later, on August 17, 1837, 17% of the news in THE SUN was local, but only one-tenth of 1% of that in the *American* was local. There were days during its first year when THE SUN was a complete blank, so far as local news was concerned, but such days were rare; while it was just as rare, on the other hand, for the *American* to devote any appreciable amount of space to the subject.

[2] But that was long before anyone had thought of an Audit Bureau of Circulations, or of a sworn post-office statement, so in claiming circulation publishers were wont to give free rein to an imagination that was usually fertile and agile in the extreme. Yet Mr. Abell's claim can be

The success of the paper was not, however, due solely to the excellence of its news policy. Its field, as well as its policy, had been chosen with fine judgment. True, when Mr. Abell first appeared in the city he had been dolefully assured that Baltimore was hopelessly overcrowded.[1] So it was, as regards the sort of papers then in existence; but a man whose intention it was to report to the community its own life could hardly have had a better town made to his own order. It was, as modern cities are measured, a small town, but at that it was the second city in the country [2] and there is reason to believe that it was approaching its intellectual and moral apogee. It was vibrantly, brilliantly alive, reaching out eager hands for whatever was new and promising in commerce, industry, art, science, philosophy. Its population was turbulent and lawless, given to furious outbreaks of mob violence, but it included many of the most daring, energetic and skillful leaders in the nation. Buccaneers some of them were, astonishingly cynical land pirates quite capable of looting their own city when no other loot was available, but resolute,

---

scaled down heavily and still leave him with a circulation that was phenomenal for the time.

[1] "To the editors of these journals Mr. Abell brought letters of introduction, and he then formed the acquaintance, among others, of Messrs. Dobbin, Murphy and Bose, of the *American;* Mr. Gwynn, of the *Federal Gazette;* Mr. Harker, of the *Republican;* Mr. Poe, of the *Chronicle;* Mr. Monroe, of the *Patriot,* and Messrs. Streeter and Skinner, of the *Transcript.* It cannot be said, however, that any of these gentlemen held out much encouragement as to the success of a new paper. In fact, the times seemed singularly inauspicious for any enterprise of the kind. The year 1837 was one of unprecedented disaster and gloom in all commercial and business circles, and all classes shared the general depression." — J. Thomas Scharf: Chronicles of Baltimore; Baltimore, 1874, p. 96.

[2] Baltimore, Philadelphia and Boston were all contenders for second place, but by 1820 Baltimore had run ahead. In 1830 her population was 80,620, against 80,462 in Philadelphia, and 61,392 in Boston. The census of 1840 showed Baltimore, 102,313; Philadelphia, 93,665; Boston, 93,383. New York having attained, after the opening of the Erie Canal, the monstrous size of 200,000, entirely outclassed any other city in the country.

clever, powerful and fearing neither man nor devil. They had covered the seven seas with their clipper ships. They had driven the Baltimore & Ohio Railroad west to Harper's Ferry and the Baltimore & Susquehanna north to the Pennsylvania line. Among them were great merchants whose house flags were known in Canton and Bombay, in Lisbon and St. Petersburg; while Callao, Valparaiso, Buenos Aires and Rio they regarded as their own particular commercial satrapy.[1] Their barges went up the bay and the Susquehanna river, across Pennsylvania, to Elmira and Bath, in New York. Their wagon trains climbed across the Alleghenies and rumbled down to the banks of the Ohio, where their loads were transferred to boats that traveled over much of the Mississippi river system; or poured through the valleys of Virginia to the Kentucky border; or toiled hundreds of miles south, into Georgia.

Three great traffic lanes converged at Baltimore, disregarding the greatest of all highways, the ocean itself. One was the line of the Susquehanna Valley, penetrating what was then the greatest farming region in America, Pennsylvania and Western New York. The second was the line of the Chesapeake Bay, along which Baltimore's commerce reached the South. The third was a man-made highway which within recent years had attained an importance equal to that of either of the others, the Great National Pike which the Federal government had driven west from Cumberland, Md., to the Ohio and beyond, and over which the Conestoga wagons rumbled in an incessant stream.

At the junction of these three great ways of commerce, Baltimore had sprung up from a trifling place in 1790 to the rich, populous and important city of 1837.[2] But recently two of

---

[1] "Our ships went principally to the Spanish Main, to Buenos Ayres, to Brazil, to Chili, Peru and Mexico." —Scharf: Chronicles of Baltimore, p. 407.

[2] It remained the second city in

these lines had been cut and badly damaged, as arteries of commerce, by an interloper, the canal which New York had dug from Albany to Lake Erie. Clinton's Ditch was a deadly menace to Baltimore, Philadelphia and Boston alike, and all three were desperately casting about to find means of averting the danger. It was Baltimore that took the most radical and spectacular step. After having found that the Chesapeake & Ohio Canal, dear to George Washington's heart, was useless for her purposes, she resorted to that still highly experimental and uncertain means of transportation, the railroad. At several places in the country factories and mines had laid down rails along which horses pulled wheeled vehicles for the transport of goods for short distances; one extended a dozen miles. But what Baltimore proposed was nothing less than to run one of these things not only over innumerable rivers, but across a system of mountain ranges two hundred and fifty miles, to Wheeling, on the Ohio. It was unheard-of. It was incredible. After ten years of prodigious effort the railroad was a long way short of Wheeling, but it had reached Harper's Ferry, which made it the longest railroad in the world [1] and an advertisement that had made the city known for its audacity to the ends of the earth.

At this time the merchant was still the dominant figure of the business world. The Industrial Revolution had barely begun in England, and the manufacturer was as yet far from occupying the position of preëminence he acquired fifty years later. Baltimore, like Fifteenth Century Venice, Genoa, and the Hanseatic towns, was a city of merchant princes, although manufacturing was already pretty well established [2] and was steadily thrust-

the United States until the census of 1860, when the development of manufacturing shot Philadelphia beyond the half-million mark, leaving Baltimore and Boston far behind.

[1] Edward Hungerford: The Story of the Baltimore & Ohio Railroad; New York, 1929, Vol. I, p. 116.

[2] J. Thomas Scharf reports in

ing forward as an important element in the city's economic life. And if there were in the group of civic leaders some Shylocks, there was at least one Antonio, a merchant capable of the princely gesture. This was George Peabody. Two years earlier, in 1835, the practically bankrupt State of Maryland had sent agents to London desperately seeking to negotiate a loan of some six millions. They failed. Then the State turned to Peabody, who chanced to be in England on business of his own, and whose word was better, in Lombard Street, than that of any of the American States. He promptly arranged the loan, but when he was offered the usual negotiator's commission, he refused to accept a cent.

It is interesting to remember that almost at the very moment when Peabody, in London, was serving the State well without desiring any financial reward, mobs were roaring through the streets of Baltimore, sacking the houses of half a dozen magnificoes of the city because these men had wrecked a bank of which they were directors.[1] For four days the city was given over to anarchy. The Mayor, Jesse Hunt, resigned. There was no organized police force in the modern sense, and the watchmen, or, as we should call them now, special constables, called in to quell the disorder were swept aside by the rioters. Finally, old General Samuel Smith, who had fought at Brandywine, Monmouth, White Plains and Long Island under Washington, and had commanded the defense of Baltimore in 1814,[2] was called on. The old soldier was now 83 years of age, but a soldier still. He put himself at the head of some hundreds of reliable men armed

---

his Chronicles of Baltimore, p. 402, that fifteen years earlier, in 1822, the town had thirteen cotton mills, with 32,880 spindles, one copper-rolling mill, three iron-rolling mills and " at least thirty " flour mills, producing 300,000 barrels a year.

[1] These were the celebrated Bank Riots. The mob made an earnest effort to lynch the whole crowd; but beyond that there appears to have been no serious effort to punish them.

[2] Scharf: Chronicles, p. 497.

with whatever weapons they could lay hands on, and swept the streets clear in short order. But Baltimore had received a shock which put an unholy fear of democracy in her heart for many years to come.

Active as the merchants were, however, they were far from monopolizing the intellectual life of Baltimore. Indeed, the great whale of the business world, the president of the Baltimore & Ohio Railroad, Louis McLane, had made his reputation outside of business. He had been successively Secretary of the Treasury, Minister to England and Secretary of State of the United States. William Wirt had been one of the ornaments of the bar until his death in 1834, and another Baltimore lawyer had just been elevated to the pinnacle of legal honor. In 1836 the Jacksonians had finally triumphed in the Senate and Roger Brooke Taney had been confirmed as Chief Justice of the United States.

By 1837 the Delphian Club had passed out of existence, but the intellectual life of the town was still feeling, to some extent, the stimulus given it by this extraordinary group. Never having more than nine members at any one time, the club managed to collect an astonishing list of young men whose names later were to mean something far beyond the confines of Baltimore. They regarded themselves as literary and artistic *dilettanti*, but the world has not looked upon them in that light. Jared Sparks's monumental work on Washington, for example, is no trifle, nor are the paintings of Rembrandt Peale, nor is the science of dentistry, which Horace H. Hayden did much to create.[1] John P. Kennedy's novels have been forgotten except by literary archæologists, but they were best sellers in their day,

[1] "Hayden shared with Dr. Chapin A. Harris the honor of being the founder of dental science in America. It is said that his lectures at the University of Maryland were the first scientific dental lectures ever given. In 1839 he founded the Baltimore College of Dental Surgery." —John Earle Uhler: The Delphian Club, *Maryland Historical Magazine,* December, 1925.

and his "Swallow Barn," a novel of Southern plantation life, "fixed the attitude toward plantation material, . . . gave matter and method for a literary tradition." [1] Uhler has calculated that sixteen members of the Delphian Club produced forty-eight books of fiction, history, travel, letters and biography, while twelve were editors of newspapers or magazines.[2] Truly, no small achievement for one small organization in one city; nor has it vanished completely. The books of the Delphian authors may gather dust on library shelves, the paintings of the Delphian artists may be interesting chiefly to antiquaries, the buildings of Delphian architects may have been pulled down, yet to this day three productions of the group enter intimately into the lives of the people of America. They are three songs. One is "The Star-Spangled Banner"; another is "The Old Oaken Bucket"; the third is "Home, Sweet Home" — all written by members of this club.

Physically, the Baltimore of 1837 was shiny new. The great bulk of the population had poured in during the previous thirty years, so relatively few of the city's structures were older than the century. Perhaps the largest and certainly the most impressive of them was the Cathedral of gray granite, begun in 1806 and consecrated in 1821. But the Byzantine architecture of the Cathedral was not the expression of the spirit of the community. That was to be found in the most conspicuous structure in Baltimore, the immense monument to George Washington, which stood on a high hill back of the town. It was a Doric column of dazzling white marble, no less than a hundred and eighty feet high, and capped with a statue of the Father of his Country sixteen feet high and weighing a ton to the foot.

Here was, in many ways, the true symbol of the city of 1837.

---

[1] F. P. Gaines: The Southern Plantation, p. 19.

[2] Uhler, *op. cit.*

Robert Mills, the architect,[1] erected more than a monument to Washington; unwittingly he erected also a permanent memorial to the city of his own day. The soaring ambition of the merchants of Baltimore, their tremendous self-confidence, their grandiose plans, their daring, bordering on recklessness, were all expressed in flinging these tons of masonry into the sky; for it must be remembered that no such architectural feat had hitherto been attempted in America. At the same time, the saving prudence that preserved them was expressed in the site chosen. Originally the monument had been intended for the square at the corner of Calvert and Lexington streets, which was then a fashionable place of residence, surrounded by the most beautiful homes in the city. But when the scope of the architect's plans became known, dwellers around the square were terrified; they had dreadful visions of lightning or earthquake overturning the thing and crushing them in the ruins of their homes.[2] So they accepted with relief Colonel John Eager Howard's offer to donate a site for the monument on the edge of Belvedere, his country estate, just outside the city. Belvedere included a high hill overlooking the town and separated only by a narrow ravine from the hill on which the Cathedral was built; and on this spot the monument was erected.

In 1837 the great column had stood for nine years, dominating the red-brick city below, a city which in a thousand pilastered doorways and in ten thousand classical lintels and architraves reflected its Grecian spirit. Architecturally, it was a city of the classical revival. The buildings were relatively low, three or

---

[1] He was a native of Charleston, S. C., and has been curiously neglected by historians. In addition to the Treasury Building, the Patent Office and the old Postoffice in Washington, and the Monumental Church at Richmond, he designed three colossal monuments, the 196-foot column to Washington in Baltimore, the 220-foot obelisk at Bunker Hill, and the mightiest monument erected to an individual since Cheops' pyramid, the 555-foot obelisk to Washington in the city of Washington.

[2] Scharf; Chronicles, p. 296.

four stories at most, so that Caucici's [1] colossal figure of Washington, handing back his commission as general of the armies, looked across the roofs of the town and the waters of the Inner Basin to the huge, red mass of Federal Hill — that eminence whose color had so impressed Captain John Smith, when he entered the Patapsco in 1606, that he regarded it as a small mountain of *bole armoniac*, or, as we should say now, Armenian clay, and so gave the site of Baltimore the dreadful name of Bolus. It was probably a beautiful city in 1837 — its air unsmudged with the smoke of factory chimneys, the water of the harbor clear and clean, the houses, for the greater part, new and well-scrubbed. True, a closer inspection might have modified one's admiration. The streets were, in most cases, muddy, rutted dirt trails, for the name and fame of John MacAdam as yet were hardly known in America and such paving as did exist consisted of rough cobblestones. Here and there an especially enterprising citizen had laid a sidewalk in front of his premises, usually of brick, sometimes of large flagstones, but there was nothing like a connected system of footways; muddy shoes were so certainly the fate of every pedestrian that no doorstep was complete without a scraper.

Sanitary arrangements were regarded as the concern, not of the city, but of the tenant of each house, who was left to his own devices. The city's nearest approach to providing a sewerage

[1] Henrico Caucici, sculptor, has been even more completely enveloped in the shades of obscurity than Mills, the architect. He is included in none of the histories of art, nor even in the very hospitable Encyclopædia Italiana. Yet it is evident that he enjoyed a considerable reputation in the early Nineteenth Century, for he received a fee of $7,500 for cutting this figure; and the figure itself, considering the vast distance from which it must be viewed, "carries" extraordinarily well. It was wrought in three sections from a monolith of Maryland marble weighing thirty-six tons; and was elevated to its present position, says Scharf, "by means of a pair of shears attached to the cap of the column by pulleys and a capstan, planned and directed by Capt. James D. Woodside, of Washington." (Chronicles, p. 433.)

system was the construction of some of the cobbled streets in the shape of a flattened V; the open gutter down the middle was flushed by rains, or when some householder emptied a tub in the street, but not otherwise. This blithe disregard of sanitation was not peculiar to Baltimore, however, but was characteristic, to some extent, of all cities of the period. Cities, a hundred years ago, were expected to be more or less pestilence-ridden; Baltimore, like others, had been scourged by cholera and yellow fever.[1] Water was drawn from wells, some of them on public property, and from springs, several of which were owned and kept in order by the city. Houses were heated mainly by wood, although some coal came from the Pennsylvania fields in barges down the Susquehanna. It has been said that one of the prime satisfactions the first directors of the Baltimore & Ohio Railroad derived from the success of their enterprise was its efficiency in bringing cheap firewood to the hearths of Baltimore.[2]

Into this town, in April, 1837, came Abell, blond, thirty-one, rather below than above middle height, bewhiskered, moderately successful, and inordinately confident, as he looked over the field with a view to establishing a new paper.

If he found it white unto the harvest, he also found in it laborers not a few. Four daily newspapers were published in Gay street alone, and two others elsewhere. In addition there were nine weeklies, and two monthlies.[3] Nor did this represent

---

[1] Cholera, which had struck heavily in 1832, was to come again in 1849. Yellow fever was epidemic in 1794, in 1819 and in 1821. The custom of smoking cigars in the street originated, says Scharf, in the belief that it was a prophylactic against this disease. (Chronicles, p. 267.)

[2] Hungerford: The Story of the Baltimore & Ohio Railroad, I, 129.

[3] The " Baltimore Director " for 1837–38 lists the daily newspapers of the period as the *American,* published by Dobbin, Murphy & Bose, in South Gay near Baltimore street; the *Chronicle,* by Nelson Poe, North Gay near Fayette street; the *Gazette,* by William Gwynn, St Paul's (*sic*) near Baltimore street; the *Patriot,* by Isaac Monroe, North (now Guilford avenue) near Balti-

any mushroom growth; all but one of Baltimore's six dailies had been in existence at least eighteen years, while the dean of the corps, the *Federal Gazette*, had attained the venerable age of forty-six. The Baltimore press already had traditions, some glorious, some otherwise. At the moment of Abell's arrival one editor-publisher was being lodged and fed at the expense of the State in the Maryland Penitentiary. He had been caught robbing the postoffice. Against this skeleton in the professional cupboard set the record of the *American*. Since its establishment in 1799 it had missed a regularly scheduled issue on one occasion only. On September 10, 1814, the editor laid down his pencil, the foreman his make-up rule and the printers their composing sticks, and all sallied out, locking the office behind them, to fight the British Army. Owing to the illness of the colonel, Editor Pechin assumed command of the Sixth Regi-

more street; the *Republican*, by Samuel Harker, South Gay near Water street; and the *Transcript*, by Skinner & Tenney, corner of Gay and Baltimore streets. To these George C. Keidel, in his list of "Early Maryland Newspapers" (*Maryland Historical Magazine*, December, 1933), adds the *Jefferson Reformer and Baltimore Daily Advertiser*. The weekly publications were the *Athenæum and Visiter*, published by Arthur & Cox, South Gay near Water street; the *Monument*, by David Creamer, North Calvert street opposite Barnum's Hotel; the *Express*, by Young & Abraham, corner of Bond and Thames streets, Fell's Point; the *Lutheran Observer*, by William S. Sherwood, with the Rev. B. Kurtz as editor; *Niles' Register*, by William Ogden Niles, Water near South street; the *Farmer and Gardener*, by Sands & Nelson, corner of Baltimore and Charles streets; the *Trades Union*, by Bull & Tuttle, corner of North Gay and Baltimore streets; the *Methodist Protestant*, by J. J. Harrod, corner of Baltimore and Charles streets. To these Keidel adds the *Kaleidoscope*, the *Maryland Colonization Journal*, the *Merchant*, the *Southern Pioneer* and the *Spirit of the Times*. The monthlies were only two in number. They were the *Baltimore Literary and Religious Magazine*, conducted by R. J. Breckinridge and Andrew B. Cross and printed by R. J. Matchett, corner of Gay and Water streets; and the *American Turf Register*, edited by J. S. Skinner, North near Fayette street. Apparently neither piety nor horse racing had secured the hold on Baltimoreans that later both acquired.

ment, while the office force, editorial, mechanical and business, was incorporated in the ranks. The Sixth did very well at the battle of North Point, and later held its sector of the fortifications protecting the city; it suffered casualties, but apparently not among the *American* personnel, for when the British eventually withdrew they all marched back, opened up the shop and the paper appeared once more, September 20, 1814. The next day it printed some verses composed the previous week by a local attorney, the title of the poem being "The Star-Spangled Banner."[1] The *American* passed through many hands, including those of C. C. Fulton, who had got his training on THE SUN, and his son-in-law, General Felix Agnus; eventually it was acquired by Frank A. Munsey, and finally, in 1923, by William Randolph Hearst.

Then there was the appalling history of the *Federal Republican*, although that tradition concerned the town as nearly as the press. In 1812 this paper was violently anti-Administration, and two days after the declaration of war it published an editorial so seditious that a mob wrecked the plant and ran the editor out of town.[2] He had, however, a backer more resolute and, as it proved, more foolhardy, in the person of one Alexander C. Hanson. Not content with having the publication printed in Georgetown, Hanson determined that it should be distributed

[1] Scharf: Chronicles, pp. 85, 86.

[2] Among its expressions were: "Our rulers have promulgated a war against the clear and decided sentiments of a vast majority of the nation. . . . We mean to represent in as strong colors as we are capable that it is unnecessary, inexpedient, and entered into from motives bearing upon their front marks of undisguised foreign influence, which cannot be mistaken. We mean to use every constitutional argument and every legal means to render as odious and suspicious to the American people, as they deserve to be, the patrons and contrivers of this highly impolitic and destructive war. . . . We are avowedly hostile to the Presidency of James Madison, and we will never breathe under the dominion, direct or derivative, of Bonaparte, let it be acknowledged when it may." This, be it remembered, was published after the nation was already engaged in war.

in Baltimore. On July 26, therefore, he brought to the city an issue containing, among other things, a bitter castigation of the Mayor, a judge and other civic authorities for not preventing the riot of June 22. He took possession of the house at 45 South Charles street, formerly occupied by the departed editor, sent out the paper from it, and assembled twenty or thirty of his friends, armed them, and prepared to stand siege. Among the garrison were two heroes of the Revolution, General James M. Lingan and General Henry (Light-Horse Harry) Lee, Washington's cavalry commander and the father of Robert E. Lee. The house was attacked by a mob that night, but it was well defended, one of the attackers being killed and twenty or more wounded. In the morning troops came to the rescue, and after some parleying the defenders surrendered to the civil authorities and were lodged in jail. Then followed a plain breach of faith, for the jail was left undefended, and that night the mob smashed its way in, lynched General Lingan and believed it had beaten the others to death, except for a few who escaped in the confusion. However, after the rioting, the victims were carried away by civilized persons, some their political enemies, and all survived, although Lee's injuries were so terrible that he never fully recovered.

This finally dissuaded Hanson from trying to publish an anti-war paper in Baltimore.

Fifty years after these events, Abell was to find himself in a position somewhat comparable to Hanson's — that is, conducting a paper not in sympathy with the government in time of war. The story of how he came through with his skin, his property and his reputation all intact, when set against the story of the *Federal Republican*, is a fascinating contrast of skillful and blundering journalism.

But in the Spring of 1837 all this was in the unguessed future. When he surveyed the field in April the newcomer had no reason to suppose that he was looking over a city that, twenty-four years later, was to be caught between the upper and nether millstones in the most frightful convulsion of the Republic's history. He saw only an alert, vigorous, aggressive city, growing in population with startling speed, already immensely wealthy and swiftly adding to its wealth by an energetic and skillful commercial policy, interested in the arts and sciences, a little given to turbulence, indeed, but indubitably a city where things happened. To a man of his type it seemed an ideal field for the establishment of a newspaper of the sort he was competent to produce.

In attempting to explain Abell's astonishing success in Baltimore due weight must be given to the fact that, although he was a young man, he was not a callow youth when he undertook his greatest venture. His thirty-one years had been spent in no bed of roses, nor was he a human hot-house plant to begin with. The descendant of a long line of New England Puritans,[1] he had been apprenticed, after a brief experience in the shop of a dealer in

[1] The widely prevalent belief that A. S. Abell was descended from a Catholic *émigré* from England is erroneous. The founder of the American branch of the family was Robert Abell. His son, born at sea on the voyage to the New World, was christened Preserved — a name that was eloquent of Robert's religious affiliation. His choice of Massachusetts in the early days of that colony. as a place of residence confirms the fact. Later, Preserved Abell removed to the town of Seekonk, in Rhode Island, where his grandson, Caleb, was living at the outbreak of the Revolution. Caleb served with distinction as an officer in Washington's army, and his son, Robert, served in the War of 1812 as a quartermaster officer. Robert married the daughter of Colonel Arunah Shepherdson, and their son was Arunah Shepherdson Abell. The wife of the Founder, Mary Fox Campbell, was a Catholic, and they were united in marriage by Archbishop Francis P. Kenrick. Their children were brought up in Mrs. Abell's faith, but Mr. Abell himself remained, somewhat vaguely, a Protestant. In his later years he liked to insist, jocosely, that he was a Hard-Shell Baptist. At his death in 1888 his funeral was conducted by the Rev. J. S. B. Hodges, rector of Old St. Paul's (Protestant Episcopal) Church, Baltimore.

West India goods, to the printer of the Providence *Patriot*, a paper of the Jeffersonian Democratic school. Take into consideration the fact that this was in New England, only six years after the Hartford Convention, and it is evident that Abell's early experience was not gained among the lords and gentlemen but decidedly among the commoners. In New England, in 1820, Jeffersonian Democracy was not the creed of those favored of fortune; on the contrary, association with that group meant the development of no small spiritual and social hardiness. Abell cherished no illusion that the world owed him a living; on the contrary, he realized clearly that if the world was to yield him a living he must show it some reason for doing so.

When his apprenticeship had ended and he had come of age, he removed to Boston [1] where he practiced his trade successfully enough to become foreman of a large print shop. It is said that in 1828, after the election of Andrew Jackson to the Presidency, he was offered a political appointment, but with the instinct of a true newspaper man he declined it.[2] More than once this sort of offer was to be renewed in later years, but it always met with the same prompt refusal from a man who cherished a deep distrust of mixing publishing and politics.[3]

Even as early as 1828 the call of New York was loud in the ears of ambitious young Americans and shortly thereafter Abell answered it. Journeymen printers were much in demand in the city at that time, and Abell, with his Boston experience, by now could qualify as a master craftsman. The problem of employment offered no great difficulties and apparently he did very well for several years. But his ambition soared above the practice of

[1] *Magazine of Western History,* January, 1889, pp. 352 *ff.:* article Arunah S. Abell, signed O. P. B. (Baldwin?)

[2] Biographical Cyclopedia, Vol. I, p. 18.

[3] This distrust, as we shall see, he transmitted to his descendants, and even to successors who were not of his blood.

his trade. He was an alert student of the trend of the publishing business, for it was still the day of small enterprises and every journeyman printer dreamed of becoming the proprietor of his own shop.

Among Abell's New York acquaintances was one who had risen to this eminence. Benjamin H. Day [1] was a job printer in a small way with a shop in Duane street and an inordinate ambition, which he discussed again and again with Abell, who was then holding a job on the *Mercantile Advertiser*, and with another printer, William M. Swain. Day had an idea that a cheap newspaper would be an invaluable adjunct to his job-printing business. Practically all the New York newspapers sold for six cents and were devoted to politics; Day imagined a newspaper selling for a penny and devoting itself to interesting news, especially about the city. He had it all worked out, even to the name. He proposed to call the paper the *Sun*.

To Abell the notion was ludicrous.[2] Had not the *Cent*, in Philadelphia, perished miserably after an existence of a few months? Had not Horace Greeley, less than a year earlier, been compelled to suspend his *Morning Post* after only three weeks? He warned Day that a one-cent newspaper, instead of advertising him, would swiftly ruin him; and for a long time the job printer did no more than toy with the idea. But in 1832 cholera swept the city and not only destroyed 35,000 lives but well-nigh ruined every business in New York. Day found himself in a position where he had to do something, so in a spirit of desperation he took the plunge. He started publication of the New York *Sun* September 4, 1833. To Abell's amazement, the thing prospered from the start. In two months it had a circulation of

[1] This was the father of the inventor of the Ben Day process of shading newspaper illustrations, widely in use before the innovation of the half-tone, and still occasionally used in cartoons and advertising illustrations.

[2] Frank M. O'Brien: The Story of the [New York] *Sun;* New York, 1918, p. 3.

2,000 copies, when the *Courier and Enquirer*, the colossus of the New York field, had only 4,500. Within a year the circulation of the *Sun* was running into tremendous figures — 12,000 to 15,000. It was evident that Ben Day had struck a gold mine.

Moreover, a year later his success began to be duplicated by a tough, weather-beaten Scot named James Gordon Bennett, whose *Herald* began to outrun the *Sun* itself. Plainly, here was the field for ambitious young printers.

Swain, who had become Day's foreman on the New York *Sun*, thought so too; and so did Azariah H. Simmons, yet another New York printer who had been observing events closely. The outcome of their thought and discussion was the signing of an agreement on Leap Year Day, February 29, 1836, whereby they bound themselves to the establishment of a penny paper in Philadelphia to be called the *Times*. Two provisions of this agreement are noteworthy as being contrary to the general practice: First, the paper was to sell for one cent, a sixth of the ordinary price of a newspaper, and, second, it was to be "neutral in politics." This latter provision might have meant that the new paper was to be devoted, as some others were, to what passed current as literature; but that possibility is eliminated by the price, for the people to whom a one-cent paper would appeal were not the people to whom polite literature would appeal. Taken together, the two provisions necessarily meant that the firm of Swain, Abell & Simmons proposed to devote its efforts primarily to the publication of news, subordinating everything else to that.

The agreement went into effect immediately, and less than a month later, on March 25, 1836, the new paper appeared on the streets of Philadelphia. However, for various reasons, the name seemed to be a poor selection, so at the suggestion of Abell [1]

[1] Biographical Cyclopedia, Vol. I, p. 19.

THE  SUN.

VOL. I.—NO. 1.] BALTIMORE, WEDNESDAY, MAY 17, 1837. [PRICE ONE CENT.

PUBLISHED DAILY, BY

A. S. ABELL & CO.

At No. 21 Light Street, near Baltimore st.

Terms of the Paper—To Subscribers, SIX CENTS A WEEK, payable to the CARRIER at the expiration of the week.

TERMS OF ADVERTISING.

1 square 1 insertion,	$0 50	1 square 1 month,	$2 50
1 do. 2 do.	0 75	1 do. 2 do.	4 75
1 do. 3 do.	1 00	1 do. 3 do.	7 00
1 do. 1 week,	1 50	1 do. 6 do.	13 00
1 do. 2 do.	2 00	1 square per year,	$25 00

☞ Sixteen lines or less make a square. If an advertisement exceed sixteen lines it will be considered two squares, if it exceed thirty-two lines, three squares, and so on. All advertisements are payable at the time of their insertion except yearlies, which are payable monthly. Cards of only two lines will be inserted for five dollars a year. All advertisements ordered in till forbid will be charged fifty cents for the first, and twenty-five cents for each subsequent insertion.

O, FAIREST OF THE RURAL MAIDS!

O, fairest of the rural maids!
Thy birth was in the forest shades;
Green boughs and glimpses of the sky
Were all that met thy infant eye.

Thy sports, thy wanderings, when a child,
Were ever in the sylvan wild;
And all the beauty of the place
Is in thy heart and on thy face.

The twilight of the trees and rocks
Is in the light shade of thy locks;
Thy step is as the wind that weaves
Its playful way among the leaves.

Thine eyes are springs, in whose serene
And silent waters heaven is seen;
Their lashes are the herbs that look
On their young figures in the brook.

The forest depths by foot unpressed
Are not more sinless than thy breast;
The holy peace that fills the air
Of those calm solitudes is there.

The N. York Star sometimes offers most valuable hints to the inhabitants of our cities, upon domestic life. The following is a true picture of many families in New York, and Baltimore.

RETRENCHMENT—A DOMESTIC SCENE.

"Why Dick," said Beau Shatterly to his friend, Abel Drugget, while standing in front of the Astor House, 'Why Dick, curse' me if your coat aint scoured,' examining the article closely with his eye glass. 'Yes,' says Abel, 'it is scoured; having nearly arranged my books and papers at the counting house, and compromised with my creditors, I determined to hold a commission over my wardrobe and other domestic matters, and turned out three trunks, the capital of better and more extravagant days, and overhauled the invoices which proved to be quite profitable [illegible] wanted a [illegible] required a button, and what with dusting, [illegible], mending, darning, and so [illegible], I find myself provided for a whole twelve months and more, when I hope to resume specie payments.' 'Well then,' said Beau Shatterly, '[illegible] commenced on the reform system.'—'[illegible] I have. I cursed old Jackson until I [illegible] Van Buren heartily—prayed that some patriot would lynch Kendall, Blair and Benton, and when tired of suffering, cursing, ranting [illegible], and so forth, I determined to endure all [illegible], to cut off every expense, and [illegible] myself against all future disaster. When the [illegible] shall have passed, I shall be ready again to [illegible], with a diminished cargo and a weather beaten ship, it is true, but I hope with the needful [illegible]. This, you will say, was a wise determination, and we should all act upon it."

"Oh, to be sure," said Beau Shatterly, 'this economy and retrenchment, as you call it, is all mighty fine and clever, but it is confoundedly inconvenient to us [illegible] the devil fly away with cotton and [illegible], and all such games at hazard, which compel us to wear a scoured coat, and touch our hats to the *patrons* of the lay. Why, Abel, now I think of it: when I dined with you last Sunday, Polly Watts, the chambermaid, waited upon us, and you gave me claret at $4 per dozen, instead of Gil Davis's superb Nuptial Champaigne. Why, man, this is fairly cutting off the supplies."

"Ah, you found that out, did you? Yes, it is all true; I drummed up my troops and called an inspection of the forces one fine sunny morning last week. Polly Smallfry, says I to the cook, what wages do you receive? "Eight dollars a month, and three for Patty the scullion." "You must take six, Polly," says I, "and dismiss the scullion.' I can't, no how sumdever take less." "Then your services are no longer required." "Mimmy, how much do you receive as chambermaid?" Seven dollars." "You must come down to five." 'I shan't do no such thing, sir, unless you will find me a silk dress, a cape, and a Tuscan bonnet." 'Can't do it, Mimmy, so you must go." "Dick, I owe you a month's wages as coachman; here it is, and a recommendation for honesty and capacity." "Why, sir, do you give up the coach?" "Yes, I keep an omnibus now. Bob, the waiter, you are a good fellow, but as you have managed my marketing for six years, and made all my purchases, I take it for granted that you have laid up a snug little sum; you are what I call comfortable." "Pretty well to do, sir, in the world. Polly Smallfry and I talk of setting up a Welch rabbit house in Thames street next May.".

Thus I went through my household troops, and soon placed the whole concern on the peace establishment. Afterwards my wife and I mounted to the garret, and under the eaves of the house we found three hundred bottles of Madeira wine, 30 years old; besides one pipe that had been twice to India, 4 quarter casks of pale sherry, 1 of old Port, and 10 cases of Lynch's Chateau Morgeaux, which lay snugly in the counter cellar. Wife, says I, this is too much of a fine article to keep in these times; so we'll send for Duncan Pell to taste—to arrange—to set up, and knock down; and it was gone. Pursuing our search for superfluities, we encountered lots of silver forks, silver tureens, silver waiters, silver plateaus, silver pitchers, magnificent china dinner setts, exquisite cut glass, superb paintings by Raphael, Rubens, Tintoretto, &c. &c. &c.; pier and mantel glasses, almost as large and as long as a church door. Mary, says I, say the word; can you part with these things, without a sigh? Willingly, cheerfully, said she with a smile, a kind look, and a squeeze of the hand. "How pathetic," said Shatterly; "why really, friend Abel, I must take a lesson from you when I fail, split me." Now, take your eye off the ladies, will you, and look over this memorandum of the sum total of facilities raised by these moveables.

Carriage and pair	$1200
Barouche	120
Buggy	100
Sleigh	60
Poney	70
Coach Dogs	40
Wines	4,200
Plate	1,500
China and Glass	500
Paintings	1,400
Looking Glasses	800
	$9,080

Here's raising the wind for you, and without missing it, my fine fellow; and do you wish to know what I have done with this money?—bought a snug farm of sixty acres, neat house, good garden, outhouses, &c., not many miles from the city, settled it on my wife and young ones, and shall plant my own corn and potatoes—raise my own pigs and poultry—milk my cows—churn my butter—bake my bread, and lay my own eggs; and when the storm is over, I shall, I hope, be found again in my roundabout, selling goods in moderation at short credits and sure profits. So Shatterly, my boy, hold up your finger [illegible] to carry me.

Paganini, whose determination to visit our country, and to put himself under the guidance of his old friends, the Watsons, had been publicly announced, is said to have actually arrived at Paris, on his way hither, to embark from Havre. We have a letter before us from the Gran Maestro to Mr. ———, at New York, in which he speaks of the delight it would give him to visit the country discovered by his immortal compatriot, Columbus. So we think, upon the whole, the American world will have a chance of being thrown into an agony of ecstacies, by hearing the greatest prodigy that ever touched the violin.—*N. Y. Gazette*.

Two years ago, one half of the American press found itself engaged in a bitter controversy in relation to the birth-place of the "illustrious" Paganini. By one he was said to be a Corsican; another made him a citizen of Rome; a third, said that he was born in Schloss Hainfield; but at last, the editor of the Boston Commercial Gazette settled the matter, by affirming that Paganini, the greatest and best of all the fiddlers, was born in the town of Lynn, and was the unmentionable kind of a son of old Mr. Mudge, the greatest and best of all the Lynn cobblers. This discovery for a while was satisfactory; but of late it has been disputed. As Paganini is soon to be with us, we shall "leave the matter for his own decision."

It is thought that the Proclamation of the President, calling for an extra session of Congress, will be hailed with great satisfaction by all parties in the country. One of the first acts of the special session, it is believed, will be to devise ways and means to release the large sums of specie now locked up in the deposite banks. It is difficult to conjecture, however, what course can be adopted calculated to afford immediate relief.

THE PUBLIC HOTELS in New York, with the exception of the Astor House, and the Clinton and American Hotels, have reduced their prices from two dollars and two and a half dollars, to one dollar and fifty cents the day—and most of them are empty at that. We are glad of it. For the last two years, the New York Hotels have rioted on the necessities of travellers.

Oseola—Florida.—The Norfolk Beacon of Monday states that two officers of the United States Army, who left Black Creek on the 9th inst., have arrived at Norfolk, who report that Oseola and Phillip, with about 800 Warriors, came into Fort Mellon a day or two previous to their departure.—There were between 2500 and 3500 Indians encamped within the vicinity of Fort Mellon, and it is presumed that by this time they have arrived at Tampa Bay. The whole body of Indians would probably embark from Tampa Bay about the last of this month for Arkansas; boats were in readiness to convey them thence.

Whilst we hope that this report may prove to be true, we most candidly confess that we doubt it. Oseola has been reported to have been captured so often, and yet has not been caught, and the Florida war has so often been closed, and yet not closed at all, that one is obliged to exercise unusual credulity before he can believe one word of any thing received in relation to Florida or the famous Indian Chieftain.

A child nine years old has arrived at New York from the West Indies, whose head measures thirty-one inches in circumference and 23 inches from ear to ear over the crown, the weight being fifty pounds. The head is free from distortion, and seems to have been formed for a person of the stature of ten or eleven feet. The sutures of the head have not closed up at the apex. The child is an idiot, and indicates no sense, except of pain when touched, and hunger, when the time of eating arrives.—*American*.

The miserable object of suffering and wretchedness, spoken of in the *foregoing paragraph*, presents one of the most revolting spectacles that man ever beheld. The sufferer, from the cradle to his present estate, has been afflicted with that most appalling of all diseases, dropsy in the head. It has endured a world of torture, and now, to gratify the avarice of the inhuman, is carted about the country as a show. We saw the poor thing a few days since, and nothing could tempt us to behold it again. While we looked on, we know not which predominated—our abhorrence of the man who made a show of the sufferer for [illegible] our pity for the sorrows and afflictions of the defenceless, unoffending victim of his avarice. Such an exhibition should not be allowed in a Christian country.

Anticipated Disorders.—The laboring portion of the New York population is becoming dissatisfied, discontented, mad by the prospect before them. On Saturday last, as we are informed by a gentleman direct from that city, a large collection of laboring men, who had deposites in the Savings Bank, assembled around that institution to demand the withdrawal of their deposites. The Bank *could not* pay them! The aspect of these men was menacing in the extreme; and their half-suppressed murmurs, and whispered execrations, but too well and too fearfully indicated the approach of one of those civil convulsions which spread desolation and terror through the moral world. It is scarcely possible that New York can escape the fury of her own population. We sincerely hope, however, that every thing will pass off quietly.

John Bull's Intelligence.—The London Morning Herald of the 16th of April copies an article from the National Intelligencer, and credits it to a paper called "the National Intelligencer, published in the city of New York, known to be the organ of the President." The same paper, whilst discussing American affairs, says that the people of the States look anxiously forward for the day which shall send the warlike Jackson, the soldier President, into retirement." There can scarcely be a doubt, that the editor of the London Morning Herald is a man of infinite information in relation to the affairs of the United States.

The *Mayor of New York*, in the midst of these days of excitement and despondency, finds himself in an unenviable situation. He has sinned against the "sovereign people," it is alledged, by ordering out a body of troops on the day that the New York Banks suspended payments, to keep the peace. That such a step was necessary, there can scarcely be a doubt; that the Mayor sought the general safety of the city is most certain; but it is now said that he called out a body of armed men to sustain the banks in their refusal to pay their just debts. The charge, we should suppose, equally absurd and foolish.

Meeting of the City Councils.—The City Councils held an extraordinary session on Monday afternoon, at the instance and call of the Mayor, when the subject of issuing small paper notes or city certificates, was taken up, and an ordinance was passed authorising the issue of certificates for the purpose of supplying small change in the absence of specie. The ordinance appoints six commissioners to issue the certificates to an amount not exceeding $100,000 in the whole, in sums of 5 cents, 10 cents, 25 cents, 50 cents, $1 and $2. It is supposed that the issue will be made as soon as practicable, and the community be thus relieved of the inconvenience which at present attends the want of small change.

The Mayor in his message to the two branches of the city government, whilst discoursing on the subject of the banks, holds the following language, which it is deemed proper to copy and preserve as a matter of future reference. We have *italicised* several expressions in the quotation we have made, in consequence of their importance.

"It is known to all that the banks of the city have suspended specie payments, *not from any want of means to meet the discharge of their liabilities*, but to prevent the removal of their specie to other cities, the prevention of which, in any other way, was impossible in their opinion, and that of most men who think on such subjects.—This suspension *will injure no one*. It may for a few days (and until well understood) check business, after which all will go on cheerfully. Men will know that the banks are *just as sound as ever they had been*, their notes will be taken as heretofore, the deposites will be made as usual, and all business with the banks and *individuals will go on as if no suspension had taken place*."

We sincerely hope that the predictions of the venerable and distinguished gentleman, who fills the office of Mayor, with so much credit to himself, at home and abroad, and with the unqualified approbation of the city, may be realized. We confess, however, that we entertain some fears in relation to the subject.

The Mayor in his message adverts to the city taxes, and affords but a sad account of the [illegible] of the tax collector.

"It may not be improper for me to inform you that notwithstanding every exertion possible has been made by the collector, yet there remains still unpaid of the taxes of 1836 the sum of $64,270,04. This has prevented the officers from commencing the execution of almost all the improvements authorised by the late acts of the Council. They have declined, with my entire approbation, from entering into any new expenditure, except the removal of the hay house at the Bel Air Market, and preparing for the stone wall of the dock. This last, payable out of the harbor fund, will be met by its own means as collected.

The collection for the present year, which will commence on the 1st of July, may justify a different course, but it can scarcely be expected, during the present pressure on the finances of almost every person."

After the subject of a small paper currency had been disposed of, both branches of the city government adjourned until to-day.

Marden's Scales.—This inimitable piece of mechanism was tested most conclusively on Tuesday last by Mr. John Henry Alexander, at his house in Saratoga street. The experiment was made in a close room, and the balance was turned by the *three hundredth part of a grain*. The weight used was a piece of paper so small that it could scarcely be perceived by the naked eye. The attainment of so perfect a balance is a circumstance of consequence to all, particularly to those who, amid the dearth of gold and silver, and the other precious metals, find it necessary to be scrupulously exact.

Mr. Marden, the inventor and manufacturer of this beautiful and exact piece of mechanism, keeps at No. 69 Pratt street, and will promptly execute all orders for scales and balances that may be given him. Baltimore may be justly proud of so able and excellent a mechanic, and we cannot doubt that he will receive that encouragement from a liberal and enlightened community to which he is pre-eminently entitled.

The literary men of the city of New York, are now doing the amiable thing for Capt. Marryatt, author of Jacob Faithful, Peter Simple, &c. Capt. Marryatt is on a tour of observation through this country, and on his return to England will probably publish a book of travels. A junket is to be given him by the literary men of Philadelphia.

FIRST PAGE OF THE FIRST ISSUE OF *THE SUN*, MAY 17, 1837

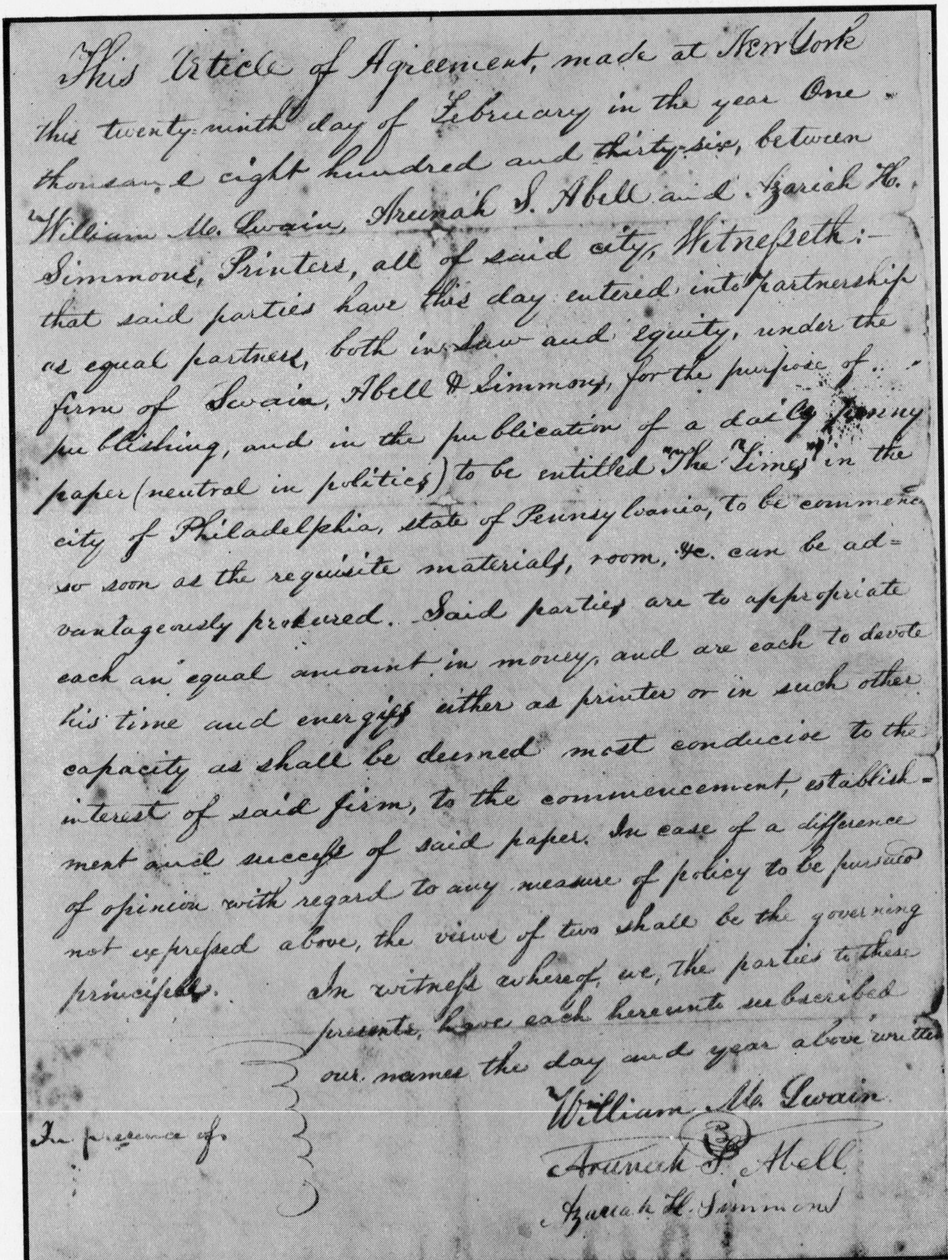

This Article of Agreement, made at New York
this twenty-ninth day of February in the year One-
thousand eight hundred and thirty-six, between
William M. Swain, Arunah S. Abell and Azariah H.
Simmons, Printers, all of said city, Witnesseth:—
that said parties have this day entered into partnership
as equal partners, both in law and equity, under the
firm of Swain, Abell & Simmons, for the purpose of
publishing, and in the publication of a daily penny
paper (neutral in politics) to be entitled "The Times" in the
city of Philadelphia, state of Pennsylvania, to be commenced
so soon as the requisite materials, room, &c. can be ad-
vantageously procured. Said parties are to appropriate
each an equal amount in money, and are each to devote
his time and energies either as printer or in such other
capacity as shall be deemed most conducive to the
interest of said firm, to the commencement, establishment and success of said paper. In case of a difference
of opinion with regard to any measure of policy to be pursued
not expressed above, the views of two shall be the governing
principle. In witness whereof, we, the parties to these
presents, have each hereunto subscribed
our names the day and year above written

In presence of

William M. Swain
Arunah S. Abell
Azariah H. Simmons

THE ORIGINAL CONTRACT BETWEEN SWAIN, ABELL AND SIMMONS, FEBRUARY 29, 1836 the new journal carried the title of the *Public Ledger;* under which name it has been familiar to Philadelphians for more than a hundred years. In the beginning, however, it seemed unlikely to do more than add another tombstone to the many already in Philadelphia's journalistic cemetery. So hard was the going, indeed, that Swain and Simmons were ready to give up in despair, and only Abell's insistence that they hang on until they were absolutely bankrupt persuaded them to cling to what seemed to be a foundering craft.[1] The man who had worked for a Jeffersonian Democratic newspaper in Providence, R. I., was not likely to be discouraged by mere indifference in Philadelphia. He knew what real opposition was; he knew that the *Public Ledger* was encountering nothing worse than public distrust of a novelty, and he felt that once Philadelphia became accustomed to the thing opinion would swing in its favor.

He was proved right in what was really an astonishingly short time, long as it may have seemed to his distressed partners. Within a year the *Public Ledger* was on a paying basis, and for the next thirty years it never failed to yield a handsome return to its founders. But no sooner was it in fairly smooth financial waters than the restless and ambitious spirit of Abell began to cast about for new worlds to conquer. Only ninety miles to the south was another great city, bigger than Philadelphia. Why not cultivate that field, too? Abell came down, looked it over, and, in spite of the gloomy reports of the editors of the fippenny-bit papers, who could talk of nothing but the Depression, he returned to Philadelphia bubbling with enthusiasm. Baltimore was obviously ripe for their sort of enterprise. Baltimore was a great field. Baltimore must be occupied at once.

But at this his partners balked. Swain and Simmons had allowed themselves to be carried along by Abell's determination in

[1] Biographical Cyclopedia, Vol. I, p. 19; *Magazine of Western History,* 1889, p. 352; Scharf: Chronicles, p. 96.

Philadelphia, and apparently it was going to work out all right. But enough was enough. For weeks and months they had stared bankruptcy in the face, and they didn't like the look of it. As the event proved, they had saved their money, but what the experience had done to their nerves was too painful to contemplate, even in retrospect. Were they now to go through all that again, in a new city, with another paper? No, they weren't — that was flat.

Nevertheless, there must have been a good deal of sportsmanship in Messrs. Swain and Simmons, for in the end they did consent to put up their share of the money for the new venture, but on one conditon only, to wit, that Abell should take personal charge of the enterprise, come to Baltimore and stay,[1] watching and guarding the new paper, sitting up nights with it, if necessary, until it was either on a paying basis or he was cured of his obsession with Baltimore. To this condition he agreed; and for this reason the history of THE SUN for its first fifty years is the history of A. S. Abell and not that of William M. Swain and Azariah H. Simmons, who are henceforth hardly even shadowy figures in the background. It was Abell, and Abell alone, who made the Baltimore paper.

In the office of THE SUN today hang two pictures of him, one from a daguerreotype of the three partners made at the time of the signing of the original agreement, the other Dabour's portrait, painted thirty years later from a photograph by David Bendann. The singular thing about them is the relative unimportance of the changes that thirty years wrought in the man. The portrait of 1866 is that of a wiser, mellower, calmer man than the one revealed in the daguerreotype; hair and mustache are white, and the figure is somewhat heavier. Existing through a stormy generation had brought Abell experience and skill, but

[1] Biographical Cyclopedia, p. 19; Scharf: Chronicles, p. 96.

no livid scars. His plans had worked as he expected them to work. Plenty of hard labor had toughened and steadied him, but he had not been spiritually vitrified by the fires of disaster.

The mature man of the portrait is plainly apparent in the photograph of the young adventurer. Indeed, the group is interesting for many other reasons than the quaint costumes and quainter whiskers that it exhibits. Here were Three Musketeers of American journalism whose record is exceptionally fine. They have the distinction of having founded two newspapers in different cities each of which has not only lasted a hundred years, but each of which has held, for every day of that century, a prominent place and usually a leading place in the press of its city. Their fortunes have varied, their managements have altered, their popularity has waxed and waned, but at no time for the last century has either the Philadelphia *Public Ledger* [1] or THE BALTIMORE SUN sunk to a position of complete insignificance in its own city, while for a large part of the time each has dominated its local field and commanded the respectful consideration of all American journalism.

Photographers later than Daguerre developed the art of retouching, so these early photographic studies are revelations of a camera that is candid indeed. What one sees in a daguerreotype is usually the truth; and what one sees in this picture [2] is an interesting combination of varying personalities. All three are frock-coated, according to the fashion of the time. All are stovepipe-hatted. All are bewhiskered as to cheeks and shaven as to upper lip and chin. Swain, standing at the observer's left, is tall and made to look even taller by his Lincolnesque hat. He is slim, mild-mannered, and his large spectacles give him a studi-

[1] The morning edition of the *Public Ledger* was consolidated with the Philadelphia *Inquirer* on April 17, 1934, but its evening edition survives under the old name.

[2] It appears as the frontispiece to the present volume.

ous look, while about the mouth and eyes there is a suggestion of latent fanaticism. He could never be dismissed as a commonplace man, but there seems to be a hint that he might develop into a John Calvin, or a John Knox — powerful, ruthless, icy, a man to command respect, but also, perhaps, fear. Years later, at the helm of the *Public Ledger*, he did just that, during the Civil War. At the right is Simmons, a little shorter than Swain, but taller than Abell and heavier than either. An open countenance, frank, fearless, but a bit truculent, suggests that here was the Porthos of the group, vigorous, impetuous, bold and strong, but perhaps a little inclined to take the bit in his teeth and bolt, unless he were carefully handled. For a short time Simmons assisted Abell in getting things started in Baltimore, but he then returned to Philadelphia, where he died in 1855.

The face of Abell is not so easily read. The broad, square chin and level, almost beetling, brows indicate determination in plenty — stubbornness, if you please. But the well-modeled nose and the wide, full-lipped mouth most emphatically are not those of a fanatic. Between the brows are two vertical wrinkles, unusually deep for thirty-one. The young man was not worried, perhaps, but he was indubitably wary. He thinks he has provided against the risks that lie ahead, and, thinking so, he will drive forward; but not for one moment will he forget that the risks are there. A man of few illusions and fewer prejudices, he is no leader of forlorn hopes, no snatcher of victory from the jaws of defeat, but a prudent, eminently reasonable individual, completely unspectacular. Swain might, under some circumstances, keep the burning deck whence all but him had fled. Not so Abell; you will never catch him on a burning deck in the first place. Simmons might hurl himself upon a phalanx, like Winkelried, gathering the spears to his own breast and purchasing victory with death. Never Abell; he would be executing a flanking movement.

The other two are good-humored, slightly smiling into the camera; Abell stands between them almost glaring. Sartorially, he is stunning — gray frock coat, trousers of a sort of plaid, a wonderful checked waistcoat and a gray beaver twice as wonderful. But his face is the face of a responsible executive, watchful, resolute, intensely serious. It is interesting and informative to turn to the man of sixty painted by Dabour. As the clothing has darkened into sober blacks and grays, the face has lightened with a fine serenity. The vertical wrinkles between the brows are now hardly traceable. The sandy fringe of side-whiskers has disappeared, and the wide mouth, shadowed by a mustache now turned white, is on the verge of a smile. This man has won success — the row of bound volumes of THE SUN in the tall bookcase behind him attests the solidity of that success. The world is still no joke to him, but at that it is a reasonably pleasant place for an honest and intelligent man. He has no quarrel with it, for he has had the strength and the skill to cope with it and it has served him well.

But all this was in the distant and doubtful future when young Abell started his press to work on the night of May 16, 1837.

CHAPTER II

☼

A NEWSPAPER FIRST AND ALWAYS

In its first issue, that of Wednesday, May 17, 1837, The Sun carried on the second page, and in the three issues following on the front page, a long address "To the Public." It was a formal exposition of the aims and ideals of the paper and, for the most part, meant little. Within the same year it is probable that a dozen newspapers made substantially the same announcement to an indifferent world; it was expected of everyone who set up a newspaper, and although Abell was destined to be known as a precedent-breaker, he restricted his iconoclasm to things of importance.

Therefore, in accordance with custom, he devoted a column and a half to a windy dissertation upon the virtues and values of newspapers in general and of one-cent newspapers in particular. Judged by modern standards, it is almost unbearably turgid, tedious and hollow; but by the standards of 1837, it was rather clear and direct newspaper writing. In 1837 American newspaper men, as a class, went far to justify Voltaire's remark that men employ speech only to conceal their thoughts. Consider The Sun's modest tribute to the penny press, which is to say, to itself:

It has tended greatly to check the vice of intemperance, that most serious obstacle to all improvement, to diffuse among its votaries a taste for higher enjoyments and worthier pursuits, to render them better men and better citizens, and more competent to maintain those great principles of civil and religious liberty, which are the foundations of all that is great in the Anglo-Saxon race on this or the other side of the Atlantic. It has diffused light where darkness had long prevailed, and roused to a just sense of their importance, as members of the social compact, and their dignity and responsibility as moral beings, those who, bound down by an artificial state of society, sought momentary consolation from a consciousness of their oppression and degradation, in habits tending to degrade still more.

If this seems to be appalling bombast now, by comparison with much editorial writing of the time it is almost a model of terse utterance.

Moreover, all the complicated rhetoric and confusing punctuation of the manifesto do not conceal two announcements that are very significant indeed. One of these is the price of the paper — one cent. The other appears in these words: "We shall give no place to religious controversy, nor to political discussions of purely partisan character. On political principles, and questions involving the interest or honor of the whole country, it will be free, firm and temperate. Our object will be the common good, without regard to that of sects, factions or parties." Almost exactly the same announcement had been made in the first issue of the Philadelphia *Public Ledger* a year earlier.[1]

What these announcements implied can be understood only in the light of contemporary opinion as to the function of a newspaper. Public journals were, indeed, ostensibly purveyors of

[1] Scharff and Westcott: History of Philadelphia; Philadelphia, 1884. Vol. III, p. 2000 *ff*. A copy of the first issue of the *Public Ledger,* in the possession of Mrs. Edward A. Robinson, of Baltimore, shows that the first issue of THE SUN was almost a duplicate, in format, of the *Public Ledger*.

news; but this function was practically always subordinated to some other. Publication of news was not an end in itself; it was rather a trick to gain circulation in order that the paper might serve some other interest of its master — usually a political interest, but sometimes commercial, or social. This employment of the newspaper as an instrumentality to serve some end other than the information of the public was not regarded as in any way questionable, but as entirely normal and right. Ben Day himself, when he projected the New York *Sun*, had no idea of undermining the system; the paper was to be merely an adjunct of his job-printing business, and when it accomplished that end he regarded its function as discharged.[1]

From this conception of the newspaper, not as an end in itself, but as an instrument for the accomplishment of some other end, two inferences were inevitable. One was that the paper's first obligation was not to print truth, but to print such selected truth as would serve its ulterior purpose. The second was that, as this ulterior purpose was always to influence public opinion in a certain way — even if only to influence opinion in favor of Ben Day's print shop — large circulation was not a prime requisite. Every propagandist knows that the quickest way to his end is to reach, not all the people, but the influential people, for if he can secure their support, they will bring in the rest.

American newspapers, therefore, being in the service usually of some political party or of an individual politician, occasionally in the service of some commercial interest, but always in the service of some one other than their readers, had little reason to try to reach the great masses of the people. Those they wished to reach were the influential, which usually means the educated

[1] "For a long time the principal object of the newspaper was to advertise the job office. It did help me in that way. When I got the printing of the American Museum to do I thought myself so lucky that I rather neglected the newspaper." — Interview with Benjamin H. Day in the New York *Sun*, September 4, 1883.

and prosperous. The *Courier and Enquirer*, of New York, with only 4,500 circulation, was yet regarded as the most powerful newspaper in the city, and with reason, for among the 4,500 were practically all the rulers of the city. Even Philip Hone, that prince of snobs, read it; and, in the manner of snobs, would doubtless have repelled with indignation the suggestion that he should read another paper because it was cheaper. There was no reason for the *Courier and Enquirer*, or for any party paper, to reduce its price in order to obtain readers it did not need.

Four newspapers shattered this tradition and set up instead the theory that the first duty of a newspaper is to its readers, with the necessary implication that its most important function is to supply them with accurate and adequate information. The four were the New York *Sun*, the New York *Herald*, the Philadelphia *Public Ledger* and THE BALTIMORE SUN. Among them they worked a complete transformation of American journalism, raising it to what newspaper men, if no others, regard as an immensely higher level; yet not one of them was established for the purpose of transforming anything or uplifting anything. They all stemmed from the little group of printers surrounding Benjamin H. Day and from one man who, although not a printer, was an acquaintance of Day. But Day was in no sense a reformer; and Swain, Abell and Simmons, like him, were merely honest journeymen, seeking a respectable livelihood. As for James Gordon Bennett, the fifth member of the group, the mere suggestion that there was anything of the uplifter in his nature is fantastic.

The origin of the New York *Sun* as a means of advertising Day's job shop has already been mentioned. The *Herald* was established after the success of the *Sun* was evident. Bennett, its founder, was a roving adventurer who had failed at half a dozen varied enterprises before he turned to journalism; he was already in his forties and a complete cynic when Day's spectacular success caused him to try penny journalism,[1] not with the faintest idea of reforming it, but with a grim determination to profit by it.

Abell, Swain and Simmons were younger men and far less colorful personalities than Bennett, but there is no evidence whatever that they were animated by missionary zeal in establishing the *Public Ledger* and THE BALTIMORE SUN. On the contrary, we have Day's word for it that his project at first aroused Swain's apprehension and Abell's derision.[2] One saw in it Day's financial ruin, the other his ridicule with his fellows. That it would work a revolution in journalism obviously never occurred to either of them. Nor is there the least reason to suppose that they were later impressed by anything other than the financial success of the new venture, for when they decided to imitate it the New York *Sun* was still regarded as an adjunct to the job shop. They invaded the realm of the penny press for precisely the same reason that motivated Bennett, namely, because there was profit there.

But as to what they actually did, there is a cloud of witnesses. Ordinarily, however, they refer to "the penny press," [3] ignor-

[1] See Don C. Seitz: The James Gordon Bennetts; New York, 1928, for a swift but lively sketch of the elder Bennett's career.

[2] "When I projected the [New York] *Sun,* I struck off the headline for the paper and took it down to the *Mercantile Advertiser* to show to Abell. He made no end of fun of it. Every time he met me he would say, 'Well, Day, how is that penny *Sun*? Ha, ha! Ho, ho!' His jokes on the penny *Sun* were eternal." — Interview with Day in the New York *Sun,* September 4, 1883.

[3] "By the sheer force of its superior circulation the penny press exerted the most powerful newspaper influence that was felt in the United States, and during this interval (1830–1840) its beneficial influence was the most apparent. It taught the higher-priced papers that political connection was properly subordinated to the other and higher function of the public journal — the function of gathering and presenting the news as it is, without reference to its political or other effect upon friend or foe. The advent of the penny press concluded the transition period in American journalism, and had three effects which are easily traceable. It increased the circula-

ing the fact that the penny press, in so far as its influence on journalism in general is concerned, consisted of these four newspapers. Not that they lacked competition; within a few years after the *Sun* first rose on New York some thirty-five penny papers were established in that city; but most of them were long since forgotten. The *Herald* and *Sun*, in New York; the *Public Ledger*, in Philadelphia, and THE SUN in Baltimore, dragged American journalism after them simply by being enormously successful. Day [1] estimated Swain's profits in thirty years in Philadelphia at $3,000,000; as Abell was an equal partner, his own share must have been as great. Day, however, seems to have been in error in supposing that Swain's money all came from Philadelphia. He shared in the profits of the Baltimore enterprise, also. At any rate, within the same period Abell was in a position to purchase Guilford, a splendid country estate near Baltimore, and to pay $475,000 for it. Bennett's fortune grew to enormous proportions. Day was the victim of his own bad judgment, for after only four years, just as Abell was starting THE BALTIMORE SUN, he sold the New York *Sun* to Moses Y. Beach for $40,000.

Whatever else they may have done, the six-cent papers never turned millions into the pockets of their proprietors; and in any commercial enterprise there is no arguing against a profit. As soon as it became evident that at least four penny newspapers were highly successful financially, their competitors began to study their methods with assiduity and respect; and not only to study, but to copy them, if possible. The penny papers that followed the old methods of journalism quickly faded; but the four that broke new paths swiftly won favor and fortune. Soon

tion, decreased the price of daily newspapers, and changed the character of the reading-matter published." — S. N. D. North, in a report on newspapers for the Census of 1880, quoted by O'Brien: The Story of the [New York] *Sun*, p. 87.

[1] In the interview cited above.

it was clear that not the new price, alone, but the new methods as well accounted for this success, and from that moment adoption of these methods by the six-cent papers was inevitable.

In its early days the penny press was regarded by the *élite* as detestable, and in many respects it was. In Baltimore, for example, Abell described the object of his paper as "to diffuse among its votaries a taste for higher enjoyments and worthier pursuits, to render them better men and better citizens," and then for weeks confined his local news almost entirely to vivid accounts of the assault and battery cases in the local police courts. It occasions no surprise that the educated part of the citizenry were unable to see in that any incitation to "higher enjoyments and worthier pursuits." Abell, it is true, never descended to publishing the backstairs gossip that made Bennett notorious in New York, but he reveled in a juicy murder case, and one of the perennial firemen's riots was his joy and delight, although, of course, he spoke of it in deprecatory tones.

The point that the *élite* habitually overlooked was that a vivid account of the beating administered to a constable at the Fish Market,[1] while it may not be edifying, is far closer to the lives and interests of the masses of the city in which it occurred than are the complimentary letters exchanged between Daniel Webster and a welcoming committee at Pittsburgh.[2] When Abell printed an account of the fight and his chief competitor printed the letters in full, the other may have been the more dignified, but Abell's story was the one that people read.

The clinching argument in favor of the penny press, however, was its price. Henry Fourdrinier's paper-making machine had been steadily reducing the price of paper for some years.[3]

---

[1] THE SUN for Wednesday, May 31, 1837.

[2] The Baltimore *American* for Wednesday, May 17, 1837.

[3] This machine, in all its essentials, is the one still in use. It makes paper in a continuous web, and its product is delivered on rolls. Four-

In 1827 newsprint, mostly hand made, was five dollars a ream, or about one cent a sheet; five years later a sheet a third larger cost only three-quarters of a cent,[1] and the price continued to decline. But the newspapers in general passed the benefit of the lower cost of paper on to their readers, not by reducing the price, but by increasing the size of their sheets. Eventually the New York *Journal of Commerce* appeared with a page thirty-five inches wide and fifty-eight inches high — that is to say, when opened, it was approximately six feet across. Yet the price remained at ten dollars a year or six cents a copy.

In Baltimore the usual price of a year's subscription was eight dollars, but all the papers sold for six and a quarter cents. This odd price was attributable to the system of coinage then prevailing in this country. The United States Mint had, indeed, been established in 1792, but for more than half a century it was unable to keep pace with the needs of a swiftly expanding population. To meet the situation Congress from time to time authorized the proffer as legal tender of various foreign coins, and the ordinary citizen of Baltimore frequently jingled in his pockets Spanish pieces of eight, Mexican reals and half-reals, and British shillings and pennies, as well as coins of the United States. The price of a newspaper was a Spanish, or Mexican, coin known locally as a fip, a contraction of fippenny, or five-penny bit.[2] It was a half-real, and as the real was one-

---

drinier was not its actual inventor. It was invented by Louis Robert, a clerk at the Essone paper mills in France, in 1798. But Fourdrinier (1766–1854) introduced it into England, and with the aid of an engineer named Bryan Donkin (1768–1855) greatly improved it.

[1] Frank Presbery: The History and Development of Advertising; New York, 1929, p. 186.

[2] "The foreign coins whose currency was most frequently legalized by Congress were the British and Portuguese, the latter generally meaning Brazilian, gold, and Mexican, silver. In the early history of the country the Spanish pillar dollar, later . . . the milled dollar, also known as piece of eight, was the very generally recognized monetary unit . . . In the retail trade of the coun-

eighth of a dollar, the fip — the picayune of Louisiana and the sixpence of New York — was worth 6¼ cents.

But to say that the competitors of THE SUN sold for a fip is merely to state the fact without revealing the truth. The fact is significant only in its relation to the value of the fip. In its first market report THE SUN quoted Western bacon at 8½ cents a pound and whiskey (from the wagon and provided you supplied your own barrel) wholesale at 30 cents a gallon.[1] A copy of the *American*, or the *Transcript*, or the *Federal Gazette*, therefore, cost approximately three-fourths as much as a pound of bacon, or a little more than a pint and a half of whiskey. No wonder the workmen of the city rarely purchased those journals. Even the little SUN, at one cent, owing to the alteration in the value of money, was more expensive than its modern descendants at twice the price; but it was still within the means of poor people. When they found that in it they could read, not only about Pittsburgh's opinion of Mr. Webster, but also how their friends and relations fared before the police judge, and how the New Market Engine Company came out in its battle the day before with the United Engine Company, they bought it in great and increasing numbers.

---

try the Spanish, afterward the Mexican, real and half-real were in common use until the middle of the Nineteenth Century. Shilling, or Mexican shilling, was the term generally applied to the real, which was one-eighth of the peso and approximately 12½ cents. But in certain Middle States, especially Pennsylvania and New Jersey, and in much of the South, the real was known as the levy, and the half-real as the fippenny, or fippenny bit. . . . In the Western part of the country the real was popularly known as a bit — a term which yet survives as a popular money of account, the terms two bits, four bits and six bits being employed to express the values 25, 50 and 75 cents. . . . By the law of 1857 all previous laws authorizing the currency of foreign coins in the United States were repealed." — Catalogue of Coins of the United States, Bureau of the Mint, 1928. In Maryland the real was always called a levy, pronounced lev-vy. The term survived until the end of the last century.

[1] THE SUN, May 29, 1837.

It is not to be inferred from this that THE SUN in 1837 was a good newspaper. On the contrary, judged by modern standards it was almost fabulously bad.[1] But in the realm of the blind, a one-eyed man is king and American journalism, in the early part of the Nineteenth Century, was a realm of the blind. What lay at its own doors it could not by any chance perceive. "We looked at the *American* of yesterday morning with some eagerness," chanted THE SUN happily one day early in its career, "expecting to find a full report of the riot of Monday evening; and we looked at it with the more confidence, from the fact that the outrage was committed at the very doors of that office, and the wounded were carried into its rooms for protection. We looked, however, in vain. The *American* was silent on the subject."[2]

In this the *American*, as a matter of fact, was true to the

---

[1] For instance, its early police court stories were frequently characterized by such remarkable statements as "the defendant, a middle-aged man whose name we did not ascertain," and again and again cases were reported in every detail *except* the decision of the court. The stories were full of editorial opinion, frequently written in what was intended to be a humorous vein, but which seems pretty heavy-footed to the modern reader, while occasionally the reporter indulged in what any modern newspaper man would identify at a glance as an outrageous fake. Names, dates and addresses, the things in which absolute accuracy is most rigidly exacted by the modern city editor, were treated by the early SUN with a casualness which makes a present-day reporter gasp. But on one point THE SUN from the very beginning maintained the same policy to which it adheres after a hundred years — it was extremely reluctant to run puffs as reading matter. Some are to be found in its columns, but never in the profusion to be found in other newspapers, even the greatest.

[2] THE SUN, June 7, 1837. The riot referred to was a battle between two fire companies. THE SUN's own account consisted of an inch and a half stating that a savage fight had occurred and that several men were injured, but it gave the name of not one of the victims, nor even the number of casualties. It had, however, aroused the indignation of some of its contemporaries among the "fipenny respectables" by ending its story with the tart comment, "No police, as a matter of course, interfered to quell the riot."

traditions of American journalism, and The Sun was violating them. A mere street brawl among firemen was beneath the attention of the gentlemen for whom the paper was published, and the presumption was that they had no desire to have it brought to their attention by their newspaper. The accepted belief was that paper and ink were too precious to be wasted on the uproars of the commonalty.

Something might be said for this view had the paper and ink been devoted to matters of genuine interest and importance; but that was rarely the case. The press was, for the most part, merely the tool of the politicians. New York, although it was already the largest city in the country, had not yet attained any overwhelming importance in the newspaper world. Its most notable figure was James Watson Webb, editor of the *Courier and Enquirer*. He was amazing enough, in all conscience, but hardly important — a sort of ten-cent Cyrano, swaggering around with pistols and a horsewhip, perpetually thrashing people or being thrashed, shooting people or being shot, and making a nuisance of himself generally. Horace Greeley was in town, but, after his disastrous experience with the two-cent *Morning Post*, he was temporarily in retirement. William Cullen Bryant, too, had not yet begun to count. The *Courier and Enquirer* had some influence, especially in New England, but it was far indeed from being a newspaper of national importance, and the rest of the New York press was completely ineffective beyond the city, although the *Sun* and the *Herald* were to acquire wide reputations within the next five years.

Vastly more important than any New York editor, so far as the rest of the country was concerned, was " a tall, lean, quick-moving man, with brilliant eyes and striking profile, always clinging to the old low shoes and silk stockings, secretary of all the public meetings, toastmaster of the dinners, welcomer of distinguished guests"[1] down in Richmond, Va. This was Thomas Ritchie, editor of the Richmond *Enquirer*, counselor of Presidents, and greatly feared of all politicians.

But the great gladiators of the press, the thunderers behind whom all other newspapers rallied from New Orleans to Boston, were a pair of Washingtonians, Francis Preston Blair, editor of the *Globe*, organ of the Administration, and Joseph Gales, editor of the *National Intelligencer*, organ of the opposition. Either of these two might have said, with regard to his half of the American press, "I am Sir Oracle, and when I ope my lips let no dog bark." In a study of THE SUN they are important, not because they were great newspaper men, but because they were the great exemplars of the newspaper system which THE SUN and its penny contemporaries were destined to overthrow.

Neither Joseph Gales nor Francis P. Blair was a product of Washington. Gales, born in Eckington, England, had learned his trade at Raleigh, N. C., where his father was editor of the Raleigh *Register*, and had been imported into Washington by S. Harrison Smith, proprietor of the *National Intelligencer*, to cover the Senate for that paper, then a tri-weekly. In three years Gales owned the paper.[2] He made it, although at various times it bore various party labels, at all times the organ of the rich, the influential, the privileged. This is not to be construed as an assertion that he was a sycophant; Gales was no more the sycophant than Alexander Hamilton was. It was the bent of his mind to believe, doubtless sincerely, that government should be reserved to the well-born and well-educated and that the intrusion of the masses into public affairs was always dangerous and usually disastrous. Naturally, to him the very name of Andrew

[1] C. C. Pearson in the Dictionary of American Biography, Vol. XV, p. 628.

[2] W. E. Smith in the Dictionary of American Biography, Vol. VII, p. 100.

Jackson was *anathema maranatha.* Clay was his hero, the Bank was his cause. As a writer he was without brilliance, but he had the gift of sententious utterance, and a clarity remarkable in an age of ornate, turgid and obscure writing. He was terribly mauled by the brilliant, if erratic Blair, but with the backing of the wealth and respectability of the country he could not be downed; and, to do him justice, his short, compact paragraphs frequently embodied a sturdy common sense that stung and infuriated his coruscating opponent.[1]

Blair was the discovery of that prince of political manipulators, Amos Kendall. Duff Green, editor of the Administration organ, the *Telegraph,* had committed the treason of adhering to Calhoun after Jackson broke with the South Carolinian, and the Kitchen Cabinet immediately began to cast about for a successor. Blair was editing a newspaper in Kentucky and he was brought to Washington to give the Administration the necessary newspaper support. And the " little man, attired in a frock coat and courtplaster," [2] amply justified the confidence reposed in him by the Jacksonians. He was a master of vituperation, but he was much more; his sarcasm was blistering, and he had a trick of allusion that poisoned the victim and charmed the readers. In 1837 Benton had at last won his long fight to expunge from the Journal of the Senate a resolution censuring Andrew Jackson, passed three years earlier; and Clay had made a series of lugubrious speeches prophesying ruin and devastation as a result. These orations Blair described as " the notes of our ever-dying swan " [3] and regarding the opposition in the Senate he observed: " The specie order can hardly keep alive the venom of

[1] William E. Smith: The Francis Preston Blair Family in Politics, Vol. I, p. 80.

[2] Parton's characterization. See his Life of Andrew Jackson, Vol. III, p. 337. The court-plaster was due to the fact that Blair had received a gash on the head in a stagecoach accident as he came to Washington.

[3] The *Globe,* January 2, 1837.

the malevolent of the Senate. They can scarcely obtain animation enough from it to draw themselves into a coil to strike, and they are evidently in danger of being frozen into a perfect torpor in this inclement weather."[1] To write a passage so completely ophidian without using the word "snake" is not easy. His choice of Joseph Surface as the name by which he constantly referred to Gales also is significant; dull men do not appreciate Sheridan.

Neither of these great lords of the newspaper world paid the slightest attention to the appearance of the little SUN over in Baltimore. Why, indeed, should they? It was not even a newspaper, as they understood newspapers, for it confessed no allegiance to any party and served no cause other than the dissemination of information. Its publisher proposed to make his living out of the newspaper, and not by acting as the Public Printer, after the manner of Blair, nor by depending on the sympathetic interest of the rich and influential, as Gales did. It was his announced purpose to print the news, first of all, and not to battle for the success of any party or any policy. Therefore he was not regarded as an invader of the field of the *Globe* and the *National Intelligencer*. He was of no interest to Blair and Gales; and they would have smiled incredulously had they been told that the prestige and renown of Abell were to survive long after theirs had disappeared; and that when the *Globe* and the *National Intelligencer* had been sleeping in the journalistic graveyard for fifty years, a critic whom no one ever accused of fulsome flattery would list THE SUN as one of "the best, bravest and widest-awake newspapers in the United States."[2]

The little Napier press in the office at 21 Light street was turned by a crank and rated at a thousand copies an hour. It must have clanked and rattled all night long, for on the morning

[1] The *Globe*, January 3, 1837.

[2] Oswald Garrison Villard: Some Newspapers and Newspaper Men; New York, 1933, p. 149.

of May 17 a copy of The Sun appeared on every doorstep in Baltimore. Fifteen thousand copies had been run off to do the job, and Abell must have hired a gang of crankmen to heave and strain at the press. The staff that got out that first issue of the paper has disappeared into the shades of obscurity. Simmons, we know, was there, and as he, like Abell, was a practical printer, it is likely that the type was set and the forms locked by the hands of the proprietors. Probably some husky Irish or German immigrant, possibly a Negro, turned the crank, but who the boy was who fed the sheets into the machine we do not know. Somewhere in the town, possibly in the office that night, was a young printer named Charles Carroll Fulton, who was to count for much in the history of The Sun and for more in Baltimore journalism; certainly he joined the paper soon after. But there is no certainty about the staff that made up that first issue.

The story of the meeting of the City Council at which it was determined to issue $100,000 in shinplasters was the local end of the biggest newspaper story of the times. Just seven days before the appearance of The Sun all but three of the banks of New York had suspended specie payments; and two days later, on May 12, 1837, the banks of Baltimore had followed suit. That is to say, the banks refused to pay gold or silver in payment of checks, but issued instead the notes of the banks themselves. The legality of this procedure remains in doubt to this day, but so long as the banks acted in concert there was nothing the individual depositor could do about it. Suspension, as Benton remarks, was " triumphant in that city whose example, in such case, was law to the rest of the Union." [1] After all, the banks had one irrefutable argument against paying specie — they didn't have the specie to pay. The country, for the last ten years, had been running through a wild orgy of speculation, in the course of

[1] Benton: Thirty Years' View, Vol. II, p. 21.

which it had piled up paper debts to an amount that it could not possibly pay. The crash was inevitable.

However, the course of THE SUN with regard to the crisis was not determined by any abstruse economic or philosophical considerations. To Editor Abell the situation was beautifully simple. The banks had received gold and silver and had refused to return it on demand. Therefore, just seven days after his paper first appeared he unlimbered his guns and opened with artillery on them;[1] Swain had done the same thing in Philadelphia.

It was an immensely popular move, because in attacking the banks the papers were reflecting popular opinion; the circulations of both THE SUN and the *Public Ledger* shot up with rocket-like speed. But there is no sufficient evidence to prove that either Abell or Swain adopted this policy merely as a means of stimulating circulation; both of them, be it remembered, were men of the people, artisans, self-educated and, at this time, not taken seriously by the commercial world. If their reasoning was that of the masses, it was because they were representative of the masses. They felt about the banks exactly as thousands of other small depositors felt; at the same time, when the thousands of others looked at THE SUN and saw their own views reflected in its columns, they were pleased with the paper.

Yet the conservatism that was born in this son of a long line of New England Puritans, and that was to show up strongly as age advanced upon him, was evident even in this early assault on the banks. Although he denounced the suspension of specie payments as plain dishonesty, he pleaded with the victimized depositors to seek redress by legal and orderly means.[2] Baltimore already had a reputation as a riotous town, and what the mob had done, as well as what it had tried to do, to the directors

[1] THE SUN, May 24, 1837.

[2] See THE SUN, May 24 and 26, 1837, for pleas for order, repeated frequently throughout the Summer.

of the Bank of Maryland three years earlier was still vivid in people's memories. THE SUN had no desire to foment fresh uproars of that kind.

Even so, the policy of the paper at this time seemed nothing short of wild radicalism to some of its readers. It was not alone by attacking the banks that Abell shocked the conservative. In a day when it was taken for granted that every newspaper belonged to some political party and when every editor, no matter how much he might vilify the opposition candidate, always spoke with deep respect of politics in general, it was stunning to read in a public journal:

> The political contests of this country are not contests for principle. They are *petit* wars and strifes between the *ins* and the *outs* . . . Who get them up? Unprincipled demagogues, aspiring office-hunters, meddling knaves, who to gratify their lust of power, and towering ambition, would abjure their God and sacrifice their country. . . . We do not attach ourselves to the chariot wheels of any political party. We are independent and we mean to remain so. We care nothing about Martin Van Buren or Nicholas Biddle and their parasites — we go for the good of the whole American people, if we know how to do so.[1]

To those who have known THE SUN during the closing years of its first century there is peculiar interest in another paragraph that appeared when it was only ten days old:

> We see it announced in the Providence papers, that the Rev. Francis Wayland, of Brown University, preached a sermon, last Sabbath a week, on the subject of the embarrassments of the times. . . . Doctor Wayland is an able man. . . . It is doubted, however, if clergymen, from the nature of their pursuits and habits, are the most judicious writers on the subjects like those which at present absorb the whole attention of the country. Practical men — merchants, artisans, artificers, laborers — all who realize the disasters of the day, are the best judges of their causes and effects.[2]

[1] THE SUN, May 31, 1837.

[2] THE SUN, May 27, 1837.

The paper's distrust of clerical interposition in political affairs is clearly no late development.

It was in the second issue, however, that Abell fixed the one policy from which it has never departed. It was in a single brief paragraph, reading, " A Professor Langdon has issued notices in New York, announcing that he will lecture on the causes that have led to the embarrassments of the country. Tickets 12½ cents, children half price. Fudge! "[1] Here is an editorial that has stood for a hundred years. The editors of THE SUN have rewritten it in, literally, thousands of columns, but on politicians, professors with panaceas, and political parsons Abell put a century's editorial deliverances into a single word: Fudge!

It is not to be supposed, however, that the proprietor of THE SUN was a lofty intelligence far above all the current prejudices. In the same issue in which he dared challenge the political supremacy of the clergy, he conformed to the popular standard of morality then prevailing. After an acid comment on the fact that the New York *Star* had devoted " a column or two " to a sketch of Paganini, in view of the violinist's approaching visit to America, he said:

> The man is a good fiddler beyond a doubt, but we do not know that the whole country should be put on the tenter-hook of excitement about him. Treat him courteously, kindly, if you please, and if he fiddles well pay him. There are some stories connected with the morality of Paganini which do not make him a second Joseph by a long shot.[2]

This is diverting, coming from a man who, fifty years later, was to prove his interest in music by such substantial evidence as a gift of $5,000 to the Baltimore Oratorio Society; but the Pecksniffian attitude was the mode of the time, and in most respects Abell conformed to his time.

The immediate cause of the success of THE SUN, the thing

[1] THE SUN, May 18, 1837. [2] THE SUN, May 27, 1837.

that shot its circulation to such a height that its editor, within seven months, could unblushingly claim 12,000 subscribers, was threefold: First, and most important, its consistent and successful effort to inform its readers about their own affairs by reporting the police court and the City Council meetings; second, the espousal of the cause of the people as against the banks, which meant the privileged classes in general; and, third, the sturdy common sense and then the pungency of its comments on local conditions.

Consider, for example, the back-handed slap at the city authorities contained in two editorial paragraphs of June 15, 1837, and how it must have delighted the taxpayers:

> Any body who may be in want of a dead dog, lying in a perfect state of decomposition, can find one in Lexington street, between Charles and St. Pauls. He is a choice article.
>
> Any body in want of a dead pig can find one in Calvert street. He has quietly reposed there three or four days, and is "as good as new."

In addition, Abell played to the contemporary æsthetic tastes of newspaper readers. His front page was given over, as was the custom of the time, to "literature" consisting of elephantine humor or swooning sentimentality. He invariably published at least one poem, frequently accompanied, or preceded, by comment more lackadaisical than the verse itself. For example, a confection entitled, "The Dying Girl to Her Mother" — and worthy of its title — is recommended to readers of THE SUN in these words: "An air of tenderness and melancholy runs through the following lines, which cannot fail to reach the hearts of all who read them. They breathe the soft and tender language of a female heart whilst yielding to the bitterest pangs that arise from unrequited and forsaken love." [1]

[1] THE SUN, June 15, 1837. The juxtaposition in the same issue of the "female heart," the dog, and the hog is one to charm the ribald.

But while these things account for the spurt that carried THE SUN far ahead of all its contemporaries, they do not account for the permanence of its success. The causes of that success make a long and involved story, as will be seen in the pages that follow; but it may be summed up briefly as the extension into ever-widening fields of the policy first applied to Baltimore. As soon as his initial prosperity brought him a little money, Abell began to thrust out. Less than a month after its establishment[1] THE SUN published its first letter "From our Correspondent" in Washington — the beginning of a service that has perhaps brought the paper more distinction than any other single feature of the last hundred years.

This first Washington dispatch still has a professional interest for newspaper men, because it happens to be at once extremely old-fashioned and extremely modern. It begins, "Without intending to violate the Sabbath," — it is dated on Sunday — "I avail myself of this moment, to drop you a line by a friend, who leaves here early in the morning for Baltimore." So a Washington correspondent of 1837 addressed his news editor. Then follows an account of the principal news event of the preceding day — the proceedings in court in the suit brought by certain interests against Amos Kendall, Postmaster-General, to compel him to accept banknotes, instead of specie, at the postoffices — written in clear, succinct, adequate English, covering the somewhat complicated legal jockeying in three hundred words. The dispatch ends with this paragraph:

> The new furniture of the Palace is now going in. It is very splendid, and I am happy to say it is of American manufacture. You will recollect that the late Mr. Monroe raised a breeze by importing his chairs from England. The President is well and, for aught that I know, is happy.
>
> *Yours truly,*

[1] On June 13, 1837.

It is a long time since the White House was the Palace and a Washington correspondent was Yours Truly, but even in that faraway time, SUN men had begun to get the idea that their readers were little interested in argument and ornamentation, and were eager for the essential facts. This is the idea on which the permanent success of THE SUN was built. Its jeremiads doubtless helped sometimes, its crusades helped, its "Fudge!" for all manner of quacks and charlatans helped much, and perhaps, considering the taste of the time, even "A Dying Girl to Her Mother" helped to some extent; but the thing that built THE SUN was news, accurate, early and comprehensive without the burden of useless verbiage. All the rest its competitors could and soon did imitate, sometimes beating it at its own game; but for years Abell contrived to be almost always just a fraction ahead of the best of them in the matter of telling his readers what was going on. Before he encountered a competitor who could rival him at that, his position was securely established and he had resources sufficient to enable him to hold his own against the stoutest rivalry.

It is all very matter-of-fact in the telling. It would be much more spectacular and thrilling as a story to tell how he won fame and fortune by denouncing corruption in high places, or by becoming the great tribune guarding the palladium of the people's liberties. Unfortunately, from the standpoint of the story, he didn't do it that way; he did it by bringing to bear all that he possessed of energy, industry and intelligence on the problem of getting the news, getting it straight, and getting it soon. He was a man of much energy, tireless industry and shrewd intelligence; therefore he dealt with the problem successfully — increasingly successfully, as the years passed.

Nevertheless, there was implicit in his course a compliment to the profession not paid it by most of the men whose names were nationally famous. It is true, the way had been opened for Abell by one man who was a real journalist, not a politician exploiting journalism. This was Hezekiah Niles, the "serene editor whose motto was, The Past — The Present — For the Future,"[1] who for twenty-five years had been teaching Baltimore with *Niles' Weekly Register* that a newspaper might be useful for recording history, as well as for fighting political battles. Niles had retired only a year before Abell came to Baltimore, and through him the town knew that journalism might be an occupation in itself, not an appendage to some greater scheme of life.

Abell, however, was the first conspicuous example of a daily newspaper proprietor who believed that to be publisher of a great newspaper is career enough for any man. He could have sold out morally a dozen times over. As soon as his newspaper became powerful — which was within a very few years of its foundation — the politicians were only too eager to use it; and as it steadily increased in strength and influence, there was hardly any office within their gift that he might not have had in exchange for throwing his newspaper's influence behind one faction or another. But apparently he was not even tempted. A newspaper man he was, and a newspaper man he was content to remain.

[1] W. E. Smith: Blair Family, Vol. I, p. 75.

CHAPTER III

☼

THE COMING OF THE TELEGRAPH

To appreciate the achievement of Abell and the others who created the modern American newspaper in the first half of the Nineteenth Century it must be borne in mind that, in the most literal sense, they did not know what they were doing. They were living in the midst of changes so profound that by comparison the changes wrought by the Revolution of 1776 were slight. These changes affected every phase of the nation's life, but no other institution found the conditions under which it existed altered more completely than did the newspaper.

Three factors intimately affect the life of a newspaper, first, the reading public, second, the system of communications, and, third, the technique of manufacturing — for printing is a manufacturing process. In the second quarter of the Nineteenth Century all three were subjected to profound modifications. In the first place, the reading public was increased enormously by the spread of popular education; and this brought into the newspaper world not merely new readers, but a new kind of reader whose modes of living and thinking differed sharply from those of the relatively well-to-do, who had constituted the newspaper audience up to that time. In the second place, the system of communications, by the introduction of the steamboat and the locomotive, underwent the most radical change it had experienced since the domestication of the horse; and within a few years the invention of the electric telegraph was to eliminate the time element altogether.[1] Robert, Fourdrinier and Donkin had revolutionized the manufacture of paper, and the introduction of the steam-driven press had affected printing almost as radically. Thus all three of the important factors in the production of newspapers were entirely different from anything known to any previous generation.

The pioneers of the penny press thus found themselves engaged in a game all the rules of which had been canceled and were no longer operative, while the new ones were still in process of formulation. To survive, it was necessary to guess what the new rules would be, and to guess correctly most of the time. Conditions demanded alert and supple intelligence, backed by sturdy common sense; for policies whose necessity is as plain as day now were then wrapped in obscurity.

It is interesting, and a little startling, to learn that Abell himself did not understand clearly the secret of his own success. At the end of his first year he attributed the rise of his paper's circulation to the fabulous total of 12,000 a day to his rigid avoidance of factional political quarrels;[2] his news policy he relegated to second place. The fact that the avoidance of dirty politics was at best a negative virtue weighed little with him, and he blandly

[1] The semaphore telegraph, although used in Europe as early as the Napoleonic era, was so expensive and unreliable that it remained sharply restricted in its use. Its effect on communications in general was relatively insignificant.

[2] "We think the chief cause of our success is the free and fearless manner in which we have proclaimed our sentiments, the candor with which we have at all times opened our columns, without respect to politics, to such communications as in our humble opinion may with propriety appear in a newspaper, and the caution with which we have abstained from indulging in the vulgarity and bitterness of party rancor." — THE SUN, May 16, 1838.

ignored the significant truth that James Gordon Bennett, in New York, had won an even greater success by the opposite policy. Bennett regaled the readers of the New York *Herald* with detailed accounts of the editor's combats, political, fistic, social and financial.

The real secret of Abell's success is to be sought in what he did, not in what he refrained from doing. What he did reveals that he understood better than most of his competitors one of the three factors that were upsetting the newspaper world. This one was the extent and direction of the changes that were taking place in the newspaper audience, the American reading public. Even though the public school system was still embryonic, literacy was spreading rapidly among the workers. Every editor knew this, but not every one understood what it signified, for not every editor of that day understood the common people. It was plain to Abell that these new readers were much more interested in events than in ideas; he knew it because he was one of them himself. The Rhode Island printer's apprentice who had earned his living with his hands could not be deceived as to what working men wanted, which was facts, not opinions or ideas. The quickening system of communications enabled him to supply them with more and more stories of happenings, and he bent every effort to meet the demand. It was this setting forth of the incidents of birth and death, life, love, labor and combat among the plain people of Baltimore, and the corollary recital of the more interesting and dramatic events outside the city that brought readers to THE SUN, not the fact that its columns were relatively free of politics.

It is not to be supposed, however, that Abell created instantly a news-gathering organization that functioned perfectly, or even well, as measured by modern standards. Less than a month after his newspaper was established Baltimore was shaken by one of the biggest murder trials in many years, when George Stewart, son of a prominent family, stood at the bar for shooting Dr. Edward J. Alcock, editor of the *Jefferson Reformer*. A change of venue having been effected, the trial began at Annapolis, and the enterprising SUN sent down a special correspondent to report it. It is regrettable that the name of this correspondent has been lost, for he deserves a derisive immortality. His first dispatch announced that the trial had that day begun with the State putting on one of its important witnesses, who occupied the stand all day, but he feared that it would be regarded as contempt of court for him to report anything the witness had said, so he didn't.[1] Abell printed the dispatch and appended to it a thundering denunciation of Star Chamber proceedings in the case of a man charged with murder. But it developed that the correspondent had taken counsel of his fears, not of the bench, for no prohibition of the publication of testimony had been issued, and the *Transcript*, a rival, carried no less than four columns of testimony. THE SUN was reduced to the humiliating expedient of copying the story from its competitor.

Nor was it the special correspondents alone who were afflicted with what seem now to be strange ideas of news. The office itself did some curious things. One midsummer day, for example, THE SUN carefully chronicled the fact that the City Council had adopted an ordinance providing for the erection of a bridge "over the Falls at the fish market," but made no mention of the

[1] The text of this surprising dispatch reads: "I have purposely omitted to send you any part of the testimony in the case for obvious reasons. To my mind it would be improper to publish detached portions of testimony, whilst the trial is pending, as an act of the kind might unnecessarily influence and prejudice the public mind, and thus conflict with the dictates of public justice. And beside all this, I am not clear in my opinion that such publications would not be illegal. I do not know that the court has placed an injunction on the press during the trial; but I understand it has manifested a strong repugnance for such publications." — THE SUN, June 12, 1837. The next day the paper announced in three lines that Stewart had been acquitted.

fact that on that same day the Philadelphia, Wilmington & Baltimore Railroad had been opened to general traffic.[1] Yet the latter event meant rail connection with Philadelphia and the north by the road that now is the trunk line of the Pennsylvania System between Washington and New York.

In the main, however, the paper did present the sort of news that interested the larger number of Baltimoreans able to read. More than that, it commented on men and events, not from the standpoint of the merchant princes and the owners of the baronial estates surrounding Baltimore, but rather from that of the working classes — that is to say, its attitude was one of bristling independence, verging on surliness, and marked by suspicion of, and some contempt for, the intellectuals. The visit to this country of the popular English novelist, Captain Marryatt, evoked this pungent paragraph:

> The Gothamites and Albanians are stuffing the Captain with adulation over green turtle and champaign [*sic*], by way of showing off for effect, and having their names recorded as the patrons of literature in the new world. Remember, the Captain is gleaning materials for a new book. . . . This way of paying fulsome homage to every adventurer who crosses the Atlantic on book speculations, belittles that proper and reserved dignity which ought to be observed on such occasions. Such persons are, at best, but tolerated spies on our manners and habitudes, and should be admitted with great caution into closer intimacy.[2]

This touchiness with regard to British authors was characteristic of the American people at the time and was, in part, a reaction to the caustic comments of Harriet Martineau after a tour of the country in 1836.[3] But aside from literary skirmishing, the attitude of the young democracy toward England still held

---

[1] The Sun, August 1, 1837.

[2] The Sun, July 18, 1837.

[3] Her Society in America was published in 1837, and her Western Notes in 1838.

more than a hint of colonialism. THE SUN epitomized that attitude in a paragraph that reads strangely today:

> The young Queen of England has been literally eaten up by the press of the country. Many crude speculations have been put forth on her charms, politics, sentimentality, freaks of temper and even hymeneal speculations. One editor pronounced the royal dame a thorough paced democrat, even dyed in the wool; and therefore recommends her to the sympathetic embraces of our Yankee President, without consulting the appetite of the little magician, if he relished a royal rib. Another sage, with specks on, declares her a second Bess, and that " she has the heart and stomach of a King "; that one of these days she might take it into her royal head to pull the Bishop of Winchester's wig.[1]

When one realizes that this eligible *parti* for a matrimonial alliance with Martin Van Buren, the Red Fox of Kinderhook, was none other than the majestic Victoria, the paragraph takes on the look of an apparition from Cloudcuckooland, rather than a summary of American newspaper comment on an accession to the British throne. It is probable, however, that this attitude of flippancy was not altogether based on a naïve ignorance. It was only twenty-two years since the end of the War of 1812, and England was still regarded as the hereditary foe; hence no opportunity to twist the Lion's tail was to be neglected.

Early in September came the first opportunity for THE SUN to demonstrate its newspaper enterprise in the grand fashion. On that day both local news and advertising were swept off the front page and Pages 2 and 3 as well; and the last page, containing the remnant of the advertising, carried also this explanation:

> The President's message, which will be found entire in this day's paper, was received at our office at 2 o'clock precisely — the transmission from Washington to Baltimore occupying less than two hours.

---

[1] THE SUN, August 4, 1837.

Its great length has excluded almost everything previously prepared for publication.

Advertisements crowded out will hereafter be attended to.

We, of course, have neither time nor room for a word of comment on this important document.[1]

Here is evidence that if THE SUN was adapting itself to the radical change in the newspaper-reading public, it was at the same time taking advantage of the still more radical change in the system of communications. Hitherto Baltimore morning newspapers had been content to wait for the President's message as it was printed in Washington papers, delivered in Baltimore the next day; then the local press would copy the story, presenting it to Baltimore readers two days after delivery of the message. But with Baltimore & Ohio trains now making the forty miles from Washington in less than two hours, an enterprising newspaper had no excuse for such slow service, and THE SUN cut the time down by twenty-four hours.

All the world, it seemed to that generation, was moving with furious speed. Consider the dizzying progress of an unknown Baltimorean of the period, as noted under the headline, "Rapid Traveling":

A gentleman of this city who left Boston on Friday last at one o'clock P. M., reached New York on the following morning in season to take the 5 o'clock boat to Philadelphia, and by the 12 o'clock boat for Baltimore he reached this city about 11 o'clock on the same day, accomplishing the whole distance from Boston in the short space of *thirty-four hours.*[2]

The italics are THE SUN's. The present regular schedules between these two cities are nine hours by rail and about half that time by air; but the difference in this respect between 1837 and

[1] THE SUN, September 6, 1837.

[2] THE SUN, September 8, 1837. The journey from New York to Philadelphia seems to have been made by the Raritan Canal, opened in 1835.

1937 is insignificant by comparison with the enormous difference between 1837 and 1827. In the tremendous years following the chartering of the first railroad in the United States the newspaper man's whole world was thrown out of place, and nimble indeed was he who could maintain his footing in the flux.

Before The Sun had completed its second year the quarters in Light street were outgrown and a better location became necessary. On February 16, 1838, the paper made its first removal, occupying a building at the southeast corner of Gay and Baltimore streets.[1] The first issue from the new building was dated February 18.

Now it might fairly claim to be of, as well as in Baltimore, for Gay street was the very spinal cord of the town. For one thing, five of the town's seven dailies were already located on that thoroughfare, making it the Park Row, the Fleet Street, of Baltimore. But aside from that, Gay street has always had a quality of its own. For nearly two hundred years it has remained a queerly contradictory street, stubbornly non-conformist, defying classification — undistinguished, but important, unimpressive, but doing an enormous business, largely ignored by the writers of literature intended to advertise the town, but beloved by artists, poets and novelists, sometimes deplored by moralists, but cheerful and friendly. It is a street in its shirt-sleeves, blandly indifferent to both the smiles and frowns of supercilious neighbors.

Its very name differentiates it from the rest. Baltimore likes to give lordly names to its streets, names associated with great events, Lexington, Saratoga, Eutaw; or with warrior heroes, Howard, Greene, Fayette, Redwood; or with illustrious statesmen, Madison, Franklin, Hamilton, Jefferson, Clay. But this

---

[1] Harold E. West: History of The Sun, published in The Sun, May 14, 1922.

thoroughfare is named for a mere surveyor, one Nicholas Ruxton Gay, who laid it out in 1747.[1] Starting at the water's edge it runs straight north for half a mile, then suddenly shoots away at a tangent to the northeast, cutting recklessly across the rectangular pattern of the city, creating crazy angles and odd-shaped little plazas where it intersects other streets, until finally, at the corner of the old Baltimore Cemetery, at what is now North avenue, it loses both name and character and becomes the Belair road.

For several miles from the harbor Gay street is now a business thoroughfare, the first half dozen blocks consisting of heavy, solid business buildings. Yet even in this, its most prosaic section, it contrives to maintain a distinctive touch, for nearly all these buildings have to do with the sea and ships. Near the water there are the Customs House and the United States Appraisers' Stores; and up and down the street are the offices of steamship lines and ship chandlers' establishments with windows filled with ships' lanterns, sextants, ships' clocks, and all sorts of mysterious objects in brass and mahogany. Even the bank that occupies one corner of this nautical thoroughfare is the National Marine.

But when The Sun established its quarters — which it was to occupy for fourteen years — at the corner of Gay and Baltimore, the street was much livelier than it is today. In 1838 there were several hotels and seamen's lodging-houses on the lower part. One, not far from The Sun, seems to have been an especial favorite of both ships' officers and actors. It was a shopping district, too, as well as a newspaper street. At this time Charles was beginning to be the street of the aristocrats, Lexington was the place of residence of substantial burgesses, what is now Baltimore (it had begun as Market street), was the main shopping center, Pratt was the seamen's thoroughfare; but all the world

[1] See an article by Emily Emerson Lantz in The Sun, April 13, 1924, for account of the origin and development of Gay street.

at one time or another had business in Gay street. It was far from being altogether lovely. The bad came with the good. If great ladies sometimes drove through it in their carriages, prostitutes haunted its sidewalks. If brilliant men knew it — Peale, and Poe, and the Booths, great Junius Brutus, Edwin the Adored, and John Wilkes Booth the Damned — human flotsam likewise floated through it. More than one election riot, involving many casualties, was staged there, and it was at the foot of Gay street that the mob piled obstructions on the tracks to stop the passage of Massachusetts troops in 1861, and there was spilled the first blood of the Civil War —

> the patriotic gore
> That flecked the streets of Baltimore.

Near High street was the boyhood home of George W. Childs and just off Gay that of John H. Hewitt, the poet-musician-editor, who made the remarkable record of having entered a poetry contest against Edgar Allan Poe and won it, of having written an oratorio on Jephtha in competition with the familiar one of Händel — it was sung in New York by a chorus of two hundred voices — and of having set up a newspaper in competition with THE SUN, maintaining the contest for three years.[1] This was the *Clipper*, whose name was recognition of the swift sailing ships that were then beginning to make the name of Baltimore familiar in every port in the world. It was published on the opposite corner of the street from THE SUN and was also

---

[1] John H. Hewitt: Shadows on the Wall, p. 53. This volume of reminiscences, published in 1877, although it is full of inaccuracies, is one of the most interesting books about the Baltimore of this period. Hewitt seems to have known everybody and seen everything, and his comments on men and events are frequently extremely piquant and sometimes illuminating. It is in this volume (p. 41) that he makes perhaps the most remarkable literary judgment ever formulated in Baltimore in these words: "Poe was not the poet he was said to be; he added but little to the literary reputation of our country."

a penny paper; but its competition apparently never gave Abell much anxiety.

It was here on the corner of Gay street that THE SUN really grew into the communal life of Baltimore and its proprietor finally emerged from the status of a roving printer into that of a solid citizen. An important contributing factor to this latter development, no doubt, was his marriage in 1838 to Mrs. Mary Fox Campbell, daughter of John Fox, originally of Peekskill, New York, a marriage that lasted through twenty tranquilly happy years until the death of Mrs. Abell in 1859.

By the time of its establishment in its new quarters THE SUN was no longer an experiment. The feasibility of the penny paper was proved and the fundamental soundness of Mr. Abell's news policy demonstrated. The circulation of the paper was the largest in Baltimore, and its advertising revenues were correspondingly large and swiftly increasing. Abell had every reason to look upon his work and call it good.

He did nothing of the sort. Precisely at this point he rose from the ranks of merely good journalists into the small category of great ones; for when money came into his hands, instead of resting on his oars to enjoy his small success, he redoubled his efforts to make his paper not merely a remunerative local concern, but a really great journal.

One of his characteristics, while it probably contributed to the success of the paper, embarrasses its historian. This was the ruthless suppression of the individuality of every servant of THE SUN. Henry Watterson might declare, "There will never be an end to the personality of journalism,"[1] but Mr. Abell's theory from the beginning was that a newspaper is the composite product of many minds and should not be associated with any personality. So consistently did he adhere to this belief that for

[1] In the Louisville *Courier-Journal,* January, 1873, quoted by O'Brien in The Story of the [New York] *Sun,* p. 167.

many years there was no such thing as a by-line in THE SUN;[1] and today it is impossible to identify more than a very few of the men who helped make it in the early days. Hewitt says[2] that Jesse D. Reed, "a man of very ordinary talent" was a member of THE SUN staff "from the day of its first issue." As he also remarks that Reed was "bitter against" his (Hewitt's) own paper, the *Clipper*, one may reasonably doubt that Reed's talent was as small as Hewitt would have us believe. Apparently Reed was for a long time the entire local staff, and possibly from his pen came the astonishing police court stories that featured the early issues. If this is the case, then he certainly possessed one characteristic of genius, to wit, a vivid imagination.

Nor is it possible to fix the exact date of Charles C. Fulton's first employment; but as he became managing editor in 1841 and had previously been a compositor and then a reporter,[3] it is likely that he was connected with the paper at, or shortly after, the time of the removal to the corner of Gay street. Fulton is important in the history of THE SUN as the first of a long series of men trained on the paper who subsequently carved out careers

[1] In fact, it was not until about 1882, after A. S. Abell had almost entirely relinquished control of the paper, that Frank A. Richardson, Washington correspondent, was permitted to append the initials F. A. R. to his correspondence. In 1884 they appeared at the end of his dispatches from the Democratic National Convention at Chicago, and so did the initials of Norval E. Foard, who will be met with in Chapters VIII and XII. For years thereafter this was the only thing resembling a by-line to be found in THE SUN, though in the days before the Civil War its Washington correspondents had signed fanciful pseudonyms, *e.g.*, Ion and Aga, to their dispatches. In 1888, at the time of the Whitechapel murders in London, a stranger calling himself McNulty was permitted to sign several articles dealing with them. He claimed to be fresh from London, and familiar with the Whitechapel scene. When his articles appeared in THE SUN he ran up a number of bills in Baltimore on the strength of them, and after his departure for parts unknown THE SUN paid these bills.

[2] Shadows on the Wall, p. 62.

[3] Biographical Cyclopedia, p. 23.

elsewhere. No small part of its contribution to American journalism consists of the procession of skillful men that for a century it has been sending to other papers. Fulton served it for more than a dozen years; then, in 1853, he obtained a half interest in the *American* and swiftly raised that once moribund sheet to the level of the chief competitor of THE SUN. During the Civil War the accident of having a relative in the Navy seems to have turned his attention to the sea fighting, and the *American* became the foremost reporter of the conflict as it developed on the sea. Fulton's pronounced Northern sympathies gave him a superior position during the war, at least in officialdom, and by the time the fighting was over, the *American* was sharply challenging THE SUN's dominance in the Baltimore field. One of Fulton's daughters married the fiery and fantastic General Felix Agnus, of the Union Army, and Agnus succeeded his father-in-law in control of the paper, sustaining, in the main, Fulton's policies.[1] So, while the two papers were antagonistic in politics and rivals in every other way, the journalistic methods and tech-

---

[1] General Agnus was born at Lyons, France, on July 4, 1839. As a young man he served under Napoleon III in the Austrian campaign of 1859, and later in the same campaign under Garibaldi. He came to the United States in 1860. He enlisted as a sergeant in Duryea's Fifth New York Zouaves on May 9, 1861, and was soon commissioned second lieutenant. On September 6, 1861, he saved the life of General Judson Kilpatrick at the Battle of Big Bethel. He was a major by 1863. On one day, March 13, 1865, he was breveted a lieutenant-colonel for "gallant and meritorious services" at the Battle of Gaines' Mill (June 13, 1862), a colonel for the same at the Battle of Port Hudson, La. (March 27, 1863), and a brigadier-general for the same during the whole war. He was often wounded, and carried several bullets in his body to the end of his life. Invalided to Baltimore in 1864, he married Fulton's daughter on December 13, and on Fulton's death took over the management of the *American*. But he did not resign from the Army until after Lee's surrender. With his fierce military mustachios, his expansive French manners, his fluent but exotic English and his love of the spotlight, he was a picturesque figure in Baltimore for many years. He died on October 31, 1925.

niques of the *American* were essentially those that Fulton had learned on THE SUN. Since he had trained his chief competitor, it may fairly be said that the influence of Abell, the journalist, absolutely dominated the Baltimore field for more than half a century.

Relatively early in the Gay street period THE SUN was joined by Thomas J. Beach, who had previously served both the *Transcript* and the *American*, and who was to have the distinction of holding the post of editor-in-chief during THE SUN's most critical days, the period of the Civil War; but John T. Crow, who, as Washington correspondent and managing editor, was to share with Beach the fearful responsibility of war times, did not join the staff until 1847.

In its new quarters the paper thrived. Three times its format was enlarged. Seven months after its arrival in Gay street it announced the installation of "a new double cylinder Napier press which will work nearly twice as fast as our former press,"[1] and four months after that it was proclaiming, "We have a circulation equal to all the daily morning papers of this city combined, and our sheet is read by all classes, from the Hall of Congress to the humble dwelling of the poor."[2] But this

[1] THE SUN, November 18, 1839.

[2] THE SUN, March 30, 1840. As a specimen of the newspaper style of the period and of the attitude the journalist thought fit to assume toward his work — at least in public — this pronouncement is interesting. Excerpts from it: "When we see the mechanic and the laborer, in their hour of rest, perusing our sheet, we feel no little gratification at having contributed to lighten their toil; when we find an apprentice boy saving a cent from his pocket money to purchase a SUN we are conscious that to him we have imparted some knowledge that may increase his appetite for more, and perhaps awaken the energies of dawning talent; and when our little diurnal is sought by the learned lawyer, the scientific physician and the pious divine, we know that even for them we have culled something that will add to their learning, communicate new discoveries in their art, and encourage them to labor for the welfare of their fellow-men. . . . It has ever been our care to conduct our paper upon such principles as

apparent complacence did not indicate any slackening of energy. THE SUN was now a part of Baltimore, and all Baltimore was fairly bursting with energy, reaching out in a dozen directions, battling strongly and successfully to retain her position as the second city of the country. No institution, really a part of the town, could fail to respond to the drive of that tremendous vitality.

A significant date, not in the history of THE SUN only, but also in that of American journalism is March 4, 1841; for on that day occurred the first great success in coöperative news-gathering. As THE SUN explained it the next morning:

> By agreement with the Postoffice Department, the Baltimore & Ohio and Philadelphia, Wilmington & Baltimore Railroad Companies ran expresses from Washington to Philadelphia, carrying President Harrison's Inaugural Address. . . . A locomotive with one car attached, under the conduct of Captain Slack, started from Washington by signal at thirty-five minutes after twelve, M., and arrived at the outer depot near this city, in *one hour and a quarter;* where the packages for Philadelphia and New York were taken by Mr. James Murray, a most distinguished express rider . . . and transmitted with the utmost dispatch to the depot at Canton, where a locomotive and car were in readiness to start for Philadelphia. . . . By the express from Washington we received the address, which was politely brought from the outer depot by the Postoffice express to the city; and . . . we had it ready in an extra for delivery at the desk of our office as promised.[1]

---

in our humble opinion would best attain the most desirable objects — the dissemination of information, the suppression of vice, the supremacy of the laws and the encouragement and reward of deeds of patriotism, honor and virtue."

[1] THE SUN, March 5, 1841. Perhaps it is advisable to explain to the modern reader that in 1841 the locomotives of the B. & O. were not permitted to move closer to the center of the city than the Mount Clare Station, on Poppleton street, in the western part of the city, the cars being drawn thence on tracks laid in Pratt street to Charles; while the P., W. & B. similarly halted its locomotives at Canton, far to the eastward. This left a gap

The significance of this is not so much in the fact that THE SUN got out an extra with the Inaugural on the same day it was delivered, or that the *Public Ledger* in Philadelphia had it by six o'clock the same evening, astounding as such speed seemed to the public in 1841; but rather in the way it opened the eyes of newspaper men to the possibilities of coöperative newsgathering.

Generations before this the exchange system had been established, whereby newspapers swapped copies, and hence news. On this occasion THE SUN hastily mailed copies of the extra to all its exchanges, thereby enabling them to beat their competitors by a full twenty-four hours; and so spectacular was the scoop that the Columbus, Ohio, *Journal* accused the *Ohio Statesman*, of the same city and on the exchange list of THE SUN, of some sort of underhand work, probably including premature publication or, as the craft says now, "breaking the release date."[1] But exchanging papers was an entirely different thing from a coöperative enterprise in which several newspapers shared the expense of newsgathering at distant points.

The handling of the Harrison Inaugural was such an enterprise. It was the first step in the long progress that has converted nearly every daily newspaper in America into a unit in an immense, closely knit organization (the Associated Press) covering the world. In furthering this process THE SUN henceforth played an important part into which it was thrust by geographical, political and financial circumstances. To begin with, it was already allied, by the circumstance of identical ownership, with the Philadelphia *Public Ledger*. Both of these papers were by now influential and highly profitable; they occupied the two southernmost of the large cities of the country, and THE SUN was the metropolitan newspaper closest to Washington. It was

---

of some four miles to be covered by the express rider; that is, a horseman.

[1] See THE SUN, March 16, 1841.

inevitable that the newspapers of New York and Boston should look to the SUN-*Public Ledger* combination for assistance in handling news from Washington and the South; compensating them by similar service from the North.

To anticipate the story somewhat, this alliance with the New York papers resulted in the establishment of the famous "horse express" across Nova Scotia in 1845. Halifax, at the time, was the first port of call for the mail steamers from Europe, but there was as yet no rail connection with that city. Therefore, THE SUN and its allies established relays of horses and riders to carry dispatches from Halifax a hundred and fifty miles across the peninsula to Annapolis, on an estuary of the Bay of Fundy; there they were placed aboard steamers which transported them to Portland, Maine, which was already connected with Boston by rail; and from Boston they were sent by rail to New York, Philadelphia and Baltimore. The entire distance was about a thousand miles and the ordinary time of transmission was approximately fifty hours. Less than ten years earlier THE SUN had been marveling at the speed of the traveler who passed from Boston to Baltimore in thirty-four hours; yet here was that speed already nearly doubled.

It was in 1832 that one of the most eminent portrait painters in the country, one of the founders and for seven years president of the National Academy of Design, began to neglect a career that had already brought him fame and fortune and to flirt with a wild idea. To be sure, Samuel Finley Breese Morse had always been a dabbler in scientific matters, inventing a marble cutting machine, and introducing Daguerre's photographic process into America; but not until he became obsessed with the powers of "the galvanic fluid" did he begin to give his friends anxiety. For the last nine years, however, he had allowed his scheme to transmit messages over long distances by the use of electromagnetism to interfere seriously with his artistic work. He had made a machine that would work, too, under laboratory conditions, and had taken out patents here and abroad; but, except for a family of brass manufacturers named Vail, in New Jersey, who had put up a little money for his experiments, few hard-headed, realistic business men took the inventor seriously.

In Washington, however, where he had spent years pleading with Congress for an appropriation large enough to enable him to try out his invention on a grand scale, he had the good luck to encounter a Marylander who was himself essentially an artist. This was John P. Kennedy, the Baltimore novelist, who had gone into politics and got a seat in Congress. The author of "Swallow Barn" had imagination and political influence as well; he got Morse's bill referred to a committee of which he was chairman; perhaps he also enlisted the support of the leading newspaper in his home town, for some one did;[1] and, finally, on February 21, 1841, "on motion of Mr. Kennedy, of Maryland, the committee took up the bill to authorize a series of experiments to test the merits of the Morse electro-magnetic telegraph."[2] The fight was bitter and close, but through the exertions of the novelist, the opposition of practical men was overcome and the painter got his money.[3] On May 25, 1844, young Alfred Vail, of the brass-manufacturing family and now Morse's third assistant, sat in a room in the Baltimore & Ohio sta-

[1] "Professor Morse found in Mr. Abell a most zealous friend to the magnetic telegraph; all the influence of THE SUN was exerted in behalf of the invention, and for an appropriation of thirty thousand dollars for the construction of an experimental line from Washington to Baltimore." — Scharf: History of Baltimore City and County, p. 620.

[2] Quoted from the record of the House by Edward M. Gwathmey in John Pendleton Kennedy, p. 41.

[3] "The bill was passed by the close vote of 89 to 83. A change of three votes . . . would have consigned the invention to oblivion. That this was not its fate is mainly due to the perseverence and foresight of the distinguished member from Maryland, Hon. J. P. Kennedy." — S. F. B. Morse in a speech at a banquet in his honor in 1868, quoted by Gwathmey, *op. cit.*

tion in Pratt street near Light, and watched a paper tape unrolling before him be mysteriously covered with dots and dashes as Morse, sitting in the Supreme Court room at Washington, tapped out the words of the first formal telegraph message ever sent: "What hath God wrought?"[1]

This was by long odds the biggest newspaper story since the foundation of THE SUN, and one of the big stories of all time. THE SUN carried it in a column headed "Local Matters" on Page 2. Under the subhead "Magnetic Telegraph," it said, "Some further experiments were conducted on the new telegraph on Saturday morning, which were witnessed by a number of spectators. Several messages were sent to and fro with almost incredible dispatch, which, although unimportant in themselves, were most interesting from the novelty of the proceeding, forcing upon the mind the reality of the complete annihilation of space, in the fact that a distinct and well-defined conversation was actually going on with persons in a city forty miles distant."[2]

This filled eleven lines in the paper. Immediately below it seventeen lines were given to the proceedings of the City Court—four cases of assault and battery and one of keeping a disorderly house. On the front page, two and a half columns were given to the Methodist General Conference and the Presbyterian General Assembly, meeting in New York and Louisville, Kentucky, respectively. What is news?

But this failure to reflect the importance of Morse's invention in the news columns cannot be ascribed to the publisher's indifference to means of speeding communications. For years Mr. Abell had been spending money like water on anything that

---

[1] Scharf: History of Baltimore City and County, p. 503. The engineer who built the line was Ezra Cornell, whose name is now bracketed by the academic world with that of the Baltimorean, Johns Hopkins.

[2] THE SUN, May 27, 1844.

promised to bring him the news even a few minutes ahead of his rivals. Not only was every important event in Washington reported by special train, if possible, but when no train was available, as in the case of the vote on the Fiscal Bank Bill, in 1841, horsemen were used. In 1841 the MacLeod trial, in Utica, New York, involved the right of United States courts to punish a British subject for an act which presumably took place outside this country's jurisdiction. In the end it was revealed that MacLeod, the defendant, was not guilty; but there was a tense moment when it seemed that the jurisdictional dispute might lead to war. THE SUN did not hesitate to set up relays of horsemen who, in conjunction with such railroads as existed, sped the news of the trial to Baltimore. It also shared with its New York associates the expense of sending the pilot boat *Romer* to London for late news. In a house on Hampstead Hill in London THE SUN kept a flock of four or five hundred carrier pigeons for use in transmitting news.[1]

The singularly uninspired treatment of the news of the first telegraphic message therefore cannot be ascribed to any lack of interest in what Morse sought to accomplish.[2] It was, rather, an illustration of the peril in which even the ablest and most alert newspaper man always lives — the peril of missing the biggest story. It is the irony of journalism that it is splendidly equipped to handle all the news except the biggest. When events transcend all previous experience, the newspaper man's ordinary humanity traps him, and he is frequently as blind as everyone else. Similar instances occurred when hundreds of newspapers, after devoting columns to the address of the orator of the day — whose very name only historians remember — at the dedication

[1] Scharf: History of Baltimore City and County, p. 620.

[2] The failure to appreciate the importance of the story was not monopolized by THE SUN. The *American* gave it twenty-three lines, and the other papers treated it similarly.

of Gettysburg Battlefield, added, "President Lincoln also spoke"; and again in 1908, when the Wright brothers made their first flight at Kitty Hawk, North Carolina, and many newspapers declined to publish the dispatch announcing the event, convinced that it was a hoax. After ninety-three years the burial of the story of the telegraph seems almost incredible; but it was, as a matter of fact, not unusual, indeed, almost normal. It dampens the pride of the craft to realize this fact, but a fact it is.[1]

However, as the electric telegraph continued to demonstrate its practicability, the press swiftly woke up to what it meant.[2] The desirability of extending lines to Philadelphia and New York was immediately apparent, and it is not surprising to find Swain, Abell's partner, among the incorporators of the Magnetic Telegraph Company, along with Morse and Amos Kendall. When funds were exhausted after the line was opened between Philadelphia and New York, Abell and Swain were among those who put up additional capital to complete the link to Baltimore.[3]

---

[1] The incredulity of the public was even greater than that of the press. Scharf relates (*op. cit.*, p. 504, footnote) an amusing illustration supplied by Hendrick B. Wright, president of the Democratic National Convention which met in Baltimore May 27, 1844, and chose for Vice-President, as Polk's running mate, Silas Wright. Hendrick, knowing Silas was in Washington, sent him a telegram asking if he would accept; and Silas immediately telegraphed back a declination. This Hendrick B. Wright announced to the convention, which was still in session, but the information was scornfully rejected and the convention adjourned until the next day to enable a committee to go by train to Washington and return with the nominee's true answer.

[2] The first telegraphic press dispatch ever sent cannot be claimed by THE SUN. It came to the Baltimore *Patriot* at 1 P.M., Saturday, May 25, 1844, and was published as follows: "One o'clock — There has just been made a motion in the House to go into committee of the whole on the Oregon question. Rejected, — ayes, 79; nays, 86."

[3] Scharf: History of Baltimore City and County, p. 507. Incidentally, the first pole of this line is still standing. It is the old Shot Tower, at Fayette and Front streets, from the top of which the lines

In the city Abell put his star man, Fulton, on the job of deciphering telegraphic dispatches, which were already sent in code, owing to the slowness of the early receiving instruments; they were capable of only about twenty words a minute.[1]

---

dropped to the telegraph office in the third story of the Postoffice, which was then at the corner of Fayette and North, now Guilford avenue. The wires were carried north over the roofs to the edge of the city. Poles in the streets came later.

[1] On May 11, 1846, THE SUN achieved a journalistic feat which had international repercussions. That day President Polk sent his Mexican war message to Congress, and THE SUN had it telegraphed to Baltimore in its entirety — the longest document ever so transmitted up to that time. In Paris the Academy of Sciences had it reprinted side by side with an authenticated copy of the original message, and this exhibit was put in the hands of Deputy Arago, who was then fighting for an appropriation for a Paris-Brussels telegraph line. Soon thereafter the Paris correspondent of the Washington *National Intelligencer* wrote, "In the Chamber, on the 18th, inst., when the proposed appropriation for an electrical telegraph from this Capital to the Belgian frontier came under consideration, Berryer opposed it on the ground that the experiments of the new system were incomplete; that it would be well to wait for the full trial of what was undertaken between Paris and Rouen. Arago answered, 'The experiment is consummated; in the United States the matter is settled irresistibly. I received three days ago THE SUN of Baltimore, with a letter from Mr. Morse, one of the most honorable men of his country, and here is the President's message, printed from the telegraph in two or three hours; the message would fill four columns of the *Moniteur;* it could not have been copied by the most rapid penman in a shorter time than it was transmitted. The galvanic fluid travels seventy thousand leagues per minute.' The appropriation of nearly a half-million of francs passed with only a few dissenting votes." — See Scharf: History of Baltimore City and County, p. 621.

CHAPTER IV

THE MEXICAN WAR AND AFTER

Two years later came a story that THE SUN didn't miss and that established its reputation as a great newspaper. This was the Mexican War.

It came at a time singularly propitious for the paper. In 1846 Abell was forty years old, that is to say, fully mature, yet with his best years still ahead of him, seasoned and experienced, well established financially and still ambitious. The city that he served, too, was at its zenith. Baltimore was now definitely the second city in the country. The next census — that of 1850 — was to show it 26,000 ahead of its nearest rival, Boston, and nearly 40,000 ahead of Philadelphia. The Pennsylvania city had, indeed, raided the great trade territory of the Susquehanna Valley, but Baltimore had compensated that loss by an important and increasing commerce with the South. Rail and water connections were making her the great trading center of the cotton-growing regions, and such gigantic mercantile houses as those of Walters and Hopkins depended largely on their commission business with that region. Enoch Pratt, the great ironmonger, drew a considerable part of his business from below the Potomac. Baltimore was one of the most prosperous and energetic cities in the United States, and no one as yet had cause to suspect that the loss of this Southern trade, fourteen years later, was to bring it into temporary eclipse.

THE SUN was still confined to four pages, but they were much larger now, approximately two-thirds of the dimensions, each way, of a modern newspaper page. The front page still carried two columns of advertising, but it had been cleared of metrical addresses of dying girls to their mothers, and windy descriptions of trips through Arabia. Such stuff was now relegated to the WEEKLY SUN, established in 1838. The greater part of the front page was given over to news, and the whole paper was carrying more and more fresh information, gathered by its own people, and less and less second-hand stuff clipped from exchanges.

With the outbreak of hostilities in Mexico the chief source of news swung suddenly to the South, while Halifax, Boston and New York became momentarily far less important. This meant that the whole group of newspapers allied in such enterprises as the Nova Scotian pony express and the voyage of the *Romer* now looked to Baltimore and THE SUN for their most important news. Thus Abell was thrust to the fore as the chief news gatherer, not for his own subscribers only, but for immense constituencies in Philadelphia, New York and Boston as well. The success with which he met this responsibility made his reputation as a newspaper man, and marked, without doubt, the highest point in his professional career.

No comprehension of the magnitude of his achievement is possible without some consideration of the physical obstacles which he had to overcome. In 1937 it is infinitely easier for a newspaper to cover a war in Ethiopia, or Outer Mongolia, than it was for him to get the news from Mexico in 1846. There were no cables. There were no continuous telegraph lines. There were not even continuous railroads, and such highways as existed were, in many cases, muddy, rutted and difficult woods roads.

The Army base of supplies and the chief news center was the port of New Orleans. The war correspondent had not yet been invented, and all newspapers depended for their information on dispatches from commanders in the field, sometimes supplemented by letters from individual officers and soldiers. The problem was to establish swift and dependable service from New Orleans to Baltimore; to solve it, Abell employed and coördinated every available means of communication, including telegraph, railroads, steamboats, stage-coaches and "sixty blooded horses."[1] The result of his enterprise was that his dispatches usually beat the Southern mails by thirty hours or more.

In the very beginning it was proved again that Fortune favors the brave. Abell's arrangements were still incomplete at the time of the first important fight of the war; his messenger reached the telegraph office at Washington only about fifteen minutes ahead of the mail. But he had filed his dispatch, marked "exclusively for THE SUN," and transmission was almost complete when the mail came in. Arrangements were immediately made to open a second line and send the news publicly. But hardly had THE SUN message been completed when a thunder storm broke over Baltimore and the manager of the telegraph office cut off the magnets to protect them from lightning. By the time the storm was over, the Washington office was closed for the night, with the result that THE SUN alone in Baltimore published the news of the battle of Matamoras.[2]

Incidentally, this story furnishes a curious illustration of the

---

[1] Scharf: History of Baltimore City and County, p. 619.

[2] See letter of S. F. B. Morse in the Baltimore *American* of May 21, 1846, copied by THE SUN the next day. Morse and his telegraph had been violently denounced by the other Baltimore papers, especially the *Patriot,* for favoritism to THE SUN and in defense he published an account of the circumstances. THE SUN had blandly let it be inferred that its own enterprise was solely responsible for the scoop.

way news was handled in 1846. In newspaper parlance, it "had everything." First, it was a battle; second, it was the first real battle of the war; third, it was an American victory; and, finally, and of great importance locally, the artillery that blew down the Mexican town was commanded by Major Ringgold, of Baltimore. What an opportunity for the rewrite man! Here is how the story in THE SUN began next day:

We received by telegraph last evening at five o'clock, exclusively for our use, and issued in an extra, by which the city was flooded during the evening, an intelligent synopsis of the following highly important, highly gratifying and joyfully welcome news from our chivalrous and noble army — small in numbers but great in deeds of valor and of skill.

There are three or four lines more about the Army, but the paragraph ends with no intimation of what had happened. Then, doubtless after drawing a long breath, the writer resumes:

We acknowledge our indebtedness to our brethren of the entire press at New Orleans for their attention in furnishing us with ample means for obtaining all necessary information. [Numerous details follow, but the news is not yet revealed.] We make use of the following paragraph from the New Orleans *Tropic*, as indicative of the feeling with which it was received in that city, and also for its testimonial in favor of a gallant son of Maryland, and an officer of whom our city may be justly proud:

"*We have met the Enemy and they are Ours.* After a painful suspense of several days, news has reached us of a blow being struck by the Americans. The prowess of our brave soldiers has made the perfidious Mexicans bite the dust. The serpent of the Mexican arms now writhes in death agony in the beak of the American eagle. Victory perches upon our banner! Honor to Major Ringgold of the Third Artillery and his brave companions for their defense of the American Camp. Cheers, nine times nine, for our country and its free institutions!"

This completed the Lead All Without Date — and never a word to explain to the reader what it was all about. Immediately following it was an insert marked "Correspondence of the Baltimore Sun," explaining that Major Ringgold was the officer left in command of the artillery by General Taylor, but explaining nothing else. Now, however, there was nothing left to do but tell the story, so it began with a credit line to the New Orleans *Picayune*, then recounted how (*a*) the steamship *New York*, Captain Windle, had just arrived from Brazos, with news (*b*) that Captain Walter, of the Texas Rangers, had got through to General Taylor with dispatches, although it seemed suicidal for him to attempt it, whereupon (*c*) General Taylor, learning that Point Isabel was threatened, had moved in that direction with part of his army, leaving Ringgold in command opposite Matamoras, and the next day (*d*) had sent Walker back as a dispatch runner and that (*e*) Walker had made his way back bringing news (*f*) that Ringgold had repulsed a Mexican attack on the camp, opened on Matamoras with his guns and destroyed the city.

By actual measurement the first definite statement that there had been a fight at Matamoras is made in the fifteenth inch of a twenty-one-inch column.[1]

It should not be inferred, however, that this hysterical style was an invention of THE SUN. On the contrary, it was the custom of the times. The admirable sententiousness that characterized the paper in its early days was plainly a virtue born of necessity. The sheet was so small that it had to be terse. Now, however, THE SUN, although still somewhat smaller than the fippenny sheets, was much larger than it was in 1837. Moreover, it was already powerful and was rapidly growing rich, so it began to develop the vices of its contemporaries, from which poverty and cramped space had protected it.

Nevertheless, in spite of what seems, by modern standards, the

[1] THE SUN, May 19, 1846.

insane wordiness of its presentation, the news was there. More than that, as the war progressed the arrangements for the horse express were perfected and THE SUN no more depended upon intervention by the Thunder God to enable it to beat its rivals. In June the telegraph line was completed to New York,[1] so through those newspapers allied with THE SUN all the newspaper reading public of the North, as well as the people of Baltimore, profited by the swift service to New Orleans. The Philadelphia *Public Ledger* was a party to the arrangement, of course, and later the New York *Herald* joined.[2] Still, even with their help, the financial burden of the service was prodigious. The share of THE SUN, according to Scharf,[3] was a thousand dollars a month. Relatively to the value of money then and now, to the resources of the paper, and to the potentialities of its field, that sum must be multiplied several times if one is to appreciate the weight of the burden in modern terms. Its expenditure indicated a policy bold to the point of recklessness.

It illustrated admirably, however, the quality of Mr. Abell as a journalist. He never wavered in his belief that the newspaper has one patron, and only one, whom it must serve at any cost. This patron is the reader. The dissemination of information he regarded as the aim and end of newspaper work, to which all else is incidental. To party, to faction, to sect, to class, he admitted no obligation whatever. Even his interest in the mechanics of newspaper production was confined to those factors which would render the news service swifter, or more accurate, or more comprehensive. He was perpetually introducing innovations in such matters as presses and other machinery, and in communications. He set up THE SUN's first newspaper carrier system, by which each carrier owns a certain territory and is responsible for

---

[1] THE SUN, June 6, 1846.

[2] Don C. Seitz: The James Gordon Bennetts, p. 122.

[3] History of Baltimore City and County, p. 620.

prompt service to subscribers therein — a system, by the way, which has never been abandoned. But, beyond seeing that he had competent bookkeepers, he apparently contributed little or nothing to what was then known as the counting-room and is now called the business office. This man, who played a prominent part in revolutionizing news gathering in America, brought to the science and art of advertising exactly nothing — except in the matter of advertising his own news service. In that he was indefatigable. But toward the merchants and others who, even then, supplied a large part of its revenues, the attitude of The Sun was, and as long as Abell lived continued to be, one of lordly indifference.

This determination always and everywhere to put accurate news ahead of everything else is a high ideal for a newspaper. It would be folly, if not effrontery, to assert that The Sun has always lived up to it throughout its first hundred years; but it is no more than obvious truth to say that the days when it has adhered most faithfully to this standard of the Founder have been its greatest days.

As the Mexican War went on, The Sun proceeded from triumph to triumph. Its couriers continued to show up the postal service in most embarrassing fashion, but in view of the terrific interest in war news the authorities no longer ventured to interfere, as they had in 1845, when Postmaster-General Charles A. Wickliffe caused the arrest of O'Callaghan, of the New Orleans *Crescent*, for sending news to the New York *Herald* by other than the postal service.[1]

On October 17, 1846 The Sun presented the first illustration that ever appeared on its front page. It was a map of Monterey, explaining the operations around that city, and was copied from

[1] Seitz: The James Gordon Bennetts, p. 122.

the Washington *Union*, which had received it from the cartographer, an Army officer who had participated in the battle. November 6 it reproduced another, this time from the New Orleans *Delta*. April 3, 1847 it had one of the battlefield of Buena Vista, "drawn by a distinguished topographical officer in the staff of Gen. Wool, and furnished to us by a friend to whom it was sent." The paper was printing more than early bulletins, too; it was carrying regularly the official dispatches from commanders in the field, and enormous quantities of other war material, including letters from officers and soldiers, the comments of European newspapers, and, rather surprisingly, a great deal of material from the Mexican press.

But the greatest day of the war for THE SUN and, perhaps, from the strictly journalistic standpoint, the greatest day in its history, was April 10, 1847. On this day it had the honor of informing the President of the United States that his Army and Navy had captured the great fortress of Vera Cruz, thereby practically assuring victory. Not only the mails, but even the official couriers of the War Department had been beaten by the ponies of THE SUN.

The way the paper handled this, by far the biggest news story that had ever appeared in its columns, fascinates and appalls the modern newspaper man. To begin with, it was placed on an inside page, appearing in the left-hand column of Page 2, the space customarily reserved for editorials. The usual masthead remained in place at the top of the column, and under it was a single-column head on which all the resources, typographical, mechanical and literary, of the whole staff had been exhausted. It had no less than eleven decks, the first five of which were devoted to exploiting the enterprise of THE SUN, announcement of the victory not being reached until the sixth. Fourteen different type faces were employed in the composition, which is as marvelous in style as in typography. First of all, stretched across the top, were three tiny cuts of running horses, obviously THE SUN's ponies. Then came the head itself:

By Special Overland Expresses of
Nearly One Thousand Miles
Exclusively for THE BALTIMORE SUN
Independent of All Telegraphic Communication!

Unparalleled Effort of
Newspaper Enterprise

Highly Important
From the South

Unparalleled. Achievement
of the
American Arms!

The Greatest Military Exploit
of the
Present Century

Fall, Surrender,
And Unconditional Capitulation of
The City of Vera Cruz
and
The Castle of San Juan D'Ulloa

The American Flag Floating in Triumph
From City and Citadel!

Garrison of 4,000 Men
Laid Down Their Arms!

American Troops
Occupying the Town and Castle!

The Stars and Stripes
Saluted by the Squadron
As They Were Displayed
From the Enemy's Battlements.

The Squadron
Saluted from the Castle!

If this seems, among other things, a howling example of bad taste, it was partially compensated two days later, when THE SUN printed, also on an inside page, the following simple announcement:

In anticipation of the publication of our paper, we sent a private telegraphic despatch to the President of the United States, communicating to him the glad tidings received by our express, and yesterday morning's mail brought us the following acknowledgment:

"Washington, April 10, 1847.

"*Gentlemen:* I am directed by the President to acknowledge the receipt of your note by telegraph, announcing, in advance of the mail, the important and gratifying achievements of the American Arms at Vera Cruz — the unconditional surrender and capitulation of the city and castle.

"For the zeal and enterprise manifested by you in running this express, you will doubtless receive deserved commendation. I am requested by the President to thank you for your obliging kindness in communicating this information in advance of your paper.

"With great respect, I am your ob't serv't,

"J. KNOX WALKER, *Private Secretary.*

"Messrs. A. S. Abell & Co., Baltimore SUN."

Just ten years earlier Mr. Abell had come to Baltimore, a wandering printer who had been successful in a small way with a precarious enterprise in Philadelphia; now he was receiving the official thanks of the President of the United States for a feat of newspaper enterprise that put him in the front rank of the country's publishers. American history is full of meteoric careers; but not many surpass this either in speed or in altitude.

At this juncture in his progress the man exhibited another characteristic that commands the respect of the craft. He was fond of money. He made a great deal, and he knew how to keep it. He spent lavishly on his news service, but he was well aware that spending in that direction would bring him greater returns in the future. He was a shrewd buyer of real estate, which means that he had some talent for and inclination toward speculation.

Yet he held that his function as a disseminator of information took precedence even over money-making. This would have been less remarkable in an impractical enthusiast; but in an exceedingly hardheaded business man who loved money, and who knew how to speculate, it is highly unusual. However, the proof is incontrovertible. During the Mexican War not once, but repeatedly, he was placed in possession of information that was bound to have an important effect on the stock market. Frequently he had this information twenty-four to thirty hours in advance of everybody else. Nevertheless, in no instance did he ever attempt to use this situation to his personal advantage. He did not wait even to get out an extra; all news that might affect the market was instantly posted on the bulletin board in front of the office of THE SUN, where it was available to everybody.[1] He believed his business was to furnish early and accurate information to the public; and he respected his profession more than he loved money. So he earned and retained the respect of the craft.

It is improbable that THE SUN made anything directly out of the Mexican War. Its circulation and other revenues increased but not in equal proportion to the terrific increase in its expenditures. Nevertheless, the adventure in the end was profitable, for when hostilities came to a close the paper found itself in a splendid position. There was no manner of doubt of its dominance of

[1] Scharf: History of Baltimore City and County, p. 620.

the Baltimore field, one of the richest in the country. More than that, its brilliant performance had given it a national reputation. The President of the United States read it as a matter of course, as did everyone else of importance in Washington, since it was the only great metropolitan newspaper available in the capital in the early morning. It was read by the editor of every important newspaper in the country, and was quoted everywhere between the Mississippi and the Atlantic.

Out of the war came, too, a development of enormous importance in newspaper history. The expense of transmitting the news over such immense distances as were involved in that adventure was too much for the resources of any one newspaper; yet it was evident that the demand for national news stimulated by the war would continue. Late in 1847 THE SUN announced the perfecting of arrangements for a daily pony express service from New Orleans; although it did not name them, this service was to be shared by the Philadelphia *Public Ledger* and the New York *Herald*.[1] The importance of this move lies in the fact that by this time the war was obviously nearing an end and these papers were preparing for a regular, daily service, maintained and enjoyed by them jointly, not as an extraordinary war measure but as routine business in time of peace.[2]

---

[1] "Nearly a twelve-month since, being impressed with the importance of laying before our readers the earliest possible intelligence from the seat of war, we established our Overland Pony Express, to bring us such intelligence as might be of sufficient importance, some thirty hours in advance of the mail. This express was arranged and established exclusively for THE BALTIMORE SUN, without consultation or previous arrangement or understanding with any other paper, and during the year has rendered most important service in the country. Several Northern papers having since joined us . . . we have just completed arrangements for a Daily Pony Express, by which we will hereafter be enabled to lay before them daily news from the New Orleans papers. — THE SUN, November 29, 1847.

[2] In connection with this pony express THE SUN was guilty of some mystification, not to say outright faking. It never explained clearly

This joining of forces by several newspapers was the first definite move toward the establishment of the great press associations, and it was only a little over a year later that the first Associated Press was set up.

In the years immediately following the war the paper prospered exceedingly. Beach and Fulton were still on The Sun, and in 1847 it made another important acquisition in the person of John Taylor Crow, then twenty-five years old. He had attracted Mr. Abell's attention as editor of the Georgetown *Advocate*, and toward the end of the war was brought to Baltimore as assistant editor.

As the business developed it became clear that the quarters at Gay and Baltimore streets were too cramped. This situation was met in a way that once more proved the boldness and foresight of the paper's management. Instead of renting somewhat larger quarters, it was determined to erect a newspaper plant that should be adequate for many years to come, and a credit to the city, as well. A suitable location was found at the southeast corner of Baltimore and South streets, where five buildings were purchased at a cost of $50,000, and pulled down to make room for what Mr. Abell intended to be the finest newspaper office in America.

It was, as the event proved, more than that. It was a landmark in the history of commercial architecture in America. Somewhere Mr. Abell had come into contact with that strange genius, James Bogardus, originally a watchmaker in Catskill, New York, who turned inventor, introducing improvements in chronometry, then in cotton-spinning machinery, then in grist mills, selling the British government a new process for manufacturing

to its readers the mechanics of the thing; although it told no lies, it was willing to let the impression prevail that the news was brought by an unbroken chain of horsemen from New Orleans to Baltimore. As a matter of fact, it employed horsemen to cover only those stretches not covered by rail or telegraphic communications.

DABOUR DEL., 1866

ARUNAH SHEPHERDSON ABELL (1806–1888)

THE SUN IRON BUILDING, 1886

postage-stamps and bank-notes, inventing a dynamometer, a pyrometer, and rubber-cutting, glass-pressing, deep-sea-sounding and drilling machines. The very fact that Mr. Abell chose a man with this bizarre record to build his newspaper office is proof that the publisher was not at this time the archetype of conservatism and caution which he became later. On the contrary, he was still on the lookout for men of original genius.

Bogardus in 1847 had erected for his own use a factory building constructed on a new principle, which he had urged in vain on builders in New York. He convinced Mr. Abell that his principle was sound and received a commission to embody it in the new Sun building. In R. G. Hatfield, of New York, they found an architect daring enough to risk his reputation on a design, and the result was the famous Sun Iron Building.

The new principle was the distribution of the weight, not on masonry walls, but on cast-iron columns supported by heavy foundations, in this case granite pillars 18 feet high, each resting on a separate plinth of the same material, embedded in the earth. Thus the iron frame became the essential part of the structure, while the walls were merely relatively light screens to make the building weather-tight. For the cast iron substitute steel, and you have the form of construction of every modern skyscraper. The Sun Iron Building rose only five stories above the street, but it was nevertheless the progenitor of the Empire State Building and of all the other dizzy towers that are the characteristic architectural feature of the American city.

In 1851 Baltimore regarded it as stupendous. Indeed, it was the beginning of the modern city, and although it fell a victim to the great fire of 1904, it had already altered the conception of commercial building, not by the novelty of its engineering only, but also by its double function as a business building and at the same time a monumental structure. Hatfield flung himself into the job with boundless, if somewhat florid, enthusiasm. Instead of attempting to disguise the columnar structure, he emphasized it. His fenestration was particularly interesting. No architect except one building a Gothic church had ever up to this time had to deal with so much window glass. Hatfield broke the line of his columns at each floor, but the windows he carried up, apparently, two stories in height. His genius was not quite equal to treating the columns as units from street to roof, however; instead he piled up three successively shorter ones, and on top of the highest perched a life-size caryatid, carrying a ponderous cornice. At the level of the second floor the base of each column was ornamented with a plaque bearing the head of the greatest of American printers, Franklin.

Startling as this ornamentation is nearly ninety years later, it was in accord with the taste of the times. No newspaper in America was more handsomely housed. The counting-room, or business office, was on the street level, occupying the corner. On the Baltimore street side an entrance to the stairway leading to the upper floors separated it from the store of Burgess, Taylor & Co., publishers and stationers, and beyond was the establishment of Vansant, hatter. The Burgess, Taylor premises ran back of the counting-room, and had another entrance on South street, where Charles West, coal dealer, also had an office, while the southwest corner of the building was occupied by the job-printing department of THE SUN. The building ran 56 feet wide on Baltimore street, and 74 feet on South.

The second floor was occupied in large part by telegraph companies — the Magnetic, the Western and the Southern — while the composing room and editorial offices were on the third. The two eight-cylinder Hoe presses occupied only a part of the basement, even with the steam-engines that drove them. The mailing room was there also, as well as a carriers' room and storage space for paper and fuel. The building was occupied September

13, 1851, and so well had Mr. Abell planned that it proved adequate to the needs of THE SUN for almost fifty-three years.

So THE SUN entered what was probably the most flourishing decade in its history — not necessarily the decade when it was greatest, but that in which its fortunes ran highest and in which everything seemed to turn in its favor. In 1853 it exhibited again its far-sighted daring. Richard Hoe had invented a new press, which he could not induce any of the New York publishers to buy. The principle involved was that of attaching a form filled with individual types to a revolving cylinder.[1] Publishers argued that the notion was an insane one because, disregarding the difficulty of printing from a curved surface, centrifugal force would fling the type all over the place as soon as the cylinder attained any speed. Hoe had met the difficulty by making his cylinder so large that the arc of the circle represented by one form was very slightly curved; by means of special quoins the form was locked on a cast-iron bed curved to fit the cylinder, and called a turtle, to which it was securely bolted. The column rules were made V-shaped, tapering toward the bottom, with the result that the more centrifugal force was developed the more tightly the type was jammed against the column rules. The first of these machines was placed in the office of the Philadelphia *Public Ledger* in 1846[2] but it was removed to Baltimore shortly thereafter. The advantage of their design was that by supplying a suitable number of feeders it was possible to make from four to ten impressions with each revolution of the cylinder, speeding up enormously the rate of printing. The press first established in the Abell-Swain-Simmons newspapers was rated at 8,000

[1] See A Short History of the Printing Press, printed and published for Robert Hoe, New York, 1902, p. 31, for a detailed description of this machine.

[2] Letter from R. Hoe & Co., to whom acknowledgment is made for their courtesy in supplying information about this press.

copies an hour, which was stepped up to 20,000 an hour in later models.[1]

Thus within the space of fourteen years THE SUN had played an important part in the development of three inventions that were destined to affect profoundly every phase of American civilization. Without the electric telegraph, the steel-framed building and the high-speed newspaper press, the United States of 1937 would be so different that imagination boggles at trying to portray it. In playing its part in these developments, THE SUN was making, not merely newspaper history, but American history.

Yet if it be admitted that the nation is not solely, nor primarily, its land, houses and machines, but its people and their habits and attitudes, then THE SUN's part in the introduction of these technical innovations was vastly less important than the share it had in the transformation of American journalism. In this it was, of course, only one force out of many that combined to form the penny press; and it was the penny press, not THE SUN individually, that did the work. Nevertheless, the fact remains that the Baltimore paper was one of the strongest, ablest and most vigorous of the group; and it was conspicuous in its adherence to the fundamental idea on which the success of all the cheap newspapers was based, that is, the idea that the function of a newspaper is to supply news. So long as A. S. Abell lived THE SUN remained, first, last and always, a newspaper. It was mildly Democratic in tone, but its party allegiance was a slight thing, which never affected its handling of the news. A generation later it became a tremendous political power, but at

[1] The relative alertness of American journalism at this time is evidenced by the fact that after the *Public Ledger* and THE SUN had been using these presses for two years, the London *Times*, in 1848, stated that "no art of packing could make the type adhere to a cylinder revolving around a horizontal axis and thereby aggravating centrifugal impulse by the intrinsic weight of the metal."

this period it hardly counted in politics because it did not choose to count.

What it believed in was getting the news, getting it early, and getting it right; and this, in turn, had a powerful effect on the development of public opinion. The old-style political sheet, filled with jeremiads, but almost void of facts, steadily lost ground from the advent of the new journalism. It was partially revived when the passions of the Civil War and its aftermath subordinated reason to emotion in the public mind, but it never resumed its old sway, because it could not stand the competition of accurate, impartial presentation of the news.

Public support came to THE SUN and with it a flood of money. In the years following 1850 all the expenses incurred during the Mexican War were recovered, and a great deal more. Mr. Abell became, for those times, a very rich man, although the popular belief in Baltimore that his newspaper was bringing him in a net income of a thousand dollars a day was apparently heavily exaggerated.[1] That was probably nearer his gross income than his net.

Storm clouds were mounting, but few people paid much attention to them in these palmy days of Baltimore and THE SUN. Long years before in the Senate old John Randolph of Roanoke had screamed, "There is death in the pot, compound it how you will!" but most rational people considered Randolph half mad, anyhow. To the north, Philadelphia, 40,000 behind Baltimore in population at the census of 1850, was developing the new industrialism, and its population was increasing prodigiously.

---

[1] On May 17, 1877, in an editorial on the 40th anniversary of THE SUN, the *Maryland Journal*, a Baltimore weekly, said: "It is not generally known, probably, that A. S. Abell, Esq., is the wealthiest newspaper publisher in the world, not excepting the proprietor of the London *Times*." It was, in fact, "generally known," but it was most likely not true. Mr. Abell's income from his extra-*Sunpaper* activities, of course, was very large.

The mercantile city on the Chesapeake was slipping behind. The Southern territory, on which it was now largely dependent, was not developing like the West, and the panic of 1857 very nearly prostrated it. Nevertheless, it continued to pour money into Baltimore, and the city still regarded itself, not without reason, as an imperial one.

Nor was its greatness confined to its wealth and population. Had not one of its merchant princes just made the princeliest gesture America had ever seen? George Peabody had removed to London, but in the city where his fortune was founded he set up the Peabody Institute and gave it an endowment to foster art, literature and music. Oh, no, Baltimore was not a city of money-grubbers only; with all its wealth and size, here was evidence that it also cared for things of the mind and spirit. Who could paint the future of such a city in any but the brightest colors? Who could regard the prospect before its leading newspaper as anything but rosy?

Politics grew daily more insane, but THE SUN very largely ignored politics. For the city and the newspaper it was the time "when the evil days come not, nor the years draw nigh when thou shalt say, I have no pleasure in them." The evil days come not — but they did. Long ago, Jefferson had heard "a fire bell in the night" in the first discussion of slavery in Congress. Now one heard little else in Congress. It was all very well to ignore politics, but politics would not much longer be ignored. One happy decade, and then the deluge, which would leave Baltimore for many years little more than a derelict, littered with the debris of the catastrophe.

CHAPTER V

☼

THE SUNPAPER IN THE CIVIL WAR

THE COURSE of THE SUN during the Civil War period is open to attack from both sides, but it needs no defense. To critics of its acts in those fearful days, it can make the all-inclusive answer of Sieyès to his critics after the Reign of Terror — "I lived." If the Civil War policy of THE SUN was not heroic, neither was it cowardly, and, most important consideration of all, it was not silly. Those were days when the brave and the foolish — or the brave and foolish — died with great speed, whether they were men or newspapers, and the cowardly ran away. Those who lived through the war in a border State were the unromantic and intelligent.

The tragedy of THE SUN was the tragedy of Maryland. Riven by internal dissension, drawn by affection in one direction and by interest in the other, suspected and reviled by both sides, exposed to all the horrors of war without enjoying its fierce exaltation, sharing the dangers, the losses and the woes of both North and South, but never with any part in the triumphs of either, it was trampled under the feet of both contestants and emerged beaten and broken. Time and again the tide of war swept over the State. Her sons were slaughtered. Her wealth was destroyed. She lived under the bayonet for four years. No matter which army happened to be in occupation, Maryland was conquered territory. She lost the war from the very beginning, and when it was over she had neither the exultation of the victorious North nor the pride in a magnificent fight that sustained the defeated South. She was beaten indeed.

All this is reflected in the experience of THE SUN. The newspaper world of Baltimore was split, like the rest of the State, the great protagonists of the two sides being the *American* and THE SUN. It was in 1853 that Charles Carroll Fulton, managing editor of THE SUN, obtained a half interest in the *American*, by now a respectable, but moribund, organ of the commercial interests of the city, and proceeded to build it into a really great newspaper, which even so early as 1860 was giving THE SUN a tremendous battle for dominance of the Baltimore field. Fulton had none of Abell's distrust of partisan politics. He flung his paper into ardent support of the Whig party, and when that organization crumbled under the shock of the battle over slavery, he went Republican. Thus at the outbreak of hostilities he was recognized as the ardent supporter of the Union cause in Baltimore, a position which he maintained throughout the struggle.

It is curious to note that it was the man from Rhode Island who espoused the Southern side, while the Pennsylvanian — Fulton was born in Philadelphia — developed in Maryland Northern sympathies more intense than those of the genuine Yankee. But Abell was no more a New Englander; he had long since become completely absorbed in Maryland. He had by this time extensive real estate interests unrelated to the newspaper property. He was active in many directions in building up the town, working in close alliance with its merchants, its growing class of manufacturers and its shipping men. These had developed important economic ties with the South. The battle for the Western trade territory had been increasing in intensity for the last twenty years, with New York and Philadelphia hotly contesting every inch; but the South still belonged mainly to Baltimore. Leading merchants, such as Johns Hopkins and William T. Walters, among many others, did an enormous business below the Potomac, while the coastwise trade down as far as Savannah supplied a large part of Baltimore's commercial lifeblood.

The social bonds connecting the city and the State with the South were even stronger. Not a few of the city's most influential families were of Virginian or Carolinian origin, while almost every prominent family in Maryland had intermarried with clans below the Potomac. Baltimore's greatest highway, the Chesapeake Bay, led straight down to the Virginia seaside resorts, and without doubt many a matrimonial alliance with Dixie was based on that circumstance, for when the city's youth met the youth of Virginia at a Summer playground, romance was inevitable. Ties of blood and of pecuniary interest alike therefore operated to swing Maryland and Baltimore toward the South. It was the State's misfortune, however, to have within her borders the capital of the North, and it was realized from the beginning that the loss of Washington would be a terrific blow to Northern prestige. The whole power of Northern arms accordingly was brought to bear upon the luckless State. Secession would have meant destruction to Maryland, no matter what happened eventually to the Southern Confederacy; and this consideration had a deterrent effect upon the Legislature when the Ordinance of Secession was presented. Moreover, there was in the State an exceedingly powerful minority sincerely devoted to the Union. Even among the merchants of Baltimore there were men like Enoch Pratt, whose sentiments and business connections alike bound them to the North; and intellectuals, such as Severn Teackle Wallis, the lawyer and at this time a leader of the Baltimore bar, whose reason told them that the cause of the South, no matter how excellent legally, was fundamentally hopeless. Thus the State, divided in its allegiance and menaced by formidable military power, was helpless and could pursue no other course than to be tossed to and fro by the tides of war.

And as the State was, so was THE SUN. Now Abell learned the uselessness in a real emergency of that policy of political skepticism which had served him admirably for a quarter of a century. In 1837 it might have seemed to him that "the political contests of this country are . . . *petit* wars and strifes between the *ins* and the *outs*," that is to say, comic-opera contests without any relation to reality; but in 1861 he was to learn how these sham battles may turn suddenly and horribly real, involving the issues of life and death for hundreds of thousands of peaceable, inoffensive men. For this development THE SUN was totally unprepared, and when it loomed upon the horizon the paper could do little except wring its hands.

From the standpoint of 1937, with the inestimable advantage of hindsight, it is easy to understand the fatuity of this course; but it would be equally fatuous to suppose that the men guilty of it were exceptionally careless or exceptionally dull. THE SUN, in its blindness to approaching events,[1] was simply reflecting the spirit of the age. The greatest and most venerated leaders of the

[1] To appreciate the completeness of this blindness, consider the comment on the election of President Buchanan in THE SUN of November 29, 1856: "The result of the late elections, by which the present majority in the House is virtually condemned, will no doubt exert a salutary influence upon the willful and impracticable theorists which it embodies. The public voice has uttered, with marked emphasis, its disapproval of the ceaseless agitation of topics which do not properly belong to national affairs. And if discretion should prevail sufficiently with the membership of the House during the coming session to make it more considerate of its own reputation, we may look for a prompt and quiet dispatch of business, a suspension of acrimonious remark, and the restoration of that spirit of nationality which will, in a measure, redeem the character of the last." The "topics which do not properly belong to national affairs" were, of course, slavery and its related issues.

nation were no more able to foresee what the future had in store than were the editors and publisher of The Sun. Nor were they, when the knowledge was forced upon them and they could no longer blink the hideous facts, much better prepared to point a peaceful and sensible way out.

The Sun's policy, up to the very brink of the abyss, was that of the ostrich. It undertook to meet the crisis by the beautifully simple process of ignoring its existence. Slavery and the questions to which it gave rise were "topics which do not properly belong to national affairs," and which it disdainfully refused to discuss. The truth seems to be that The Sun, within the previous twenty years, had suffered the usual effects of exceedingly great prosperity — it had grown fat and somewhat greasy. It indolently accepted the current morality of its time, unhesitatingly published advertisements of love philters, dubious matrimonial notices and the announcements of slave traders;[1] on occasion it even allowed its editorial columns to be prostituted to the uses of obvious quacks.[2] This was a degeneration from its

[1] See, for example, the issue of December 2, 1856: "*Personal.* — *A Lady* of refinement desires the acquaintance of a wealthy Gentleman with a view of Matrimony. Address Ella Mabary, Baltimore P. O." There are many ads like this one in the issue of Friday, December 5, 1856: "*Cash for Negroes.* — We wish to purchase immediately a lot of young and likely *Negroes,* for which the highest *cash* price will be paid. Persons having Negroes to sell will please call at No. 11 *Camden st.,* Baltimore, or address through postoffice. All letters promptly attended to. Negroes received to board. J. M. Wilson."

[2] For example, on Thursday, December 4, 1856, there appeared, not in the advertising, but in the editorial columns, under the masthead of the paper, this paragraph: "We find upon our table a variety of pamphlet extracts from a number of publications of high authority, both English and American, commending in the most enthusiastic terms the remarkable skill of Dr. Turnbull, a Scotch physician, and chronicling numerous cures of blindness and deafness which he has wrought. He has acquired a special reputation in the treatment of those diseases, quite unapproached by any past or contemporary practice. Of our own knowledge and observation we do not speak. — But we have the

own standards, for in the early days THE SUN did little editorial puffing, although it was the accepted practice among newspapers in general. By 1860, though, even with war clouds visibly mounting, it was capable of devoting part of its editorial space, day after day, to a wandering eye doctor, to a singer, to a midget. Other papers did likewise, so the public presumably accepted it as a matter of course; but there had been a time when THE SUN was above that sort of thing.

Its news enterprise, however, showed no sign of slackening. In 1858 it received a press cablegram from England during the few minutes that the ill-fated first cable was in operation; and as 1860 brought in what was obviously to be the bitterest Presidential campaign on record, THE SUN mobilized its forces to present the most complete report possible. Thomas J. Beach was editor, and for his assistant Mr. Abell had acquired another man from the Georgetown *Advocate*, where he had found Fulton. This was John Taylor Crow, already mentioned in Chapter IV, a native of Prince George's county, Maryland, who was destined to render unusually long and distinguished service to THE SUN. Norval E. Foard was in Charleston, although his connection with THE SUN was to be formed a little later. Who was in Chicago covering the Republican National Convention is not known; nor who was on the desk the night news of the nominations there came in. The desk man is certainly no hero of journalism, for he allowed THE SUN to announce in its headlines the next day the nominations of *Abram* Lincoln and Hannibal *Hamblin* for President and Vice-President respectively. The editorial writer also referred to Lincoln as Abram, but he man-

---

assurance of professional authority in this city that he has effected the most wonderful results and is now demonstrating his professional power in Baltimore. The importance of this subject gives it a public character, and we are therefore induced to invite the attention of persons interested to the acknowledged ability of Dr. Turnbull. He is to be found at Barnum's Hotel."

aged to spell Hamlin's name correctly. His comment, though, deserves a conspicuous place in the museum of newspaper mistakes; it read, "The nomination does not strike us as being a very strong one. . . . The issue is made, however, and sectionalism on the part of the Republicans must constitute the distinctive feature of the campaign." [1]

As the Summer progressed THE SUN seemed to be far less interested in the Presidential campaign than in a fight it had on its hands in Baltimore city. The acquisition of a great park for the city was to the fore; the paper indorsed the project, but disapproved the site chosen, the area now comprised in Druid Hill Park, and violently opposed the method of financing the deal, which was the imposition of a tax of one cent on every street-car fare in Baltimore. Largely ignoring the questions of Secession and slavery, on the issue of the park tax it loosed all its thunder. The hated *American* was strongly in favor both of the Druid Hill site and of the tax, and this circumstance did nothing to reduce the heat of THE SUN's denunciations.[2] It might seem to be weak and hesitant on national affairs, but its roaring on the question of the park tax left no man in doubt as to where it stood.

---

[1] THE SUN, May 19, 1860.

[2] A specimen of the fighting style of those days is an editorial of July 20, 1860, some excerpts from which follow: "Our readers are fully aware of the unqualified terms in which we have denounced the city passenger railway affair, the corrupt and fraudulent process by which it was foisted upon this community, the parties to the lawless and outrageous transaction, and the wrongs deliberately devised and practiced against the citizens of Baltimore in connection with it. We have the same unqualified sentiments for those who are affiliated with such transactions in any way; and also for those who advocate or palliate such disreputable things. . . . If the Baltimore *American,* or any other paper professing to serve the people, dare to avow its sanction of so odious, outrageous, intolerable and wicked a scheme as this, we hold its professions as nought, and denounce it as the insolent and audacious *enemy of the people — or a confirmed lunatic*. It may take its choice of the alternatives. We are not quite so mad as to impale ourselves upon either horn of such a dilemma."

As a matter of fact, its policy in national affairs, while hesitant, was never equivocal. THE SUN did not attempt to carry water on both shoulders. Its position did not merely seem to be, but really was, anomalous, because it was for the South but against Secession; and therefore, like countless citizens of Maryland, it found its voice almost stifled, its arm almost paralyzed. There are dignity and pathos in its utterance on the last birthday the country was to celebrate as a united nation:

With all the blessings of freedom heaped upon us, as it were, with a profusion of benevolence, we are prone to rebel against the privileges we enjoy, and in divided counsels, vicious purposes and factious opinions, make a mockery of the great and glorious theory of self-government. Let us hope that we shall not grow wise only when it is too late; but that whatever troubles and conflicts beset the way, each recurring fourth of July may find us knit in bonds of union firmer than we ever were before.[1]

Pious hopes and sincere laments, however, availed nothing. The momentous election day arrived, and the result was precisely what had been foreseen; although he lacked a million votes of a popular majority, Lincoln carried the Electoral College easily. For once THE SUN's emotions overcame its professional instincts; although for months its front page had been loaded with news of the campaign, it announced the result of the election under a one-column head half-way down from the top on Page 2: "The Presidential Election — Lincoln Elected President and Hamlin Vice-President of the United States." Its comment was brief and lugubrious: "As we cannot offer to the readers of THE SUN one word of congratulation upon so inauspicious a result, we are disposed to do no more than announce the fact this morning, and await the developments that may ensue." [2]

After forty-eight hours, however, it recovered the power of articulate utterance; and then it spoke directly to the point and

[1] THE SUN, July 4, 1860. [2] THE SUN, November 7, 1860.

with a moderation it never exercised toward municipal opponents:

> The South needs the utmost measure of forbearance and of such devotion to the Union as she has never in all her trials been required to exercise before, to govern and guide her in this emergency. The act of deliberate secession, which has been ascribed to her as a thing of choice, will be, should the necessity ever occur, most repugnant to her. . . .
>
> We can but insist, therefore, at such a crisis as this, upon common decency in the treatment of States and people occupying so anomalous a position as the South must do, in the Union or out of it. In the Union she must remain for a time, at least, subject to a power she can neither recognize civilly, socially nor politically. And in all that time, with an uncertain future before her, must live on the hope of an emancipation from the most odious thraldom that could be inflicted upon her. Out of the Union she could only exist burthened with regret as an unwilling separatist, having chosen an undesirable political independence because her first choice has been rudely and offensively denied to her, with an equality of the rights and honors of confederation.[1]

But while demanding the utmost fairness in the treatment of the South, THE SUN was little disposed to permit anyone else even the expression of an opinion. When George William Brown, the newly elected Mayor of Baltimore, in his inaugural address remarked, "Surely no cause has yet arisen to justify the overthrow of the noblest and most beneficent government ever established by human wisdom," THE SUN's comment was tart:

> In view of the very important fact that Mr. Brown was elected as the representative of a principle, exclusive of national politics in municipal affairs, we certainly read with some surprise a dissertation, very brief it is true, towards the close of his remarks, upon that very theme. It is not our purpose to express an opinion about Mr. Brown's views of national or State affairs; but we regret that as

[1] THE SUN, November 9, 1860.

Mayor of Baltimore he should have deemed the occasion a proper one in which to speak in his official character upon such subjects. The State of Maryland has no representation in the mayoralty of Baltimore, and must speak, whenever it shall be necessary, for herself.[1]

Still it was with the authentic voice of Maryland, of the sincere and fair-minded men of Maryland, whether they inclined to the North or to the South, that THE SUN itself spoke a few days later:

It were an easy thing to denounce Republicanism on one hand and Secession on the other, and round a succession of periods on the value, importance and glory of the Union. But in so doing we should constantly realize conflicting sentiments, which a sense of justice and equality would thrust before us. . . . We have no precedent, no light, no guide, by which to aid us in the solution of an apparent inextricable complication of antagonisms.[2]

Eventually, however, the welter of confusion began to reduce itself to order and the course of the paper became clear:

Nature, interest and affection have defined the necessities which will control our conduct. Our lot is cast with that of Virginia, and the lot of Virginia is cast with that of the Southern States. Calmly, therefore, inviting calm deliberation on the part of all around us, we can but await the issue, confiding it to the wisdom and providence of Almighty God.[3]

A noble and knightly attitude, no doubt, but not a particularly effective one for a State caught between two belligerents; and, as it turned out, a pretty bad guess as to what Maryland would do. The soundest word in it is "necessities," for both Maryland and THE SUN were to be controlled, not by their preferences, but by hard necessity, crudely but vividly represented by the guns with which Ben Butler presently had Federal Hill

[1] THE SUN, November 13, 1860.
[2] THE SUN, November 16, 1860.
[3] THE SUN, November 19, 1860.

bristling. When an eminence commanding the heart of a city is crowned with enough artillery to blow that city into the next county, artillery commanded by an officer praying for an excuse to use it, the doctrine of free will becomes purely academic as far as that city is concerned.

The desperation with which the luckless border State caught at every shred of hope, however fantastic, is reflected in the editorial columns of THE SUN, which presently attained a complete divorce from reality. The *Star of the West*, attempting to relieve Fort Sumter, had been fired upon by the guns of South Carolina; and THE SUN said next morning:

> Secession and disunion do not by any means necessarily mean war. . . . Indeed, we do not despair of the time when the reunited States will, in a spirit of genuine fraternity, reimburse the seceding States themselves the expense of this painful episode in our national history; or at least take their stock of arms off their hands at a fair valuation. We are more disposed to hope for this than to predict bloodshed.[1]

A prediction that the nation would eventually pay South Carolina the cost of the powder and shot with which she had fired on the flag was, indeed, a marvel of prophecy. But the alternative was simply too dreadful for THE SUN to face. It was not solely a matter of sentiment, or of slaves, although both bound Maryland to the South. Abell, the hardheaded Rhode Islander, did not lose sight of the economic consequences for an instant.

> It has always been our opinion and belief that our material interests, as well as our rights pertaining to the institution of slavery, were identified with the South. That our commerce is, in the main, with the South, and that if we are to grow, thrive and prosper as a manufacturing city, our sources of prosperity must be in the South. With Virginia, North Carolina, Kentucky, Tennessee and Georgia cut off from us as customers, we do not see what is to sustain this

[1] THE SUN, January 12, 1861.

community, or requite the employment of capital in business enterprise.[1]

Forty lean years were to prove all too well that this reasoning was accurate.

But it was not given to THE SUN, even in its blackest mood, to foresee the curious fate that was in store for Baltimore. Other cities, Richmond, in Virginia, for example, and Chambersburg, in Pennsylvania, suffered more of the horrors of war, but they also experienced something of its exhilaration. Baltimore got nothing but its degradation. The city was never shelled, never burned. The only fighting it saw was rioting. But from beginning to end it bore the brunt, not of fire and sword, but of the lies, the tyrannies, the treasons, the petty spites and jealousies, the stupidities and brutalities, the moral dirtiness and nastiness that are as inevitable accompaniments of war as are fire and sword.

It began even before the new President assumed office. As Mr. Lincoln made his leisurely way toward Washington, a cheap-John detective, anxious to make a name for himself by appearing to do something to earn his pay, cooked up a blood-curdling story of a great conspiracy to assassinate the President-elect as he passed through Baltimore. Historians since have proved that the whole thing was a fabrication,[2] but in the hysterical state of the nation at that time it proved to be easy to convince Mr. Lincoln's advisers, and apparently the President-

[1] THE SUN, January 16, 1861.

[2] See Matthew Page Andrews: History of Maryland, p. 510. Especially consult Ward H. Lamon: Life of Abraham Lincoln, p. 511 *ff.*, who avers that for ten years he believed the story implicitly and finally discovered its baselessness, not through any protestations of Baltimoreans, but through examination of the documents furnished by the detective which, scrutinized in cold blood, were patently fraudulent. Even James Ford Rhodes (History of the United States, Vol. III, p. 304) does not attempt to defend the story, and all Henry Cabot Lodge can say is that subsequent events seemed to indicate that there was something in it.

elect himself; and so he was led into one of the most deplorable errors of his career. Instead of following the published schedule, he left the rest of the Presidential party at Harrisburg, Pa., took an earlier train and sneaked though Baltimore at half-past four in the morning of February 22, 1861. When news came from Washington of his arrival there, The Sun said, "The story was not credited — nine out of every ten believed it a ruse to prevent a large gathering at the Calvert Station, where he was expected to arrive. The people would not believe that they deserved such treatment at the hands of the President-elect, and did not think him capable of such conduct." But the story was only too true. When the train arrived Mrs. Lincoln and her children were on board, but not the President-elect.

The effect of this blunder upon public opinion in Maryland was stunning. To appreciate it, one must bear in mind that at this time Abraham Lincoln was practically unknown in the East, this being the State's first contact with him. The immediate effect was to give everyone, those whose sympathies lay with the North as well as others, the impression that the country was moving into the most fearful crisis in its history with a poltroon at its head. Even the Republicans were abashed by the conduct of their leader, and in no position to resent the withering comment of The Sun:

Had we any respect for Mr. Lincoln, official or personal, as a man, or as President-elect of the United States, his career and speeches on his way to the seat of government would have cruelly impaired it; but the final escapade by which he reached the capital would have utterly demolished it, and overwhelmed us with mortification. As it is, no sentiment of respect of whatever sort with regard to the man suffers violence on our part, at anything he may do. . . .

A brief review of this stupendous folly is all we can attempt. . . . We have information that Mrs. Lincoln warmly opposed the project. . . . At all events, it is true that while Mr. Lincoln went by another route, he affectionately left Mrs. Lincoln to come by that on which the cars were to be thrown off the track at some point between Harrisburg and Baltimore, when a horde of ruffians was to " rush down a steep embankment and destroy in a moment the lives of all on board." And the route was followed by Mrs. Lincoln when no one knew that Mr. Lincoln was not on board, and she arrived safely in Baltimore and passed on to Washington. So there is to be some pluck in the White House, if it is under a bodice.[1]

Naturally, after this, The Sun gave up all hope of the new Administration and, for that matter, so did the greater part of the people of Maryland, whatever their sympathies. Not until long afterward did Baltimoreans begin to realize that there was any quality of greatness in the man — not until the damage was already done. At this time they were able to see no good in him, and even the great First Inaugural drew from The Sun the scornful comment:

The argumentation of the address is puerile. Indeed, it has no quality entitled to the dignity of an argument. It is a shaky specimen of special pleading, by way of justifying the unrighteous character and deeds of that fanaticism which, lifted into power, may be guilty, as it is capable, of any atrocities. . . .

There is no Union spirit in the address; it is sectional and mischievous, and studiously withholds any sign of recognition of that equality of the States upon which union can alone be maintained. If it means what it says, it is the knell and requiem of the Union and the death of hope.[2]

If this seems downright incredible to a generation bred up in the belief that the First Inaugural is one of the great monuments of statesmanlike reasoning, read it again with the assumption that it was delivered by a man of whose sincerity you have no convincing proof and of whose personal cowardice you have what you consider very convincing proof. The greatness of the

---

1 The Sun, February 25, 1861. 2 The Sun, March 5, 1861.

address is dependent upon the sincerity that today we know was behind it. The First Inaugural, spoken by a coward and a hypocrite, would have deserved THE SUN's bitter scorn; and circumstances, aided and abetted by some extremely competent and industrious human liars, had given Maryland much reason to believe that the man who spoke was a coward and to suppose that he was a hypocrite.

This tragic misconception of Lincoln's character was to contribute largely to the series of events which were to bring down upon the city the concentrated fury of the North. No fair-minded review of the situation can acquit Baltimore of all blame for what followed, but certainly history can furnish few other instances of a city so completely unlucky. The great, central misfortune from which all the others stemmed was the people's loss of confidence in all leadership. Southern men had little faith in Jefferson Davis. For one thing, he was much too far away to do them any good. Northern men had little more faith in Lincoln. For one thing, he was much too close for comfort. Only forty-five miles away, he was assembling soldiers and cannon at an appalling rate. It is notorious that the most dangerous thing on earth to innocent bystanders is a terrified man with a gun. History was to prove that Lincoln, as a matter of fact, was almost the only cool-headed man left in the country; but in the Spring of 1861 Baltimore didn't know it, and that night trip of February 22 had convinced the city that he was a badly frightened man. It followed logically that nobody could know, when the artillery opened up, what the target was going to be. Baltimore had already been accused of conspiring to assassinate the President when she had done nothing of the sort; what assurance had she that she would not next be accused of trying to destroy the government, and therefore be chosen for the first assault of the assembling army?

When leaderless people find themselves facing a grave crisis, there is no predicting what they will do; but it is safe to predict that it will be something foolish. "We have no precedent, no light, no guide," lamented THE SUN; and it was true. Therefore Maryland, blundering along in darkness, imagined vain things, said and did silly things, thereby intensifying the distrust in which she was held. "We have too much reason to believe," averred THE SUN hysterically,[1] "that a deliberate purpose is entertained, and a plan maturing, if not matured, by which the State of Maryland is, if possible, to be attached to the Northern confederacy and literally sold to the black Republicans."

Yet, even with the approaching menace growing more appalling every day, life had to go on. Babies were born and old people died, hucksters chaffered in the streets, housemaids scrubbed marble steps and polished brass rails just as they had for generations. Mr. Abell, flung into politics against his will, was nevertheless still the publisher of a newspaper and still responsible for making it a going concern. With the nation splitting asunder, he could nevertheless devote his editorial space one day [2] to a proud announcement that THE SUN was appearing in a dress of "new copper-faced type," made essential by the increase in its circulation. Apparently some one — could it have been the *American* gang? — was spreading rumors that THE SUN was losing all its subscribers because of its pronounced Southern leanings. One might think that the obvious way to nail such a canard would be to give the exact figures; but in 1861 that wouldn't do at all. Instead, THE SUN saw fit to call upon various doubtful witnesses, including its own pressmen, mailing clerks and newsprint purveyors, to testify that its circulation was larger than it had ever been before, and was still increasing. Precise calculation from this confused accounting is impossible,

[1] January 16, 1861. [2] March 25, 1861.

but the evidence indicates a circulation somewhere between 30,000 and 40,000 copies daily.[1]

Wars might come and wars might go, but Abell remained the publisher whose first business was to make sure that his paper came out on time and served the largest possible number of readers. To add to his difficulties at this juncture, however, his partner, Swain, over in Philadelphia, was going fanatically Unionist. In 1855 Simmons had died. The other two had purchased his interest from the estate, but they had not divided the properties. Swain was still owner of half THE SUN and Abell of half the *Public Ledger*. The partnership had proceeded in perfect amity for twenty-four years, but it could not withstand the shock of civil war. For all his mildness of manner, Mr. Abell was a man of convictions as strong as those of his more explosive partner. On the surface they managed to maintain good relations for three years longer; but divorce was inevitable from the outbreak of war, and it came before the war was over.

---

[1] THE SUN's deliverance on the subject reads as follows:

"In the city distribution of THE SUN, Thirty-One carriers are engaged, each of whom has a regular route, to be served and improved by his own attention and enterprise.

"Besides these, more than twenty Book Stores in different parts of the city supply themselves with THE SUN for sale, according to a pretty regular demand at their counters.

"In addition to these, Sixty youths are regularly furnished with copies of THE SUN every morning, according to their demand, for sale in the city and suburbs. . . .

"THE SUN is sent every morning to no less than Six Hundred and Eighty-Nine Postoffices, extending over a vast area of the United and Confederate States of America.

"It is also sent in packages to Sixty-Five different agents representing cities, towns and large villages, in which it is served by carriers at the houses of the residents. . . .

"The circulation of THE SUN is from Twenty to Twenty-five Thousand greater than that of all the other daily papers in Baltimore, printed in the English language, combined; being very nearly, if not quite, three times the total amount of all the other daily papers printed in English put together."

On April 14 Fort Sumter fell. Bitterly as it hated the necessity, THE SUN recognized the fact. The headline over its story of the beginning of the bombardment read, "Opening of Civil War." It was not yet able, however, to accept all the implications of war, including the necessity of suppressing one's opinions. Its comment on the event is eloquent of the survival of free speech to that date:

In the attack upon Sumter they have done . . . just what any nation would do under the same circumstances. And in fact they have done that thing which, *had they not done*, they would have been the subject of scoff and ridicule up and down the whole gamut of black Republican insolence.[1]

Events now moved far too fast for THE SUN, or for Baltimore and Maryland, to keep pace with them. So the confused and leaderless community moved further and further from reality. It is hard to imagine anything with less bearing on the situation that actually existed than THE SUN's comment on Lincoln's call for volunteers:

Let us suppose Baltimore sending out militia and volunteers for the subjugation of the South, and our doom is written beforehand. . . . We are for the Union, first, last and always; but it must be the Union as our fathers formed it, the Union designed by Washington and his compatriots, a Union of equal rights. No other can exist, fight as we may to maintain the idolatrous image of it.[2]

The day after this unrealistic utterance was published came the crash, the event that definitely obliterated Baltimore as a free city and converted her into an Ishmael, her hand against every man and every man's hand against her. THE SUN's story of the events of that day is, in the main, pretty accurate — marvelously accurate, considering the confusion and passion that tore the city — but, fortunately, there is another detailed

[1] THE SUN, April 15, 1861. [2] THE SUN, April 18, 1861.

narrative available, one written by the gentleman whose sore misfortune it was to be Mayor of Baltimore in 1861, that same George William Brown whom THE SUN had tartly rebuked for speaking up for the Union in his inaugural address.[1] It is possible that Mr. Brown's account may be swayed by his personal bias in some of the details, but no one has proved that he told anything but the truth about the main course of events.

This point requires emphasis because the story, to modern ears, resembles a chronicle out of Bedlam rather than a sober narration of the doings of men presumably sane. From start to finish, the mismanagement of the affair was complete; yet when one takes into consideration the concomitant circumstances, there is an ironic logic about it, a sort of insane inevitability. Perhaps it was impossible for the men concerned, situated as they were, to act otherwise than crazily.

Baltimore's responsibility, to take that phase of the situation first, went back many years. During the 50s the city had suffered the characteristic degeneration of swiftly growing American municipalities. The citizens were too busy making money, especially in real estate, to pay strict attention to their civic duties; they had supinely permitted the city government to fall into the hands of a political ring of the worst type. These gangsters were for the most part associated with the Know-Nothing party, an early prototype of the Ku Klux Klan of the 1920s. The result had been a gradual disintegration of the police and the courts and an enormous increase in lawlessness. Only in 1860 had a fight, aided if not led by THE SUN, resulted in breaking the hold of the ring on the city government and the election of the reform candidate, Brown. The time had been too short, however, for the reorganized police to regain complete control of the city; and the popular excitement attending the

[1] Baltimore and the 19th of April, 1861, by George William Brown. Published by the Johns Hopkins University Press, 1887.

beginning of the war made it still harder to control the riotous element. To this extent the city of Baltimore cannot escape blame.

However, Baltimore was not to blame for the fantastic conspiracy story cooked up by the detective; and it was this story, as yet implicitly believed in the North, that largely determined the attitude of Federal officers, civil and military, toward the city. There was, furthermore, a strong local feeling that Maryland should not permit the Federal government to transport troops across her soil for the purpose of attacking Virginia — a feeling not confined to Southerners, but shared by many Union men. It is easy to understand, then, why Federal commanders felt that in entering Baltimore they were invading hostile territory. As a matter of fact, that is exactly what they were doing, so far as popular sentiment was concerned.

But Federal commanders erred in jumping to the conclusion that, because this popular sentiment existed, therefore Baltimore officials would not do their duty. This error doubtless was assisted, although it really should have been eliminated, by an incident that occurred on April 18. The Mayor of Baltimore was advised that a troop train carrying a detachment of artillery (regulars) and a battalion of Pennsylvania militia, would arrive at the Bolton Street Station at two o'clock and that the troops would be marched across the city to Camden Station, there to entrain for Washington. The Mayor immediately ordered the marshal of police, George P. Kane, with fifty men to the Bolton Street Station, and when the troops arrived they were escorted across the city by the police. There was some booing and jeering, but the presence of the police deterred the riotous element from starting any serious disorder.

Unfortunately, the military authorities seem to have conceived the singular notion that the presence of the police had promoted, rather than repressed, disorder. At any rate, it was determined not to apprise the city authorities of the arrival of the next detachment. As a result, Mayor Brown was sitting quietly in his office the next day when he was told that a train bearing troops — they turned out to be the Sixth Massachusetts Infantry and some Pennsylvania militia — was already in the President Street Station, and that the troops were preparing to march across to Camden Station.

Here Mayor Brown made his great mistake. He assumed that if trouble occurred it would start when the troops were trying to entrain for Washington, so he rushed Marshal Kane, with every available man, to Camden street, thus putting them nearly a mile away from what proved to be the real danger spot. Then the commander of the troops, Col. Edward F. Jones, contributed his bit to this tragedy of mismanagement. Instead of promptly detraining his 1,700 men, forming them in columns and pushing rapidly across the city to Camden street before the inhabitants realized what was going on, he delayed. There were railway tracks in the bed of Pratt street, the thoroughfare connecting Camden and President Street Stations, but they were unfit for use by locomotives and the practice was to haul cars through Pratt street by means of horses. Colonel Jones decided not to detrain at all, but to have the men hauled in the cars from one station to the other; and the delay involved proved fatal.

The first nine cars got through all right. A mob had, indeed, formed around Camden Station, but Kane and his patrolmen had the situation well in hand and no trouble developed. But other mobs formed at President street and along Pratt street. This was a wide avenue along the water front, with ship chandlers' stores on one side and wharves on the other. Among other maritime supplies lying around were several ponderous anchors. Members of the mob, determined to halt the cars, seized these anchors and dragged them upon the tracks at the foot of Gay street. A cartload of sand came by, and they seized that and dumped it on the rails, too. When the driver of the next car saw what was ahead, he immediately unhitched his team, hitched it to the other end of the car and started back to President Street Station, compelling all the cars behind him to return, too.

The colonel commanding seems to have passed on to Camden street with the first detachment, and Captain Follansbee took command of the remaining troops. He now detrained them, formed them in column of squads and pushed forward along Pratt street. Then the firing started. It has never been determined which side fired first, but shooting soon became general.

Mayor Brown, in the meantime, had joined his police marshal at the other station, and was there when word came that there was fighting in Pratt street. Leaving Kane to collect police reinforcements, he ran down the street toward the riot. To his amazement, he met the troops, there at the foot of historic Gay street, coming at the double, a man turning occasionally to fire wildly at the mob that pursued them. He says that it was upon the tip of his tongue to ask the officer in command why on earth he didn't halt, deploy his men across the street, turn on the mob and let them have it; but he remembered, first, that he was a civilian with no right to instruct a military officer, and, second, that he was Mayor of Baltimore with no right to suggest that citizens of his own city be shot down. So he restrained himself to the suggestion that the troops quit running, which they did. Then he placed himself beside Captain Follansbee, at the head of the column and, his hat in one hand and his umbrella in the other, marched with the troops, through flying bricks, cobblestones and bullets until, between Light and Charles streets, they met Marshal Kane with fifty policemen, coming at a run. The officers flung themselves between the troops and the mob, formed a line across the street with revolvers drawn, and the riot was over. But four soldiers and eleven citizens were already dead, thirty-six soldiers and an unknown number of civilians were wounded, and Baltimore was ruined. From this time on, whatever was said against her was accepted as gospel by the North.

Seventy-five years after the event it is easy to perceive the comic element in the whole affair. The spectacle of a regiment of the United States Army, under arms and supplied with ball cartridge, being chased through the streets at a run by the rabble of Baltimore, finally to be rescued by fifty city policemen, certainly is one of the most astounding in military history. Nor is His Honor as personal escort of a column of troops any less absurd. "I cried out, waving my umbrella to emphasize my words," says Mr. Brown in one place; but unfortunately even the brandishing of the mayoral umbrella did not quell the riot.

But after one has laughed, it is but fair to remember that there was death in the air of Pratt street that day, and that when Mayor Brown took his place beside the captain, he had no assurance whatever that he would live to reach the next street corner. Municipal politicians who do not hesitate to take their lives in their hands in the line of duty are not common; for all the absurdity of his situation, George William Brown represented his city bravely and well. After seventy-five years, he looms up in its history as a heroic figure, umbrella and all.

The troops left in the President Street Station were hastily returned to Philadelphia. Those at Camden Station entrained for Washington, while a cordon of Kane's policemen held back the mob. As the train passed through the outskirts of the town, old Mr. Robert W. Davis, out inspecting a piece of property beside the railroad tracks, shook his fist at it. A jittery soldier instantly shot him down and he died there in his own field.

The battle of Pratt street had the curious effect of at once isolating and unifying Baltimore. The town now clearly realized that it had become No Man's Land. THE SUN, wringing its hands, found only this small crumb of consolation in the situation:

It is with profound regret that we record this morning the scenes of bloodshed which took place in our city yesterday. . . . The result of the unequal conflict, in which the blood of our citizens has been shed and their lives sacrificed, has had the effect to obliterate almost every shade of difference among us, and to unite us as one people, zealously devoted to the honor, the interests and the welfare of our State.[1]

Even the *American* was staggered by the death of Baltimoreans in the streets of their own city. Its devotion to the Union cause was pronounced, but not to the extent of making it view with equanimity the shooting of citizens of its city.

Whatever differences may have, or do yet exist, the blood of our citizens shed in our streets is an irresistible appeal to us all to unite as Marylanders, to meet firmly and together the responsibilities clustering thickly about us. . . . Let us first seek unity among ourselves and then act. In such a crisis as this all other considerations must give way to our duty towards one another, and to the State and city.[2]

But what was Baltimore to do? Only a small minority of the citizens were enthusiastically in favor of joining the Confederacy. An even smaller minority enthusiastically favored joining the North. What the great bulk of Baltimoreans favored intensely was avoiding getting shot in their own streets. After April 19, it was plain that the next detachment of Federal soldiers would have to fight every foot of its way across the city; perhaps a detachment of Confederates would have been greeted with cobblestones and pistol bullets, too, but that was an academic question, since the Confederates were far away.

What the city actually did was convert itself into an armed camp, prepared to fight anybody who came along. The Mayor, with a delegation of prominent citizens, rushed to Washington to plead with the President and the War Department not to

---

[1] The Sun, April 20, 1861.

[2] The *American*, April 20, 1861.

bring any more troops through Baltimore. Since it was possible to get troops into Washington by other routes, this was temporarily agreed to; but it is eloquent of the atmosphere of suspicion that enveloped the place that the word of the President and the Secretary of War was not enough. The city authorities burned the railroad bridges north of the town, thereby making it impossible to move troop trains. In the meantime, citizens by the hundred were mustered into military organizations and armed, while earthworks were thrown up commanding various approaches to the city. Baltimore settled down to stand siege.

The military activity was not, in fact, directed against the United States any more than it was intended as support of the Confederacy. Union men, as well as Southerners, were enlisted in the armed bands that patrolled the outskirts of Baltimore; they were animated by a sincere belief that the government in Washington was in completely irresponsible hands, as likely as not to destroy Baltimore through some irrational whim, and that, therefore, the only safety of the city lay in such protection as its own citizens could give it.

The situation was intolerable, of course, yet it existed for nearly a month. Trade was at a standstill and the city's economic life was crumbling visibly. Baltimore, however valiant, couldn't fight the whole world. From the standpoint of the Federal government it was equally bad. Baltimore lay athwart the principal line of communication between the North and its capital. In addition, Baltimore was a seaport, with direct waterways to Virginia and the South. So long as the city was in hands unfriendly to the Union, the Confederacy might, theoretically, throw an army into it from the Chesapeake Bay and take Washington in the rear. Obviously, the first move of the Union forces must be to wipe out this threat behind them.

Accordingly, on the night of May 13 Benjamin F. Butler, brigadier-general of Massachusetts Volunteers, marched into the city and occupied Federal Hill, an eminence just south of the inner harbor and commanding the heart of the city. Not a shot was fired, no shadow of resistance was offered, and, without doubt, countless citizens breathed easily for the first time since April 19 when it was known that Federal troops were in occupation. But here again Baltimore's singular ill luck attended her. Almost any other officer would have been a better choice for this mission than General Butler. In the first place, he commanded Massachusetts troops, including the Sixth Infantry, who naturally had a grudge against the city that had handled the Sixth so roughly; and in the second place this officer's personality would have provoked Job to rebellion.

His first move was to arrest Ross Winans, a member of the Maryland Legislature, and pop him into jail under no charge except a general one of rebellion; and when Winans's counsel sued out a writ of *habeas corpus* in the Federal court — not a court of the State of Maryland — the military authorities refused to recognize it on the ground that the writ of *habeas corpus* had been suspended by the President.[1] This was raw work, but Butler had an irresistible argument in his favor in the shape of fifty guns trained on the city. More than that, on the same day Colonel Hare, with a detachment of New York Volunteers, had seized the city's supply of arms, kept in a warehouse at the corner of Gay and Second streets. Butler was soon removed from command by General Winfield Scott for acting without orders; but nevertheless he was made a major-general for "capturing" Baltimore, which honor seems to have been resented by the city more than all his arbitrary acts.

Now at last the war was actually on. With Federal artillery scowling down from Federal Hill, with blue-coated patrols incessantly passing through the streets, with Ben Butler swearing

[1] Andrews: History of Maryland, p. 522, footnote.

that at the first sign of disturbance he would blow down the Washington Monument — a beautiful target from Federal Hill — even THE SUN's almost pathological optimism wilted and it had to make up its mind what to do.

Three possible courses were before Mr. Abell — to turn his coat, after the fashion of the Know-Nothing Governor Hicks, and sing the song of the military overlords; to stand on his rights and fight for free speech; or to shut up.

The first course was unthinkable for an honest man. Moreover, even had Mr. Abell been scoundrel enough to follow it, he would have profited nothing, for any singing he might have done in favor of the Federal side would have been drowned by the stentorian voice of Fulton, of the *American*, who had been a Union man from the beginning, and could consistently bellow the Battle Hymn of the Republic, which he was doing right lustily.

What would happen to him if he followed the second course was soon demonstrated. Ross Winans was already languishing behind the bars, and on May 25, at the request of the Federal commandant in Pennsylvania, General Nathaniel P. Banks, commanding in Baltimore, arrested one John Merryman, a citizen of Baltimore, and lodged him in Fort McHenry, without a warrant and on no specific charge. This time application for a writ of *habeas corpus* was made directly to the Chief Justice of the United States, and the Marylander Taney issued it. But General George C. Cadwalader, in command of the fort, would not permit the United States marshal to enter the place, and flatly ignored the writ; and there was nothing the Chief Justice could do about it save record his indignation.[1] So Abell learned

[1] "The Secretary of War was appealed to, as was Lincoln. Neither would order Cadwallader to surrender Merryman. Whereupon Taney issued his famous decree, and ordered it sent under seal to the President, with a stinging rebuke." — J. Fred Essary: Maryland in National Politics, p. 179.

quite early in the war the important lesson that in a terrified nation there are no civil rights. If the lesson needed emphasis, it came a month later when George P. Kane, marshal of police, he who had so sturdily defended the Sixth Massachusetts on Pratt street, was deposed from his office and jailed; and on September 12, when a clean sweep was made of the city administration, who went behind the bars unanimously, and with them — which may have been more impressive to Abell — Thomas W. Hall, of the *South*, and Francis Key Howard, of the *Exchange*. This mass jailing was downright frenzy, for Henry May, a member of the Congress of the United States, was imprisoned by the military, and also one of the strongest Union men in Baltimore, Severn Teackle Wallis. Mayor Brown now had leisure to reflect in jail on the rewards that come to mayors who risk their lives in their country's service.

Apparently the Federal government was still indulging its fondness for detectives in Baltimore, for the military authorities had enlisted a Falstaff's army of spies and informers, including, of course, all the greatest rascals in the city; these were restrained by no inconvenient respect for truth and the information they brought in produced fantastic results.[1] The British Ambassador, astounded, wrote home, "A war has been made, at Baltimore, upon particular articles of dress, particular colors, portraits of Southern leaders, and other supposed symbols of disaffection. The violent measures which have been resorted to have gone far to establish the fact that Maryland is retained in the Union only by military force. They have undoubtedly increased the dislike of the people to their Northern rulers."[2] Things went to the point at which the military authorities for-

---

[1] Andrews: History of Maryland, p. 524.

[2] Letter of Lord Lyons, September 16, 1861, quoted by Andrews, *op. cit.*

bade the sale of infants' socks of red and white, the Confederate colors.[1]

Through this Bedlam it was Mr. Abell's task, not only to find his own way, but also to conduct a large business enterprise upon which hundreds of inoffensive people were dependent for their living. Even if his own life, liberty and fortune had not been in jeopardy, this responsibility for the welfare of his employés must have imposed a measure of caution on any decent man. In "The Vicomte de Bragalonne" D'Artagnan warns his companions on a hazardous enterprise, "Gentlemen, we walk between the Bastile and the gallows." Abell might have used the very words, had he been of a romantic temperament, to John T. Crow, his Washington correspondent, and Thomas J. Beach, his editor; for the Bastile, represented by Fort McHenry, was swiftly filling with Baltimore newspaper men, and a quite literal gallows was no impossibility when the authorities were lending a willing ear to the tales brought to them by every conscienceless rogue in the city and jailing honorable men on such testimony. But Abell was as completely unromantic as any man who ever walked in shoe leather, and his instructions to the staff were dry, matter-of-fact and to the point. They can be epitomized in two words: "Shut up."

And shut up The Sun did. It was, if you please, an unheroic course, but it was the only course possible in view of the character of the paper and the condition of public affairs. It would not turn its coat, and it could not speak what it believed to be the truth and live. The mortality among Baltimore newspapers was terrific. On September 14 W. W. Glenn, publisher of the *Exchange*, joined Howard, his editor, in Fort McHenry and the paper was suppressed. In February Col. Samuel S. Mills, publisher of the *South*, and Thomas S. Piggott, the new

[1] Scharf: Chronicles, p. 616.

editor *vice* Hall, in jail, were arrested and that paper went out. In August William H. Carpenter, editor of the *Maryland News Sheet* (and later literary editor of THE SUN), went to jail and his paper was suppressed. In September, 1863, the *Republican* was suppressed and Beale H. Richardson and his son Francis (later to be Washington correspondent of THE SUN), with Stephen J. Joice, were arrested and put through the Confederate lines; Francis Richardson, attempting to return, was imprisoned for the remainder of the war, as we shall see in Chapter XII. Two weeks later, the *Daily Gazette* was suppressed and E. F. Carter and W. H. Neilson went to jail. The following May the *Transcript* was suppressed. In September the *Evening Post* met the same fate, and in November, 1864, the *Evening Loyalist* fell under the military ban.

In the midst of the reign of terror, however, Abell must have enjoyed one good laugh. This came on June 30, 1862, when Fulton, of the *American*, the thunderous defender of the Administration and the North, was laid by the heels by a military patrol and, despite his voluble and vociferous protestations, lodged in Fort McHenry. He did not stay long. After forty-eight hours he succeeded in convincing the War Department that the offending dispatch which had caused his arrest was in reality a confidential telegram for the information of an editor, and not intended for publication, so he was released. Abell, however, must have been more, or less, than human to fail to get some amusement out of the incident. At the same time, it emphasized anew the fact that under the military régime the best of intentions were no guarantee of safety; if Fulton could be arrested, nobody was safe.[1]

---

[1] The following letter from General John A. Dix, then commandant at Fort McHenry, is among the Gist Blair papers, and has been kindly supplied by Mr. David Rankin Barbee, who is engaged upon a history of the Washington corps of correspondents. It is dated August 22, 1861, from Fort McHenry, and is addressed to Montgomery Blair

The blunders of military government were not, however, the only threat to a man in Abell's position. One of the most revolting features of war is the opportunity it affords for the venting of personal spite and the perpetration of all sorts of crime under the guise of patriotism. West has a story [1] which, although it is not documented, is so typical of what happens in time of war as to be highly plausible. It reads:

At one time an order for the closing of THE SUN and the arrest of Mr. Abell was actually issued by the War Department and was about to be transmitted to the commander of the forces at Baltimore when Mr. Abell received information of it. He had an earnest

(1813–83), counsel for the defendant in the Dred Scott case and Postmaster-General in Lincoln's Cabinet:

"I have had the idea that some of the rabid Secession papers in Baltimore should be stopped. THE SUN has, all say, changed its tone. I had an interview with the agent and informed him that the publication would not be permitted if it persisted in the course it was pursuing. The Provost Marshal had a visit subsequently from the proprietor, who assured him that there should be no future cause of complaint.

"The other papers are the *Exchange,* the *Republican* and the *South.* Their circulation is as follows:

Exchange	1200
South	1000
Republican	700

"For a city of 230,000 inhabitants, these are certainly very scanty subscription lists. Indeed their regular subscribers are not so many. I have no doubt these three papers would rejoice at a forcible discontinuance by the Government. They are all losing money, and are supported by private subscription, as I am informed. In that case they would be glad to be made victims.

"Without any reference to them, the question is, whether we should lose more than we should gain by suppressing papers having so little power to do mischief. THE SUN presents a different question. It has a circulation of 12,000, and if it advocates doctrines which, carried into practice, would constitute treason as defined by the Federal Compact, it will present a strong argument in favor of the exercise of an arbitrary power to prevent their promulgation through a press so widely circulated."

It will be observed that General Dix overlooked a number of the Baltimore papers of the time.

[1] Harold E. West: The History of THE SUN, published by THE SUN, May 14, 1922.

and effective protest entered against such a proceeding and the execution of the order was suspended.

The motive which had instigated it was betrayed a day later, when two noted politicians called on Mr. Abell at his office and offered to buy THE SUN. They anticipated that with the fate of other prints which had been suppressed, and their editors imprisoned, staring him in the face he would be only too willing, if not thankful, to retire from his dangerous position and be rid of his precarious property at any sacrifice. They intimated as much. They were accordingly surprised and disappointed when they found their design was thoroughly understood and they were told that THE SUN was not for sale at any price.

So, grimly silent, THE SUN stood and took it. Crow, at Washington, walked with cat-footed sureness among a thousand pitfalls; one slip on his part, and an eager provost-marshal would have pounced. But he made no slip. Beach, at Baltimore, night after night got out the paper with a United States marshal at his elbow, scanning every edition, searching for some excuse to close THE SUN and throw the staff into jail; but the most hawk-eyed scrutiny revealed nothing. When news of Confederate victories arrived, mobs surged through the streets and besieged the building, demanding that THE SUN hang out a United States flag. The flag was displayed and the mob passed on. Day by day THE SUN lived; and like the Abbé Sieyès's feat, the mere living was a mighty achievement.

No doubt there was many a day when Abell wished heartily that fate had thrown him into almost any position other than that of a newspaper proprietor in a border city. He was too old to join the flood-tide of Maryland youth rushing away to join the two armies. Young fellows with no responsibilities, such as James Ryder Randall, might shoulder a gun and march away, bursting into fierce, exultant song:

> The despot's heel is on thy shore,
> Maryland, my Maryland!

but that was not for a publisher of 55 to imitate. Solid business men of his own age, such as Johns Hopkins and Enoch Pratt, might leap into the business of purveying munitions and supplies to the Army, cleaning up enormous fortunes; but a newspaper was no war baby. The great commission merchant, Walters, seeing his business shot from under him, might close his office and warehouses and retire in cold disgust to Europe until the madness was over, whiling away the time by beginning the art collection that was to make his name and that of his son famous two generations later. But a newspaper couldn't be carried away. Abell's friend, John W. Garrett, president of the Baltimore & Ohio Railroad, might attain fame as an unofficial adviser to the President — the original dollar-a-year man — at such times as he was not hurriedly replacing rails and bridges destroyed by Early's cavalry; but a newspaper could not assist the transportation of troops and guns.

Abel's part in the war was nothing profitable, nothing glamorous, nothing emotionally satisfying. It was merely to keep his readers informed of the course of events as well as he might, without bringing down on his head the erratic and unpredictable wrath of a government which, in Baltimore at least, showed itself as savage toward its friends as toward its enemies. It was arduous work but profitless, important but inglorious, extremely dangerous but dull. Few positions behind the line of battle were less enviable.

All the usual nuisances and inconveniences attending a state of war were present. The economic life of the country was disrupted and every man trying to do business was subjected to a thousand harassments. Prices mounted dizzily as the war wore on. Paper and ink became more and more difficult to obtain, and, as war traffic clogged the railroads, transportation difficulties in Baltimore became almost insuperable. Finally, in 1864, The Sun was forced to take a step which must have cost its proprietor much heart-burning. It ceased to be a penny paper. The price was raised to two cents, where, except for relatively short intervals, it has remained ever since. But day by day it came out, somehow. Day by day the military patrols continued to pass its door, instead of battering it in. Day by day the marshal at Beach's elbow stayed his hand. And it continued to appear every day until the Confederate armies collapsed and peace returned to the shattered land.

Beach did not survive to see the end. He died in 1864, and his four-inch obituary in THE SUN did not even mention his birthplace, or whether he was married or single. A great war was roaring to its climax, and its repercussions in newspaper offices were so devastating that even the death of an editor had to be passed over with little notice.

On the fall of Richmond THE SUN made no comment whatever except by way of an announcement that the city of Baltimore was to be illuminated; but in the same issue it devoted eight inches of its editorial space to an obituary of Zenus Barnum, proprietor of Barnum's City Hotel. The day after Lee's surrender THE SUN chose to discuss the excellencies of the Baltimore United Fire Department, a volunteer organization which had just been disbanded. But military affairs did not pass without any discussion; four inches were given over to an illuminating exposition of the identities of General Robert E. Lee, General George Washington Custis Lee, General William H. Fitzhugh Lee, General Fitzhugh Lee, cousin of the others, and General Henry (Lighthorse Harry) Lee, progenitor of them all. But by the next day THE SUN considered itself justified in making the cautious announcement, "The End Approaches," and in filling half a column with a masterly statement of the obvious.[1] It expressed no opinion of the merits of the Southern cause or of the Northern cause, of the valor of the Southern

[1] THE SUN, April 11, 1865.

Army or of the Northern Army. It neither favored nor opposed anything. Only by implication, indeed, did THE SUN come out in favor of peace. After setting forth at length the reasons that led it to believe the surrender of Lee and the Army of Northern Virginia signalized the collapse of the Confederacy, however, it did commit itself to one opinion. The surrender, it declared,

> has been so considerately and skillfully prepared as to save the feelings and do justice to the bravery of our vanquished fellow-countrymen, while, of course, it evinces that quality of magnanimity which all ages of the world have regarded as befitting the conqueror in the field. On the supposition that such action is inspired by the good offices of the President, it gives evidence of such humane and liberal purposes of administration on his part, whatever may be the efforts of others in a contrary direction, as may be possible hereafter.

Humane, liberal, magnanimous — here is, indeed, a different judgment of Lincoln from the one expressed by THE SUN four years earlier. Things were clearer, now, including the "efforts of others in a contrary direction," a bit of prophecy which was soon to be all too well justified.

And then three days later, came the last shot, the terrible shot that, because it was fired by a Baltimorean, hurt Baltimore pride worse than all the cannonading. The city was to have no luck, not even at the end. As the firing in Pratt street began the war, so the pistol of John Wilkes Booth ended it, not in honorable battle, but in murder. But the tragedy evoked from THE SUN an expression that is a higher tribute to the war President than all the eulogies of his friends. "Had we any respect for Mr. Lincoln, official or personal, as a man or as President-elect" that bitter editorial in February, 1861, had begun; now the same newspaper captioned its editorial, "The National Bereavement," and said:

> Not alone in the North, but doubtless to a very large extent in the South, had a trust grown up that Abraham Lincoln possessed

the qualities of head and heart which would enable him as readily as any other citizen who could possibly have been chosen to the position, to successfully accomplish the important work of reconciliation, of reconstruction and true national union. His humane disposition, his practical views, his skillful treatment of delicate and difficult questions as they have arisen, the fortitude with which he had met all exigencies, and his evident and firm purpose of action, had come to be recognized, in the light of recent events, more fully than ever before, and a degree of confidence and hope had grown up in regard to him in quarters where, at one time, such a result had not been anticipated. This confidence and hope are now rudely dashed down by the diabolical and astounding act of the assassin, and the country is again thrown, more or less, into a state of apprehension and uncertainty.[1]

---

[1] THE SUN, April 17, 1865.

CHAPTER VI

THE LAST YEARS OF THE FOUNDER

NEITHER Mr. Abell, nor his city, nor his newspaper emerged unscathed from the conflict of the 60s. He was fifty-five when the fighting began, but he was more, much more, than merely fifty-nine when it ended. Men, even civilians behind the lines, live fast in war time. Biologically they may not be much altered, but psychologically experience is telescoped; maturity comes with a rush, and old age follows fast.

In 1861 Mr. Abell was near the height of his vigorous maturity; in 1865 he was already old. He had twenty-odd years yet to live, for he was a rugged man, but they were years of gradual senescence. Never again was he to startle the newspaper world with daring and ingenious innovations. THE SUN had been the first to adopt the high-speed press, the first to adopt the electric telegraph, the first to adopt metal frame construction for a big office building; but hereafter, for almost a generation, it was to permit others to do most of the experimenting, devoting itself to the safe and sane. It was to permit the next great newspaper innovation to be taken from under its nose. When a Baltimore watch-maker, Ottmar Mergenthaler, finally solved the long-studied problem of mechanical typesetting, THE SUN was reluctant to adopt this revolutionary contraption, and, as we shall see in Chapter XI, the linotype had been in use in New York newspaper offices for some years before it was accepted by the principal newspaper in its inventor's home town.[1]

In this The Sun once more reflected with striking clarity the condition of its community. The notion that because Baltimore was never captured by the Confederate Army, never burned, never even bombarded, therefore it suffered only negligible damage in the Civil War is grotesque. Richmond and Atlanta, laid in ashes by invading armies, suffered worse material damage than was inflicted on Baltimore, but it is to be doubted that any war-ravaged town of the far South suffered more moral damage than the Maryland city endured; and its economic losses were terrific.

What happened to Baltimore was what happened to Abell and The Sun — it grew old in four years. The zest, the vigor, the enterprise were burned out of it. The prostration of the South swept away the only market in which its dominance was unchallenged. Its business men made desperate and fairly successful efforts to develop commerce with the West, but there they had to meet the stern competition of Philadelphia and New York, and even sharper and more vigorous rivalry from the new cities of the West — Chicago, Cleveland, Detroit, St. Louis. From being third city in the United States in 1860, Baltimore dropped to fifth place in 1870, to sixth in 1880, to seventh in 1910 and to eighth — Los Angeles having come

---

[1] It should be added (as will also appear in Chapter XI) that a large part of the hesitation of the Abells was due to a fear that the linotype would throw a great many printers out of work. There were men in the composing room in those days who had been setting type on The Sun since its first years. They were not only employés of the Founder, but friends. He feared, and his sons feared after him, that these old-timers would be unable to master the linotype, and that in consequence its introduction would imperil their jobs.

up in the meantime—in 1920. As a brilliant servant of THE SUN [1] once wrote:

There was a period of eclipse in THE SUN's history. It came with the Civil War, and it was also a period of eclipse in Maryland's history. The city and the State suffered under a crushing load of Federal tyranny and under the despotism of the gutter and sewer over manhood and freedom. Maryland was the Belgium of the South, and she sat in chains for four years. . . . The days of Reconstruction were still days of peril. . . . No man knew what the morrow would bring forth. Every man had to watch his step to keep his business head on his shoulders. Thus, Caution became the watchword of THE SUN in place of that earlier word Enterprise. And this war habit, engendered by fear, survived long after the cause had been removed.

What had been the most vibrant, energetic and aggressive of American cities became a slow, plodding, dull town, and the newspaper that had risen with it became conservative, stodgy, dull, too. It was an old man's town and an old man's newspaper, both aged, not by the process of time, but by a frightful catastrophe which had taken the spirit of youth out of them. Mr. Abell reverted to his earlier belief that politics was a dirty game, unworthy of an intelligent man's attention. Once in a while there would be a momentary flash, as when THE SUN paid its respects to the notorious Louisiana returning boards during the Hayes-Tilden contest:

Since the day of the Star Chamber there never was a more arbitrary and odious instrument for the suppression of the popular will than these returning boards, nor a more ingenious organization to deceive and defraud the community.[2]

But such outbursts were rare. Even in this case THE SUN took the final election of Hayes to the Presidency rather apa-

---

[1] O. P. Baldwin in an article in THE SUN, May 14, 1922.

[2] THE SUN, November 22, 1876.

thetically. It still furnished its readers with a careful, comprehensive news service, scrupulously accurate and usually well written. But conservatism was its watch-word and it seemed in the 70s to develop the typical old man's heresy, that of regarding all vigor as folly.

For Philadelphia and for Richmond, when Lee surrendered, or certainly when Johnston surrendered, the war was over. Such fighting men as had survived came back to their homes and were welcomed, in Richmond sorrowfully, in Philadelphia jubilantly, but in both cases warmly and sincerely. But the fighting men of Baltimore, whether they wore the Blue or the Gray, came back to find a town divided against itself. On half a dozen battlefields Maryland regiments, U. S. A., had come into collision with Maryland regiments, C. S. A.[1] Neighbors and even kinsmen shot and bayoneted one another, and while the soldiers might have been content to forget it, their families could not have been expected to do so. The result was that the town was poisoned with animosities so bitter that even today, more than seventy years after the firing ceased, one still hears occasionally echoes of them. Naturally, this hindered, when it did not paralyze, communal enterprise of all sorts. Southern cities could devote themselves whole-heartedly to repairing the ruin; Northern cities could turn, with similar singleness of purpose, to exploiting the new era of industrial and commercial expansion. The singular and depressing fate of the border city was to be so rent by the passions of the late conflict that it could do nothing unitedly for years after the fighting stopped. It was ruled

[1] Baltimoreans of all degrees of competence and veracity have delighted in telling over and over the tale of the war of Maryland against Maryland, especially the incident of the Battle of Front Royal, where the First Maryland Infantry under Stonewall Jackson smashed the First Maryland Infantry under the Federal General Nathaniel P. Banks. See, for more competent examples, Andrews: History of Maryland, pp. 531 *ff.*, and Scharf: Chronicles, pp. 635 *ff.*

by men who, although at or near the summit of their physical and intellectual powers, were psychologically old men, made so by four years of terror. Safety First was their motto, caution their highest virtue, depression their normal mood.

THE SUN, throughout these drab years, was such men's ideal newspaper. Sober, staid, dignified, it ignored with lofty scorn the vulgarities of politics; it presented the news and considered its duty done. Even when local politics, in the 70s, grew incredibly rotten, and the city government fell into the hands of banditti as conscienceless as Ali Baba's Forty Thieves, THE SUN remained apathetic. It was for the second Abell, George W., to rouse it again in the New Judge Fight of 1882; Arunah S. Abell was done with politics. The picturesque and idealistic apologist quoted earlier [1] puts a lofty interpretation upon this apathy:

> The policy was not entirely inspired by timidity. THE SUN had no sympathy with the freebooters and despots who had made themselves masters of the Democratic party, but it had no sympathy with the Republican rascals who had lorded it over the people of Maryland in their hour of power, and it preferred to keep silence rather than help the sewer rats back to the places they had prostituted and fouled.

But it is probably more nearly accurate to say that the first Abell, like all men, was the plaything of destiny, and the conservatism of his old age was but the common history of men.

A dying city and a dying newspaper, one might have said of Baltimore and THE SUN in the fifteen years immediately following the Civil War; and the saying would have had much color of truth. But it would have been a false judgment, grotesquely false. It was precisely this battered generation, precisely these prematurely aged men, who were to build for Baltimore a new sort of greatness and a new sort of fame that were

[1] Baldwin, *op. cit.*

to compensate her all her loss. George Peabody had made his donation to the city just before the war began, but the Peabody Conservatory of Music was not formally opened until 1868, and Asger Hamerik became director in 1871, just when the city's fortunes seemed to be at their lowest ebb. Johns Hopkins died on December 24, 1873,[1] leaving a will setting up the hospital and endowing the university that have not only made his name immortal,[2] but that also established his city for years as the scientific capital of America, as Hamerik and his successors had already made it a musical capital. Enoch Pratt at the same time was meditating the establishment of the public library that stood for years as the American model of its kind. William T. Walters, in the intervals of piecing together broken-down railroads in the South, eventually to weld them into the Atlantic Coast Line, was amassing the basis of the art collection which, immensely enriched and enlarged, his son Henry was to give to the city of Baltimore many years later.

These war-scarred, apathetic men, these apparently dull, stodgy men were incapable of the daring and brilliant feats of

---

[1] Incidentally, THE SUN missed the story by a curious freak of chance. It was Christmas Eve, and every man who could possibly be spared had been given liberty. The counting room, or business office, had only a solitary occupant and the editorial rooms were operating with a skeleton staff. To avoid interruptions by drunken loafers, the city room door was locked, and when an ancient Negro servant came with a note from Dr. Alan P. Smith, the attending physician, announcing Mr. Hopkins' death, he was turned away by the watchman, one Adolph Schuch. Not knowing what to do, he wandered across the street to the office of the *American*, where he was fervently assured that he had come to the right place, and so went home satisfied, leaving THE SUN people to read the biggest news of the day in their rival's columns.

[2] The university was incorporated on August 24, 1867, during Mr. Hopkins's lifetime, and the first board of trustees was organized in 1870, but it was not until 1874 that the trustees elected Daniel Coit Gilman president and he began assembling the first faculty. The first lectures began in October, 1876. The hospital was opened in May, 1889, and the medical school in 1893.

commerce and engineering which had made the city famous in its lusty youth. They could not bring back the clipper ships. They introduced no such innovation in transportation as the railroad. They erected no colossal monuments. But out of their work Baltimore gained a reputation in the worlds of science and art as splendid as the one she had had in commerce and industry. They brought into the city a new element — scholars and musicians, men learned in the lore that the New World as yet had had little time to acquire. "Music," lamented John H. Hewitt in his old age, "has always been, and still is, my frailty." [1] Unconsciously he epitomized his age; in Baltimore, and in all America, for that matter, music was not an art, it was a frailty; but it became an art, to be taken seriously, in Baltimore when the Peabody Conservatory began to draw into the city numbers of distinguished men who had given their lives to it. It came to be taken very seriously indeed by as unemotional a person as A. S. Abell, as his subscription of $5,000 to the Oratorio Society amply proves. Likewise, when Daniel Coit Gilman arrived and began to draw to him such teachers as Gildersleeve, Remsen and Rowland and such pupils as Walter Hines Page and Woodrow Wilson, he introduced into the city an element that enriched its life as much, if in a different way, as it had been enriched by the vigorous, daring business men of its youthful days. If the intellectual and social life of Baltimore has grown mellower and richer than it was in the days when the Plug Uglies rioted around the polls on election day, much of the credit must be laid to the work of these men whom the Civil War had made old at sixty.

Nor was the least among them A. S. Abell. If he had lost the hardihood and fire of the days when he and Day and James Gordon Bennett were revolutionizing journalism in the United States, he had gained in tolerance and understanding, in sym-

[1] Shadows on the Wall, p. 65.

pathy and generosity. This is a history of THE SUN, not a biography of Abell, but it is appropriate to mention here that at this time he gained a wide and lasting reputation for the assistance he rendered privately to countless distressed Southerners. He never advertised this activity and for the most part there is no record of these transactions, but there is some mention of them in every tribute paid to the man at the time of his death. What is of record is the strikingly large number of Southerners, especially Virginians, whom he drew into the service of THE SUN immediately after the war. The more salient men among them will be noticed in later chapters. This was anything but charity. All of them were highly competent, and they strengthened the staff of THE SUN immeasurably.[1]

The great public work that Mr. Abell performed in this era was that of an advocate of reconciliation and of actual, as well as technical, peace. This work is difficult to describe, because there was nothing striking or spectacular about it. His method was not dashing attack, but quiet, persistent, unremitting pressure. He put in charge of the Washington bureau — replacing Crow, who had been brought back to Baltimore after Beach's death — that Francis A. Richardson who had been imprisoned during the war for pro-Southern utterances, knowing that Richardson could be relied on to treat the defeated States sympathetically; and the new correspondent's dispatches from

[1] But the most eminent literary man on the staff at this period was no *émigré*, but a native Marylander. He was Edward Spencer, known now principally as the recipient of Sidney Lanier's celebrated description of how he became a poet, but in the late 70s and early 80s a contributor to the stateliest of the Northern magazines, a historian and a dramatist. His Maternus, a tragedy of ancient Rome in five acts, is extant and is interesting as one of the last American efforts to write a play in blank verse and in the style of Racine. He also wrote a light opera, The Great Electric Light, dealing with the advent of electricity for lighting.

the capital soon began to make an impression on fair-minded men everywhere. Of him we shall hear more anon.

This course of The Sun must have seemed a labor of Sisyphus through many weary years, for at no other period of our national history has statesmanship been so completely displaced in Washington by cold cynicism, blind hate and hawk-eyed greed. Claude G. Bowers, in "The Tragic Era," has painted an unforgettable picture of the scene; but no one can picture, because it is almost imperceptible in the orgy, the work of such forces as The Sun, making steadily, although with countless heart-breaking setbacks, toward fairness, justice, tolerance and that reunion which was the only gateway to true peace. Yet in the end these were the forces that prevailed; and everyone who had a part in that work can claim to have had a part in the re-establishment and preservation of this Republic. Perhaps, were any perfectly accurate estimate of history possible, it would show that The Sun was never so great, that Abell was never so great as in these days when he was old and the paper seemed half dead.

When the 80s approached, the founder of The Sun was through, as a newspaper publisher. He was still nominally head of the paper, but his three sons, Edwin, George and Walter, were taking an increasingly important part in the conduct of its affairs and the old man withdrew more and more from active participation. He had already become a sort of monumental institution in the city, as is well illustrated by the flowery dedication with which J. Thomas Scharf, the historian of Baltimore, often quoted in these pages, inscribed a volume to him in 1882, [1] "partly in testimony of the author's esteem and his enduring gratitude for many kindnesses, ancient and recent;

[1] It was Volume I of the History of Western Maryland, published by Everts in Philadelphia, 1882.

partly, also, as a tribute of the author's genuine admiration for, and appreciation of THE SUN, the model newspaper of the United States. This great Structure, as it was Mr. Abell's creation, will also become his monument. It is a Perfect Piece of Work, "not built by envious show," yet symmetrical in all its Parts, and the Pride of the Generous Architect swells chiefly at the Fact that, as it was reared with no man's ruin and to no man's hurt, so there are none who witness its Prosperity with Envy or wish its solid columns less stately in their vista. . . . Its influence in the community must ever be on the side of virtue, honor, justice, and enlightenment. The Founder's Sons may be expected to maintain in its pristine integrity, develop, enlarge and beautify the original work; but neither They nor the Public will ever fail to uphold him for its creating and perfecting.

Even one year earlier the ebullient Scharf's reference to "its solid columns" might have been suspected of having some sardonic allusion to the tremendous dullness of THE SUN; but in 1882 George W. Abell had flung the paper into the New Judge Fight and that was anything but dull. However, although A. S. Abell was still in service, the New Judge Fight really belongs to the next phase in the history of THE SUN, and will be treated in detail in that connection.

Meanwhile, despite the political lethargy of the paper, it had continued after the Civil War, as before, to be enterprising in newsgathering, and in the improvement of its mechanical and circulation equipment, though it brought in no real innovations. In 1867 the use of the stereotype was introduced, and in 1879 the first telephone appeared in the Iron Building. In 1882 Baltimore was dazzled when the Iron Building became the first business house in the city to be illuminated by electricity. No less than 170 bulbs were employed for this purpose, and the burghers were fairly blinded. This was one in the eye for the *American*, too, which had had the impertinence, a few years earlier, to erect on the opposite corner a structure one story higher than the Iron Building, which set a local poetaster to singing:

Our go-ahead *American* no obstacle will shun,
But boldly runs its *columns* up above the daily SUN;
And now the mighty question is, though both spread wholesome leaven,
Which of the two aspiring sheets will make its way to heaven?

In June, 1876, the Founder showed a touch of his old form by delivering 5,000 copies of THE SUN in San Francisco in 3 days, 11 hours and 29 minutes. The Union Pacific Railroad had been completed on May 10, 1869, and on February 25, 1874, the first through freight train from the Coast had reached Baltimore, but passenger service was still slow: in fact, the normal trip took a week. In 1876 one Henry C. Jarrett decided to run a train from New York to San Francisco in record time. Mr. Abell at once entered upon negotiations with him, and it was arranged to take aboard the 5,000 copies of THE SUN at Harrisburg, Pa. Their arrival in San Francisco made a sensation, and they were all sold. The record made on the trip was not approached within at least 24 hours for 20 years, and it was not until 1933 or thereabout that regular passenger trains began to equal it.

For five years after the New Judge Fight of 1882, the Founder continued to come down to the office every day and to act as nominal head of the institution. It was his ambition to round out half a century in harness, and he achieved it. But in 1887, on the fiftieth anniversary of his paper, he called his three surviving sons into full partnership, frankly gave over the conduct of affairs to them, and while he never formally retired he considered his active service at an end.

The press of the United States treated THE SUN very handsomely on the occasion of its anniversary, which was celebrated in the office by the publication of a four-page historical supplement. It had lived down the worst of the animosities resulting from the war, and the honesty of its course was now recognized in the North as well as the South. But among the felicitations was one that Mr. Abell prized especially as coming from a personal friend as well as a great man. It read:

Accept my congratulations on the fiftieth anniversary of your management of THE BALTIMORE SUN, with the hope that your influence for good may long continue to guide its course.

The signature was, "Grover Cleveland."

It was a long and weary road that the Rhode Island journeyman printer had traveled before he held the personal friendship of the President of the United States; but he never doubted that it was to be only the first short stage in the journey that the institution he had founded was to make. There is no record that he indulged in prophetic speculation, however. He was not a romantic man. One of his contemporaries, though, gave free rein to fancy, and produced a picture of THE SUN in 1937 that makes entertaining reading now:

There are few of us who can reasonably expect to see THE SUN's centennial birthday. But we may permit our imagination to picture it then. Its headquarters will then be in a building covering an entire block, fifteen stories high, and with six elevators running day and night, and making the trip from bottom to top in five seconds. Its size will be quadrupled. Its local circulation will amount to about half a million in a city containing two millions of people. Its editions will number four each day. It will be delivered by pneumatic tubes, in the dining room of each subscriber's house, within a radius of fifty miles. Those who live farther off than that will get their papers by balloon. Reporters will not visit public meetings; by a combination of the phonograph and telephone, they will sit in the office, hear everything that is said, and they will write it out as fast as it is uttered, by means of electric needles on wax sheets. The matrix thus formed will then have metal poured in it, and, as soon as the plate has cooled, it will be put on the press. The movable types and the intelligent compositor will be things of the past, and all the articles will be printed with perfect accuracy, under the amended criminal code, making the misspelling of a word in a newspaper punishable by death with slow torture. It will have branch offices in all the principal cities, including Teheran and Timbuctoo, and special correspondents in every town in the world having more than one thousand inhabitants.[1]

---

[1] The Baltimore *Argus,* May 14, 1887. In view of the fact that some literary archæologist may run across the present volume in 1987, and be interested to know how nearly right this prophet was, here is a tabulation of the various items, showing the prophecy on the left and the fact in 1937 on the right:

Prophecy	*Fact*
Building a block long.	It is.
Fifteen stories high.	Four stories.
Six elevators.	Three elevators.
Size of paper quadrupled.	More than that, in number of pages, but not in their size.
Circulation, 500,000.	Morning and evening nearly 300,000, Sunday, more than 200,000.
City, 2,000,000.	City, 825,000.
Editions, 4.	Editions, 11 (regular).
Pneumatic tube city delivery.	Unheard of.
Balloon rural delivery.	THE EVENING SUN maintained airplane delivery on the Eastern Shore of Maryland for a short time. Didn't pay.
Reporters sit in office and write stories of meetings held elsewhere.	They do get reports by radio sometimes, and by telephone often.
Use electric needles.	The teletype is something like that.
No more movable types.	Not for many years, except for special purposes.
No more intelligent compositors.	There are still intelligent compositors.
Death for misspelling.	Unfortunately, no.
Branch offices in all important cities, including Teheran and Timbuctoo.	But Teheran and Timbuctoo are no longer important. Bureaus in Washington, London, New York.
Special correspondents everywhere.	Correspondents in all great news centers, and Associated Press and other news service agents everywhere else.

Mr. Abell survived the semi-centennial of THE SUN a little less than a year. He died on April 19, 1888. "His death," according to his obituary in THE SUN ALMANAC for 1889, "was the result of a gradual decay of the vital powers due to advanced age, though he was confined to his room only two weeks during his last illness." It occurred at his home at the northwest corner of Madison and Charles streets and his body was buried in Greenmount Cemetery.

But THE SUN, by that time, had already experienced a rebirth. Under his sons it was a different sort of newspaper, maintaining Mr. Abell's ideals, to be sure, but discarding many of his methods and introducing others more in keeping with the times. THE SUN, in fact, has been three distinct newspapers, under three distinct types of management, the individual, the partnership and the corporate. The death of Mr. Abell marked the end of its first phase; the second SUN emerged under the younger Abells.

It is a curious irony of history that A. S. Abell, who never believed in personal journalism, was one of its most perfect exemplars. All his life he insisted that THE SUN was the entity and that all personalities must be subordinated to it. As we have seen, he never permitted a by-line to appear in the paper as long as he was in active control. He suppressed the individualities and, as far as possible, even the identities of his men to an extent that seems, to modern practice, unjust and even tyrannous. THE SUN, the composite personality, was his ideal; and he would tolerate no other conception of a newspaper.

And yet there was never a newspaper that followed the sinuosities of its proprietor's experience more exactly. How much he wrote for it at any time is a matter of doubt, but it is certain that in his later years he wrote not at all; nevertheless, when he was young, rash and radical, so was THE SUN; when he became prosperous, sedate and dignified, so did THE SUN; when he was bewildered and terrified by what resembled the crash of matter and the wreck of worlds in 1861, so was THE SUN; and when he emerged from the war a prematurely aged man, THE SUN began to exhibit the symptoms of weariness.

The fact remains, however, that this man's work survived him. The institution he founded, now that he has been nearly fifty years dead, still flourishes and still adheres to the principles he laid down a hundred years ago. It stands to reason, therefore, that while his personality indubitably did sway his paper, it must have been founded on something more permanent than the genius of one man. Without doubt, this permanent element was Mr. Abell's conception of the newspaper as an independent institution, devoted to the publication of news, and bound to the service of no other aim whatsoever. This was his great contribution to journalism, and to the country as well. He found the press a servant, a lackey, valued only as it served the whims of the great; he left it a burgess, a freeholder in its own right, sometimes, indeed, an arrogant overlord, but never again a flunkey at anyone's beck and call.

Let Scharf have the final word. After all, he spoke no more than truth when he said of Mr. Abell's work: "As it was reared with no man's ruin and to no man's hurt, so there are none who witness its prosperity with envy." And the man himself comes far nearer than most men to deserving the lordly epitaph: "Ever on the side of virtue, honor, justice and enlightenment."

CHAPTER VII

☼

THE FIGHT FOR A CLEAN JUDICIARY

It was not until the New Judge Fight of 1882 that The Sun asserted a real political leadership in Maryland. For nearly two decades after the Civil War there had been, in fact, no overt and obvious need for it. The local situation, as politicians called it then, and call it now (neither the language nor the methods of practical politics seem to change with the years) — the local situation was not good, but it was not intolerable. These were the difficult years of adjustment, following the great impact of battle. While they lasted and for quite a while afterward, city and State politicians seemed pygmy creatures. Their factional squabbles and petty pilferings appeared trivial and puny.

Of course the inevitable happened. It would have happened in any community, but in Maryland, where the Democratic nomination was equivalent to election, it was certain to come. Gradually there grew up a political ring which completely controlled the county, city and State governments. The continued quiescence of The Sun offered every opportunity for the spoils type of politician, because there was no other agency in the State that could effectively block his game, even if the spirit and desire to do so had been present. The result was that there came into being in Maryland one of the most smug and unsavory political organizations ever put together. The fact that it was under the domination of men who, by birth and background, were above the level of the average political boss, far removed from the thug type and, in the case of at least one, personally honest, with a lust for power rather than money, did not prevent corruption from flourishing.

However, as one looks back upon the dominant figures in the State and city Democratic organizations of that time, contrasting them with the leaders of the present, it isn't easy to decide whether the progress that has been made in politics is all gain. Either view is defensible. It is true there no longer exists in the State a machine comparable to that of two generations ago, under which all branches of the government were ruled with a rod of iron, the will of the people counted not at all, and oligarchic control centered in men who wielded their power arrogantly and fostered a system that was clearly ugly, evil and vicious. Those things have largely disappeared. But in their place we have immense confusion, incompetency, vacillation, ineptitude, an utter lack of force, capacity and party responsibility, which, under universal suffrage, crowds the City Councils and Legislatures from the lower ranks of the citizenry, and except for the few more glamorous offices such as those of Mayor, Governor and Senator, has practically killed the public service habit of the better grade of men in Maryland. There have been some illuminating exceptions here, but in the main, as to both caliber and character the level of the public service is lower than it was.

In these days there is no man or group of men at the top capable of delivering a party primary. There is no real control that does not slip and slide all over the political lot; no coherent, well-oiled and smoothly working machine, the engineers of which are able to say this shall be done or that shall not be done, and enforce their edict both ways. In consequence, the idea of serving the State and city in the smaller, but sometimes very vital offices, is no longer cherished by first-rate men, for they naturally shrink from the petty and vexatious primary fights that stand in the way. Corruption has been exchanged for confusion; malign competence for innocent (more or less) blundering. From the moral point of view the swap is, of course, a good one, but from the purely practical standpoint of results attained there is at least room for debate. There has been a deterioration in personnel and a degeneration of structure. That is the price Maryland seems to have paid for the disappearance of the old type of political leader and the scrapping of the old-fashioned political organization. No doubt it was worth it, but such are the facts. That is, such are the facts except as they apply to judges. There the story is different — quite dramatically different.

The difference is due almost entirely to that fight made by The Sun in 1882. Whatever the sins of omission and commission committed by the paper before and since, beyond question in that campaign it performed a truly important public service. The value of its service is not to be reckoned in terms of the successful outcome of the actual contest. Its true measure is to be found in the fact that it was only a start. There was then established a policy which for more than fifty years has been followed with undeviating consistency and striking success. The proof of this is in the long, shining record of the Maryland judiciary and the remarkable attitude toward it of the State's press, people and politicians today. The principle for which The Sun, shaking off its post-war lethargy, fought in that campaign, and which, through half a century of steady adherence, has become indelibly imbedded in the minds of Maryland people, is briefly this:

Whatever else politicians do, they must keep their predatory paws off the bench. A non-political judiciary that will interpret fairly the law and administer justice without political taint or touch is more vital to the community than anything else. A good judge is entitled to reëlection regardless of his party affiliation; a poor judicial candidate, pushed by the politicians, should never be supported for party reasons. That was the position THE SUN took in 1882, and from it the paper has never receded an inch. The city bosses have never forgotten the lesson of their great defeat. They have never again given THE SUN a chance to raise the people against them, on the judiciary issue.

It really is an interesting record — this education of a community to the point where it is no longer necessary to make a slam-bang fight, with every gun roaring and the throttle wide open, to prevent politicians from packing the bench with their creatures. An illuminating and impressive instance occurred in Baltimore in the election of 1934. Things political, in that year, were in the hands of a little group of small-bore politicians without any real party authority. Three judges of the Baltimore Supreme Bench were to be elected. Each party was called upon to nominate three, which gave the voters a choice from six. Under the direct primary certain candidates whose qualifications had been questioned got by the gate and on the ticket. They were pushed by little factional groups and personal campaigns. There were also on the ticket two sitting judges — one a Republican, Judge Robert F. Stanton, who had served fifteen years and had a good record; the other, Judge Rowland K. Adams, a Democrat, who had been appointed by Governor Albert C. Ritchie, and was recognized as in the first rank as a lawyer and a man. There had also been nominated, by the Republicans, Mr. J. Frank Supplee, who had given excellent service as a United States commissioner. Of the new candidates he was clearly the best qualified by experience and proved capacity.

The election was held in the Fall of 1934, a year when the New Deal prestige and the Roosevelt popularity were both very high. The Democrats had carried the State two years before by the stunning and then unprecedented majority of 130,000. The Republican party in the city was at its lowest ebb in years, dispirited and demoralized, without leadership or hope; deprived of Federal as well as State and city patronage. That the local Democratic ticket would sweep the city was a foregone conclusion. Among the politicians and political observers the belief was practically unanimous that the three Democratic judges would be elected. But THE SUN argued that Judge Stanton as well as Judge Adams should be retained on the bench, and that Mr. Supplee was better qualified than any other for the third place. In other words, it asked the voters to elect two Republicans and one Democrat. The notion was scoffed at by all the political experts. They conceded the possibility that Judge Stanton would pull through, but the idea that Mr. Supplee could win was characterized as a silly dream of impractical idealists.

Nevertheless, THE SUN continued to urge the voters to vote for two Republicans, Stanton and Supplee, and one Democrat, Adams. It made no flaming fight. It did no denouncing of the political bosses. As a matter of fact, there was none big enough to be worth denouncing. Nor did it denounce the other judicial candidates. It confined itself to stressing the names of Stanton, Adams and Supplee as the best qualified. When the votes were counted it was discovered that all three had been elected — Adams, the Democrat, by plurality of 50,000; Stanton by 25,000 and Supplee by 9,000. Stanton and Supplee were the only Republicans elected to any office in the entire city.

But let us return to the battle of 1882. The dominant figure in THE SUN organization at that time was George W. Abell, the second son of the founder. He was a vigorous, virile man, of real courage and great capacity, and the possessor of a sound newspaper heart. By that is meant that he had clearly in his head the conception, fundamental in every decent newspaper office,

GEORGE WILLIAM ABELL (1842–1894)

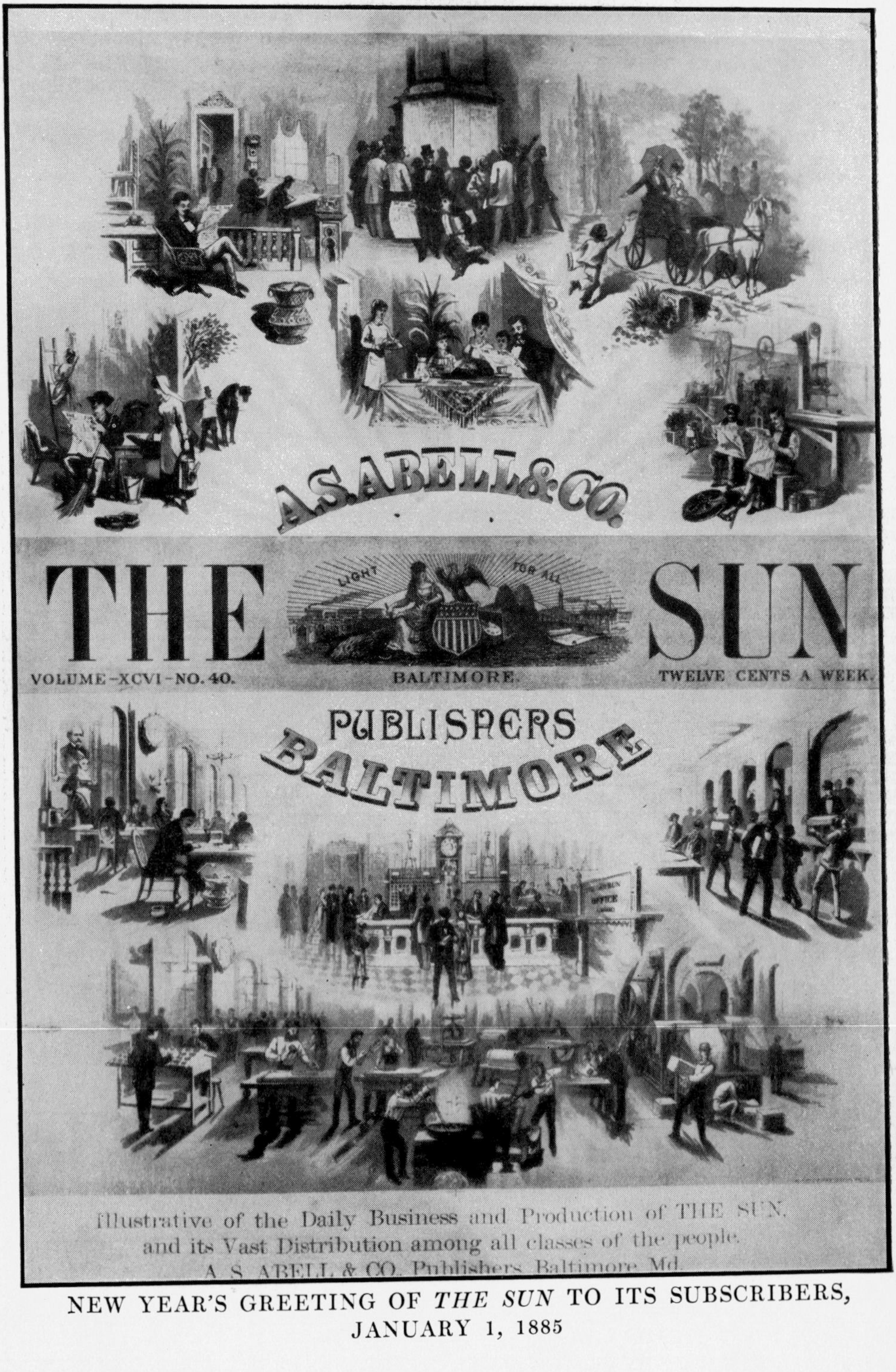

NEW YEAR'S GREETING OF *THE SUN* TO ITS SUBSCRIBERS, JANUARY 1, 1885

that if it is not news it must not be put into the news columns, and if it is news it must not be kept out. There was another thing about George Abell, which was just as true of the other Abells who succeeded him as publisher and of the men who succeeded them: he could not be reached. That is, there was no social, business, religious or political influence that could divert him from a course he had once taken.

When the war between The Sun and the bosses began, the latter, being practical men, conceived that the thing to do was to find out what the proprietors and publishers of The Sun wanted and give it to them. It took them a good many years to discover that there was nothing they wanted and that they could not be given anything. With George W. Abell, the bait used was the ambassadorship to the Court of St. James's, which only made him laugh. With his successors, Edwin F. Abell and Walter W. Abell, the temptations took not only that form, but also the form of suggestions that if The Sun would just say whom it wanted for this or that office, the organization would name him. The Sun, however, had no candidates, and the Abells would not go into conferences with the bosses, would not deal or dicker with them, would express themselves politically only through the editorial columns. There was nothing that could be done with such men. It is interesting that the ambassadorship offer to George W. Abell, which came during the first Cleveland administration through Senator Arthur Pue Gorman,[1] and was unhesitatingly rejected, was later ingeniously distorted into an explanation of the unrelenting fight of The Sun against Gorman. Mr. Abell, it was alleged, wanted to be Ambassador and never forgave Gorman for refusing to recommend him. It

---

[1] During the second Cleveland administration news reached The Sun office that the President was considering offering Edwin F. Abell a place in his Cabinet. Mr. Abell informed the President at once that he could not accept any political office, and the matter was dropped.

was wholly without truth, but that did not prevent its wide circulation among the faithful. One heard it from embittered Gorman men so late as 1906.

On the staff of The Sun at the time of the New Judge Fight were a number of interesting men, most of whom stayed with it for the duration of the war and long after. Of that staff, there is only one living today — Harold E. West, who in 1882 was sixteen years old and a copy boy. He became one of the best reporters The Sun ever had.[1] The managing editor of the paper was Colonel Oakley Philpotts Haines, who had come to The Sun from the Richmond *Enquirer*. Henry J. Ford was city editor, in charge of the local staff. He later resigned to go to Pittsburgh as managing editor of the *Dispatch* of that city, then be-

[1] Mr. West was born in Baltimore November 14, 1866. Educated in the public schools, he went to work in The Sun office on October 3, 1882, a month before the New Judge election. His main duty was to answer its one and only telephone. His father had been interested in telephones, and young Harold not only knew how to operate the instrument, but also how to repair it — a frequent necessity. At eighteen he became a reporter, and thereafter, until 1924, he covered or worked on most of the big stories of the time, from Cardinal Gibbons' investiture with the red hat to the march of Coxey's Army on Washington, and from the inauguration of Presidents to the trial and execution of murderers. He acted, at various times, as city editor, telegraph editor, State editor, Virginia editor, and night editor, and also edited The Sun Almanac. In 1910 he became Sunday editor, and in 1916 became city editor of The Evening Sun. He once left The Sun office to be editor of the Staunton (Va.) *Dispatch-News,* but he was soon back. On May 14, 1922, on the eighty-fifth anniversary of The Sun, a history of the paper from his pen was published as a special supplement; it has been drawn upon heavily for the present chronicle. On January 1, 1924, Governor Albert C. Ritchie, struck by his able handling of public service matters in The Sun, asked him to be a member of the Maryland Public Service Commission. But he was reluctant to leave the paper, and the directors were reluctant to see him go. Finally they solved the problem by passing a resolution, unprecedented in Sun history, retiring him as an Army officer is retired. On January 12, 1925, he became chairman of the commission, and on the expiration of his term in 1936 he continued on its staff.

came professor of political economy at Princeton, and in 1920 was appointed a member of the Interstate Commerce Commission. Other members of the editorial staff were Charles W. Fairbanks, night editor; Oliver P. Baldwin, telegraph editor; William H. Brogden, financial editor; William H. Carpenter, literary editor; Norval E. Foard, State editor; Henry D. Beall, exchange and Virginia editor. The editorial writers were Dr. S. Z. Ammen, Frederic Emory, Edward Spencer, Major Thomas W. Hall and Judge Pere L. Wickes, the two latter not being regular members of the staff, but special contributors during campaigns. To Major Hall, a Confederate soldier and distinguished lawyer, were attributed most of the more devastating editorials of the battle. Among the reporters was Charles W. Dashiell, who later became city editor. The Washington correspondent was Francis A. Richardson. Other reporters included John T. Morris, John T. Doyle, Harry Sultzer, Louis Garthe, William A. Murray, William H. Davis, Dr. Horace A. Brooks, William B. Krout, Edward P. Duffy, Edward Ingle, George Morrow and Albert Richardson.[1]

These were the men who manned THE SUN in 1882, and most of them stuck with it until the tremendous smash of the Gorman-Rasin machine in 1895, when Maryland elected its first Republican Governor. The three leading figures of the Democratic machine were William Pinkney Whyte, Arthur Pue Gorman and I. Freeman Rasin.[2] Mr. Whyte was a man of

---

[1] Sketches of Messrs. Haines, Baldwin, Foard, Ammen, Dashiell, Francis A. Richardson and Duffy will be found in Chapter XII, and of Mr. Morris in Chapter XI.

[2] Mr. Gorman was born in Howard county, Maryland, on March 11, 1839, and at thirteen became a page in the United States Senate, Elected to the Maryland House of Delegates in 1870, he became its Speaker. He was sent to the United States Senate in 1881, and remained there until 1899, when he was defeated as a result of THE SUN's war upon him. He returned to the Senate in 1902, and served until his death on June 4, 1906. He was a candidate for the Democratic Presidential nomination in 1892 and 1904.

breeding, background and culture, a good lawyer, an eloquent speaker, an agreeable companion, but a ruthless ruler of the organization. He had been Governor, then United States Senator, and in 1882 was Mayor of Baltimore. For years he exercised dictatorial power over the Maryland Democracy. But at the time of the New Judge Fight of 1882, Gorman had supplanted him in the Senate and a break between them had started. On the surface, Mr. Whyte had voluntarily retired from the Senate, but the retirement really came because he realized that while he sat in fancied security, Gorman had stacked the cards against him in the Legislature. The details of that affair have no place here, but the upshot was that Mr. Whyte, leaving the Senate because of "family reasons," accepted the nomination for Mayor of Baltimore and was in that position when the fight began. He was on his way to political retirement but he still retained much of his power and the machine was regarded as his.

This was true, however, only to a limited extent. The insiders knew better. Gorman's congenital talent for manipulation and management had made Mr. Whyte rely upon him, but the disciple was all the while engaged in undermining the master. The election of Gorman to the Senate in 1880 was a tremendous shock to Mr. Whyte, and such was the paucity of published political news in those days that the people of the State had no understanding of what had happened. The State machine, to them, was still the Whyte machine. As a matter of fact, it was still that to THE SUN. Cold, cruel, calculating, shrewd, selfish, utterly devoid of sentiment, almost of emotion, but with a great

---

He was an intimate of Matthew S. Quay and the other corruptionists of his time, and is remembered in Maryland as a foremost exponent of machine rule at its worst. Isaac Freeman Rasin, familiarly known as Free, was for many years Gorman's chief henchman in Baltimore, and hence the Democratic boss of the city. He filled only inconsiderable offices; his chief energies were devoted to political manipulation. Born in 1833, he died in Baltimore on March 9, 1907.

and definite charm, Gorman pushed his way into the State leadership so unostentatiously that it was after 1882, not before, that the fact was recognized. Naturally, Mr. Whyte never forgave him and in the later and greater battle between THE SUN and the machine he was with THE SUN. He hated Gorman so long as he lived, with an intense and deadly hatred.

Of Gorman's preëminent ability and skill as a politician there was never any question; of his character there was a great deal. But the outstanding trait of the man was his perfectly extraordinary imperturbability. There was never so impassive a person. His self-control was almost beyond belief. In victory and in defeat, in sickness and in health, among friends or facing foes, he was exactly the same. Nothing ever disturbed or affected for a moment his suavity, urbanity, poise. The testimony of members of his family and of his closest friends was that none had ever seen him flustered, known him to lose his temper, exhibit exaltation, excitement, depression, discouragement, regret, remorse, delight or glee. He was a truly remarkable politician. If this were a story of Maryland politics instead of the story of THE SUN, most of the present volume could be devoted to his personality and career. Suffice it to say that, while in 1882 he was still nominally a lieutenant of Mayor Whyte and a freshman in the Senate, in a short time he had become a great national figure in the Democratic party, and not only bossed the machine in his State, but was the leader of his party in the Senate, chairman of the Democratic National Committee, first a friend of Grover Cleveland, and later denounced as a traitor by that uncompromising and fearless man. In this history, however, Gorman is important only as he relates to THE SUN, and this is true, too, of that other remarkable politician, Rasin. Grim, cunning, unscrupulous and yet curiously sensitive to criticism and attack where Gorman was completely insensitive, Rasin was a type of political boss now almost extinct. His city machine was a marvel of compactness and strength. Corrupt to the core, it was none the less intelligently run. Rasin joined with Gorman in shelving Whyte and for nearly thirty years they maintained a political partnership, held together by mutuality of interest, but with neither trust, friendship nor respect on either side. At the time of the New Judge Fight, other figures in the city machine included John J. Mahon, then leader of the downtown Fourth Ward of Baltimore; Frank Kelly; J. Frank Morrison, who was then head of the Crescent Club, a famous organization of the time; Henry G. Fledderman; and Robert J. (Doc) Slater, who ran a gambling house. There, too, was Frank A. Furst, devoted to Gorman personally, a friend also of Rasin, a supporter of both but never really part of the machine — more a patron than anything else, and because he was greatly beloved in the community, a tower of strength to it.

The fight narrowed down to the question of the freedom of the judges. That was the real stake all the time. However, it is interesting to see how gradually The Sun worked up to it, how cautiously it laid its foundations and stirred its public. As, today, one goes back over those old files, straining the eye to read that small type, puzzling over the baffling make-up and the trite and stilted headlines that seem purposely designed to obscure or conceal the news rather than attract attention, surprise is felt that it was possible under such circumstances to create a militant public sentiment or get the facts home to the people. One could never tell upon what page one would find an editorial, and often it was necessary to read the piece through before one knew it *was* an editorial. Yet, somehow they rang the bell and the people rallied. At the start, probably the most effective thing The Sun did was to print on its first page (along with the advertisements) interviews with leading citizens who indicted the machine for operating fraudulent primaries, concocting false ballots, and innumerable other crimes against the community. It was on August 14, 1882, that the first editorial appeared in which THE SUN really sounded the note of battle, and laid down the principle for which it intended to fight. It was long, cloudy and unnecessarily verbose, but its concluding sentences were clear enough. "One conviction," it declared:

often hidden from view in the dust and smoke of local politics, is rapidly asserting its controlling power as a motive of public action, and no party in this State or city can succeed, or even live, which does not obey it. This controlling conviction is a deep sense of the necessity of honest, faithful and good government, administered by competent men; of *good laws interpreted by good judges.* It is this conviction which is rapidly overmastering every purpose less worthy in its character and which will soon assert its complete supremacy.

A week later there was another editorial which started out in an extremely impersonal not to say vague fashion, and then suddenly got extremely concrete and detailed. It asserted that the local Democratic machine was steeped in iniquity, that the time had come to call a halt on its arrogant and unscrupulous leaders, and that THE SUN proposed from this time forth to oppose corruption within the party, particularly when the foul fingers of corrupt politicians reached toward the judiciary. At that time, Mayor Whyte was at Long Branch, then a fashionable resort. There, too, was the Washington correspondent of THE SUN, Francis A. Richardson, who sent in a long interview with Mr. Whyte on national politics, in which he made a plea to all Democrats to get together in the effort to elect a Democratic President, thus bringing the Federal administration back to the Jeffersonian standard. To this THE SUN's reply was:

Let us first get a City Council which represents the reform sentiment; let us secure a judiciary that will not wink at crime nor spare a criminal who might be useful as a ward politician; let us secure a Congressional delegation, if possible, which will have the ability to speak and vote in Congress the true Democratic sentiment of a conservative people. We shall then, building on a secure foundation, reforming first at home, be able with clean hands to aid in bringing back the Federal administration to the Jeffersonian standard.

Not for weeks later did Mr. Whyte, or Rasin either, for that matter, take THE SUN seriously. They regarded these editorial outbursts with tolerant amusement, secure in the conviction of their own invincibility. The result was that by the time the bosses awoke to their danger, THE SUN, by weeks of editorials, letters from readers, and interviews, had given impetus and organization to an independent citizens' movement too strong to be resisted. Before the middle of September the paper, getting hotter all the time, was daily denouncing "The Monster of Machine Politics." From that time on, day in and day out, except Sunday when there was no *Sunpaper*, it hammered the bosses with everything it had, asserted that the registration lists reeked with fraud, that the primaries had been manipulated, and that the convention was a farce and the machine ticket an insult to all decent citizens.

President Arthur was then in the White House and an effort was made to nullify the force of THE SUN's attack by asserting that it was "imperiling the Democratic chances for the Presidency." This THE SUN denounced as bosh. It was tired, it declared, of this attitude of the bosses that any criticism of them was an effort "to turn the State over to the Republicans." "The time has come," said THE SUN, "for every honest man, disregarding such nonsense, to stand up and say what he thinks and believes."

The Supreme Bench of Baltimore City in 1881 consisted of George William Brown, chief judge;[1] Robert Gilmor, Jr.,

[1] He has been encountered in Chapter V as the heroic Mayor of Baltimore who tried to prevent the attack on the Sixth Massachu-

Henry F. Garey, George W. Dobbin and Campbell W. Pinkney. Judge Pinkney, who was related to Mayor Whyte, sat in the Criminal Court. The terms of Judges Gilmor, Garey, Dobbin and Pinkney expired in the Fall of 1882. There had been for several years suppressed resentment over the conduct of some of the judges, particularly Judges Pinkney and Garey, who seemed to have a monopoly of the Criminal Court bench. The provision of the Maryland Constitution obligating the judges to rotate annually among the courts was disregarded. The primary to elect delegates to the judicial convention was held on October 4, and the convention the next day. The machine ticket included William A. Fisher, Pinkney, Garey and Gilmor. There was some hesitation about Judge Gilmor, but his friends insisted he had served the party as well as either Garey or Pinkney and was thus entitled to be returned. And, notwithstanding much criticism, Mayor Whyte insisted upon the renomination of his relative, Pinkney. In the convention the vote stood — Pinkney 178, Fisher 176, Garey 178, Gilmor 160. Judge Stewart, who got the most applause, received only 26 votes. THE SUN declared that "the bosses had to crack the whip to get their ticket nominated over the dissatisfaction in the party ranks."

After the convention THE SUN threw itself with great vigor behind the movement for an independent ticket, which blossomed

setts Infantry on April 19, 1861, and got into jail for his pains. He was appointed to the Supreme Bench of Baltimore in 1872, and remained there until 1888. Born in Baltimore of Irish descent, he was educated at Dartmouth and Rutgers, and began the practice of the law in 1839. He was prominent in the reform movements of the days before the Civil War, and was elected Mayor of Baltimore in 1860 with the support of THE SUN. When the first trustees of the Johns Hopkins University were appointed in 1870 he was one of them. He was also a trustee of the University of Maryland, of the Peabody Institute, of the Enoch Pratt Free Library, and of St. John's College, Annapolis. He died in 1890.

out on October 14, with an "address to the people," signed by 350 of the leading business and professional men of Baltimore. On October 18 there followed a great mass-meeting at the Concordia Opera House, then the biggest hall in Baltimore. There, amid vast enthusiasm, the Independent ticket was nominated. Judge Fisher, named by the bosses, was also named by the Independents. In a hot speech Major Richard M. Venable asserted that "the machine managers had put him on their ticket as a disinfectant." The other three nominees were Judge Stewart, Edward Duffy and General Charles E. Phelps. All were natives of Baltimore except General Phelps, who had been born in Vermont, was brought to Baltimore as a child, served in the Union Army and was a Republican. In 1864 he had been elected on the Unionist ticket to Congress, and there he opposed the Republican party's Reconstruction policy in the South. He was nominated again in 1876 by the Conservatives, but after his term expired returned to the practice of the law in Baltimore. Mr. Duffy was also a Republican, but Messrs. Fisher and Stewart were Democrats, so that the ticket was evenly divided between the parties. It was endorsed by the Republicans, and also at a tremendous meeting of colored citizens. However, the Democratic bosses induced certain Republicans to nominate what was known as the Straight-Out Republican ticket — Luther M. Reynolds, George C. Maund, John C. King and John R. Kenly.

The campaign that followed was short but intense. THE SUN led the attack with great energy and devoted more space to politics than ever before in its history. The election, held on November 7, resulted in a smashing victory for the New Judge ticket. Fisher received 52,594 votes, Stewart 33,318, Duffy 33,320 and Phelps 32,718. On the Old Judge ticket Garey received 22,946, Gilmor 21,883 and Pinkney 21,273. On the Straight-Out Republican ticket John C. King received 1,046,

George C. Maund 1,022, Luther M. Reynolds 492 and John R. Kenly 8.

The Supreme Bench reorganized with Brown, the holdover, as chief judge, Fisher in the City Court, Stewart in the Court of Common Pleas, Phelps in the Criminal Court, and Duffy in the Circuit Court. One of the first acts of the reorganized bench was to pledge itself to an observance of the constitutional obligation for a rotation of the judges in the courts, which has since been rigidly adhered to. Thus was broken the domination of the Baltimore courts by a political machine. So decisively was it broken that it has never been revived. It was the beginning of the political education of a community.

CHAPTER VIII

A SPOKESMAN OF CLEVELAND DEMOCRACY

FOR more than a decade following the 1882 campaign the political history of Maryland was largely a record of the feud between the Independent Democrats and reform element on the one side and the old bosses of the Democratic machine on the other. THE SUN, despite its vigorous and successful fight for a clean judiciary, resumed a good deal of its former quiescence in other directions. Once more it " advocated happiness in a guarded way " and let an implacable group of sturdy Baltimoreans, led by Severn Teackle Wallis, Charles Marshall, William Cabell Bruce, John K. Cowen, William L. Marbury [1] and

[1] Mr. Wallis (1816–94) was for many years leader of the Maryland bar. He was born in Baltimore and lived there all his life. In 1861, as we have seen in Chapter V, he was imprisoned by the Federal military authorities, though he was opposed to Secession. Released in November, 1862, he returned to his law practice, and in 1870 became provost of the University of Maryland. He was a man of literary tastes, but took an active interest in politics, though he never held office. There is a vivid sketch of him in William Cabell Bruce's Recollections; Baltimore, 1936, p. 134 *ff*. Colonel Charles Marshall had been military secretary to General Robert E. Lee during the Civil War. After the war he settled in Baltimore, and became a conspicuous member of the bar. Mr. Bruce, who is still living, was a United States Senator, 1923–29.

others, fight without effective journalistic support. Some of them were bitter toward THE SUN in those days; it was twitted for its timidity, sneered at for its failure to follow up the logic of its 1882 victory.[1] But it was not all timidity — not by a long shot. THE SUN was held in a rigidly hostile attitude toward the dominant Gorman-Rasin machine. It never gave that machine the least encouragement, or supported any of its candidates. If it did not go further it was mainly because it was unhappily aware that back of the struggle between the machine and the independents was a struggle between two great railroads — the Pennsylvania and the Baltimore & Ohio, then both up to their necks in politics. Gorman, United States Senator and boss of the Democratic organization in Maryland, was a Pennsylvania Railroad man; Mr. Cowen, then general counsel and later president of the Baltimore & Ohio, and by many regarded as one of the ablest men who ever lived in Maryland, sup-

---

Mr. Marbury, who died in 1935, was for long a distinguished Baltimore lawyer.

[1] Mr. Cowen sometimes took advertising space in THE SUN to denounce it. One of his advertisements is quoted at length in Mr. Bruce's Recollections, p. 183 *ff*. He accused it flatly of having been corrupted by the awarding of city, State and Federal printing to its Book and Job Printing Office. "That THE SUN," says Mr. Bruce, "should have been willing to publish such a letter as this in its advertising columns excited not a little surprise, but it is only fair to say that, at that time, in pursuing the political course it did, it was voicing the conservative instincts of thousands of Maryland Democrats quite as honorable and upright as Cowen himself, who, deeply disgusted as they were with the scandalous abuses to which he referred in his letter, shrank from looking for relief to any agency but the party that, whatever might be its shortcomings, included in its membership at that time an overwhelming preponderance of the wealth and intelligence of the State of Maryland." Mr. Cowen's charges, of course, were without ground, and later on, when THE SUN joined him, he admitted the fact. Since that time, says Mr. Bruce, "it has, on the whole, been the most effective single upholder, in the State of Maryland, of all those essentials of good government, under our democratic forms of civil polity, which Wallis and Cowen championed so long, and, in the end, so successfully."

plied a large part of the brains behind the anti-Gorman fights. So long as the machine kept its hands off the judiciary and put up decent men for the higher offices, there was some ground for The Sun to feel that a flaming fight was not called for. At any rate, it did no blazing for some years, except when a judicial vacancy occurred. Then it hammered home its basic principle and got results. Exceptionally good judicial appointments were made by the organization Governors.

However, in the 1884 Presidential campaign, its support of Grover Cleveland was certainly much more than perfunctory. If ever a newspaper was whole-heartedly for a Presidential candidate, The Sun was for him — in 1884, in 1888 and in 1892. Cleveland was its kind of Democrat. He was the sort of leader who aroused genuine enthusiasm in the Abell family. While they voiced in The Sun great admiration for his integrity, courage and capacity, the quality that seemed to appeal to them most was his steadfastness. For twelve years The Sun's editorials constantly emphasized that he was a "safe" man, a leader who could be "trusted," a President whose policies were "sound." Those were the traits that endeared him to the Abells, and it is easy to understand why. They were a conservative family and they ran a conservative newspaper. Their distaste for radical proposals and visionary economic experiments was congenital and profound. This was as true of the sons and grandsons of A. S. Abell as of himself. The qualities of safety, soundness and integrity which they admired and extolled in Mr. Cleveland they exemplified in themselves as individuals and in the paper they owned and published. After Mr. Cleveland's first election, the support of The Sun was so intelligent, consistent and effective that a personal bond sprang up between the President and the Abells. More than once he sent for George W. Abell to come to the White House, and wrote him many personal notes in his small copper-plate handwriting. Also there was a real personal friendship between Mr. Cleveland and the Washington correspondent of THE SUN, Francis A. Richardson. It was Mr. Cleveland who, in his first term, made THE SUN one of the seven papers subscribed to by the White House. It has been on file there ever since — but for Grover Cleveland, as for Woodrow Wilson, it was the President's favorite paper, the one which he personally read.

In 1905, years after Mr. Cleveland had left the White House forever and was living at Princeton, wholly out of public life, the writer of this chapter, then a reporter, was sent up by THE SUN to get an interview with him. Joseph Jefferson, the actor, was dying in Florida. It was thought to be a matter of hours. He and Mr. Cleveland had been warm friends, fishermen together, comrades. The idea of O. P. Baldwin, then managing editor, was to get Mr. Cleveland to talk of his recollections of Jefferson and publish them when Jefferson died. The reporter, at Princeton, went to the Cleveland house, sent in word that he was from THE SUN, and was shown into the drawing-room. Soon Mrs. Cleveland, beautiful and charming, came in.

"Which *Sun* are you from?" she asked.

"THE BALTIMORE SUN," was the reply.

"Oh," she said, "I'm glad of that. If you had been from the New York *Sun* Mr. Cleveland would not have seen you, but THE BALTIMORE SUN is different. If you will come back in an hour, I think I can arrange it."

In an hour's time, again in the drawing-room, Mr. Cleveland, smoking an old corn-cob pipe and dressed in rough tweeds, came in, shook hands, sat down. "How," he asked, "are my friends the Abells? Which one is running the paper now?" And then, "How is my friend Frank Richardson?"[1] When these ques-

---

[1] During Mr. Cleveland's second term (1893–97) Mr. Richardson dissented from some of his public acts and criticized him vigorously, and as a result there was an interruption in their friendship. But it

tions had been answered, he was told The Sun wanted him to talk about Mr. Jefferson.

"Why," he said, "I can't do that. He is my friend and you tell me he is dying. I can't talk about him. It is shocking."

He was told that Mr. Jefferson's death was hourly expected, that unless his reminiscences could be got at once it would not be possible to print them in The Sun simultaneously with his old friend's obituary, that, of course, nothing would be printed until he died. Mr. Cleveland looked out of the window, and smoked silently for several minutes. Then he swung around and for half an hour talked about Jefferson, told fishing stories, described the man, his charm and versatility, told how and why they had become friends. The reporter went back to the Princeton Inn, wrote two thousand words of the Cleveland reminiscences, and wired them to The Sun. Jefferson did not die for three weeks, but when he did The Sun printed a Cleveland tribute the following morning that was reprinted all over the country.

It is an interesting fact that Mr. Cleveland also had a personal relation with the Baltimore city boss, Rasin, between whom and the Abells — all of them — there was never anything but hostility. To The Sun the name of Rasin was synonymous with corrupt politics; to Rasin, The Sun was the real enemy he feared, the one with the most power to wound. Even in the days of its quiescence he recognized that and was afraid of it. How the Cleveland-Rasin friendship came about no one seemed to know. Perhaps friendship is too strong a word, but there was a relationship that induced Mr. Cleveland to consult Rasin about small appointments long after he had broken with Gorman and that kept Rasin thoroughly loyal to him through three campaigns — so loyal, in fact, that in his last fight in

---

seems to have been resumed after
Mr. Cleveland left office.

1892, when Gorman himself was a candidate for the nomination and went out to the Chicago convention with a trunk full of Gorman buttons, Rasin stuck to Cleveland and could not be budged. He never let the Maryland delegation vote solidly for Gorman, did not vote for him himself, and was certainly instrumental in frustrating the Gorman-Hill conspiracy to defeat Cleveland. Mr. Cleveland got the details of this from the Abells and showed his appreciation in various ways after his election.

It is an example of the straightforwardness of Mr. Cleveland that The Sun was apprised by him of his contact with Rasin and understood the reasons. It is also typical of Mr. Cleveland that on the larger appointments he always named for Federal offices in Maryland not only men of complete independence but men who were strongly anti-Rasin as well as anti-Gorman. That, under these circumstances, the Rasin loyalty to Mr. Cleveland never wavered is one of the most remarkable incidents in the career of that remarkable boss, because certainly the things he got in the way of patronage from Mr. Cleveland were far overbalanced by the things he failed to get.

The Cleveland break with Gorman is part of the political history of the country. It came in his first term and strengthened the bonds between the President and The Sun. Elected on the pledge to lower the tariff wall, Mr. Cleveland succeeded in getting through the House a measure that lived up fully to the platform pledge. In the Senate it was hung up in committee, and more than 600 amendments were written into it. It was finally passed in such form that Mr. Cleveland refused to sign it, but let it become a law without his signature. For this emasculation for the benefit of the "special interests" a small group of Democratic Senators was responsible. Among them, Gorman was perhaps the most influential. His particular concern, it was generally understood, was for the sugar people. In any even it was a disgraceful performance, which led Mr. Cleveland to brand those Senators as traitors guilty of "party perfidy and dishonor."

In this tariff fight THE SUN was strongly on the Cleveland side for three reasons — first, because of its confidence and trust in Mr. Cleveland; second, because the bill as he desired it was a clear redemption of the party platform pledge; third, because, wholly aside from Mr. Cleveland, THE SUN was a low tariff paper. One of the fundamental and cherished convictions of the Abells was of the iniquity of the high protective tariff of the Republican party. Hence the paper's reaction against Gorman was violent. It denounced him editorially in as strong terms as those used by Mr. Cleveland, all of which Gorman took with his customary imperturbability. He did not want a fight with THE SUN and, in various ways, had done his best to ingratiate himself with its representatives. For example, in the first Cleveland convention of 1884, where he was practically in command, he gave THE SUN correspondent a copy of the platform before it was reported to the convention, and its contents were clearly outlined in THE SUN the day before its adoption. In the campaign that followed, Gorman was chairman of the Democratic Executive Committee, and practically made the fight. His skill and ability undoubtedly contributed to the result. For three days the outcome was in doubt. New York State was close. The Cleveland majority there, when the final count was completed, was under 1,200. The excitement while the uncertainty lasted was, of course, intense. For three consecutive days THE SUN printed editorials urging the people to be calm. Finally, on Friday night, Gorman telegraphed THE SUN from New York as follows:

> No doubt that Cleveland and Hendricks will have 219 electoral votes. We have New York. The Republican claims of the two Virginias and Indiana are claims of desperation.

Following the election, Gorman returned to Baltimore and a tremendous mass-meeting of Democrats in Baltimore paid tribute to him for his part in bringing about the victory. THE SUN had one editorial in which it did likewise. Perhaps the recollection of that modicum of praise made it a little more bitter in its denunciation of the Senator for his subsequent "betrayal" of the President and the party. At any rate, THE SUN never found occasion to speak favorably of Gorman from that year, 1884, until his death more than twenty years later. It did not by any means wage an incessant campaign against him. There were long periods when it almost ignored his existence. But whenever it did refer to him editorially, it was with contempt.

It is interesting to note that neither in the years they fought him nor in their years of peaceful reporting of the news, was there any personal contact between the Abells and Gorman. There were occasions when certain of his friends came to THE SUN office to sound out the paper, but these were not many and never successful. One of Gorman's closest political and personal friends — General L. Victor Baughman of Frederick county, Maryland — had married Helen Abell, fourth of the five daughters of A. S. Abell, and there were those who thought that here was a political pipe line into THE SUN office. But it was wholly imaginary. General Baughman, charming, attractive and ambitious to be Governor, was never able to bring his SUN brothers-in-law and Senator Gorman together, though he tried. All the Abell men liked General Baughman, but when it came to holding political conferences with him, neither George Abell, Edwin, nor Edwin's son, Walter, each successively publisher of THE SUN during the Gorman régime, was interested.

It would be hard to exaggerate the importance of the great fight upon Gorman that was finally to come in 1895, either politically or journalistically. Both sides threw everything they had into the fray — weight, brains, punch and cash. Quarter was neither asked nor given. The risks on both sides were large. In no political contest in Maryland before or since had feeling run so high, bitterness been so great, or the stakes seemed so big and vital. It really was a great battle — the kind of battle which will not occur again.

The fact is that both State politics and metropolitan journalism have changed since that day. Both are paler in hue. There are no more political bosses like Gorman and Rasin, and no more newspaper owners like the Abells. Both the politicians and the publishers may be better — in some ways they undoubtedly are; but they are certainly different — very different, indeed. So far as the metropolitan newspapers are concerned, they are today less local, more national; less personal, more general; less disposed to impress upon their readers the details of State politics, more inclined to be comprehensive in their field. This change is due partly to the growth in population, partly to quickened interest in national and foreign affairs, partly to the steady increase in the power and size of the Federal authority, and partly to the undreamed-of advances in the facilities for the transmission of news from all over the world. These things have broadened the scope and added to the interest of the big daily newspapers, but at the same time they have diminished unavoidably that intense interest in State and city politics which once characterized such journals as The Sun.

In the last decade of the last century and the first decade of this, during the sessions of the Maryland Legislature The Sun maintained at Annapolis a bureau of four men — two editors and two reporters — and printed during the three months of each session always one and sometimes two or more solid pages of the proceedings, a great deal in small type. It recorded not only every bill introduced but the report of every committee on every bill. The Sun reports, in fact, were almost as detailed as the journals of the House and Senate. Its editorials on legislative affairs were written on the spot. One man covered the House; one man the Senate; one man the Governor's office, and the fourth man was in charge, as head of the bureau. At the start this man was William H. Davis and his chief aide was Thomas J. Ewell. Mr. Davis was later succeeded by Norval E. Foard, the State editor. With the latter in the bureau during the sessions when THE SUN's long-delayed fight to the death on Gorman was most intense — 1896, 1898, 1900 and 1902 — were Thomas J. C. Williams, Charles F. Daley, O. Augustus Hayward and Mr. Ewell. Mr. Foard was an extraordinary man. Small, bald-headed, with bright black eyes, he had a real instinct for politics and a journalistic style well suited to THE SUN of those days. He was a great friend and admirer of Gorman — to such an extent that he had named his son after him — Arthur Pue Gorman Foard. But in 1895 when THE SUN finally launched into its great attack upon Gorman, Mr. Foard also broke with him, and deep enmity replaced their friendship. From then on Mr. Foard intensely despised the Senator and intensely regretted having named his boy after him. But he never could do anything about it except curse with great fluency and force whenever the fact was mentioned in his presence.

After Mr. Foard died in March, 1906,[1] the Annapolis bureau dwindled to three men, then to two, except in the last rush month, when an assistant to the local political man was sent down to help out. Simultaneously, as the paper expanded its Washington bureau, its foreign service, its financial pages, its sporting section and other departments, the space for legislative news grew less and less, until today the two or more pages that used to be devoted to the Legislature have dwindled to a few columns.[2]

---

[1] There is a more extended account of him in Chapter XII.

[2] During the 80s and 90s THE SUN used to give a dinner at Annap-

As for the politicians, the reasons no more Gormans and Rasins are bred to battle as they were in the 90s are several. One, already noted, is the direct primary, which has done away with the convention system of nominations. While it has not lessened the power of a compact organization, none the less it breeds litters of little bosses rather than big leaders. Another reason is the virtual elimination of the utility corporations and railroads from politics and particularly from the lobby. When these corporations were deep in politics they tended to build up one, or, at most, two bosses. It was all to their interest to be able to deal with one man, or two men, rather than have to dicker with a lot of little politicians. Also, it was much less expensive. Hence, it was intelligent in those days for the public utilities of Maryland to be on the Gorman-Rasin side — and they all were, except the Baltimore & Ohio Railroad. These corporations were the chief source of revenue for the machine. They played ball with the bosses from start to finish. But with the setting up of a Public Service Commission in 1910 they began to go out of politics. It had become, under the Corrupt Practices Act, illegal for them to contribute publicly to campaign funds and a very great risk was involved in doing so surreptitiously. With the Public Service Commission in operation, it paid to be out of politics, rather than in. As soon as this fact sank in they joyfully embraced the opportunity to get out.

When the extraordinarily bitter battle with Gorman came on at last, in 1895, THE SUN was in the hands of perhaps the most peace-loving and philanthropic of all its publishers — Edwin F. Abell. Mild mannered and gentle, there was nothing, superficially, of the militancy of his brother George about him, little to

---

olis at the end of every legislative session, in honor of the judges of the Court of Appeals. To this dinner the officers of the State Senate and House of Delegates were always invited.

FROM A PHOTOGRAPH MADE IN 1892

EDWIN FRANKLIN ABELL (1840–1904)

UNION ARTILLERYMEN ON FEDERAL HILL, 1862, WITH BALTIMORE UNDER THEIR GUNS

THE SUN IRON BUILDING AFTER THE FIRE OF 1904

make you think of him as a son of his hard-driving, decisive, determined father.

Up to the death of his brother George he had apparently paid little attention to The Sun. He knew all the people on the editorial staff and in the mechanical and business departments, but he knew them as a friend, not as one of their bosses. Edward H. Fry, now cashier of The Sun, recalls him during George Abell's régime. "He seemed," says Mr. Fry, "to have not very much to do, but all day long a stream of people trickled into his office, and most of them came out with little pieces of blank paper about an inch and a half long and two inches across, which Mr. Abell had torn off old envelopes. On these pieces of paper Mr. Abell would write '$5 — E. F. A.,' or '$10 — E. F. A.,' or '$15 — E. F. A.,' or '$20 — E. F. A.' That was all. But when those little pieces were brought down to the cashier's window we paid out the amount mentioned just the same as if they were certified checks. We never knew the names of the people presenting them, but each piece of paper we put on a steel spike and at the end of the week we tallied them all up and charged them to Mr. Abell. He must have had close to a hundred such friends who called more or less regularly during the year."

There were others who received orders on various merchants for supplies. One of these was a former Union colonel who had married an extravagant young wife and fallen upon evil days. Whenever the colonel received a pension check his wife cashed it and spent the proceeds for finery, leaving nothing for household supplies. Mr. Abell accordingly sent an order to Courtney & Fairall, grocers, instructing them to give the colonel whatever he needed and to send a monthly bill to The Sun office. One day, happening to glance through a file of accumulated bills, he noticed that the colonel was getting a Smithfield ham every week at the uniform price of $4. This seemed strange, for Smithfield hams, like any other hams, vary considerably in weight. So Mr. Abell sent Herbert West, an office boy, to Courtney & Fairall's to investigate. He discovered that the weekly ham bill actually represented a gallon of Sherwood whiskey. But he only laughed, and the colonel continued to get liquid hams until his death three or four years later. When he died Mr. Abell went to his somewhat drab funeral.

It is a curious thing that this kindly man should have been the directing head of the paper in its most tumultuous period, and that during his directorship it should have had more bitter enemies than in all the years that preceded his régime and all the years since. The truth is that under his gentleness there was in Edwin, as in his brother George, a streak of iron. He could be an implacable foe as well as a generous friend. When he made up his mind to fight, he fought. And in 1895, fighting for THE SUN seemed not only right but necessary. It became not alone the part of public righteousness, but sound business policy as well. There was, to be sure, a certain amount of danger for THE SUN in making the battle, because it took it clear out of the party to which it had adhered since its first publication, but there was danger in not making it, too — probably more. The reasons it seemed impossible for the paper to continue longer the complaisant course it had followed since 1882, can be listed as follows:

First, it had become a matter of journalistic self-respect. The arrogance of the "dual despotism of Gorman and Rasin" was so great, and the abuses which had grown up were so flagrant, that the situation had grown intolerable.

Second, the pressure upon THE SUN from the independent elements who had been fighting Gorman and Rasin for more than ten years without adequate newspaper support, became very great. To have gone on failing to respond would have earned for the paper the lasting contempt of many of the best men in the community. The time had come when tolerance from the side lines was no longer a tenable position.

Third, there was the entry into Baltimore of Charles H. Grasty, who in 1892 became the publisher of the *Evening News*. He not only threatened the influence and leadership of THE SUN as a community factor, but, for the first time since the Civil War, gave the paper real competition in both circulation and advertising.

The old Reform League of Baltimore, of which Charles J. Bonaparte [1] was an early president and which included in its membership and among its officers many influential Baltimoreans,[2] began to voice its views through the columns of the *News* rather than of THE SUN, and its conferences — or, at all events, many of them — were held in Grasty's office. He was no aloof publisher like the Abells, with a distaste for personal political contacts and articulating only through his editorials. On the

[1] Mr. Bonaparte was a grandson of that Jerome Napoleon Bonaparte, King of Westphalia, who married Betsy Patterson, of Baltimore. Born in Baltimore June 9, 1851, he died on June 28, 1921. He was an ardent civil service reformer, and once served as president of the National Civil Service Reform Association. Theodore Roosevelt was greatly interested in the same cause, and the two became fast friends. Mr. Bonaparte was Secretary of the Navy and then Attorney-General in Mr. Roosevelt's Cabinet, and had a hand in the Bull Moose movement of 1912. He was prominent in the life of Baltimore for many years. During the early days of THE EVENING SUN he frequently contributed signed articles to its editorial page.

[2] Among them, in addition to the reformers named at the beginning of this chapter, were William Keyser, Roger W. Cull, John E. Semmes, John C. Rose, Joseph Packard, S. Davies Warfield, Karl A. M. Scholtz, Alfred S. Niles, Archibald H. Taylor, Charles Morris Howard, Summerfield Baldwin, William Reynolds and Henry W. Williams. The League survived until the time of the World War, with Mr. Niles as president and Mr. Scholtz as secretary. When Mr. Scholtz finally resigned in 1917 he destroyed the dossiers of all the politicians that the organization had denounced for election frauds. "Limitations," he said long afterward, "had set in, many were dead, and others had become reputable church members, so I deemed it but charitable to forgive and forget."

contrary, he was a warm, charming, friendly fellow, a grand companion, who loved to talk, liked his drink, and understood not only the newspaper game, but the game of politics, too. He comprehended the fact that fighting the machine was the soundest possible business policy for his newspaper, that the harder he fought the bosses and the worse the bosses hated him, the stronger his property became and the surer his prosperity.

The sum of all this was that in 1895, when the Gorman-Rasin leadership ruthlessly ran the steam-roller over its opponents, THE SUN was practically forced into fighting. Had it refrained, with the sort of impetus Grasty had then achieved, he might easily have emerged from the battle, even if he lost, the dominant newspaper figure in the field, with the strongest paper. It is true the fight could not possibly have been won without THE SUN, but from Grasty's standpoint winning the election was not the point at all. The important thing journalistically, he always argued, is to assume the sound position and make a good fight. If that be done, you always win, no matter how badly you lose. No newspaper man ever believed more completely in this paradox than Grasty. It was one of the basic axioms in his newspaper creed.

This was the sort of competition the gentle Edwin F. Abell found in the field when, in 1894, he was elected president of the A. S. Abell Company, and it did not take him long to recognize its formidable nature. The decision to fight in 1895 was his entirely. It was not the result of any polling of opinion among his editors. In those days, indeed, editors were told, not asked, and while there were some able men on THE SUN at the time, there was none with the initiative or nerve or confidence sufficient to tell an Abell how he thought THE SUN should be run. The managing editor, Colonel Haines, was certainly not of that type; nor was Mr. Baldwin, then chief editorial writer. There were, in fact, some Gorman men and even some Rasin men on the staff. There were no Abell brothers left and both Edwin's sons and his nephews were very young men. It was his responsibility and he quite unemotionally accepted it, not rushing into the fight with a loud whoop, but waiting, watching, letting the situation develop, gradually making the position of THE SUN clearer day by day in its editorials, finally making the declaration of war in a ringing denunciation, written by Major Thomas W. Hall, that echoed through the State and was quoted to the last day of the campaign.

It was really a momentous decision to make. In those days the party label had vastly more power than it has today, and party treason was to many an unforgivable crime. Maryland was an overwhelmingly Democratic State, and THE SUN was a Democratic paper. Grasty, with his *News*, was never within a party enclosure and had no party fence to jump. But THE SUN had been inside all its life and when it went over the fence it was a tremendous shock to thousands, bitterly resented for years to come. From that day in 1895, for nearly ten years, no SUN reporter ever attended a Democratic political meeting without having to listen to abuse of the paper. For years it was the favorite target of the Democratic sharpshooters and their bitterness was genuine and intense. Having once jumped the fence, it did not return for five long years. The first result of its jump was the election of a Republican Governor — Lloyd Lowndes — the first the State ever had. That, from the standpoint of the regular Democratic readers of THE SUN, was surely pretty bad, but it did not compare in iniquity with the course of the paper the following year, 1896, when it dared support a Republican candidate for the Presidency.

CHAPTER IX

THE WAR UPON THE DEMOCRATIC STATE MACHINE

THERE was nothing hurried nor impulsive nor emotional about the process by which THE SUN entered the battle of 1895. If ever there was a carefully measured newspaper campaign, this was it. No one can review the facts without concluding that the directing minds in THE SUN organization knew exactly what they were going to do many months before the time came to do it. There is reason to believe that within that organization Charles W. Dashiell, the city editor, perhaps had as much to do with making effective THE SUN's policy, once it had been laid down, as anyone — more, in fact, than the managing editor, Colonel Haines.[1] The decision, of course, was made by Edwin F. Abell, and the editorials were not in the city editor's province, though concerning many of them he was consulted. But the job of presenting the political news of the city and State was in his hands, and it was carried out with great skill and effect.

The interesting thing about the newspaper half of this furi-

[1] Biographical sketches of both Mr. Dashiell and Colonel Haines are in Chapter XII.

ous battle is the contrast between fighting tactics of THE SUN and those of its competitors. Mr. Grasty, with his *Evening News*, was completely independent of party ties, and darted in and out, stinging Gorman and Rasin like a hornet with his cartoons and editorials, laughing at them, jeering at them, inflicting slight wounds, drawing blood, bruising their feelings, but never able to hit hard enough to reach a vital spot or jar the solid foundations of their organization. Across the way from the Iron Building, at the southwest corner of South and Baltimore streets, was the Baltimore *American*, the recognized Republican organ. It always supported the Republican ticket, State and national. However, its Republicanism was recognized as mainly routine in its nature and its assaults upon the Gorman-Rasin machine were neither forceful nor effective. The fact is that, except during the white heat of a campaign, it petted the Gorman-Rasin organization and maintained friendly relations with its leaders. They could get propaganda into the columns of the *American* they could not get into any other paper. Its chief political reporters were Democrats, personal friends of both Gorman and Rasin. One of them, actually and without concealment, for years held a political job given to him by Rasin. That would have meant automatic dismissal from either THE SUN or the *News*.

The character of THE SUN and the character of its owners precluded it from being either a sharpshooter like the *News* or a friendly enemy like the *American*. Steeped as it was in the Democratic tradition and with an unbroken record of nearly sixty years of adherence to the Democratic party, its support of the Republican ticket was a sensational matter, indeed. It required much thought and great preparation. Nearly a year ahead THE SUN began to lay the foundation. It inaugurated a campaign of education. It began with long, impersonal editorials on the evils of machine policies, on the abuse of power, on the dangers of dictatorial control. Then it moved its guns up a little and dwelt upon the vital necessity of honest elections, emphasizing the known frauds in the city registration and the bribery of voters in the State. The next step, taken in the Spring of 1895, indicted Gorman for his "betrayal" of his party in the Senate and his treachery to President Cleveland. Coming still closer, The Sun pointed out the peculiarly mercenary nature of the Rasin machine in the city. For weeks before the convention was held, it was heavy with warnings that the Gorman-Rasin outfit, if unchecked, would bring disaster upon the Democratic ticket in the Fall. All the time it pressed home the fact that it was with the President, that the true Democracy was the Cleveland Democracy, that Gorman was not a Democrat and Rasin a mere mercenary. There were months of this sort of campaigning before August, when The Sun finally got the range and opened with artillery. From then on its big guns roared every day.

While the course of the paper had been determined early in the year, there were several ways by which Gorman and Rasin might have compelled it to reconsider. One was by renominating the sitting Governor, Frank Brown; a second was by nominating Judge William A. Fisher; a third was by nominating Thomas G. Hayes, a Confederate veteran and eager reformer. To all three of these The Sun was favorable, but not one suited the bosses, and The Sun never believed they would. Governor Brown had shown entirely too much independence at Annapolis and was suspected by Gorman of cherishing Senatorial ambitions. Judge Fisher had a fine record on the Baltimore bench, but he was a sturdy Cleveland Democrat and had said some bitter and unforgivable things about Gorman. As for Mr. Hayes, despite his independence and fiery temper, Gorman was disposed to take him, and did promise him his support. However, when Mr. Hayes's name was mentioned, Rasin became violently hostile, and would not hear of him. It was impossible to nominate a city man over the Rasin protest, and so, two days before the convention, Gorman dropped the Hayes idea without so much as saying a word to him. The consent of John E. Hurst, an eminently respectable wholesale dry goods merchant of Baltimore, was obtained, and word was sent down the line that he would be the party candidate for Governor. The convention was held on July 31, 1895, in the old Academy of Music, Baltimore.

Mr. Dashiell took a group of picked reporters to the convention hall to cover the proceedings, but there was very little to do, the proceedings being cut and dried and brought to a close at the earliest possible moment. Only one ballot was taken. Hurst received seventy votes, Fisher thirty-one, Jones five and Hayes two. There was no proposal that the vote be made unanimous for fear of an uproar.

Dashiell wrote the lead to the story. The headlines tell what happened:

Gormanism Wins

The Dictator's Wishes Carried Out
By the Convention

Democracy "Not In It"

Mr. Hayes accuses Mr. Gorman
of Base Treachery

His Words Plainly Spoken

Shakes His Fist in Mr. Gorman's Face
But No Reply is Made

How the Deals Were Fixed

An Interesting Account of the Convention from Beginning to End — A Throng of Straight Democrats in the Galleries Who Showed What They Thought and Felt — Mr. Bernard Carter had a Hard Time of it as Chairman and also while Nominating Mr.

Hurst — Judge Fisher's name Enthusiastically Received — Resolutions Indorsing the National and State Administration — Notes and Incidents.

An hour or so before the convention, Mr. Hayes, recognizing that Gorman had thrown him overboard, rushed to the Carrollton Hotel, forced his way into the Senator's room and denounced him as a traitor and a crook, shook his fist in his face, declared he would devote the remainder of his life "to dethroning you from the dictatorship now held by you over the party." The imperturbable Gorman remained completely silent during this violent tirade. He did not look at Mr. Hayes, nor speak, nor move. It was as though he had not heard a word.

Following the convention, Dashiell, with others who had covered it, returned to the office and went into a conference with Colonel Haines, Oliver P. Baldwin,[1] Edwin F. Abell and Walter W. Abell, who was then being trained for the management of the paper. It was agreed in that meeting that THE SUN would not support the ticket nominated under such conditions, but it could not be determined just what the paper's course would be until after the Republican State Convention, which would be held on August 15, two weeks later. The leading editorial on the Democratic convention and its action concluded with this paragraph:

> We believe we have done our duty in a faithful endeavor to save the Democratic party from the consequences of what we believe to be a false step. Together with the great majority of the Democratic party and of the people of Maryland we await the final result, trusting that it will be for the best interests of the people and for the honor and well-being of the good old State of Maryland. That decision, we believe, will be an honest one. It will not be bought with money or secured by the intrigues and cajoleries of officehold-

[1] Then an editorial writer and later managing editor. There is an account of him in Chapter XII.

ers and politicians. Politicians, bosses even, may be bought at so much per head; voters even, at primary elections may sometimes be bought by the dozen, and conventions may be thus packed and misled, but the people of a whole State, especially the State of Maryland, cannot be corrupted.

This sounded ominous. The next day no comment was made editorially on the political situation, and leading figures in the Democratic party, sent by Gorman, came to the office in an effort to induce the Abells to agree that if the paper could not actually support the ticket it would not oppose it. They pointed out that Mr. Hurst was a highly honorable and respected citizen and declared that he could be depended upon, if elected, to give the State a good administration. These gentlemen received no satisfaction whatever. A Hurst Business Men's Association was formed and an imposing committee from it called upon Edwin F. Abell, pleading for support. They were courteously but coldly received.

By that time everybody in The Sun organization knew that the paper was going to fight. Those closest to Mr. Abell had known it for months. However, there was still the danger that the Republicans, being a stupid lot, would nominate for Governor a man whom The Sun could not support. Such a man was William T. Malster, who was a prosperous iron foundry owner in Baltimore, but would have made an impossible Governor.[1] At one time his selection seemed assured, and it was with great relief that The Sun saw the situation change and the leaders swing behind Lloyd Lowndes, an able banker of Cumberland and a man of high character. Undoubtedly The Sun aided in bringing this about, for the fact became known that it would support Lowndes but would not support Malster.

The Republican State Convention of that year was held at

[1] Some years later he became Mayor of Baltimore — and turned out to be impossible.

Cambridge, a country town on the Eastern Shore of Maryland, on August 15. Mr. Malster, who had carried only one district in Baltimore city and who had practically no strength in the counties, dropped out before the convention met and his name was not even presented, his friends scrambling to get on the Lowndes bandwagon. John C. Rose, counsel for the Baltimore Reform League, was made chairman of the convention. So keen was the interest in the proceedings that not only were all the Baltimore newspapers represented, but also the newspapers of Washington and Philadelphia. There was only one telegraph wire out of Cambridge and, with so many dispatches being written, no paper would be able to get a complete story of the convention out of town. Dashiell had foreseen this situation. He had four men in Cambridge and had arranged with the commander of the State Shell Fish Commission to take one of them over to Oxford, on the north bank of the Choptank river, a distance of ten or twelve miles. The telegraph operator at Oxford turned out to be a very competent man. Although his day ended at 6 o'clock, he had been engaged to remain on duty as long as he might be required, and he and The Sun reporter both kept at work until 1 o'clock in the morning. In the meantime, the other reporters who had remained in Cambridge were squabbling over the wire and getting only fragmentary stories through. The Sun was the only paper to have a complete story of the convention next day.

Immediately after the convention it sailed into action, and for nearly three months it volleyed and thundered. At once the thing became a personal fight between the paper and Gorman. The Republican party and its candidates were largely obscured. The independent Democrats and the Reform League did heroic work, but they were in line behind The Sun. As for Mr. Grasty and his *Evening News*, they were overshadowed and almost forgotten. Gorman made a series of brilliant speeches in counties and city, but The Sun tore them to pieces, indicting him as a party traitor, a corrupt politician, a menace to the State and a disgrace to the country. Highly influential in the Democratic National Committee and with many friends among his Senate colleagues, Gorman brought into the State as speakers Senators Gray, of Delaware; Faulkner, of West Virginia; Daniel, of Virginia, and others. The largest campaign fund ever known in the State was accumulated from forces inside and out. The Baltimore precinct and ward executives, for the first — and, perhaps, the last — time, actually had more money on election day than they could use. As much as $120 a precinct was paid out — an unheard-of sum. In those days there was no Corrupt Practices Act in Maryland and the buying of votes was a recognized industry, practiced particularly on the Eastern Shore of the State. It was believed — and charged — at the time that part of the huge Gorman campaign fund came from the Sugar Trust, whose friend he was. At any rate, its size was enormous, and the lack of restriction upon expenditure made the job of dislodging the machine a Herculean one.

The strategy of Gorman was first to defend himself, and second to attack The Sun. Denunciations of the paper, its editors and proprietors were a feature of every mass-meeting in every county and every ward. Anti-Sun resolutions for all the counties were prepared at headquarters and a good many of them adopted. The Sun treated these denunciations humorously. It never for a moment permitted itself to get angry or seem disturbed, but every time a resolution was passed it turned a little more heat on Gorman. Here is a sample of its editorial treatment of one of the earlier resolutions:

THAT AWFUL *SUNPAPER*

According to dispatches from Annapolis, at a meeting held there yesterday to ratify Mr. Gorman's ticket some frightened office-holders and office-seekers passed a resolution "condemning" The

Sun for attacking Mr. Gorman and his machine. This grieves us, grieves us to the heart. The Sun feels almost as badly cut up as a judge would feel who should be " condemned " by an offender whom he had just sentenced. But really we do not think the meeting meant any harm. Those who voted for the resolution were simply carrying out orders. Although the words of their resolution seem harsh, they were actually very complimentary. What they intended to convey was something like this:

" *Whereas*, in accordance with orders from Mr. Gorman, we must express our opinion of The Baltimore Sun,

" *Resolved*, that it is a journal of too much honesty and independence to suit our ideas, and that if it keeps on talking out of meeting, we will be elected to stay at home;

" *Resolved*, that it has given so truthful an account of the situation in this country as to encourage the friends of honest government and greatly impair the influence of our local bosses;

" *Resolved*, that this sort of thing won't do at all, don't you know, and that that awful *Sunpaper* ought to be deprived of free speech;

" *Resolved*, that we hope these resolutions are in line with what Mr. Gorman expects;

" *Resolved*, that the unbought democracy of Anne Arundel county expects every man at this meeting to do his duty; and, therefore, lastly and chiefly;

" *Resolved*, that this meeting do now adjourn and take several drinks, and that the chairman be instructed to send the bill to Mr. Gorman, who, with some others, it is understood, will pay the freight in this campaign.

" (*Signed*) Peter Thirsty and John Always Dry."

It is needless to say that these resolutions were adopted with great applause, and that the last was greeted with deafening and unanimous enthusiasm. We thank the gentlemen of the Anne Arundel machine for their kind expressions, and had we been present would have been glad to join them after adjournment.

In the main, however, The Sun's editorials were deadly in their earnestness and annihilating in their day in and day out reiteration of the issues. Here are some of their titles:

Clevelandism and Gormanism.
It Is The Democratic Masses Who Are After Him.
The Democrats Revolt Against Gormanism.
Senator Gorman's Great Example As A Bolter.
The Issue Is Gormanism.
Destroy The Bosses And Rescue The Party.
A Bad School Of Politics For Young Men.
Regularity The Last Refuge Of Cornered Bosses.
The People's Strike For Freedom.
Strike While The Iron Is Hot.
No Chance For Reform Within The Party.
Fraud, Fraud, Fraud.
Rescue The Democratic Party From The Wreckers.
Horatius Gorman And His Bridge.
Liberate The Democracy From Moral Slavery.
The Plain Issue Plainly Reviewed.

There was a blistering one on the morning of the election entitled " Bury the Bosses Today " and winding up as follows:

> The Democrats of this city and State must unload their twin dictators or Democracy in this part of the country will be suffocated in the choke-damp of mercenary and machine-ridden politics. The thing to be decided is whether there is to be a Democratic party in Maryland or a Gorman party opposed to the national Democracy and the Democratic President, leading a contemptible existence for the private emolument of Mr. Gorman, Mr. Rasin and their friends.

There was no effort in the campaign to keep the news columns free from editorial expressions, nor was there any pretense of giving the opposition equal news space to present its case. THE SUN of those bitter days was untroubled by any feeling of obligation to be fair to the other side. Its news columns for three solid months bristled with anti-Gorman, anti-Rasin attacks. It printed hundreds of letters and interviews from Democrats assailing the bosses. It brought out against them William Pinkney Whyte, Thomas G. Hayes, William Keyser, William Cabell

Bruce, Judge William A. Fisher and other conspicuous party men in ringing declarations. A sentence from Mr. Hayes is typical. " My grievance," said he in The Sun, " consists in the evil of having the Democratic party dominated by Gorman and Rasin. Remove that evil by a removal of their damnable and destructive influence. Then, and not until then, am I conciliated."

The Sun, of course, printed the news of the other side. It suppressed no material fact. It gave space to every Gorman speech — and he made at least ten in the campaign — and it told fully the stories of the Gorman-Rasin mass-meetings, rallies, demonstrations and parades. But how! An illustration is afforded by the contrast between its headlines on two meetings in the same week in October. The first was a Democratic meeting in the big Music Hall, Baltimore (now the Lyric Theater). It was an immense affair. Mr. Hurst and the other candidates were there and spoke, and Senator Gorman made the big address. The Sun's headline next morning was:

GORMAN STILL AT IT

Three days later another meeting, smaller in size, was held at the Germania Maennerchor Hall in the interests of the Republican ticket. A telegram assailing Gorman from Carl Schurz, which The Sun had secured, was read. The headline over the account of this meeting was:

THE PEOPLE SPEAK

Each story fitted its headline. On the Friday night before the election, Gorman had arranged to close the fight with an enormous meeting to be preceded by a parade. There were 15,000 stalwarts in line. Unlimited money had been provided. Some of the marchers got as much as $3; others only 50 cents. There were bands, floats, banners and fireworks. The marching ward-clubs turned out in costume. Hundreds of signs, reading "Down With The Sun," were carried by the faithful. John J. Mahon, Frank Kelly, Doc Slater, Frank Morrison, all the Rasin lieutenants, marched at the heads of their clubs or divisions. In Eutaw street, near Baltimore, a reviewing stand was erected, and here Gorman, Mr. Hurst, Henry Williams, the machine candidate for Mayor of Baltimore, and all the other city and State candidates, reviewed the troops. At the head of the procession, to clear the way, was a large float upon which was mounted a great bell, the sound of which could be heard long before it was seen. Harold E. West wrote the account of that parade, and his story ruined it. He featured the bell. He likened the parade to a funeral procession. All through the two columns of his piece one almost heard the bell. A dozen times he used the sentence, "And the bell tolled on." And here was the headline Mr. Dashiell put on the story:

And The Bell Tolled
As The Gorman-Rasin Followers
Marched Along
With Bands And Bombs
But It Was A Great Night
For The Ring "Boys"
And For Small Boys, Too
Who Made Up A Very Large Part
Of The Procession
With The Out Of Town Men

Besides These, There Were The "Eminently Respectable" Section, Many Officeholders Who Had To Turn Out, And That Bugaboo Which Summarizes All The Arguments Of The Ring, The Mixed School, Presided Over By A Man Dressed As A Colored Woman, And, Possibly, Representing The "Maiden With The Raven Locks" About Which The Hurst Business Men's Association Has Been So Eloquent.

That was the headline to the story. The story itself began with these words:

> When Lord Chesterfield was in his last illness, and his death was only a matter of a few weeks, his physician advised that he be taken for an easy drive in his carriage. As the equipage proceeded slowly along it was met by a lady, who remarked pleasantly to the great invalid, " Ah, my lord, I am glad to see you able to drive out."
>
> " I am not driving out, Madame," answered Chesterfield, " I am simply rehearsing my funeral."

Despite their confidence in Gorman and their belief in the potency of unlimited money, the machine politicians knew that they were beaten when they read Mr. West's story. It was the climax of a thrilling campaign and the election day that followed was the most tumultuous and disorderly that had ever occurred in Baltimore. " Rowdyism Rampant " was THE SUN's headline the following morning. For weeks the Reform League had been uncovering registration frauds in the city and THE SUN had been raising a great pother about them. It had succeeded in forcing the resignation, or rather removal, of two of the election supervisors, and Governor Brown, at its insistence, had named, in place of one of them, Charles J. Bonaparte. Literally, for weeks there had been a constant row in the board and the whole town was in a state of immense excitement over the effort of the machine to steal the election. The Reform League had called for watchers in the tough downtown wards, and on election day there were many volunteers. Some of them were treated pretty roughly. Alfred S. Niles, later a judge, was assailed in an election booth and knocked down. Two heelers jumped on William P. Riggs, but found it was a mistake. Mr. Riggs, as husky as they make them and a famous Princeton football guard, battered both of them up pretty badly. A Negro was shot and killed, and there were innumerable fist fights all over the town, which the police did little to stop.

When it was all over, it was found the bosses had been beaten in every direction and every possible way. Lowndes had close to 20,000 majority — a huge figure in those days before the women voted and when the total vote in the State was less than one-third what it is today. Alcaeus Hooper, a Republican, was elected Mayor of Baltimore. Gorman had lost the Legislature, Rasin the City Council. A Republican United States Senator was assured. The rout was complete.

CHAPTER X

☼

THE THREE BRYAN CAMPAIGNS

THE CONDITION of the Democratic machine in Baltimore city and the State of Maryland after its defeat in 1895 was bad, but not desperate. The bosses were down, but not out. It was a great feat to beat them, but beating them by no means dealt them a death blow. The fundamental fact that the primaries are the key to all politics had not then been grasped either by THE SUN or by its allies in the anti-Gorman-Rasin battle. It is the primaries that are vital to the machine everywhere and all the time. So long as it controls that gate, it controls the nominations. Beating the bosses' ticket in the general election is exceedingly painful and it may seem destructive at the time, but the fact is that it is anything but fatal. The only way to put a political machine out of business permanently is to unhorse it in the primaries. That is where it lives. From any general election defeat it can recover, but defeat it in the primaries and it dies.

The Gorman-Rasin machine was never beaten in the primaries and was never really broken up. THE SUN and the reform elements overthrew the organization in the general election, turned the State and city over to the Republicans, and rooted thousands of small Democrats out of thousands of small municipal and State jobs, but they never touched the real source of Gorman-Rasin power. The bosses still remained in possession of their inner citadel; still commanded their organization army. Their machine, defeated and dismayed by the prospect of lean years with no patronage for the boys, was still intact. Even two years later, when, following up its fight, THE SUN succeeded in throwing Gorman out of his Senate seat, his control over the machine was still unimpaired. Neither he nor Rasin was ever really ruined as a leader — defeated, yes, but not destroyed. With them, after 1895, it was a question of watching their step, keeping the organization together, waiting for the reform tide to ebb, as it inevitably does. Then they came back, though it took them six years to do so, and in that period they sustained two more general election defeats.

Naturally, the election of the Lowndes ticket by such a smashing majority, after so long and bloody a fight, was the cause of great rejoicing in THE SUN office. However, the greatest care was taken not to give the least indication of this in the columns of the paper. With an almost painful modesty THE SUN refrained from claiming credit at all — and it printed only three or four of the hundreds of congratulatory letters that flowed in from all parts of the State. It not only emitted not a single gloat, but it deprecated its own part in the fight and congratulated "the people." Such journalistic gloating as there was came from the *News* and the *American*. The former had played a spectacular if secondary part in the fight and really had considerable reason for self-congratulation. So, too, had the Reform League and the various independent Democratic leaders who had been fighting Gorman and Rasin for years without results until THE SUN swung into action. But all THE SUN had to say of the result was to call it "The People's Victory."

For this extreme modesty, not at all characteristic of victorious newspapers, there were several sound reasons. One was that the Abells — particularly Edwin F. Abell and his son Walter W. — were genuinely modest men, and the thought of crowing over the victory was offensive to them. A second reason was that THE SUN had not come out of the battle unscathed. It had lost a lot of friends and made a lot of enemies, and meanwhile, its rival, the *News*, had gained. The *News* wasn't a Democratic paper and its course thus aroused neither rancor nor resentment among the old-line Democrats. It risked nothing, had nothing to lose. Still a third reason for THE SUN's caution was its apprehension that the conduct of the Republicans in office would not be of a kind to commend them to the better people of the State. Being primarily responsible for putting them in power, THE SUN was uneasy as to their behavior. In an extremely short time these feelings were found to be amply justified. Governor Lowndes, himself a man of the highest character and real capacity, was helpless against the hungry hordes of Republican politicians who suddenly found themselves with their feet in the trough. The Legislature broke all records for waste, graft and inefficiency. The lobby was open, bold and piratical beyond belief. Public utility corporations were blackjacked by the Republican bosses and in turn pitched in to run the Legislature and corrupt the legislators. It was at this session that Sydney E. Mudd, later Congressman from the Fifth Maryland district, but then Speaker of the House of Delegates, defined an honest man as "a —— who will stay bought." That remark as well as anything else describes the sessions of 1896 and 1898, during both of which the Republicans were in control.

The 1896 saturnalia was somewhat mitigated by the election of William Cabell Bruce, a man of unquestioned integrity, great courage and unusual intellectual equipment, as president of the Senate. But he could accomplish relatively little. After disgraceful dickering and dealing, George L. Wellington was chosen as the first Republican Senator from Maryland since the

Civil War. It was a scandalous and unsavory session, and in THE SUN office there was great relief when it was over. However, it was many a long day before THE SUN found itself able to return to the Democratic fold and again espouse a Democratic ticket. Having once put its hand to the plow, it could not turn back. Within a few months of the close of the 1896 Legislature it was plunged into another campaign — this time a national one, in which principles and not personalities were involved. For the first time in its existence THE SUN found itself compelled to oppose a Democratic candidate for the Presidency. The nomination of William Jennings Bryan on his 16-to-1 free silver platform left it no choice. Every economic belief of the Abells, conservative to the core, was outraged by that platform.

While, according to its settled policy, THE SUN carefully laid the foundation for its 1896 fight, and was a long time engendering real heat, yet there never was a moment when there was any doubt inside the office as to its course. Nor was there any doubt among the editors and owners that its fight would be costly. It had lost much circulation and some advertising as a result of the 1895 campaign, but these losses were trifling compared to those it was to suffer in 1896. The bitterness developed against the paper was almost unbelievable. The effort to damage it was deliberate, organized and determined. Back of it was Gorman, smarting under THE SUN's blows the year before and now plunged into the Bryan fight, not because he was not anti-Bryan and anti-free silver, but because he saw an opportunity to secure at least a measure of revenge. It also seemed to him good policy to weaken THE SUN as much as possible just ahead of his own fight for reëlection to the Senate. Not in the whole hundred years of the life of the paper has there ever been such vilification and abuse heaped upon it and the Abell family. Democratic meetings were largely devoted to lambasting them. They were accused of selling out to the Money Interests, of being for the rich and against the poor, of favoring the powerful against the downtrodden and oppressed.[1]

On June 10, nearly a month before the Democratic National Convention met, the Maryland State Convention had met at Ford's Opera House in Baltimore and, by a resolution which was adopted by a vote of 87½ to 27½, declared in favor of the maintenance of the gold standard, opposed the free coinage of silver at the ratio of 16 to 1 and declared further that

> the safety of the masses of the people can only be found in a sound and honest currency, and it is because we perceive that the hope of relief held up to them by the advocates of the free and unlimited coinage of silver at a ratio nearly, if not quite, twice the real value of silver bullion, will assuredly prove delusive, that, true to the history and traditions of our party we declare our hostility to a policy so fatal, in the absence of an enlightened international agreement regulating the whole subject, to the early establishment of which agreement we believe the efforts of the government should be steadily directed.

At a still earlier date the Republicans of Maryland, at their State convention, had opposed the free silver movement, declaring:

> We believe in the gold standard upon which to base our circulating mediums, and are opposed to the free and unlimited coinage

[1] It was understood in the office at the time that about 20,000 subscribers, mainly in the Maryland counties, stopped the paper. Most of them, of course, were back in a little while, but bitterness against it continued for ten years, at least. A story in point used to be told by Albert J. Almoney, secretary of the State Senate and editor of a paper at Rockville. On the day after the Baltimore fire of 1904, a copy of THE SUN, printed in the office of the Washington *Star*, was delivered to an aged Rockville subscriber who was a faithful Bryan man. It was a meager sheet of eight pages, much unlike THE SUN of ordinary times. The old fellow turned it critically this way and that. He looked at it first with scorn, and then with a vast satisfaction. "There," he said at last, "you ——, you're trimmed to suit me now."

of silver until an international agreement of the important commercial countries of the world shall give silver a larger use.

The Republican National Convention at St. Louis, on June 18, adopted a gold plank and opposed the free coinage of silver except by international agreement, pledging itself to promote and maintain the gold standard until such agreement could be obtained. This convention nominated McKinley and Hobart. The gold plank of the platform received a much larger vote in the convention than the candidates. The gold Democrats in the National Democratic Convention refused to abide by the platform and candidates of the Chicago convention and, at Indianapolis on September 3, 1896, adopted a platform denouncing the plan for the remonetization of silver and declaring unequivocally for the maintenance of the gold standard. They simultaneously nominated Palmer and Buckner to run against Bryan and Sewall.

For months before the meeting of the Democratic convention in Chicago The Sun had hammered away against free silver. One of the chief apostles of silver was Senator Teller, of Colorado, who, it was expected, would be nominated if the free silverites could get control of the convention. He had been in the movement led by Gorman to emasculate the Wilson Tariff Bill and had been a party, also with Gorman, to the embarrassment of President Cleveland at the time of the gold purchases. He had been a Republican and a Populist, and The Sun pointed out the menace of the candidacy of such a man on the Democratic ticket.

In its issue of July 6, 1896, the day before the convention met at Chicago, it printed a long editorial on the situation, in which it said, among other things:

It is idle to disguise the fact that the worst fears concerning the action to be taken at Chicago are likely to be realized. The leadership of the party, for the time being seems to have passed into wild and reckless hands. Demagogues pandering to a passing popular craze in certain sections of the country are in the places where statesmen, guided by principles and restrained by a conscientious regard for national, as distinguished from partisan interest ought to be. Men who seek to make up by the violence of their language for the feebleness of their ideas are temporarily in the saddle. It appears to be an hour of triumph for passion over reason.

After denouncing the betrayal of the party pledges for tariff reform and the movement in Congress to discredit President Cleveland, THE SUN went on:

It is at such a time and with the rank and file of Democracy in such sour and angry temper that the crafty and leather lunged demagogue finds his opportunity. Political quackery flourishes apace in such an atmosphere, and the delusions of the free silver cult, promising to make times better by making money cheaper, and to lighten all debts, national, state, municipal, and individual, by making dollars out of fifty cent pieces by act of Congress finds a ready army of believers. Broken down and discredited politicians, bankrupts alike in ability and character, step to the front in this delirium of monetary hallucination.

We shall hope against hope until the deed is done, that Democracy will not have its name thus degraded. But we are satisfied that in any event nothing more than the name of the national Democracy, along with the section of its momentarily misled and deceived voters, can be sold and delivered to the free silver syndicate. The honest, intelligent manhood of the party may be overcome by its machinery at Chicago this week, but it will assert itself at the polls next November, and will be the final master of the situation when the madness of this hour has all spent itself in the sound and fury of a foolish and forefated campaign.

No political convention in THE SUN's career up to that time had ever been covered as fully and completely by it as was this Chicago convention. Francis A. Richardson, its Washington correspondent, was then at the height of his powers. He had charge of the staff sent to Chicago and himself wrote the leading dispatch each day. He had a singular facility for getting at the inside of what was going on and discovering the under-the-surface currents which swayed political movements. No paper in the country had more thorough and accurate accounts of the proceedings. Throughout the convention THE SUN kept hammering away at the free silverites. The delegates split after the adoption of the silver plank in the platform, 162 refusing to vote for a nominee for President and 250 refusing to vote for a nominee for Vice-President. The Maryland delegation also split. Of the sixteen delegates, only four voted for Mr. Bryan. General John Gill, a prominent figure in Baltimore's financial life, was so disgusted with the platform which had been adopted that he left the convention before the balloting for President began and came home without leaving his proxy with John E. Hurst, who was chairman of the delegation. As a result, Maryland's total vote in the convention was fifteen instead of sixteen.

On July 11, the day after Bryan was nominated, THE SUN, in an editorial on "The Candidate and the Platform," spoke of him in complimentary terms, but foreshadowed its own refusal to support him in these words:

> The election of McKinley would not produce irreparable injury, and would mean, at worst, but a short reign for Protection. But free silver coinage at the ratio and under the conditions proposed in the Chicago platform would open the doors of our national household to dangers, the extent of which we cannot foresee and to evils of which we could not rid ourselves for many years to come, if ever.

THE SUN's position throughout the campaign which followed was that the Populists, the demagogues and the self-seekers had stolen the livery of the Democratic party and that the ticket that had been nominated at Chicago was not a Democratic ticket and did not represent Democratic policies. Major Thomas W.

Hall wrote the leading editorials. He wrote at home, seldom coming to the office except for conferences with the Abells and Colonel Haines. Gorman made two or three speeches in the campaign, and his own words and his own record were turned against him with telling effect. Before the combat was half over, substantially every important business and professional man and institution in Maryland had been lined up by THE SUN against the Bryan candidacy.

The third-party movement, which came to a head in Indianapolis with the nomination of Palmer and Buckner in September, was not encouraged by THE SUN. Its principal effect was to give the people of the South, to whom the name Republican was anathema, a place to go, but so far as Maryland was concerned THE SUN advocated support for McKinley as the best means of destroying the ideas advocated by Bryan.

All the work against Bryan by THE SUN, outside its editorial columns, was directed by Mr. Dashiell, the city editor. He it was who developed a series of anti-Bryan interviews with leading business and professional men of the city and State and pointed out to them the line of argument to be taken. He worked night and day on this enterprise and spared neither himself nor the members of the city staff. Bryan himself addressed two meetings in Baltimore on September 19, both of which attracted huge crowds.

On October 22, President Cleveland made an address at Princeton University on the "Higher Americanism," which, without mentioning names, warned the people of the country against demagogism and pointed out the ways in which the people of the country were about to be misled. On the following day THE SUN had a long editorial commending this address and making practical applications of it to the issues of the campaign. It was taken generally as a statement of the President's opposition to the Bryan candidacy and the free silver platform adopted in Chicago and brought him violent denunciation from the Bryan followers.

Things got hotter and hotter as the campaign drew to an end, and denunciation and abuse of THE SUN became more intense. On Saturday morning, October 31, three days before the election, it printed a page of short extracts from the addresses of President Cleveland, John G. Carlisle, Bourke Cockran, Thomas F. Bayard, William Pinkney Whyte, Governor Charles T. O'Ferrall of Virginia, former Governor Robert M. McLane of Maryland, General James M. Longstreet, the famous Confederate soldier, Senator George Gray, of Delaware, and various conspicuous Baltimore Democrats, under a two-column heading, "Things for Democrats to Think About." This was the first two-column heading ever to appear in THE SUN.

On the day before the election, in an editorial entitled "A Last Word to Working Men," it predicted the election of McKinley and went on to say:

> The last word of argument before the vote is taken is to the great body of our working people. In their hands, Tuesday's decision rests. As we have said many times before we say now again on the eve of election — free silver coinage could bring nothing but injury and loss to them. The prospect of higher prices for all the necessaries of life is not one on which wage-earners can look with any comfort. It will not help them in the least to be obliged to pay more for their provisions, their clothing, their fuel, and their rent. Yet this is all that Mr. Bryan has to offer them. He has claimed in a glittering general way that if the prices of all products are raised, the prosperity of what he calls the producing classes will spread eventually to all other classes, including wage-earners. But that is far too vague a vision of benefit to win the vote of any level-headed workingman.

In another editorial on the same day, under the heading of "Bryan's Defeat Will Vindicate True Democracy," it had this to say:

Alike to wage-earners and to farmers, the free silver party has failed to make out its case. Human history and experience are against it. The fixed laws of finance and trade are against it. The American sense of national honor and business honesty are against it. The common sense of the average citizen who reads, thinks and reflects is against it. Therefore, when the votes come in we hope and believe it will be decisively voted down. True Democrats will rejoice at that result, for the defeat of Bryanism will be the vindication of true Democracy.

Its editorial on election day, November 3, was a brief one, urging the people to go to the polls, vote according to their convictions, and return at once to their homes or places of business, and not to linger around the polls.

The result of the election was a sweeping victory for McKinley, Maryland going for him by 30,872, which was the largest majority given to any candidate by the State since the Democrats took control in 1867, when Oden Bowie was elected Governor. It was more than 11,000 greater than Governor Lowndes had received in 1895. McKinley received 61,954 votes in Baltimore to 40,845 for Bryan, while Palmer only got 1,318. On the day after, The Sun had this to say editorially:

The result leaves no doubt of the sentiment of the people of the United States upon the leading issue of the campaign. The attempt to fly in the face of common sense and common morality by declaring fifty cents to be one dollar has been rebuked and repudiated as it deserved. The specious arguments of the advocates of free coinage have failed to mislead the voters of the country, who have brushed aside these sophistries and once more put themselves on record on the side of sound business principles, fair dealing and general good government. It is in the highest degree creditable to their strength and integrity of character that they were not swerved from the path of right and sense by the appeals to their prejudices and their cupidity. The answer which they have made to those appeals should convince the professional politician and demagogue for the future that honesty is the best policy in dealing with the American people.

The next day THE SUN summed up the result and made its own party position clear in the following:

The great conspicuous and paramount lesson taught by Tuesday's election is not only in the rebuke administered to Altgeldism [John P. Altgeld was the Governor of Illinois who had pardoned the Haymarket rioters in Chicago], Debsism and Tillmanism, but also to Gormanism and every other ism that is comprehended in Bryanism. The people have repudiated everywhere and with the utmost indignation and contempt the idea that because a man may have voted and acted with a particular party, and called himself by the name of that party, he, therefore, has lost all right of private judgment, all freedom of individual action, all responsibility for his own political opinions and acts, but is bound, at the risk of being called a "traitor," "a limping, contemptible, cowardly fellow," to servile obedience to the decrees of the national convention of his party. Tuesday witnessed the emancipation of some millions of American freemen from the shackles of party slavery. Patriotism, common sense and common honesty were recognized as possessing superior claims to the consideration of the voter over the party whip and the appeals of the boss pleading for regularity. Those shackles will never again be riveted and felt to anything like the extent that has existed heretofore. A moral revolution has taken place, and the independent voter has become a power in politics whom party managers and machine politicians can no longer afford to leave out of their calculations.

The election, in spite of the intense excitement, was one of the quietest, if not the quietest, that had been held in Maryland for many, many years. It was in striking contrast to the election of the year before, when there was open rioting and a man was killed. This change had been brought about by the adoption by the Legislature of 1896 of the Reform League's Election Law, prepared largely by John C. Rose, counsel for the league,[1] and fought through the Legislature under the leadership of THE SUN, with the support of the Lowndes administration and against the solid opposition of the Democratic machine.

In 1897 was fought the last of THE SUN's major combats with the machine. It was the climax of them all, for it resulted in the personal defeat of Gorman, the only one he ever sustained in his long political career. After it had retired him (at least for a while) to private life, THE SUN moved back toward the Democratic fold — and glad it was to get back, for the Republican Legislatures and City Councils it had brought into office were sickening in their plunderings.

Gorman, after the 1896 fight, believed that THE SUN had had enough and that he could secure reëlection to the Senate without a fight. Those were the days before the direct election of United States Senators. They were chosen by the State Legislatures, and it was not necessary for Gorman to be an open candidate. He could stay in the background, work for a Democratic majority at Annapolis, and slide in through the caucus method. That was his plan, but THE SUN knocked it higher than a kite. No sooner had the campaign for the Legislature opened than the paper tore the curtain aside and showed Gorman as the hidden manipulator. It called for the election of a Republican Legislature to defeat him. It again made Gormanism and Rasinism the issue, and with it were joined Mr. Grasty and his *News*, the Honest Money League, organized by Democrats to defeat Bryan

---

[1] Mr. Rose became United States district attorney at Baltimore in 1898, was promoted to the Federal district bench in 1910, and went to a circuit in 1922. He was district judge in Maryland during the World War. Thanks to his stern refusal to countenance spy-hunts and the persecution of radicals, no one was jailed for sedition in Maryland during the whole course of the war. His career on the bench, indeed, was in the best traditions of the Maryland Free State. He was born in Baltimore on April 27, 1861, and died on March 26, 1927.

in 1896, the Reform League, and all other anti-Gorman, anti-Rasin forces. Far in the background but financing the Republican organization was the Baltimore & Ohio Railroad.

It was a bitter fight. In the midst of it, Gorman, desperate and recognizing The Sun as the chief force against him, addressed a public letter to Edwin F. Abell, offering to turn the management of the campaign over to The Sun and declaring that he had no personal ambition and was willing to retire. But Mr. Abell was not to be tempted by this approach of a Greek bearing so highly suspicious a gift. "No, no, Mr. Gorman," said The Sun next day, "the fly will not walk into your parlor."

After that, there were no more overtures, and it was a slugging match, with no quarter asked and none given. Sun reporters had a hard time at Democratic meetings and The Sun was the target for every Gorman orator in every ward and county. The finish was amazingly close. Democratic managers, looking back, claimed that with $2,000 more in one or two counties they could have saved the day for Gorman, but that is doubtful. Certainly if they had had twice as much money they could not have stemmed the tide in Baltimore city. The Republicans got the Legislature by the slenderest kind of majority. Louis E. McComas, of Hagerstown, was elected Senator to succeed Gorman, and Democratic Maryland for the first time found itself with a Republican Governor, two Republican United States Senators, a solid Republican delegation in the House of Representatives, a Republican State Legislature and a Republican Mayor of its largest city — for practically all of which its leading Democratic newspaper, The Sun, was responsible.

After the Gorman defeat, the Abells felt that the job they had started out to do had been done and that The Sun was justified in returning to its Democratic moorings. It supported Bryan on his stand against imperialism in 1900. In the State campaign of 1899 it gave tepid aid to John Walter Smith, the Democratic candidate for Governor of Maryland, and four years later it was ardently in favor of Edwin Warfield for the same office. During those years it also supported two Democratic candidates for Mayor of Baltimore — Thomas G. Hayes and Robert M. McLane. But in 1904 it went off the reservation again to deliver a final lick at Gorman, then trying to induce the Maryland Legislature to send Bernard Carter, a distinguished lawyer but a strict organization man, who was counsel in Maryland for the Pennsylvania Railroad and the Bell Telephone interests, to the United States Senate. The Sun favored Isidor Rayner, who had been counsel for Admiral Winfield Scott Schley, the hero of Santiago, in his controversy with Admiral William T. Sampson. After a terrific battle the city boss, Rasin, fell in line for Rayner, and he was elected. It remained in doubt, however, whether Rasin was converted by The Sun's arguments, or by the Rayner money that reached him through Harry Welles Rusk, a Congressman who was both a Rasin man and a friend of Rayner. After this combat The Sun advocated the Seventeenth Amendment to the Constitution of the United States, providing for the direct election of Senators. It was submitted to the States by Congress on May 16, 1912, the Legislature of Maryland promptly ratified it, and it was proclaimed on May 31, 1913.

The Sun's partiality for Rayner was largely due to his adroit handling of the case of Admiral Schley in the controversy just mentioned. When, after the Battle of Santiago, an effort was made by a naval clique to deprive Schley, who was in actual command, of the credit for the victory, and to give it to Sampson, who was miles away, The Sun leaped to the charge at once, for Schley was a Marylander. Largely through its insistence, a Court of Inquiry was called to investigate the matter, and Rayner, who was then Attorney-General of Maryland and a very eloquent orator, appeared as Schley's counsel. The majority of the court reached a decision, approved by the Secretary of the Navy on December 21, 1898, that criticized Schley's battle tactics and otherwise used him somewhat harshly. But Admiral George Dewey, the president of the court, dissented. His minority verdict not only approved Schley's tactics, but also gave him full credit for the victory. Inasmuch as Dewey was then still the hero of the nation, this was generally accepted as a great triumph for Schley, and Rayner became a hero on his own account in Maryland. He served in the Senate from 1904 until his death in 1912. He made many speeches, chiefly aimed at Theodore Roosevelt, and was an able opponent of centralization in government, always a *bête noire* to THE SUN. He had been in the House of Representatives for three terms, 1878–80 and 1891–95, and was Attorney-General of Maryland from 1899 to 1903.

In 1907 THE SUN made a vigorous fight for Austin L. Crothers, Democratic candidate for Governor of Maryland (it will be described at length in Chapter XIV), and thereafter, down to the present, it has always supported Democrats for that office. In 1915 it departed from its usual neutrality in primary battles to support the Democrat Blair Lee against the Democrat Emerson C. Harrington. When Harrington won, it advocated his election, and he was elected. Through its influences both parties were induced to include planks in their platforms providing for the appointment of a non-partisan commission to plan a reorganization of the State government, which had become cumbersome and extravagant. Governor Harrington appointed a commission headed by Dr. Frank J. Goodnow, then president of the Johns Hopkins University, and it recommended a budget system that was adopted by the State Legislature. Later, during the long administration of Governor Albert C. Ritchie, which began in 1920 and ended at the beginning of 1935, another commission was appointed and a further reorganization of the

State government was effected. The Sun and Governor Ritchie usually saw eye to eye, and when he went before the Democratic National Conventions as a candidate for the Presidency, in 1924, 1928 and 1932, it was on a platform largely made up of traditional Sun doctrine — State's rights, the strict separation of executive, legislative and judicial powers, economy in government, and so on. Lower down the scale of office, The Sun has supported Democrats somewhat less consistently. In 1911, as we shall see in Chapter XVI, it had a war with J. Harry Preston, Democratic Mayor of Baltimore, which went on during the greater part of his eight years in the City Hall.

Its support of Bryan on the issue of imperialism in 1900 was followed by active opposition to him in 1908. On August 13 of that year was printed an editorial headed "Mr. Taft's Election Will Better Promote the Public Welfare" and concluding with the words, "We support him from a sense of public duty." The Sun's opposition to Bryan this time was due to his advocacy of the public ownership of railroads. He had made a tour of Europe early in the year, and came back filled with the notion, then new in the United States. The Sun could not endure it. In 1912, as will be recorded in Chapter XVI, it had an important hand in the first nomination of Woodrow Wilson at Baltimore, and in 1916 it supported him again. In 1920 it was for Cox against Harding, in 1924 for Davis against Coolidge, in 1928 for Smith (very ardently) against Hoover, and in 1932 for Roosevelt against Hoover. In 1936, however, it found itself unable to advocate the reëlection of Roosevelt, though neither was it able to develop any enthusiasm for Landon. This last campaign will be mentioned again in Chapter XXI.

CHAPTER XI

☼

THE SONS OF THE FOUNDER

On the fiftieth anniversary of The Sun, in 1887, the three surviving sons of the Founder, Edwin F., George W. and Walter R., became partners in A. S. Abell & Company, and on his death the next year they inherited his own interest in equal parts. They thus became joint proprietors of The Sun, The Weekly Sun and The Sun Job Printing Office, which last had been in operation as long as The Sun. There had been another son, Charles, but he was already dead, unmarried. There were also five daughters, but though they were amply provided for out of the Founder's large estate, they got no shares in The Sun and its appendages.

The three sons were charged with carrying on the paper according to the principles laid down by their father, and they did so with filial devotion. At the start, the middle son, George W., was the active editor and publisher. His elder brother, Edwin F., was chiefly interested in the management of the Abell estate, which was made up in the main of real property, and included many warehouses in the business center of Baltimore and a ring of land around the city, later to be developed as suburbs. The park-like and opulent Guilford, now the chief residential show-place of the city, was held by the heirs of the founder until March 6, 1907, when it was sold for $1,000,000 to a syndicate of real estate developers. Walter R., the youngest of the surviving sons, was a man of literary tastes and a lover of travel. Educated at Mount St. Mary's College and Georgetown University, he was interested in books rather than in journalism, and though he frequently contributed both prose and verse to THE SUN, he took little hand in the shaping of its editorial policy and almost none in the gathering of news. Born in Baltimore on February 11, 1849, he was but forty-two years old when he died on January 3, 1891. He left his share in the paper in trust to his son, Walter R. 2d, and his two daughters, with his two brothers as trustees. On their deaths the brothers were succeeded by Charles J. Bonaparte and later by John J. Nelligan, of the Safe Deposit & Trust Company of Baltimore.

The setting up of this trust made a continuance of the old simple partnership impossible, and in 1892 it was decided to incorporate the business under the name of the A. S. Abell Company of Baltimore City. The certificate of incorporation was filed on August 9 of that year, naming Edwin F., George W., Arunah S. 2d and Charles S. Abell, William H. Heindle and George H. Karsner as incorporators. Arunah S. 2d (d. July 28, 1914) was the elder son of Edwin F. Abell, and Charles S. was the son of George W. Abell. Mr. Heindle was the head bookkeeper of THE SUN [1] and Mr. Karsner was the cashier. The

[1] He lived to be 88, and in his last years was one of the landmarks of THE SUN office. Born at Red Lion, Pa., November 21, 1828, of Pennsylvania German stock, he was ten years old before he could speak English. He came to Baltimore as a boy, and got a job in THE SUN counting room. He eventually became head bookkeeper, and when he died on June 14, 1916, had been in the service nearly sixty-four years. He was retired on a pension at Christmas, 1904, but continued to come to the office daily. From 7 A.M. to 4 P.M. he sat in the editorial rooms, diligently reading THE SUN, including all the advertisements.

existence of the corporation was limited to forty years, and its capital stock was fixed at $300,000, divided into 3,000 shares of a par value of $100 each. Six shares were set aside for the six incorporators, leaving 2,994 to be swapped for the interests of the partners in the old partnership. As trustees under the will of their brother, Edwin F. and George W. Abell had to seek judicial authority to make this trade. It was granted to them by an order of the Circuit Court of Baltimore City on August 8, 1892. They received, as trustees, a full third of the stock, or 1,000 shares, but as individuals each had to be content with 997 shares. The incorporators, with the exception of Charles S. Abell, were elected the first directors of the company, with George W. as president and general manager and Edwin F. as secretary and treasurer.

This change, forced upon the two Abells by the death of their brother, was made with regret, for a simple partnership, with its easy informality, was far more to their taste than a corporation, with its precise and solemn charter, its meetings of stockholders and directors, its minutes in legal jargon, and its disquieting impersonality. On August 10, 1892, the day after the new company began business, the stockholders held a meeting and passed the following somewhat melancholy resolution:

As this is the last day of the existence of the time-honored partnership of A. S. Abell & Co., which owned and conducted for so many years the daily and weekly SUN, established fifty-five years ago by the senior partner, Arunah S. Abell, and as this is also the anniversary of the birthday of the founder of these journals, and is the day of beginning of the corporation formed to carry on the business heretofore conducted by the said Arunah S. Abell and the said partnership composed of Edwin F. Abell, George W. Abell and the late Walter R. Abell, it is becoming to mark by some appropriate action the sense of this meeting of the stockholders of the new corporation, of the importance of the event today consummated, and of the responsibilities assumed.

Therefore be it resolved by the stockholders in meeting assembled, That, while regretting the necessity which led to a termination of the former partnership of A. S. Abell & Co., which for so many years conducted the business of the daily and weekly SUN and THE SUN Job Printing Office in Baltimore city, we hail with satisfaction the new organization which has sprung up in its place, and we pledge ourselves to exert our best ability to conduct the new enterprise on the same lines and on the same principles of honor and integrity which so eminently characterized the old management, in the hope and belief that the same success will attend our labors which crowned those of our predecessors.

The history of the A. S. Abell Company of Baltimore City for the next few years was the uneventful one of a relatively small but highly successful corporation. At the annual stockholders' meeting on May 10, 1893, the board of directors was reduced from six members to the more workable compass of three, and Edwin F., George W., and Edwin's son, Arunah S. 2d, were elected. On motion of Charles S., the son of George, a dividend of 12 per cent. was declared as of December 31, 1892, and another of 4 per cent. as of April 30, 1893. In those days, it appears, dividends were declared by stockholders, not by directors. The next year there was the same story, the minutes filling only a few lines. The three directors were reëlected, and the regular dividend of 12 per cent. was sweetened with an extra of 6 per cent. Thus the stockholders received $54,000 for the year on a putative investment of $300,000, which was certainly pretty good in the midst of the worst Depression before that of 1929. The gory political battles of the 90s, described in the preceding chapters, made THE SUN many virulent enemies, and lost it some circulation and even some advertising, but it continued to show a good profit every year. The surviving corporation books do not record the paper's transactions in detail until after the fire of 1904, but it is a fair deduction from the reports of these later years that the dividends distributed before 1904 did not run much above half the actual profits. A formidable surplus, approximating the annual gross revenue from operations, was quickly accumulated.

Down to the time of the fire, and even for a few years thereafter, THE SUN continued to cling faithfully to the austere business practices of the Founder. There were no advertising solicitors, circulation figures were never given out, and anything resembling typographical display in advertisements was strictly forbidden. If any advertiser wanted to attract notice with large type, each letter had to be painfully made up of small letters. The column rules could not be broken, so they sometimes ran through such synthetic large letters. The advertising rates were based on an archaic square system, going back to 1837. A square was sixteen lines "or less," and if an advertisement ran to, say, seventeen or eighteen lines it was charged for as two squares. The original rates were 50 cents a square for one insertion, 75 cents for two, $1 for three, $1.50 for a week, $2 for two weeks, $2.50 for a month, $13 for six months, and $25 for a year. Small notices of two lines were taken at $5 a year. In the course of the years the square shrank from sixteen lines to six, and then to four, but it continued to be used in measuring space. During the 90s the published "terms of advertising" were as follows:

For 2 lines, 1 day	$ .40
For 3 lines, 1 day	.50
For 1 square (4 lines), 1 day	.60
For 1 square, 2 days	.90
For 1 square, 3 days	1.20
For 1 square, 4 days	1.50
For 1 square, 5 days	1.80
For 1 square, 1 week	2.10
For 1 square, 2 weeks	3.90
For 1 square, 1 month	6.00

The following notice was printed under these terms:

FOUR LINES constitute a SQUARE. If an advertisement exceeds four lines the price will be in exact proportion. All advertisements are payable at the time of their insertion. Marriage and Funeral Notices twenty-five cents each, and must in all cases be indorsed.

The second sentence indicates that the original plan of charging every run-over, even of a single line, as a full square had been abandoned with the shrinking of the square. The rate of $6 a square a month, it will be noted, worked out to slightly less than six cents a line. But inasmuch as there was an additional charge of five cents a line whenever copy was changed, and most of the larger local advertisers naturally changed theirs daily, the cost to them approached eleven cents.[1] Their advertisements, however large, appeared under classified headings, and they had to bring their copy to the office, and, in many cases, to pay for its insertion in cash, and on the spot. When, as sometimes happened, it was impossible to determine how much space a given piece of copy would fill, the advertiser, if notoriously solvent, would be given credit until the next morning. But before noon the office collector, Abraham G. Cole (who completed fifty years with The Sun on May 15, 1936, and is still in active service) would call upon him with a bill, and he was expected to settle at once. On every such bill, printed at the top, was the following somewhat saucy notice:

We do not insure the insertion of any advertisement on any specified day or days, nor do we insure the number of insertions within the time required by the advertiser. Advertisements will, however,

---

[1] This was the rate until May 18, 1911. Advertisements of department stores were classified as Dry Goods, jewelry stores went under Jewelry, and hat stores under Hats, and when an advertisement did not lend itself readily to classification under one of the regular headings it was placed under Miscellaneous. Even national advertising was so classified, and until 1907 it was billed at the same rate as want-ads, which for single insertions was 60 cents a square, or 15 cents a line.

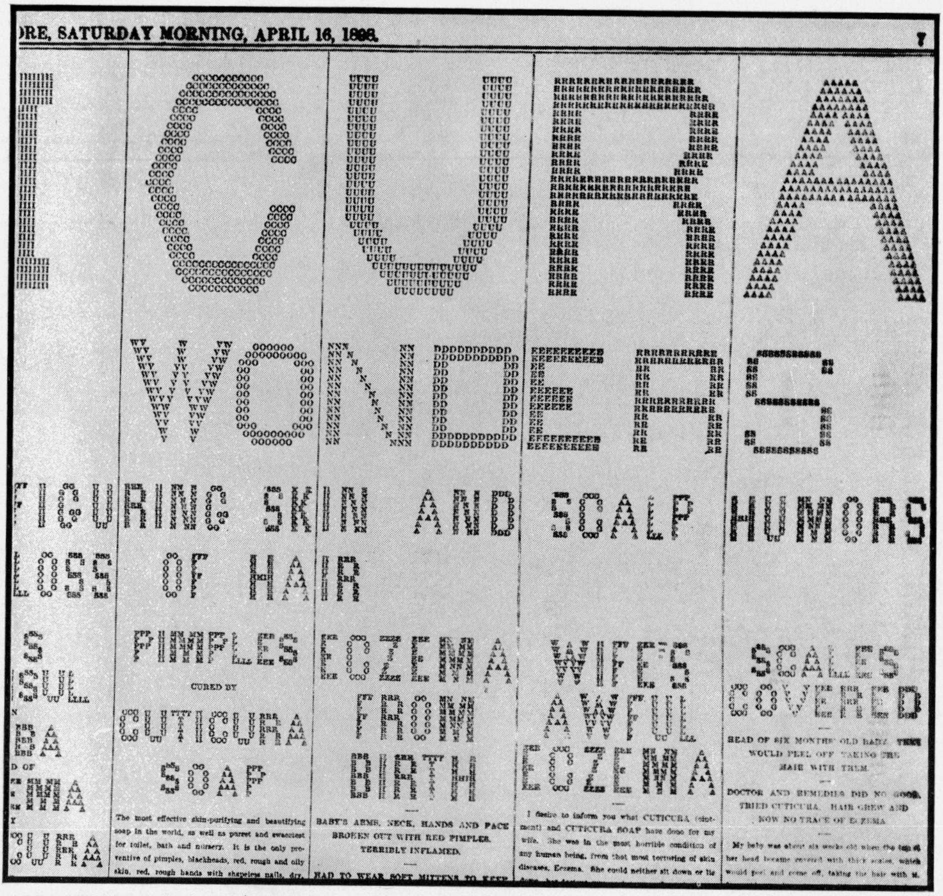

AN ADVERTISEMENT OF 1898, SHOWING HOW THE RULE AGAINST THE USE OF LARGE DISPLAY TYPE WAS CIRCUMVENTED BY MAKING LARGE LETTERS OF SMALL ONES

DRY GOODS. DRY GOODS.

ALL CARS TRANSFER TO BALTIMORE'S BIGGEST, BEST STORE

STEWART & Co.

HOWARD and LEXINGTON Sts

New York Connection—James McCreery & Co.
High-Grade Merchandise at Popular Prices

1-Piece Cloth Dresses Are Decidedly The Vogue

There Are Many Good, Practical Reasons Why This Should Be So

What smarter or neater garment can a woman wear during the early fall and winter? The One-Piece Dress is a change from the regular order of styles that have prevailed for the past few seasons. Its neat, graceful lines cannot fail to appeal to the woman who knows and appreciates dignity and refinement in her dress.

They come in serges, broadcloths, voiles, hairline striped worsteds and eoliennes.

Black Voile Mourning Dresses For $25.00

Women's One-Piece Dresses For $18.50

Women's One-Piece Dresses For $25.00

Black Silk Crepe de Chine Dresses For $38.00

Women's Separate Coats

54-Inch Black Chiffon Broadcloth Coats For $25.00

Full-Length Black Broadcloth Coats For $18.00

Cashmere Waterproof Coats for $12.50

Women's Tailor-Made Suits

Special Lot of Custom-Tailored Suits at $30.00

Braid-Trimmed Chiffon Broadcloth Suits for $35.00

—Third Floor—Stewart & Co.

Reception & Evening Wraps & Coats, $28, $35, $40, $50 to $100
Motor & Traveling Coats, $15 to $75
Black Cloth Coats, $10 to $75
Rain Coats of Various Favored Fabrics, $18 to $25

CHINA AND GLASSWARE.

J. SETH HOPKINS-MANSFIELD CO.
4 and 6 W. FAYETTE ST.

FINEST DISPLAY IN THE CITY
Original Designs in HIGH-GRADE NOVELTIES AT EXTREMELY LOW PRICES.
Rich Cut Glass
LIBBEY & HAWKES
Wedding and Anniversary Gifts
Fine China—Rock Crystal Magnificent Plates
Mahogany Trays
Artistic Brass Goods
WHAT EVER IS GOOD WE SELL
SPECIAL TABLES FILLED WITH BARGAINS From 25c to $7.50
Kitchen Utensils
OUR PRICES ARE LESS THAN ELSEWHERE

J. SETH HOPKINS-MANSFIELD CO.
Fayette St., 1 Door West of Charles

CHIROPODY.

Dr. Frazier Co.
CHIROPODISTS
Painlessly Extracting Corns
209 N. LIBERTY ST.
BALTIMORE, MD.

JEWELRY.

MADE IN ENGLAND.
OUR ANNUAL IMPORTATION OF SHEFFIELD WARE
TRAYS, PLATTERS, VEGETABLE DISHES, ETC.
THE JAMES R. ARMIGER CO.,
310 N. CHARLES ST.

MISCELLANEOUS.

"A MODERATELY GOOD CLEANER IS ABOUT AS GOOD AS A MODERATELY GOOD EGG"
"YOU CAN RELY ON EMIL FISHER"
A Ladies' Tailored Suit Cleaned for $2.50.

LADIES' TAILORS.

INDIVIDUALITY IN TAILORED GOWNS.
S. GINSBERG,
LADIES' TAILOR,
419 N. Charles street.
I make them for $30 and upward.

J. SIRIANNI,
NOW AT 1007 M'CULLOH ST

TO THE LADIES.

L. RUBENSTEIN,

FURS.

REPAIRING AND REMODELING OF ALL KINDS OF FURS.
B. FEIKIN, 124 North Eutaw St.

FUR REMODELING.

October Fur Remodeling
ONLY BEST WORK
At prices that are sure to please.
Established Since 1846
A. SIGMUND & SON,
300 N. CHARLES ST.

SHOES.

GEORGE POLLOCK,
FALLING ARCH AND DEFORMED FEET.

WEDDING INVITATIONS.

VISIT THE SHOP OF UNUSUAL THINGS
LYCETT'S,

MANICURING.

MISS SIMPSON,

STORAGE BATTERIES.

STORAGE BATTERIES RECHARGED AND REPAIRED BY EXPERT ELECTRICIANS.
SPECIAL RATES TO GARAGES.
CHAS. ELLIOTT & Co., 482 N. Charles st.

AN ADVERTISING PAGE OF 1910, SHOWING THE USE OF CLASSIFIED HEADINGS OVER STORE ADVERTISEMENTS have their full number of insertions when the time can be made up, and when accidentally left out and the number of insertions cannot be given, the money paid for the omitted insertions will be returned to the advertiser.

Some of the largest local advertisers — for example, M. Posner, owner of the principal department store — always sent their money with their advertisements, and even after this draconian system yielded to the progress of human reason there were old-fashioned local advertisers who followed it as a habit. National advertisers had been dealt with more gently, even from the earliest days. There is a moldering ledger dated 1842 which shows that the primeval patent-medicine manufacturers of that time were permitted to settle monthly. The deadline for advertising copy was 6 P.M. and advertisers who got to the office late, or who violated any of the other rules for their governance, were treated very cavalierly. In 1902 or thereabout one of the largest of them was taken to task for tardiness by the clerk who received his copy at the counter. He replied hotly that he could get along without advertising in THE SUN. Edward Crummer, the business manager of the paper, who happened to be within earshot, thereupon suggested that he try staying out for three months. "THE SUN," said Mr. Crummer acidly, "doesn't want you to spend your money for space if you think it is unprofitable." This exchange, overheard by a counting-room employé who had lately come to THE SUN from another Baltimore paper, gave him such a shock that he was a week recovering. The advertiser decided to go on in the paper, though he continued to protest bitterly, and destiny was on his side, for the rules he complained of did not long survive the fire of 1904.

Mr. Crummer, who died on September 26, 1906, at the age of sixty, after forty years of service with THE SUN,[1] twenty-

[1] He was born in Baltimore May 21, 1848, and was a descendant of Gen. John Armstrong (1758–1843), a hero of the Revolution and later

five of which had been spent as business manager, believed as a cardinal article of faith that it was immoral and unthinkable for a great public journal to broadcast its circulation. THE SUN, in fact, had made no mention of the subject in its own columns since June 22, 1839, when the Founder, in the grandiloquent manner of the time, had offered $1,000 to anyone who could prove that he didn't print as many papers daily as all the other Baltimore sheets combined. The test for a reader, in the view of Mr. Crummer, was not the number of copies a newspaper sold but what news it printed in every copy, and the test for an advertiser was not the number of potential buyers reached but the number of actual buyers brought into his store. In 1898 he supplied *Printers' Ink*, the advertisers' organ, with the material for a paragraph printed in that journal on March 23. It ran as follows:

THE SUN is a well established and ably conducted and influential daily paper, and is by long odds the leading daily in Baltimore. It has a fixed hold upon a large class of readers who have become habituated to it and cannot be brought under the influence of another paper. It is run on principles of a generation ago and has become notable for features that are excellent although old-fashioned and peculiarly its own. Though the only 2-cent paper in Baltimore, it has a larger circulation than any other daily. It is widely read in and around Baltimore and as far west as Pittsburgh. Only once during the history of THE SUN have the publishers made known its circulation, and that was in December, 1894, when they stated to the American Newspaper Directory that the smallest

Minister to France and Spain, and Secretary of War during the War of 1812, who married a sister of Chancellor Robert R. Livingston, of New York, and of Edward Livingston, author of the Penal Code of Louisiana. Mr. Crummer's elder brother, Daniel, was a member of a firm of architects which had an office in the old SUN Iron Building. This connection got young Crummer a job in THE SUN counting-room when he left school, and he remained there all his life. Despite his high way with advertisers, he was a mild man whose chief recreations were driving in the country and collecting antiques.

edition during that year had not been less than 66,432. Its present circulation is probably about 40,000 copies. Some of THE SUN's characteristics are that it will not break column rules for advertisers, or admit full-face type in its pages, or allow illustrations or cuts. Its prevailing rate is 60 cents per square (four lines agate) per insertion, and its rates are sustained absolutely and to the letter.

From November, 1882, to May 23, 1892, a couple of months before the incorporation of the property, THE SUN printed six pages daily, 19½ by 25 inches over all, and made up in nine columns. The inner pages, printed on the two sides of a single sheet, were headed *Supplement*. The first leap in 1892 was to eight pages, and simultaneously the size of the page was reduced to 17¼ by 21½ inches, and it was arranged in eight columns.[1] This change was made possible by the installation of two new presses, capable together (at least in theory) of printing 96,000 eight-page papers an hour, and of turning out, at lesser speeds, papers of as many as thirty-two pages. "It can be claimed for THE SUN," said the announcement, "that it has kept pace with the progress of the age." If it lagged a bit when the linotype type-setting machine was invented it was mainly for the reasons noted in Chapter VI. The inventor, Ottmar Mergenthaler, was a German domiciled in Baltimore,[2] but the first trial of his invention was made in the composing room of the New York *Tribune* on July 3, 1886. It was not until ten years later that the Abells decided to abandon hand composition and put in a battery of machines. This step was taken only after long and careful preparation. In order that the printers of THE SUN might have time to master the new contraption, a door was cut in the wall of the composing room,

---

[1] The present size is 16⅞ by 22⅞, in eight columns.

[2] He was born in Württemberg May 11, 1854, and died in Baltimore October 28, 1899.

linotypes were installed in the building next door, and all hands were given months of instruction. Some of the older men found it very difficult to manipulate the keyboard, but the younger ones took to it readily, and within a few years one of the latter had become the champion linotype operator of all time. He was William H. Stubbs, then only twenty-two years old. On October 3, 1899, in competition with the previous champion, a Philadelphian, he set 66,717 ems [1] of corrected matter in five hours and thirty-three minutes, or 12,021 ems an hour. He won thereby a purse of $1,000 and " a handsome gold medal," the latter presented to him by THE SUN chapel of Baltimore Typographical Union No. 12 " in recognition of his great performance." He lived to be president of the union, and a great hero among the printers of the whole country. On the night of January 10, 1914, he made printing history again by setting fourteen columns of THE SUN in seven hours flat. It was estimated that he struck the keys 145,000 times. Said THE SUN a few days later:

> He set ordinary news matter, dumped his takes, made his corrections, and carried the corrected lines to the corrector. In the seven hours he left the machine forty-two times, losing as many minutes, though no account of this was taken. Stubbs has always been accustomed to a nine-line-to-the-minute speed, and he nearly equaled the capacity of the machine. In the last hour he set 11,375 ems, or 459 lines, and left his machine five times. In the night's work he handled all sorts of copy — manuscript, typewritten, reprint, sporting reviews and names. He had no pick-ups or recasts, and inserted his heads and dash lines. The accuracy of the record is vouched for by Fritz Mergenthaler, a half-brother of the inventor of the linotype, who has charge of THE SUN's battery by night.

[1] For the benefit of readers unacquainted with printing it may be explained that an em is the printer's measure of width. It occupies as much space as a capital M, the widest of the letters, in the pica size of type. Thus, 1,000 ems occupies much more space than 1,000 average letters. A pica em is about 1-6th of an inch in width.

These feats have never been surpassed. In 1904 Mr. Stubbs was asked by the Mergenthaler Linotype Company to take charge of its exhibit at the St. Louis Exposition, and THE SUN proudly lent him for that purpose. In May, 1914, he was finally lured from his machine to become a member of the staff of the International Typesetting Machine Company, manufacturers of the Intertype, and later he joined the staff of the Mergenthaler Company. He was the author of "Stubbs' Manual: A Practical Treatise on Keyboard Manipulation," still the standard textbook for linotypers. He died on January 21, 1933.

The editorial rooms and circulation department likewise produced heroes during the closing years of the century. That of the former was John T. Morris, then a reporter and later city editor. Early in 1896 he obtained some information which forecast action by the Baltimore Grand Jury, and it was duly printed in THE SUN. The next day the jury haled him before it, and demanded to know the name of his informant. Mr. Morris, replying grandly that a SUN reporter never betrayed those who gave him their confidence, refused to tell, and the jury cited him for contempt to the judge presiding in the Criminal Court. The judge decided that, if there was any contempt, it had not been committed in his court, but advised the jury that it could jail Mr. Morris on its own motion. This it did, and he languished in the City Jail for four or five days. Then the jury's term ended, and he was released.[1] The Maryland Legislature was in session

[1] Mr. Morris had another brush with the law on New Year's Day, 1913. Boarding a pay-as-you-enter trolley-car in Baltimore, he paused at the door to drop his fare into the box. While he was so engaged, three policemen entered, and one of them tried to crowd past him. Mr. Morris, who was a large and powerful man, interposed an elbow, and after what seems to have been a warm exchange of words he was arrested and charged with disorderly conduct. Released on cash bail of $51.45, he was fined five cents the next morning. After he had left the Police Court, protesting bitterly, the magistrate discovered that under the law he should have been fined at least $1. So he was recalled,

at the time, and on April 2, 1896, it passed an act (Article 35, Section 2 of the Maryland Code) giving newspaper men the immunity commonly enjoyed by lawyers, physicians and clergymen. To this day, in Maryland, they are not required to divulge to any State court or jury the sources of the news they print. The law was given a test on May 12, 1925, when Hamilton Owens, editor of THE EVENING SUN, was tried for contempt at Westminster, Md., for refusing to give the Grand Jury of Carroll county the name of a Westminster reader who had written a letter to the paper,[1] saying that the county was overrun by bootleggers. The question before the learned judges, Parke, C. J., and Forsythe, J., was whether a letter to the editor was "news or information" within the meaning of the act. After due deliberation, they decided that it was, and so Mr. Owens was liberated.[2]

The other great intramural event of the era is thus described by Mr. James W. Dove, assistant business manager of THE SUN, who has been digging out of the records of the office, for years

and the five-cent fine remitted. He had left THE SUN in 1900 to become a police commissioner, but his term had expired, and the policemen did not recognize him. In 1887 he was sent to Rome by THE SUN to cover the diamond jubilee of Pope Leo XII as a priest, and President Grover Cleveland intrusted him with a copy of the Constitution of the United States as a present to His Holiness. When he got back he was made a colonel on the staff of Gov. Elihu E. Jackson, and thereafter he was always known as Colonel Morris. He had been trained in the law, and practiced at the bar after his retirement as police commissioner. He was born in 1860, and died on August 2, 1917. He was a Ph.D of Manhattan College, New York.

[1] It had been published January 23, and was signed A Daily Reader.

[2] The text of the act follows: "No person engaged in, connected with, or employed on a newspaper or journal shall be compelled to disclose in any legal proceeding or trial before any committee of the Legislature or elsewhere the source of any news or information procured or obtained by him for and published in the newspaper on and in which he is engaged, connected with, or employed."

past, a SUN chronicle that has been frequently levied upon for these pages:

On February 13, 1899, "Denny went to Towson." [Towson is the county seat of Baltimore county, ten miles from the city.] The great blizzard began on Saturday night, February 11, and completely overwhelmed Baltimore and the State. The storm continued through Sunday and raged all day Monday, February 13. The total snowfall in twenty-four hours ending 8 P. M. February 13 was 15½ inches. Business was almost entirely suspended, many stores were closed, wires were down, the mail service was at a standstill, all street-car lines were obliged to stop, and travel by steam railroads and boats ceased for two or three days. In many streets and roads the drifts were ten or more feet deep. The temperature ranged from six degrees below zero on February 11 to seven above on February 12, when the wind from the north reached thirty miles an hour. Saturday and Sunday were bad enough, but Monday the streets were almost impassable. On this day, A. J. Dennistone, a SUN carrier, refusing to let the blizzard interfere with the delivery of the paper to his subscribers, covered his north Baltimore suburban route completely, reaching the end of his territory at Towson at 4 P. M., after a sixteen-hour struggle through the storm, part of the way by wagon and part on foot. Other carriers also made deliveries, but Dennistone's route was through open country and the most difficult. His feat established a tradition of THE SUN Carrier Service and to this day carriers are reminded in heavy weather to "remember when Denny went to Towson."

On May 1, 1894, George W. Abell died, aged fifty-two. He had been the active editor and publisher of the paper since the death of the founder in 1888. Trained for the law at the University of Maryland and admitted to the bar in 1864, he had elected to follow his father in journalism, and after some experience in the counting-room had devoted himself to the editorial and news departments. He was an extremely able journalist, and his marks remained upon THE SUN for many years after his death. That unhappy event left Edwin F. Abell as the only surviving son of the Founder. But he did not hesitate to take command, and some of his bold and successful editorial ventures have been described in the preceding chapters. A reorganization of the publishing corporation was quickly effected. Edwin F. was elected president on June 12, 1894, and his son, Arunah S. 2d, was made secretary and treasurer. At the same time another of his sons, Walter W., was made a director. The three ran The Sun in harmony until 1901. Charles S. Abell, the only son of George W., had been one of the incorporators of the company in 1892, and had been left 500 shares of its stock by his father's will in 1894, but he did not appear as an active participant in the management until April 19, 1898, when the board of directors was increased to four members, and he was made one of them. On June 6, 1901, the offices of secretary and treasurer were separated, and Charles S. Abell was elected secretary, with Arunah S. 2d remaining as treasurer. At the same time the new office of vice-president was created, and Walter W. was elected to it.

It was after the death of Edwin F. Abell, in 1904, that differences between the three sets of heirs of the Founder began to be manifest. First, there were his two sons, Walter W. and Arunah S. 2d. Next there was Charles S. Abell, the only son of the dead George W. Finally, there were the heirs of Walter R. Abell, represented by the Safe Deposit & Trust Company as trustee in the years after Edwin F. Abell's death.[1] The stockholders' and

[1] At the start Charles J. Bonaparte succeeded Edwin F. Abell as trustee. But inasmuch as Mr. Bonaparte was a Republican and actively interested in politics, it was soon found that his participation in the affairs of The Sun was embarrassing to the paper, so he retired as trustee of the Walter R. Abell share in it. He was followed by John J. Nelligan, an officer of the Safe Deposit & Trust Company, and later by the company itself, with Mr. Nelligan remaining as its representative. Mr. Bonaparte continued, until his death, as trustee of

directors' minutes show a certain jockeying for control as early as 1894, but it was not until 1904 that any really serious friction developed. The ultimate result of that friction was that the Abell grandsons, in 1910, surrendered control of the paper their grandfather had founded in 1837. Of that revolution in its history there will be more in a later chapter.

---

the other property of the Walter R. Abell estate. When he died he was succeeded by the Safe Deposit & Trust Company, which has been trustee for the whole estate ever since.

CHAPTER XII

☼

THE SUNPAPER AT THE TURN OF THE CENTURY

The Sun, in the closing years of the century, had a number of men on its staff whose names are still alive among the newspaper men of Baltimore, among them, Norval E. Foard, Oakley Philpotts Haines, Oliver Perry Baldwin, Francis Asbury Richardson, Edward P. Duffy, T. J. C. Williams, John Pleasants, Charles W. Dashiell, George Morrow, Samuel Z. Ammen, and Robert Karl Beer.

Some of these were Virginians — in fact, there was a strong Virginian flavor in the office down to the retirement of the Abells. Mr. Foard had sent out the first news of the Confederate investment of Fort Sumter, though at that time he was not working for The Sun. Born in Alexandria on July 10, 1837, he began newspaper work at the age of twenty on the Baltimore *Republican*, of which we shall hear more presently. The late 50s were turbulent days in Baltimore, and Mr. Foard covered, among other events, a number of Know Nothing riots, including the subsequent trials of their perpetrators. He also covered the visit of the Prince of Wales (later King Edward VII) to Baltimore in 1860, and the visit of the *Great Eastern* to Annapolis roads. Going to Charleston, S. C., when the war clouds began to gather late in 1860, he joined the staff of the *Guardian* there and also became assistant to the correspondent of the Associated Press. It was in the latter capacity that he reported the firing on the *Star of the West* and the beginning of the Civil War. He also covered the adoption of the South Carolina Ordinance of Secession on December 20, 1860. Transferring to the Charleston *Courier*, he went to Montgomery, Ala., as its correspondent, and reported the inauguration of Jefferson Davis as President of the Confederate States, the framing of the Confederate Constitution, and all the other exciting events of February and March, 1861. When the Confederate government moved from Montgomery to Richmond he followed it, and was soon in the field as a war correspondent for the *Courier*. His fighting spirit aroused, he joined Company A, Seventeenth Virginia Infantry, and took part in the first battle of Bull Run, July 21, 1861. Later he entered the Confederate Treasury and was put in charge of the printing of Confederate bonds. The end of the war found him in the quartermaster's department at Augusta, Ga.

He came to Baltimore in 1865, joined the staff of THE SUN, became the editor of THE SUN Almanac when it was established in 1876, and later was made State editor of the paper, in which post he served until his death on March 26, 1906, with the exception of a period of several years in the 80s, when he succeeded Henry J. Ford as city editor and was himself succeeded by Charles W. Dashiell. As we have seen in an earlier chapter, he was for many years in charge of THE SUN staff covering the biennial meetings of the State Legislature. When he died the Maryland Senate passed a resolution describing him as " a loyal and devoted son of Maryland, whose life was wholly devoted to the public interest." The first part of this was inaccurate, but his knowledge of Maryland affairs was truly remarkable, and he was the author of two books that were long accepted as authorities on the State: "Maryland: Its Resources, Industries and Agricultural Conditions," 1893, and "Maryland As It Is," 1903.

Mr. Richardson, like Mr. Foard, was an alumnus of the old Baltimore *Republican.* His father, Beale H. Richardson, was the proprietor of the paper, and in 1860, when he was but twenty-three years old, Mr. Richardson himself became its managing editor. When the Civil War came on, it showed strong Southern sympathies, and in September, 1863, it was suppressed by General R. C. Schenck, the Union commandant in Baltimore, who ordered the two Richardsons sent into the Confederate lines. They went to Montgomery, Ala., and the elder remained there until the end of the war, editing a paper. But young Frank was not content to submit to the suppression of the *Republican.* Running the blockade from Wilmington, N. C., to Nassau, he boarded a British ship for New York, and prepared to return to Baltimore to challenge his oppressors. But when news of his presence in New York got to General John A. Dix (of "If any man attempts to haul down the American flag, shoot him on the spot" fame), then busy suppressing the draft riots, he was arrested and sent to Baltimore a prisoner. Later he was locked up at Fort Delaware, and there he remained until March, 1865, when he was released by President Lincoln. He then went to Washington to resume practice as a journalist, and after a year as a reporter of Congress for various groups of newspapers he became a Washington correspondent of THE SUN in 1866, and after 1872 was the head of its bureau. He held that post until 1901. His thirty-five years of service have been surpassed by but one other Washington correspondent — the late O. O. Stealey of the Louisville *Courier-Journal,* who served two years longer. Mr. Richardson covered every national convention from 1872 to 1900, and his dispatches from Wash-

PHOTOGRAPH BY BLACKSTONE

WALTER W. ABELL (1872-)

CHARLES W. DASHIELL
(1858–1898)

FRANCIS ASBURY RICHARDSON
(1838–1926)

OAKLEY PHILPOTTS HAINES
(1837–1909)

ington greatly enhanced The Sun's reputation for news-getting enterprise and accurate reporting.

In 1867 he reported the proceedings of the convention at Annapolis which framed the present Constitution of Maryland. In its early sessions the question of appointing an official reporter came up, but Judge Albert Ritchie (father of the later Governor, Albert C. Ritchie) argued from the floor that "the reports of Mr. Richardson in The Sun are so accurate, fair and complete that no official recorder is needed." So none was appointed and to this day Mr. Richardson's dispatches constitute the sole record of that historic gathering. In 1923 they were reprinted by Philip B. Perlman, Secretary of State of Maryland, as "Debates of the Maryland Constitutional Convention of 1867." More than once the Court of Appeals of Maryland has cited them in its decisions. The convention was composed, as The Sun said at the time, "of the very flower of Maryland manhood," and one of its chief purposes was to restore the civil rights of the people of the State, invaded since 1861 by the Union military. The Bill of Rights that it adopted is still the chief pride of the Maryland Free State, especially Article 6:

> Whenever the ends of government are perverted, and public liberty manifestly endangered, and all other means of redress are ineffectual, the people may, and of a right ought to reform the old, or establish a new government; the doctrine of non-resistance against arbitrary power and oppression is absurd, slavish and destructive of the good and happiness of mankind.

Mr. Richardson came of a family that had immigrated from England to Maryland in 1640. The original grant of land near Bel Air, Md., remained in its possession for more than two hundred years. Mr. Richardson (whose given name of Francis was usually reduced to Frank) was born in Baltimore on January 10, 1838, and died in Washington on March 6, 1926. He was for sixty years a familiar figure in Washington, for he continued to live there after his retirement in 1901. A man of independent means, he was fond of entertaining, and in his early days was the Beau Brummel of the Washington correspondents. He knew everyone worth knowing in the administrations of thirteen Presidents, and also had a wide acquaintance among State politicians, far and near. His wife died childless in 1886, and he never remarried. When he died himself forty years later his executors found among his papers a note directing that his body be cremated and his ashes buried at the foot of her grave in the churchyard of St. James's Protestant Episcopal Church, at My Lady's Manor, near Baltimore. After his retirement he lived at the Cosmos Club in Washington, and there it was that he died. His days of professional idleness were anything but empty. He frequently wrote letters to THE SUN, and later to THE EVENING SUN on public questions, and in them he displayed a number of extremely marked aversions. He was especially contemptuous of William Jennings Bryan, and when Prohibition fell upon the country he denounced it with great vigor. He also liked to write about political history, and there was an immense amount of it in his memory. He was one of the early members of the Gridiron Club and also of the Alfalfa Club — Washington's two famous dining organizations. He wrote but one book — "Baltimore Historical and Biographical," published in 1871. When he retired in 1901 the Washington *Star* said of him:

THE BALTIMORE SUN has throughout its career had Washington correspondents of ability and high character. Eliab Kingman, whose signature was Ion; Francis J. Grund, who used X,[1] and

[1] Mr. Grund represented THE SUN in Washington from January, 1874, to March, 1855. He was a distinguished figure in the Washington journalism of the time, and the elder James Gordon Bennett once printed a eulogy of him in the New York *Herald*. He was born in what is now Czechoslovakia, but was brought to the United States early in life. He was at one time editor of the New York *Age*. He died in 1863.

A. G. Allen, who used Aga — all were writers of note in their day. But none of them attained the wide reputation and sustained a high distinction for so long a period as Mr. Richardson.

To which THE SUN itself added at the time of his death on March 6, 1926:

Not only did he play an important part in the creation of THE SUN's might and influence under the Abells; he also became a powerful force for good in the generation that followed the Civil War. Few political publicists of the period were so potent in championing the rights of the defeated South against the onslaughts of hate that came recurrently from the more narrow-minded of the North. Mr. Richardson in that service was as bold as a lion and as deadly as an adder in quick, short thrusts at the oppressors. In sober truth, he was one of the strong workmen in the rebuilding of the nation upon just and enduring lines.

But despite these strong Southern sympathies, he was very critical of latter-day Southern politicians, and when they were in the saddle in Washington in 1915 he wrote of them as follows in a characteristic letter to THE EVENING SUN:

The Southern Democrats are in the majority of the high places and the germs of socialism and populism and dangerous isms generally run in broad streaks all through them. They are constantly on the lookout to grab money out of the Treasury and at the same time to strike down the hands which put money in the Treasury. Through the absurd and senseless rule of counting seniority in service as a lien on prominent committee assignments, men are put at the head of committees who have no conception of the duties and are utterly unable to perform them intelligently. This obtains to a considerable degree in the Senate, but it is perfectly shameful in the House. Dozens of instances are apparent, but the mention of one may suffice. A man from Kentucky, for the reason only that he was longest in service on the committee on the District of Columbia, was put at the head. As is known, this committee is by far one of the most important of the House, calling for a man of capacity and enlarged experience. It is said there is not a town of 5,000 population in the entire district of its chairman. He stated himself recently on the floor of the House that there was not a private residence in his district costing as much as $18,000. Yet he is put as a kind of despot over this magnificent city, largely controlling its purse and dealing potentially with the delicate and difficult municipal problems which center around such a community as this. He is like Mr. Bryan. He thinks nothing is done right unless it is done his way.

Oakley Philpotts Haines was managing editor of THE SUN from 1881 to 1906, and was thus on the bridge during the bitter political battles of the 90s. He was born at Petersburg, Va., December 29, 1837. His father was the editor and proprietor of the Petersburg *Constellation*, a leading paper in its day, to which both Thomas Jefferson and Edgar Allan Poe had contributed. The father died in 1841, when young Oakley was but four years old. The boy was educated in the local schools, and in his late teens was taken by his mother on a tour of Europe — then a rare adventure for young Americans. On his return in 1855 he went to work on the Petersburg *Express*, and was soon the star reporter of its staff. In 1861 he reported the proceedings of the convention which took Virginia out of the Union, and when the Confederate Congress began its sessions in Richmond he went there to cover them for the Richmond *Enquirer*. The *Enquirer* soon sent him to the front, and he reported many of the sanguinary battles fought in Virginia. At Seven Pines, May 31, 1862, he found himself directly behind the Confederate picket lines, and came close to losing his life. Once the war was over, he migrated, like so many other excellent Virginians of his generation, to Baltimore, and in January, 1870, he became night editor of THE SUN. In February, 1881, he was promoted to the post of managing editor, which meant, in those days, chief editor, and he continued in it until failing health forced him to retire from active service in March, 1906. He died on March 5,

1909. Mr. Haines, despite the fact that his whole manhood was spent in a busy newspaper office, was a man of literary tastes, and his father's early association with Poe had much influence upon him. He was fond of reading poetry, and he wrote a great deal of charming prose for the magazines of the 70s and early 80s. In an editorial tribute to him, printed the day after his death, THE SUN said:

> Mr. Haines was a newspaper statesman. In addition to this, he was endowed with the rare faculty of understanding human nature and of making THE SUN's policies understood by those from whose intelligence, common sense and clear judgment he attracted sympathy and support. His intensity of purpose was remarkable, and in later years on more than one occasion after a severe political campaign his health would show the effect of the strain when the mental tension was over. His loyalty to THE SUN was unswerving. THE SUN's interests were his interests. He had but one purpose to serve, and that was THE SUN. His fund of knowledge seemed unlimited, and whether the simplest commonplace subject or one of deepest thought, he was thoroughly familiar with it in all its detail.

His successor as managing editor of THE SUN, Oliver Perry Baldwin (appointed March 31, 1909), was also a Virginian, though there was some New England blood in his veins. He was named for his father, who had been given the names of Oliver Perry in memory of an earlier Baldwin's death while serving under the immortal commodore during the War of 1812. The first Oliver, born in New York of Connecticut stock, himself served a year or so in the Navy, and then embarked on adventure of his own, working his way down the Mississippi on a raft. He contracted yellow fever, and on recovering settled down in Lexington, Va., writing for the *Gazette* of that place. Then he went to the Richmond *Examiner* and then to the Richmond *Dispatch*, staying with the latter paper until the collapse of the Confederacy brought him to Baltimore in search of a living. He clung to conviction; he was the last Whig Senator in the Virginia

Legislature, and would have no dealings with the Know Nothing party. During his newspaper career he had married Eliza Lee Sheffey, descended from the Sheffeys and Hansons of Frederick, Md., but then living with her family in Staunton, Va. On the old Staunton estate, which still stands, although considerably altered by later occupants, the second Oliver Perry Baldwin spent much of his boyhood.

He was born in Richmond on September 2, 1850, so that he was not yet eleven years old when the Civil War broke. His father, not suspecting that Richmond would be the Confederacy's last stronghold, and fearing for the safety of his family (now a numerous one), sent the whole brood down to Staunton while he continued his newspaper labors at the capital. The Valley, however, soon became the cockpit of the armies, and before long the children were brought back to Ashland, sixteen miles from Richmond. Nothing could have been better from the viewpoint of young Oliver, who, on almost any fine day, could saunter out and see Gray cavalry chasing Blue or occasionally, to his dismay, Blue cavalry chasing Gray. It seemed to him like a fine game for his special benefit, until the first day he saw a soldier fall and fail to rise. The village changed hands several times, and this, plus the tightening pressure on income, made education difficult; sometimes the children were taught by neighboring clergymen, sometimes by their parents, and sometimes not at all. At length came the report that Lee had surrendered, and in the distance could be seen the columns of smoke rising from Richmond. Young Oliver and a neighbor's boy ran to the patched-up railway, hauled on the track a hand car hidden in the bushes, and pumped their way to town to survey with their own tear-filled eyes the ashes of the Confederacy. Yet never in life did the Virginians feel that the Confederacy had been really wiped out; and never among them all was there a more wholly unreconstructed rebel than Oliver Baldwin.

The *Dispatch* had come to grief with Appomattox, and in 1866 the elder Baldwin came to Baltimore. Here he joined the staff of THE SUN, where he continued until his death in 1878. Once settled, he brought his family north, planted it in East Baltimore and then in the quiet suburb of Waverly. Probably one reason for going to Waverly was the existence there of Dr. Marillat's school, a semi-military institution wherein several of the teachers were old Confederate officers. Here young Baldwin made some of the warmest friends of his life, including the Ridgelys of Hampton, members of an ancient Maryland family, and Robert L. Owen of Oklahoma, later a United States Senator. From Marillat's school Mr. Baldwin went to the University of Virginia, completing the law course in three years. There he formed another warm friendship with John Sharp Williams of Mississippi. Returning to Baltimore in 1873, he practiced law for nine years and mixed a little in politics, serving in 1875 as a Baltimore county member of the House of Delegates. For that office he ran as a Potato Bug, *i.e.*, an insurgent Democrat who was disliked by the regular factions of both parties. The next year he became regular in order to give oratorical support to Tilden. But in 1882 he left the law for his father's old calling and his father's old office, the Iron Building, advancing in regular course until he became managing editor. When THE SUN fought Gorman and Rasin no one fought more furiously than he, and when THE SUN supported Wilson in the campaign of 1912 no one supported him with more vehemence.

To his work he brought a blazing zeal perfectly fitted for the strongly partisan journalism of his hey-day. To the end he never lost that zeal nor his old-fashioned views. He was always convinced that ladies could never wish to vote, and that women who were not ladies should not be allowed to. He regarded the pioneer suffragists as public menaces, and by tongue and editorial pen assailed them with a passionate fury almost beyond belief in a man of such courtly ways in his private relations. He was literally almost stricken dumb when two Baltimore ladies whose intelligence he regarded as highly as their characters came to his office and revealed themselves as advocates of the Nineteenth Amendment. If anything, he was even more opposed to the Eighteenth. He never touched liquor, yet it lifted him to a perfect fury to think that he, and others, should be told they could not. He was an equally bitter foe of bigotry in religion. He treasured alike the warm friendship of Cardinal Gibbons, for long the only American of the red hat, and that of Bishop John G. Murray, primate of the Episcopal Church in America. On the withdrawal of the Abells from active management of The Sun in 1910 he retired as managing editor, but he continued as a member of the editorial staff, and his editorials maintained their old vigor to the end. In his later years he wrote many editorial-page articles over the *nom de plume* of An Old-Fashioned Fellow, and in them he rioted in his picturesque prejudices. He kept pretty close to the office in those days, going out only rarely to interview public men who interested him, and sometimes returning with a waggish affectation of amazement that politicians whose ideas he loathed were nevertheless often agreeable and intelligent fellows — "even Vermonters," he exclaimed to his amused colleagues after a call on Calvin Coolidge. He was often ill in his later years, but whenever his doctors allowed him he came to the office and filled dozens of half-sheets of copy-paper with his cramped but extremely legible handwriting. He died in Baltimore on June 20, 1932.

Six months before, on January 8, he had completed fifty years of service with The Sun. But he was not the oldest Sun man in the office, for "Admiral" Edward Paul Duffy, the paper's ship-news reporter, beat him by a week. Mr. Duffy came to the paper on January 1, 1882, and remained continuously at work until a short while before his death on February 13,

1933, his seventy-eighth birthday. Indeed, his connection with THE SUN really went back to 1873, for in that year he became a carrier for the paper at Ellicott's Mills (now Ellicott City), a county town ten miles from Baltimore, and soon afterward he began sending in news items to the State editor, N. E. Foard. For a while the honor of being a reporter was his only reward, but just before his first Christmas in the service he sent a letter to George W. Abell, suggesting that some further emolument would be welcome, and Mr. Abell sent him a trunkful of books and a check for $50. Soon afterward young Duffy gave up his carrier route, and went to work in the printing office maintained at Woodstock College, a Catholic institution near Ellicott's Mills. There, coached by Father Camillus Mazella, afterward a cardinal, he learned to set type not only in English but also in Latin and Greek. He continued at Woodstock and as a volunteer reporter for THE SUN until 1879, when he enlisted in the Navy, and was assigned to the old frigate *Trenton,* then the American flagship in the Mediterranean, as ship's printer to Rear-Admiral John C. Howell. He made the trip to Gibraltar in the historic *Constellation,* of which Lieut.-Com. Charles V. Gridley, afterward captain of Dewey's *Olympia* at Manila Bay ("You may fire when you are ready, Gridley") was executive officer. After being transferred, along with Gridley, to the *Trenton,* Duffy asked Gridley for permission to establish a ship's newspaper aboard. Gridley was puzzled, but finally put the matter up to Admiral Howell. The idea appealed to the admiral, but he could not see how it could be worked out.

"Leave that to me," said Duffy.

"All right," replied the admiral, "you may establish the paper, but I'm going to be censor. You can't say anything rough about the President of the United States, the Secretary of the Navy, or me," intimating that the bars were down for anybody and anything else. That was the beginning of the

Trenton Herald, the first newspaper ever published on a ship of any nation in the world. The supply of ship's type was not sufficient for the job, so when the *Trenton* reached London, Duffy bought a new supply, and from that time on getting out the fleet newspaper was not so difficult a job. He continued the paper as long as he was with the fleet.

Meanwhile, he continued to keep his eye open for news. When, on the trip outward, the old *Constellation* rescued the crew of the sinking bark *Olive*, he wrote a dispatch that appeared in The Sun before the Navy Department received any word of the matter. Arriving at Alexandria, Egypt, he witnessed the departure of the obelisk which now stands in Central Park, New York, and described it at length. Later, at Naples, he saw the liquefaction of the blood of St. Januarius in the cathedral there, and was so vastly impressed that he took two columns to tell about it. He sent in so much good stuff that Mr. Abell wrote to him in 1881, saying that a job on The Sun awaited him at the end of his enlistment, and at the beginning of 1882 he was on the staff.

After a few weeks of police reporting he was made ship-news reporter, and in that post he flourished for more than half a century. At the wheel of his launch, the *Sunbeam*, he met all the ocean ships that made Baltimore harbor, and in the course of time he acquired a really enormous acquaintance among ship captains of all nations. On January 1, 1907, on his completion of twenty-five years in service, he was given a gold watch by the A. S. Abell Company, and on January 1, 1932, he received another. His proper territory embraced only Baltimore harbor, but not infrequently he bulged out into Chesapeake Bay. In the middle 80s there was a famous oyster war in Virginia waters, with Governor William E. Cameron and a new dredging law ranged on one side and a larger number of rebellious oystermen on the other. The admiral went down to cover it, and in the little port of Chesconnessex was taken for a spy in the employ of the

Governor, and narrowly escaped lynching. He was a peppery fellow, especially in his later years, and full of confidence in himself. When, in 1920 or thereabout, he was given a young assistant, his indignation was boundless. When he died in 1933 all the craft in Baltimore harbor, both American and foreign, lowered their flags to half-mast. THE SUN said of him next day:

> He did not appear to change physically; scores of his fellow-workers, now fat and bald, saw in his last months almost exactly the figure they had seen when they entered THE SUN's employ as striplings — the stocky, erect body, the up-tilted head, the fearless eye lighted up now and again by sheer devilment. Nor was there change in his quality. His bold physical bearing reflected his mental and moral qualities and his outlook on life and until the end one expected from him the clipped, terse sentence, expressing the swift, unafraid thought. To generation after generation of SUN men, "the admiral" was a permanent institution. His original appearance in the office more than half a century ago was beyond anyone's memory and his final disappearance was beyond anyone's belief.

The scholars of THE SUN staff at the end of the century were Dr. Samuel Zenas Ammen, a Virginian of Swiss ancestry, and Dr. Robert Karl Beer, a German. Dr. Ammen was born at Fincastle, Va., on October 22, 1843, and at the outbreak of the Civil War was a student at the Botetourt Military Academy there, and less than eighteen years old. But when the older boys went into the Confederate Army he followed, and in August, 1861, was mustered in as a private in Company D, Eleventh Virginia Infantry. His regiment saw hard service under Longstreet, Ewell, Pickett and A. P. Hill. In 1863 or thereabout he transferred to the Confederate Navy, but he was soon back on land, and at the close of the war he was in command of a troop of guerrilla cavalry. After Appomattox he followed Robert E. Lee to Washington College (now Washington and Lee University), and there he took his master's degree in 1869. While a student he founded the Kappa Alpha fraternity, still flourishing in the South, with 26,000 members. On his graduation, General Lee offered him the assistant professorship of modern languages at Washington College, but he had already accepted a post as classical master at Milburn Academy in Kentucky. In 1870 he came to Baltimore to teach Latin, Greek and Chemistry in Dr. Robert Atkinson's School for Boys, but his tastes ran toward writing rather than toward teaching, and in 1881 he joined THE SUN as an editorial writer. He continued as such until 1911, when he retired. For a time he was also editor of THE SUN Almanac. Dr. Ammen was a heavy reader and an extensive traveler, and his range of knowledge was very wide. His precise, military set-up and his great amiability, especially to the younger members of the staff, made him a salient and favorite figure in THE SUN office. In 1893 his *alma mater* made him a D. Lit. *honoris causa.* In 1915, four years after his retirement, he prepared the following brief characterization of himself for THE SUN's morgue:

> Mr. Ammen's interests were chiefly intellectual. He cared little for active pursuits, though a careful investor. He kept up and increased his knowledge of Latin and other classical learning, adding acquirements in French, Italian and Greek literature. From a boy he was much occupied with chemistry and physics and the sciences generally, accepting the evolution hypothesis. In his later years he was interested in archæology and studies dealing with the beginnings of civilization, religion, art, political institutions, etc. In person he was robust, and of about five feet nine inches in stature. His health was remarkably good, a fact which he attributed to habits of moderation in diet and drink, coupled with carefully tempered optimism.

Dr. Ammen died at Daytona Beach, Fla., January 5, 1929. His colleague in learning, Dr. Beer, was born near Cassel in Germany on May 8, 1842, and was the last of a long line of Lutheran theologians, the founder of which was a monk who became converted to the reformed religion in Luther's time. He was educated at Bonn and Marburg, and later went to Paris, planning to study medicine. But his father induced him to turn to the family profession, and he took orders. In his early thirties he came to America, first teaching in a school in New York and then moving to Baltimore to become pastor of St. Jacob's Lutheran Church. But he disliked the pulpit, and in a little while was operating a school of languages in Baltimore, editing a pedagogical paper, and writing books, one of which, "Beer's Pharmaceutical Dictionary," ran through many editions and was published in three languages. Finally he joined the staff of THE SUN, where he served for ten years as the office encyclopedia. He knew Greek well enough to make speeches in it, and he was proficient too in Sanskrit, Hebrew, Latin, French, Spanish and Italian, beside German and English. He also had more or less acquaintance with half a dozen other languages. In 1904 his health failed, and he died on December 27.

The others must be mentioned more briefly, though they are all remembered in THE SUN office. T. J. C. Williams was born on a tobacco plantation in Calvert county, Maryland, on August 6, 1851, and was the son of a Protestant Episcopal clergyman. He studied law and in his early days was associated in its practice at Hagerstown, Md., with William T. Hamilton, who was a United States Senator from Maryland from 1869 to 1875, and Governor of the State from 1880 to 1884. But the law was eventually abandoned for journalism, and Mr. Williams attracted attention throughout the State by the editorials he wrote for the Hagerstown *Mail*. In 1891 they brought him an invitation to join the staff of THE SUN, and he remained an editorial writer for the paper until 1910, when he was appointed judge of the Juvenile Court of Baltimore. He served in that place for nineteen years, and became known for his mild but shrewd dealings with young delinquents. In 1906 he published an elaborate history of Washington county, Maryland, in two volumes. He was a vestryman (the only vestryman then in The Sun office!) of St. Michael and All Angels' Protestant Episcopal Church, Baltimore, and during his time the church saw three successive rectors become bishops. On the evening of December 11, 1929, he went to a meeting of the vestry, and just as it ended he dropped dead. He was often in charge of The Sun as *locum tenens* for Mr. Baldwin. A mild and urbane man, round and smooth of face and of courtly manners, he was much liked in the office.

His colleagues John T. Pleasants and Charles W. Dashiell were also extraordinarily popular. Mr. Pleasants, like Messrs. Foard, Haines, Baldwin and Ammen, was a Virginian, born at Petersburg on October 1, 1860, as the son of Dr. John M. Pleasants, then Mayor of the town. He was too young during the Civil War to remember anything of it afterward, but he remained a loyal Virginian to the end of his life. As a young man he became a reporter for the Petersburg *Index-Appeal*, and later worked on a paper in Wilmington, Del. In 1891 he joined the staff of The Sun, and there he remained as an editorial writer until his death on March 6, 1911. A man of handsome person, amiable manners and constant good humor, he was the *beau ideal* of an old-time editor.

Mr. Dashiell, who died on August 16, 1898, at the early age of forty, was the city editor of the paper for about fifteen years. Born in Baltimore of an Eastern Shore of Maryland family of Huguenot origin (its first American representative, James Dashiell, settled in Somerset county, Maryland, in 1666, and it provided two signers for the first State Constitution of 1776), he joined the staff of the Baltimore *Morning Herald* at twenty, and after a brief service there and a little while on the Baltimore *Bulletin*, came to The Sun as a reporter. His promotion to the city editorship followed quickly. In the history of American journalism there have been few more popular city editors. His staff adored him, and his name is still venerated in the office. He was the first president of the Journalists Club of Baltimore (1884), and when he died the whole journalistic craft in Baltimore went into mourning.

A dozen years after his death his young daughter, Virginia, applied to Charles H. Grasty, then publisher of THE SUN, for a post on the reportorial staff. "Your name is enough!" exclaimed Grasty. "It would disgrace me forever if the news got out that a daughter of Charlie Dashiell had wanted to come on THE SUN, and I had not found a place for her." Miss Dashiell, who turned out to be an excellent reporter, was married in 1918 to John W. Owens, then political reporter of THE SUN and now its editor. She died on May 30, 1926.

George Morrow, who died in 1915 after thirty-three years of service on THE SUN, was in one respect at least the perfect editor, for he was never known to make a mistake, even in spelling. Nor did any other man's mistake ever pass under his eye without a challenge. He was, in his later years, assistant city editor, but his alertness always extended beyond the bounds of the city room. As the evening's proofs began to come down from the composing room he went through them rapidly but carefully, and when the first edition came up from the pressroom he gave it the same diligent scrutiny. If there was a word that didn't parse he detected it instantly; if a name was misspelled he corrected it; if there was a misstatement of fact he set it right. His mastery of all the different kinds of information that a newspaper man needs was really astonishing, and he was always adding to his stock. THE SUN's high reputation for accuracy in his day was largely due to his vigilance. His self-chosen rôle of office mentor might easily have made him unpopular, especially among young and impatient reporters, but he was so amiable that even the most careless of them was all for him. Tall, straight, white-haired and very quiet in manner, he did his invaluable work without offending anyone, and it left an indelible impress upon the office. Born in Washington county, Maryland, he made his first contact with newspapers as a printer at Greencastle, Pa., just over the Mason & Dixon Line. At seventeen, he came to Baltimore and worked on the old *Gazette*. There followed two years in St. Louis, after which he edited a paper at Towson, the county seat of Baltimore county. He came to THE SUN in 1882 and was successively court reporter, telegraph editor, night editor, and assistant city editor.

CHAPTER XIII

☼

THE GREAT BALTIMORE FIRE OF 1904

At 10.50 o'clock on Sunday morning, February 7, 1904, a day of bitter cold and high winds, an automatic fire alarm sounded from the establishment of John E. Hurst & Company,[1] wholesale drygoods merchants, at German street and Hopkins place, in the heart of Baltimore's business district. A few minutes later Archibald McAllister, a private fire-patrolman employed by the property owners of the neighborhood, saw smoke emerging from the cellar grating in the sidewalk and sent in another alarm. A couple of engines were soon unlimbered at nearby fire plugs, and John A. Conlon, a watchman in the National Exchange Bank across the street, settled down behind a barred window of the bank to watch what promised to be a diverting show. Suddenly there was an explosion, part of the front wall

[1] This firm, one of the pillars of Baltimore when the city was chiefly a jobbing center, was founded on May 17, 1831, and was thus six years older to a day than The Sun. Starting as Battee & Hurst, it became Barry & Hurst in 1832, Hurst & Berry (not Barry) in 1841, Hurst & Company in 1857, Hurst, Purnell & Company in 1869, John E. Hurst & Company in 1895, and John E. Hurst & Company, Inc., in 1919. It was liquidated in 1932. Its senior partner in 1895, John E. Hurst, was the Gorman-Rasin candidate for Mayor of Baltimore in that year. The Sun's opposition to him has been noted in Chapter IX.

of the Hurst building blew out, the bank window blew in on Mr. Conlon, he was knocked down, his clothing caught fire, and he was given the scare of his life. Rushing out into Baltimore street, he seems to have fallen into a swoon, and when he came to he found himself in the Maryland General Hospital. Another patient lay beside him: a Mr. S. F. Ball, of West Fayette street. Mr. Ball had been taking a Sunday morning stroll along Baltimore street when the blast fetched him. It was a full block away, but flying debris cut both his hands and blew a hole through his hat.

The firemen put down the explosion to gasoline stored in the cellar of the Hurst building, but that explanation, on later investigation, turned out to be inaccurate. There was, in fact, no gasoline in the building. In all probability, it was smoke that had gone off. How the fire started was never determined, but the most plausible theory was that some passer-by dropped a lighted cigar or cigarette butt through the cellar grating, and set aflame the cotton batting stored below. Whatever the cause, the firemen found on their arrival that they faced a very serious blaze, and when the explosion followed before they had got fairly into action they began turning in additional alarms with great zeal. By 9 P.M. twenty-one had been sounded, every piece of apparatus in Baltimore was in service, fifty firemen were injured, including their commander, Chief George W. Horton, and engines were arriving from Washington, Wilmington, Philadelphia and New York, and all the smaller towns of Maryland and lower Pennsylvania. The first to get in were three from Washington. They made the forty-mile run by a special train of the Baltimore & Ohio Railroad in thirty-two minutes — probably a record for the trip to this day. Some of these visiting engines remained in service for four or five days and nights, and a few never got home at all, for the fire overtook them and burned them. Many pieces of Baltimore apparatus went the same way, and for weeks after the fire their grisly skeletons were visible amid the ruins.

It was the greatest fire in Baltimore's history, and one of the largest ever seen in the United States. Whipped by stiff winds, it burned almost a week, and when it died down at last, stopped by Jones' Falls, a stream running through Baltimore from north to south, the entire wholesale center of the city, covering an area of more than a square mile, was a wreck. All save two or three of the city's office buildings were burned, and all save two of its downtown hotels, and all save a few of its banks. The office buildings made magnificent torches, once they were fully alight, and the largest of them, the Calvert Building at Fayette and St. Paul streets, and the Continental, at Baltimore and Calvert, sent up pillars of yellow flame to a height of hundreds of feet. But though their wooden floors were consumed completely, and all the contents of their constituent offices, their steel structures held out without substantial damage, and so did their brick-and-stone skins. After the fire they were all rebuilt, and still remain in service after a third of a century.

The total loss was never figured out with any accuracy, but it must have run close to $100,000,000. Of this amount, probably not much more than half was covered by collectible insurance. The big national and international companies all paid up more or less promptly, but some of the small local companies went bankrupt, and their policyholders were out of luck. Rather curiously, only one man was reported killed, and he may have been imaginary, for there were conflicting reports about his name, place of residence and station in life, and in the excitement of the ensuing weeks the police neglected to locate his corpse, if any. Nor was there any need to succor the homeless, a distressing necessity after most big fires, for only a few people had lived in the burnt area, and they quickly found refuge with friends living outside. When, some days after the fateful Sunday, the Maryland Legislature met in special session at Annapolis and proposed "to relieve the distressed," the head of the city charities, John M. Glenn, reported that he knew of no one who was in distress. Offers of financial and other aid were also received from many cities, but to all of them the reply was made that Baltimore needed none.

The old SUN Iron Building was at least half a mile from the Hurst building, and in consequence the afternoon was well along before there was any serious threat to it. Great clouds of smoke beat upon it, propelled by a wind from the west, and it was bombarded by sparks and flying brands, but the reporters of the city staff kept on covering the fire as if it offered no menace to their own headquarters. It was a swell day for young journalists, and they enjoyed it immensely. Their city editor, Herbert A. Hallett, was a hard driver, but he did not have to urge them now. They compiled long and ever-lengthening lists of buildings burned, with the names of the owners and occupants, the probable losses and the amount of insurance, and they wrote column after column of strange tales about the vagaries of the fire, and interviews with various public officials and private eyewitnesses. THE SUN, in those days, was not a paper to get excited and descend to indecorum, even in the presence of a fire that was destroying the heart of Baltimore. It got out no extra, but devoted itself to preparing a full report for early next morning, with all names spelled precisely right and no essential fact forgotten. The other papers published extras, but not the imperturbable *Sunpaper*.

Toward the end of the afternoon, however, a certain amount of seething began to be visible in the Iron Building. The fire, by that time, had crossed Charles street, and was whirling crazily down Baltimore street. The firemen, worn out and hopeless, had sent for dynamite experts from the suburban stone quarries to help them, and toward 4 o'clock these brethren set off six charges of one hundred pounds each in a building at the southwest corner of Charles and German (now Redwood) streets, a block south of Baltimore street. The idea was that demolishing buildings would halt the fire. With so much wind blowing, it was a bad idea, but nevertheless it was cherished all that melodramatic afternoon, and toward 6 o'clock there were some violent detonations very close to the Iron Building, followed by the inevitable rumors that a dozen, or a score, or a hundred people had been killed. When the bombardment got so close it was determined to remove the files of the *Sunpaper* to places of safety, along with its mailing lists, record books and other valuables, and the work was carried out promptly by the staff of the counting-room, with some friendly aid from volunteers passing by.

While it was in progress the preparation of next morning's first edition went on. The reporters continued at work, and so did the compositors. Form after form was filled with the story of the fire, and each was stereotyped and sent to the pressroom as it was completed. Finally, all that remained to be done was to finish the first page, which lacked only the headlines of the story and its general introduction. Twenty minutes would have sufficed to finish the job.

At this juncture one of the compositors, alarmed by the shower of sparks that fell on the skylight of the composing room, by the nearby explosions and by the glare shining through the windows, left his work, and without saying anything to his fellows, ran down to the editorial rooms and told Walter W. Abell that every man in the composing room was in danger of being burned alive. Mr. Abell did not believe it, but he was reluctant to keep the men at their posts, even if they only thought they were in danger. So he gave the order to clear the building.

That order caused the nearest thing to an insurrection that was ever seen in THE SUN office. First came a delegation from the composing room, headed by George Nichols, the assistant foreman, declaring profanely that the alarmist did not represent the printers, and that they wanted to stick to their work and get out the paper. Then came a delegation from the pressroom, headed by Mike Donovan, the foreman, arguing that the boys were all ready to go down there, and that the fire, after all, was still almost a block away. Finally, City Editor Hallett added his protestations, saying that in fifteen minutes more the paper would be out. But Mr. Abell had given the order, and it was manifest by now that any delay might be dangerous and could only be very short. The men accordingly gathered up their belongings and filed out, grumbling. Mr. Abell himself made a trip from the top to the bottom of the building, to make sure that no one had been left behind.

At 11.30 in the evening the cornice was set afire by falling brands, but this blaze was quickly put out. Fifteen minutes later, however, the *American* Building directly across South street broke into furious flame, and it was seen that the Iron Building, after standing four-square for fifty-four eventful years, was doomed at last. The last men to leave it were Mr. Abell and Harold E. West. They went to the corner of North and Fayette streets, a block away, still hoping against hope. When some brands lodged on a window sill of the fourth floor Mr. West returned to the building and put them out with a fire extinguisher. Later he put out another blaze on the second floor. All the windows had been shut, and there was still a faint chance that the wind might change, and send the fire driving some other way. But by midnight the heat of the burning *American* Building so greatly expanded the confined air in the Iron Building that some of the upstairs windows blew out, and in twenty minutes the heavy linotype machines on the fifth floor were falling through the blazing editorial and counting-rooms to the pressroom in the cellar. At 12.30 the walls caved in with a huge upheaval of sparks, and that was the melancholy end of one of old-time Baltimore's most famous landmarks. It had been erected in 1851. Many warehouses in the burnt area had been built in imitation of it — that is, they had cast-iron fronts. But these cast-iron fronts, under the impact of so vast a fire, turned out to be very vulnerable. They cracked and warped the instant the flames reached them, and then went down, carrying along floors and brick side-walls. Making them had been one of the most flourishing of the minor industries of Baltimore for half a century; they were cast in foundries which also made iron hitching-posts, lamp-posts, fire-plugs and elegant dogs and deer for ornamenting lawns. But even before the fire, cast iron had been challenged by steel and concrete, and when the rebuilding began they had it all their own way.

When the danger to the Iron Building first became apparent negotiations were opened by telegraph with the Washington *Evening Star* to print next morning's SUN in case the building had to be abandoned. A special train of the Baltimore & Ohio Railroad was engaged and it stood waiting at Camden Station from 4 P.M. onward. Up to the last, however, it was hoped that the Iron Building would escape, and that it would be possible to issue THE SUN as usual. When, at 11 P.M., its imminent destruction became certain, orders were given to proceed to Camden Station. The melancholy Washington expedition consisted of a detail from the editorial staff, headed by Allen S. Will, the telegraph editor, with Harold E. West second in command, and including the whole force of the composing room and mailing department, the stereotypers, and several clerks of the counting room. City Editor Hallett remained in charge of the reporters left in Baltimore. Work on next morning's paper did not cease until the very moment of departure. The trip to Washington was made quickly, and the *Evening Star* office was found to be in complete readiness. By 2 o'clock in the morning Monday's edition of THE SUN was on the *Star* presses, and by 4 o'clock such of the regular carriers as could be rounded up were beginning to deliver it in Baltimore. On February 9 THE SUN announced proudly that "no other Baltimore morning paper could be obtained yesterday." This was a slight exaggeration, for, though the *American* had not appeared on the morning after the fire, the *Morning Herald* had been on the streets alongside THE SUN.[1]

THE SUN's first Washington edition contained a long and, considering the circumstances, very vivid and coherent account of the fire, though the difficulties of printing a paper in a strange plant were revealed by the fact that a group of fire notes headed "Gathered at Random," and running to two-thirds of a column, appeared on both Page 2 and Page 3 of Monday morning's paper. Two other articles, each briefer, were similarly duplicated. But these were inconsiderable and perhaps inevitable slips. The fire by no means monopolized this first refugee issue of the paper. There was a long dispatch about the opening of the Russo-Japanese War, with a big map of the scene of the conflict, probably borrowed from the *Star*. The *Star*, of course, already had Associated Press wires running into its office, and

[1] The *Herald's* editions of February 8 and 10 were produced in the plant of the Washington *Post*, but the issue of February 9 was printed in Baltimore at the office of the *World* and parts of it were set up in the office of the *Catholic Mirror*. The *World* plant was outside the burnt district and undamaged. Beginning February 11 and for five weeks, the *Herald* was issued from the plant of the Philadelphia *Evening Telegraph*. The *Evening News*, Monday afternoon, February 8, was also printed at the office of the Washington *Post* and continued there until its own plant was in operation in Baltimore on February 22. The *American*, beginning February 9, was published from the building of Frank A. Munsey's Washington *Times*, where its publication was continued until February 27. Then the paper moved back to Baltimore and was printed with *News* equipment, beginning with the issue of Sunday, February 28. Mr. Grasty and General Agnus had an agreement, made before the fire, to open either plant to the use of the other paper in case of fire or other emergency.

without any delay THE SUN's night report was switched to them. Some headlines of the first two days: Two Burned at Stake, Mr. [Mark] Hanna Weaker,[1] Guards Kill Miners, Wreck Near Richmond. And titles of editorials: Financing the Canal, The Cape Colony Elections, Endowing Research, Is Australia Decadent? There were also plenty of store advertisements. And theater announcements, for none of the Baltimore theaters had been burned — Ada Rehan and Otis Skinner, in "The Merchant of Venice," at Ford's Opera House; Percy Haswell, in "The Two Orphans," at Chase's in North Charles street, and the Oratorio Society warbling "Israel in Egypt" at the Lyric.

During the next week or two THE SUN printed only a few formal editorials on the fire, but there was a good deal of undisguised editorializing in its news articles. On Tuesday, February 9, it ventured upon a caustic criticism of the conduct of the Fire Department, alleging that the fire engines had been badly placed on Sunday, that their water had been wasted on buildings already doomed, and that dynamite had been used too late. There was another article denouncing the storage of gasoline in warehouses, and calling for remedial legislation by the City Council, though, as we have seen, there was actually no gasoline in the Hurst Building. There was another mocking at fire-proofing, and directing attention to the fact that many of the most elaborately fire-proofed buildings had been among the first to go. In general, the paper took a somewhat gloomy view of the situation in Baltimore. The fire, though it was officially under control at 5 P.M. on Monday, actually went on burning for a full week. No one knew what the net loss would be, and there were serious doubts that parts of the burned area would ever be rebuilt. "Many men formerly prosperous," said an editorial of Monday, "will be ruined by the events of the last twenty-four hours." This was indeed the case, but there were plenty who

[1] He died on February 15.

were not ruined, and they were presently hard at work, planning the rebuilding of the city.

The Legislature of Maryland, meeting in special session, was induced by Governor Edwin Warfield to cut a lot of legal red tape, and a commission headed by Colonel Sherlock Swann, and including three much-respected business men, Charles K. Lord, Reuben Foster and John T. Graham, was given what amounted almost to sovereignty over the burned district. This commission cleared off the debris in the streets, widened some of the narrower ones, and arranged for hauling the wreckage of the destroyed buildings to the mud flats of the upper Patapsco river, where it made a lot of valuable new ground and incidentally obliterated the malaria that had been one of the curses of Baltimore for two centuries. But though things were going ahead briskly within a few weeks, and Colonel Swann and his associates were full of a rosy optimism, there remained some Baltimoreans who believed that the town was crippled beyond recovery, and one of them was its 36-year-old Mayor, Robert M. McLane. On May 30, nearly four months after the fire, he so far yielded to his unhappy vapors as to shoot himself. He was succeeded by E. Clay Timanus, a jovial fellow of large bulk. Under Timanus there was no more despair, and by the beginning of the Summer Baltimore was rising from its ashes, and in the end turned out to be much better laid out, and much cleaner and livelier than the Baltimore of old.

While The Sun continued to be printed on the presses of the Washington *Star* it was brought to Baltimore every morning by a special train of the Baltimore & Ohio, which had itself lost its home office in Baltimore and was otherwise badly damaged by the fire, but gave quick and effective aid to every other victim. The carriers met the train at Camden Station, and proceeded to their routes as usual. Papers for mail subscribers, of course, were dispatched from the Postoffice in Washington. Bright and early on Monday, with the fire still raging unchecked, The Sun opened Baltimore headquarters in the building of THE SUN Book and Job Printing Office at the southwest corner of Calvert and Saratoga streets. This was several blocks north of the burning area, and made a very convenient location. The building had been erected in 1900. It contained two quadruple Hoe presses and a complete stereotyping outfit; they had been installed a year or more before the fire against just such an emergency. Unfortunately, only enough linotypes were in place to serve the Job Office, and there was a delay of nearly two months while a battery sufficient for the needs of THE SUN was set up. Meanwhile, some effort was made to recondition the equipment in the ruins of the Iron Building, but most of it was found to be beyond repair.

It was thus not until April 6 that THE SUN came home to Baltimore: it had been printed in Washington exactly two months. Its first issue from the Job Printing Office contained a graceful editorial of thanks to the Washington *Star*, which had been a ready and eager friend in a day of desperate need. The *Star* replied with an editorial saying that it was made desolate by the departure of THE SUN comrades, all of whom were charming fellows and high-toned journalists. The staff quickly settled down in the Job Printing Office; in fact, most of the reporters had been working there all the while. Their copy had been sent to Washington by messenger every afternoon, and by telegraph every evening, and there set up in the *Star* composing room by SUN printers. Now they were all home again, and they soon discovered a comfortable saloon in an alley near the Job Printing Office, kept by a German who drank thirty-five glasses of beer a day and wore a beard of such cut that he came to be known to them as Weber-and-Fields. All their favorite saloons of the old days had perished in the fire, along with all the night-hawk lunchrooms that they had patronized.

The months following the fire were prosperous ones for the

Baltimore papers, at least in gross income. Thousands of firms and individuals, burned out, had established temporary quarters in the ancient residence section just north of the burned area, and all of them were eager to notify their customers and clients of their new addresses. There were stockbrokers' offices in fashionable Mount Vernon place, lawyers' offices in boarding houses, real-estate offices in saloons, and at least one bank in the parish house of a church. By the middle of its first week in Washington THE SUN was crowded with announcements of these campers-out, and as such announcements multiplied they tended to increase in size, so that they made serious inroads on the paper's news space. It had seldom printed more than ten pages before the fire, but now it went to twelve, and then to sixteen. Its expenses, to be sure, were very heavy, but its takings were also heavy. The insurance on the Iron Building and its contents was soon collected, and the directors began to amass funds against the new building that loomed ahead. But on the heels of the fire came a calamity that forced these plans to be shelved for a time. This was the death of Edwin F. Abell, the president of the publishing corporation, on February 28, exactly three weeks after the beginning of the fire.

Mr. Abell, who was born in Baltimore on May 15, 1840, was the eldest of the twelve children of Arunah S. Abell, the Founder. All his brothers had preceded him in death: Charles S. on December 3, 1875; Walter R. on January 3, 1891, and George W. on May 1, 1894. He entered the counting-room of THE SUN at the age of 16, but before the death of his brother, George W., as previously stated, he had devoted most of his time to the management of their father's large estate, and had thus given little attention to the paper. On his brother's death he found himself in charge of it, and thereafter his whole energies were given to it. He was a man of retiring habits, with no political or other visible ambition, and he cared little for society or club life. He never sat on public committees, went to banquets, or did any of the other things commonly expected of newspaper proprietors. His one dissipation was collecting walking-sticks, of which he had a large number, some of historical associations. Rather curiously, he was never known to carry one. He was an extremely shrewd judge of real-estate values, and greatly increased the worth of the family property.

His foresight was revealed by the erection of THE SUN Book and Job Printing Office in 1900.[1] That was his idea, and it turned out to be a capital one when the fire came and THE SUN needed a temporary home in Baltimore. The other Baltimore papers were hard put to find quarters. The *Evening News*, after two weeks in Washington as the guest of the *Post*, did its printing in an old warehouse near Calvert Station, and the *Morning Herald*, after a few days in Washington and five weeks in Philadelphia, returned to an abandoned street-railway powerhouse in South Charles street. But THE SUN had clean, convenient and comfortable quarters in the Job Printing Office, and once adequate equipment had been installed there, it was as well served as it had ever been in the Iron Building. In fact, it was better served, for the Iron Building had been built for small presses and hand composition, and with the coming of larger presses and the linotype it had been badly crowded. Moreover, it faced Baltimore street, one of the busiest thoroughfares of the city, and had only narrow South street beside it, so that the delivery of papers in the early morning hours was sometimes incom-

---

[1] Mr. Abell was twice married. His first wife, the daughter of Henry R. Curley, was the mother of his three children — Walter W. and Arunah S. Abell 2d and Mrs. James Dudley Morgan. His second wife, who survived him, was the daughter of Francis B. Laurenson. On February 29, 1904, both branches of the Baltimore City Council passed resolutions noting his death, and on March 1 the General Assembly of Maryland passed others, and the State Senate adjourned as a mark of respect.

moded by traffic. The Job Printing Office was in a quieter neighborhood, with a wide and little used street running beside it.

Nearby, in Calvert street, was the office of the *World*, an evening paper, and the only Baltimore daily that had escaped the fire. But though the *World* thus started out with a great advantage over the other Baltimore newspapers, it was a small and little heeded sheet, and the competition for the advertising that followed the fire was between THE SUN on the one hand and the *News*, *American* and *Herald* on the other. Of these rivals, the *News* was the most formidable, and by far. It had been forging ahead since the political battles of the 90s. To most Baltimoreans it appeared as the exponent of a new and exciting kind of journalism, grounded on a fearless independence, and not a few of them believed that it was overhauling THE SUN, and would eventually become the principal newspaper of the town. Moreover, it had the advantage of being an evening paper, for even in those days the trend of advertising was toward the evening field. Nevertheless, THE SUN, aided by a row that Mr. Grasty had with his principal local advertisers early in 1905, managed to corral the major share of the post-fire advertising, and the stockholders were told at their annual meeting on March 31, 1905, that "the increase in both advertising and circulation for the year was most satisfactory." It was not until the next year that the officers of the company began to realize that Grasty's competition was really serious, and that the paper would have to revise its archaic and unyielding practices if it were to retain its leadership.

The *American* and *Herald* gave it little concern, save in the Sunday field. The former had the romantic prestige which went with its having been the first newspaper to print Francis Scott Key's "Star-Spangled Banner," written on a ship in Baltimore harbor during the British bombardment of Fort McHenry in 1814. But otherwise it was of little influence and it offered no serious rivalry to THE SUN, either in news-getting or in advertising patronage. It survives today as the Sunday edition of W. R. Hearst's Baltimore *News-Post,* a combination of Grasty's *News* and the Scripps-Howard *Post.* The *Herald* was of even less consequence. It was owned, at the time of the fire, by Wesley M. Oler, a Baltimore ice and coal dealer who had developed into a financier and later became president of the American Ice Company. It suspended publication in 1906. The real competitor of THE SUN at that time was the *Evening News.*

Soon after the fire of 1904, for the first and last time in its career, THE SUN had to face the defalcation of an old and trusted employé. He was even then an elderly man, and is now long dead. The detection of his shortage was due to John J. Nelligan, who had become a member of the board of directors during the Spring following the fire. Mr. Nelligan had been trained in the office of the Safe Deposit & Trust Company, Baltimore's oldest fiduciary corporation, under a remarkable financier, B. F. Newcomer, and he appeared on the board as the representative of the heirs of Walter R. Abell (d. 1891), for whose interest in THE SUN, though not in the rest of the Walter R. Abell estate, he had been appointed trustee on the retirement of Charles J. Bonaparte. He was a man as prudent and alert in business as his old chief, and he was destined to serve THE SUN, save for a brief interval, until his death in 1935. One of his first proceedings was to look into the financial management of the paper. He suggested that the care of its money ought to be better safeguarded, and that all appointed to handle it should be given definite prerogatives and responsibilities, and properly bonded. When the recreant employé heard of what was afoot he went at once to Walter W. Abell, the new president of the company, and confessed, explaining that he knew the bonding company's experts would discover his shortage, and that he preferred to break the news himself. There was a melancholy special meeting six days later to accept his resignation. The man put in charge of THE SUN's cash after that was William J. Morris, who continued to hold the post until 1914, when he resigned to enter the employ of the Edwin F. Abell Estate and was succeeded by Edward H. Fry, who is still in service (1937). Mr. Fry came to THE SUN on November 7, 1887, and is thus one of its oldest employés. Mr. Morris, if he had not resigned in 1914, would be the oldest of all today, and by far, for he entered the counting-room in June, 1879.[1]

---

[1] As of January 1, 1937, the active employés of thirty years or more service were as follows:

Name.	Department.	Date Employed.	Years of Service
Hacker, Oscar C.	Composing Room	Aug. 15, 1885	51
Cole, Abraham G.	Credit and Collection	May 15, 1886	50
Fry, Edward H.	Accounting	Nov. 7, 1887	49
Poole, Walter A.	Editorial	June 28, 1890	46
Culver, William J.	Composing Room	July 1, 1893	43
Webb, William A., Sr.	Composing Room	July 1, 1896	40
Shaughnessy, Thomas	Composing Room	Jan. 15, 1898	39
Miller, Harry R.	Composing Room	Feb. 15, 1898	38
Gosnell, Edgar C.	Composing Room	Aug. 15, 1899	37
Kent, Frank R.	Editorial	Jan. 15, 1900	37
Greenfield, William E.	Composing Room	July 15, 1900	36
Warfield, Murray L.	Editorial	Sept. 15, 1900	36
Ellis, Edgar	Library	Jan. 7, 1901	36
Morrow, Andrew H.	Composing Room	June 15, 1902	34
Fitzell, William L.	Accounting	Aug. 2, 1902	34
House, Thomas F.	Pressroom	July 15, 1903	33
Childress, Henry J.	Stereotype	Dec. 1, 1903	33
Funkhouser, Charles S.	Bookkeeping	Feb. 22, 1904	32
Malone, Joseph J.	Mailing Room	Nov. 15, 1904	32
Duennebier, Louis H.	Composing Room	July 15, 1905	31
Stidman, G. Fred	Commercial Art	May 15, 1906	30
Trott, Frank B.	Composing Room	June 15, 1906	30
McKinsey, Folger	Editorial	July 1, 1906	30

Mencken, H. L.	Editorial	July 30, 1906	30
Dove, James W.	Business Office	Oct. 1, 1906	30
Heusi, John H. G.	Circulation	Oct. 15, 1906	30
Taylor, George W. A.	Business Office	Nov. 17, 1906	30

On the same day there were five carriers of thirty years or more service: Charles E. Utermohle, 36; Charles W. Davis, 34; John A. Seipple, 34; George P. Spamer, 31, and William G. Miller, 30. There were four retired employés who had served thirty years or more: John R. Hackney, composing room, 54; William H. Pentz, editorial, 48; Frank Clemens, pressroom, 40, and Frederick Strehlau, editorial, 30.

CHAPTER XIV

NEW MEN AND NEW ENTERPRISES

WITH the death of Edwin F. Abell in 1904, and the succession of his son, Walter W. Abell, to the presidency of the publishing corporation,[1] a general overhauling of THE SUN's ancient practices began. On July 10, 1905, after what seems to have been a considerable amount of debate and misgiving, its first advertising solicitor was engaged. He was Harry Martin Leitch, who had been working for the *Morning Herald*, and a sop was thrown to the *manes* of the Founder by calling him a " rate demonstrator " and instructing him to confine his activities to " explaining the rates " to inquiring advertisers. His salary was fixed at $25 a week, and on June 28 the board of directors solemnly approved his appointment. Mr. Leitch, of course, did not take his instructions too seriously. He was one of the best adver-

[1] Walter W. Abell was then but thirty-two years old. He was born at Litter Louna, his father's estate near Baltimore, on February 28, 1872. After a short period in the National Marine Bank of Baltimore, in which the Abells were interested, he became a director of the A. S. Abell Company on June 15, 1894. He was elected vice-president on June 6, 1901, and president on June 21, 1904. He resigned on April 19, 1909, but as trustee of his father's estate and on his own account he is still largely interested in THE SUN.

tising solicitors ever heard of, and he remained in the service of THE SUN until his death at the age of seventy-five on December 19, 1935. Confining himself to the local field, he was presently tracking down and bringing in advertisers who had never advertised before, whether in THE SUN or elsewhere.[1]

His appearance in the counting-room, which a few years later came to be called the business office, was matched by some other revolutionary changes. On May 31, 1905, the board appropriated $2,000 for the promotion of circulation outside the city limits of Baltimore, on April 19 it decided to have the books of the paper examined twice a year by a public accountant, on September 28 it engaged the firm of Haskins & Sells, of New York, to set up a new system of accounts in the business office, and on October 25 " the president was authorized to increase the number of pages of THE SUN to fourteen on days during the week on which business and news demanded it," and a resolution was passed indicating that the paper already had a representative in the foreign advertising field, though whether he was permitted to solicit advertising does not appear. By the beginning of 1906 the appointment of undisguised advertising solicitors, shamelessly designated as such, is revealed by the minutes. These were days of rapid change. They brought a great many strangers into THE SUN's organization, among them, one Joshua S. Cosden, a youngster from the Eastern Shore of Maryland. He was

[1] Mr. Leitch had spent twenty-two years on the *Herald* before coming to THE SUN, so his total service ran to fifty-two years. One of the Baltimore firms that he converted into a steady and very successful advertiser was the Stieff Company, silversmiths. When he died the directors of the company held a special meeting and passed resolutions describing him as " one of our most valuable and loyal friends, associates and advisers for nearly thirty years." Mr. Leitch once described his professional function and theory as follows: " I want the advertiser to feel that, in advising him on advertising, I am as careful of his money as I am of my own. High pressure salesmanship? I want none of that! "

put to work in the business office at $10 a week, but though he was raised to $15 on July 26, 1905, he seems to have got on badly, for the minutes for August 30 of the same year record his discharge by Mr. Crummer " for failing to report for duty." This Cosden then went to Oklahoma, got into the oil business, and picked up a large fortune. He is the only alumnus of THE SUN ever to become a multi-millionaire. But there have been plenty who have become university professors, diplomats, corporation executives, bankers, novelists, dramatists and the editors of other newspapers.[1]

Mr. Leitch's operations as a " rate demonstrator " were very successful, and a great deal of new business began to flow into the columns of THE SUN. On the death of Mr. Crummer in September, 1906, William L. Unduch, who had been in the business office since boyhood, succeeded him as business manager,[2]

[1] One of the last-named was Edwin L. James, now managing editor of the New York *Times*. Mr. James was born at Irvington, Va., in 1890, and educated at Randolph-Macon College. He joined the staff of THE SUN in 1910. As a reportorial novice he stumbled into a murder story, and telephoned to the city editor, Allen S. Will. Mr. Will said he would send a more experienced man to handle the story. " The hell you will! " replied young James. " This is my story, and I am going to handle it." And he did — very well. Two years later the same city editor fired him, and he went to Pittsburgh, where he became assistant news editor of the *Dispatch*. By 1915 he was on the New York *Times*, and he has been there ever since, as reporter, copy-reader, war correspondent, Paris correspondent, chief of the European correspondents, assistant managing editor, and finally managing editor. He traveled a great deal in his European days, and in one year, 1930, the *Times* carried dispatches from him dated London, Berlin, Vienna, Paris, Moscow, The Hague and Warsaw. His predecessor as managing editor of the *Times*, Carr V. Van Anda, was also an old SUN man, having served as night editor from 1886 to 1888.

[2] Mr. Unduch had entered the business office in 1897 and remained there until 1912. From 1909 to 1913 and again in 1918 he was amateur billiards champion of Maryland. On March 24, 1928, he was shot and killed as the climax of a quarrel with a friend. The friend, who was defended by Harry W. Nice, now Governor of Maryland, pleaded self-defense, and was acquitted by a jury on April 26, 1928.

and the reforms inaugurated in 1904 went on at an accelerated tempo. On October 1 the force was augmented by James W. Dove, who, like Mr. Leitch, had been on the *Herald*, and had continued in the employ of its receivers after its suspension in July.[1] Mr. Dove was full of ideas that were to bring him, in the course of time, to a high place in THE SUN organization. He not only believed in soliciting advertising; he also believed in writing attractive copy, and then taking that copy to potential customers to tempt them. This scheme worked so well that he presently brought in a number of advertisers who have remained steady customers of THE SUN to this day. In May, 1906, an art department had been set up, with G. Fred Stidman as artist, photographer and manager, and it was soon engaged upon preparing drawings for these advertisers.

On the day that Mr. Stidman's appointment was approved, the board decided to reduce the rate for various classifications of want ads, including Situations Wanted, to 10 cents a line flat, with a minimum of 20 cents. Although other classified advertising rates have been more than tripled since then, as circulation has increased, this low rate for Situations Wanted ads to those seeking work and whose ability to pay may therefore be limited has never been raised. In October, 1907, the rates for local display advertising were 17 cents a line for transient advertisements, 16½ cents for 1,000 lines used in a year, 16 cents for 2,000 lines, and so on down to 10 cents under 150,000-line contracts. These local rates were made effective January 1, 1908, when THE SUN's first rate-card, giving rates based on total

---

[1] Mr. Dove was born at South River, Anne Arundel county, Maryland, where his father was postmaster, in 1881. The family moved to Baltimore four years later, and soon afterward the elder Dove died. The son quit school at fourteen, and went to work in the business office of the Baltimore *Morning Herald*. In 1906, when the paper suspended, he was in charge of its advertising. He has been on the business staff of the *Sunpapers* ever since, and is now assistant business manager.

lineage, was issued. All previous cards quoted rates based on monthly insertions. The old monthly rates for local advertisers — of $1.50 a line a month for six week-day issues and $1.75 a line a month for week-days and Sunday, with an extra charge of 5 cents a line for changes in copy — remained optional, but only the smaller advertisers took advantage of them, for, as we have seen, the rates worked out to 11 cents a line, and the larger advertisers could now buy space for 10 cents.[1]

While local display advertising has always been accepted for either the morning or evening issue separately, all classified ads, except legal, and all national advertising since the start of THE EVENING SUN have appeared in both morning and evening issues on week-days at a single rate. This plan of selling advertising for both issues in combination proved so successful that the *Sunpapers'* advertising, counting the lineage in all issues (morning, evening and Sunday), reached a total of 15,125,000 lines in 1918 — the largest amount of advertising ever locked up into forms and printed in a single newspaper office in a twelve-month period up to that time. THE SUN has always carried the great bulk of the classified ads of Baltimore. In August, 1936, for instance, the number of them in the morning and Sunday issues (many of which appeared also in the evening issue) was double the number printed anywhere else in the city.

Under date of January 29, 1908, the following revolutionary minute appears in the directors' minute book:

[1] The rates for national advertising were made 20 cents a line for 1,000 lines, running down to 16 cents for 5,000 lines or more if used in one year. The national, or general, rates were again increased some time after the advent of THE EVENING SUN, when they were advanced to 20 cents for 5,000 lines, covering both morning and evening issues on week-days and the Sunday morning issue. The transient rate was made 25 cents; 1,000 lines, 24 cents; 2,000 lines, 23 cents, and 3,000 lines, 22 cents. These rates appeared for the first time on the national rate-card dated March 15, 1916. They were further advanced by easy stages, as circulation grew, to the present minimum national rate of 50 cents.

CHARLES SHEPHERDSON ABELL (1876–   )

WALTER R. ABELL (1849–1891)

ARUNAH S. ABELL 2ND (1865–1914)

Upon the statement of the business manager, Mr. Unduch, that he believed the telling of the circulation of THE SUN to advertisers would result in more revenue to the paper, the following resolution was adopted:

Resolved, That the circulation of THE SUN may be told to advertisers in the discretion of the manager.

On February 26 there followed this:

Resolved, That black type not over seventy-two points in height, the style to be determined upon by the Board of Directors, be used in advertisements in THE SUN, daily and Sunday, excepting on the first and last pages and beside editorials and death notices.

And on April 4 this:

Resolved, That black cuts not exceeding seventy-two points in height and 150 in width may be used in THE SUN in advertisements at the discretion of the business manager, all black cuts exceeding this height and width to be stippled, tooled or Bendayed.

This was a year and a half after the death of Mr. Crummer, a little over four years after that of Mr. Edwin F. Abell, and twenty after that of the Founder. The revolution had got under way slowly, but once it was in progress it moved very fast. It came to a dramatic climax in 1909, when a Baltimore corsetière sent in copy for an advertisement including a half-tone showing a lovely female creature stripped to her whalebones to exhibit the efficiency of a dollar reducer model. It was passed by Business Manager Unduch only after hours of doubt and soul-searching, and the staff of the advertising department came to the office next morning expecting to find indignant subscribers canceling their subscriptions by the hundreds, and the Abells in a great state of perturbation. But nothing was heard from the subscribers, and nothing from the Abells. THE SUN was on its way.

Nor was there progress only in the business office. The editorial rooms were also undergoing a gradual transformation during the same years. The old SUN had been extremely enterprising in news-gathering, and its accuracy was almost fabulous, but it had been, on the whole, a somewhat stodgy paper, and its reporters were not usually encouraged to indulge their literary fancies. There was a saying in the city rooms of the other Baltimore papers that no one could hope to beat a SUN reporter in gathering news, but that anyone could beat him in writing it. In December, 1891, when a hole was dug in the sidewalk before the Iron Building to admit a new press, Col. A. B. Cunningham, then editor of the *Herald*, wrote in his paper that what THE SUN really needed was " to dig a hole in the roof and put some brains in upstairs." No notice was taken of this gibe, for THE SUN, in those days, never admitted the existence of contemporaries in Baltimore. Its first apparent mention of them since the 60s, when it had denounced the *American* with a ferocity noted in an earlier chapter, was in its issue of February 8, 1904, the day after the fire, when it reported the burning of the *Herald* and *American* buildings. Two years later, in 1906, it went so much further that Baltimore was genuinely astonished. On April 19 of that year the directors had resolved to employ Folger McKinsey (The Bentztown Bard),[1] as exchange editor, and on April 26 he began contributing a daily column of prose and

[1] Born at Elkton, Md., August 29, 1866. In his late teens he ran a weekly newspaper at Ocean Beach, N. J., and was much in the company of Walt Whitman at Camden. After service on various Maryland country papers he joined the Baltimore *News* in 1898 and became its managing editor. In 1906 he went to the Washington *Post,* but remained only a short while. His daily column in THE SUN, mainly in verse, was a great success, and he was often called upon to read his poems to Maryland audiences. He published a book, A Rose of the Old Régime, in 1907. He is the author of Baltimore, Our Baltimore, the official song of the Baltimoreans, set to music by Emma Hemberger. It is played at every concert of the Municipal Band. Mr. McKinsey is still on the staff of THE SUN, and still doing his column. Originally it was headed Maryland Musings, but now it is called Good Morning.

verse to the paper. He was The Sun's first columnist, and the *Evening Herald* offered felicitations on May 17 in an editorial headed "The Sun Hires a Poet," and running as follows:

The Baltimore Sun, which is celebrating its sixty-ninth birthday today, is the Uncle Joe Cannon of the newspaper world. The older it grows the more chipper and vigorous it seems to become. In its middle age it was solemn and perhaps a bit ponderous. Today it is showing daily evidence that its corpuscles are bright red and its eye clear. It is printing a big paper, full of pictures and good humor; its editorial policy is positive and freespoken; it has hired a staff poet. All in all, it's a very healthy and happy oldster.

Baltimore without the *Sunpaper* would cease to be home, sweet home. Who of us hasn't absorbed it, with our matutinal coffee and rolls, for years and years and years? Who of us didn't learn to read by studying its want ads? Who of us hasn't been influenced and led by its arguments and opinions? What politician of Maryland has been able to get along without its aid? In what great public question has it failed to show the way?

Certainly, The Sun in its field is one of the most influential newspapers journalism ever saw. When it was young and rash it gave a helping hand to that dream of a riotous imagination — the electric telegraph. In its old age it dragged a man from the cave of oblivion and, despite the efforts of practically all the rest of the human race, made him a United States Senator. For sixty-nine years it has been in the forefront of the fray.

It would be impossible to estimate the value of such a journal to the community in general. No doubt, when all is said and done, it has exerted more influence for the good in Baltimore than any other agency.

May it live to a hundred! May it live to be a thousand!

Instead of passing over this editorial loftily, The Sun reprinted it in full on its own editorial page on May 19, with the following gloss by O. P. Baldwin:

A word fitly spoken is like apples of gold in pictures of silver, and we may be pardoned for characterizing in that way the above remarks from our sprightly and able afternoon contemporary. Our contemporary calls The Sun the "Uncle Joe Cannon of the newspaper world," probably because, like the Speaker, while old, it is yet lusty and strong, and people like both The Sun and the Speaker. But it is said that the Speaker sets himself up as an arbitrary ruler and Czar without a Douma. In that respect The Sun is wide apart from Mr. Cannon. It never undertakes dictation, and when it advises its readers it does so with modesty and diffidence.

One expression which our contemporary uses causes us some pain. It says "The Sun has hired a staff poet." Poets cannot be hired. Their minds are far above sublunary things. The fragrance of a lily, the modest beauty of the primrose and the buttercup, the field daisy, the gushing fountain under the spreading tree, the song of the birds which he terms the flowers of the air, the twinkling star — it is these things which fill the mind of our poet. And if perchance the weakness of the flesh should call him down to earth for food, it is such airy nothings as pie and mint julep alone that can satisfy the poetry of his soul. Hire a poet! Perish the expression. *Poeta nascitur*, not hired. You might as well talk of hiring a zephyr.

This amiable exchange was something new for The Sun, and thereafter its relations to the other Baltimore papers were measurably more frank and easy than they had been before. The men of The Sun staff, of course, and especially the younger men, were always on good terms with the men of the other papers; they frequented the same saloons after the day's work was done, belonged to the same Journalists Club, and made merry together in other ways. But the paper itself, until after the fire, proceeded on the lofty assumption that there was only one actual newspaper in Baltimore, and that that one was itself. In more than one way, this was close enough to the truth to pass muster. The Sun had what amounted almost to a monopoly on certain kinds of news. It was common for a reporter for another paper, going to a house of mourning for obituary material, to be told that he would find what he wanted in the *Sunpaper* the next morning. Nor was its advantage confined to obituary material. In 1895 J. Edwin Murphy, now managing editor of The Evening Sun, was appointed bicycle editor of the *Evening News*, and one of his jobs was to try to persuade the Baltimore Park Board to rescind an order barring bicycles from Druid Hill Park. One day, after a meeting of the board in which the matter was discussed, he called on Douglas H. Thomas, one of its members and a prominent Baltimore banker, to ask what had been done. Mr. Thomas looked at him in a pitying sort of way and replied: "If you will just read the *Sunpaper* tomorrow morning you will find out."

The first years of the new century were happy years in The Sun office. One of the survivors of those years, describing them in The Evening Sun of April 15, 1935, spoke of "the placid and lordly life of a Sun man under the Abell régime." "There was never on earth," he said, "a more pleasant newspaper office. It was full of charming fellows, and the Abells carried it on as if it were a good club rather than a great industrial plant." A considerable formality prevailed, and nearly everyone above the rank of office boy was mistered, at least by his superiors. Salaries were far from princely, but whenever a reporter did a good job of work he got a substantial bonus in cash, and at Christmas there were gold pieces for the business office boys and turkeys for all hands, from the managing editor and business manager down to the charwomen.

If a member of the staff fell ill, his salary went on as usual, not merely for a few weeks, but for months and years. In fact, it was implicit in every contract for services — they were all verbal — that the party of the second part should remain on the pay roll for life, or at least until and if he committed some grave and unforgivable offense against the honor and dignity of the paper. In 1903 or thereabout there had been a cleaning out of heavy drinkers and one of the victims was a star reporter, but it was rare afterward for any members of the staff to be discharged, and when it happened it was solemnly recorded in the minutes of the corporation. A SUN man was well received everywhere in Baltimore, and, indeed, in all the region south of the Mason & Dixon Line. His paper was notoriously solvent and notoriously honest, and its proprietors had no itch for public office. Some very good journalists were bred in the office in those days.

Down to 1901 the paper had no Sunday edition.[1] There were, at that time, two Sunday newspapers in Baltimore, the *American* and the *Herald*, and both were somewhat brisk and up-and-coming sheets, with illustrations in half-tone, then a novelty in journalism, and primeval attempts at comic supplements in color. But THE SUN, characteristically, disdained all such devices to attract readers: the Sunday issue that began in 1901 was exactly like any other issue, and sold at the same price, 2 cents. No advance announcement of it was made, either to readers of the week-day SUN or to advertisers. Wells Hawks, formerly a *Herald* reporter, was at that time press agent of the Academy of Music, the principal Baltimore theater. Getting wind of the new SUNDAY SUN through the gossip of reporters and printers, he called up the Iron Building on the afternoon of the day before the first issue, and asked if an advertisement of his theater would be accepted. "Yes," he was told, "if you send it down." He sent it down, and so scored a scoop on the other theaters. The explanation of the secrecy which surrounded the first issue, as given to inquirers, was that it was feared that if what was afoot became generally known, the office would be swamped with advertisements! This first issue appeared on October 6,

[1] But on Sunday, July 3, 1881, it had astonished Baltimore by bringing out an extra reporting the shooting of President James A. Garfield by Charles J. Guiteau in Washington the day before. So far as can be discovered, that was the only time THE SUN ever came out on Sunday before 1901.

1901. Simultaneously, THE SUN began using illustrations now and then in its week-day issues — an innovation almost as surprising to Baltimore as the appearance of the *Sunday Sunpaper*. But these illustrations were kept off the first page, which was largely given over to advertising.[1]

THE SUNDAY SUN continued to sell at 2 cents a copy until April 5, 1908, though the price of the other two Sunday papers was 3.[2] It was enlarged a bit from time to time, but remained essentially a daily paper with a few Sunday features. There were no comic strips, no color pages, and no separate magazine section. On June 10, 1909, it began to give a reproduction of some famous but innocuous painting, sometimes in sepia and sometimes in full color, with each issue, for example, Gilbert Stuart's portrait of Washington, Rosa Bonheur's "Horse Fair," and Turner's "Grand Canal of Venice." This was kept up for fifty-three weeks, but without noticeable effect on circulation. The first Sunday editor was O. P. Baldwin, who, as we have seen in Chapter XII, had been a member of the staff of THE SUN

[1] They were so rarely printed before 1904 that in 1902 or thereabout a book of those that had appeared was issued as a sort of marvel. There were about fifty in it, including maps. The whole edition of this book seems to have perished in the fire of 1904.

[2] The subscription price by mail was $1 a year. On April 5, 1908, it was raised to $1.50, and on the same day the price of a single copy, sold on the street or delivered by carrier, was increased to 3 cents. But a week later the old rates were restored, and they continued in force to May 15, 1910, when the price of the Sunday issue was dropped to 1 cent, or 50 cents a year by mail. On January 1, 1911, the price became 3 cents a copy again, or 15 cents a month by mail, or $1.50 a year. On February 4, 1917, there was another lift to 5 cents a copy, or 25 cents a month by mail, or $2.50 a year. On April 4, 1920, the price for a single copy outside Baltimore became 8 cents, or 35 cents a month by rural carrier, or $4 a year by mail, but the city price of 5 cents a copy was maintained. On April 8, 1928, it was raised to 10 cents a copy, where it still remains. But the paper is delivered to city subscribers at 5 cents a copy, and to country subscribers at 45 cents a month. The price by mail is $5.20 a year. In combination with THE SUN and THE EVENING SUN it is delivered to city subscribers by carrier at 25 cents a week.

since 1882. When, in 1906, Oakley P. Haines was forced by illness to retire from active service as managing editor, and Mr. Baldwin was given his duties, it was resolved to go outside The Sun fold for a new Sunday editor with experience in editing larger Sunday papers, and to increase the size and scope of the paper itself. Three entries in the minutes of the board of directors record this radical break with the programme hitherto followed. At a special meeting on July 7, 1906, the following resolution was adopted:

> *Resolved*, That the president is hereby authorized in his discretion to increase the size of The Sunday Sun to any number of pages, up to and including twenty-four.

At another special meeting nine days later there were proceedings described in the minutes as follows:

> The meeting was called for the purpose of selecting a Sunday editor. Walter W. Abell nominated H. L. Mencken, and Charles S. Abell nominated Harold E. West.[1] Mr. Mencken was selected by the votes of Walter W. Abell, J. J. Nelligan and A. S. Abell. Charles S. Abell voted for H. E. West. The president stated that he was not sure Mencken could be secured, but would communicate with him at once.

The third entry, dated July 25, follows:

> The president reported that he had engaged H. L. Mencken as Sunday editor, as authorized by the board meeting of July 16, at $40 a week. Mencken will begin his duties on July 30.

But The Sunday Sun continued to be a relatively unimportant appendage of the week-day Sun, and though it presently put in its first engraving plant and blossomed out in large illustrations, sometimes running to the full width of the page, and even indulged itself now and then in something hard to dis-

---

[1] There is a sketch of Mr. West in Chapter VII.

tinguish from jocosity, it never went to the length of printing comic strips. They never appeared in THE SUN, in fact, until January 1, 1911, when the apparition of its first comic section (it now runs to sixteen pages in color!) brought many an old subscriber to the verge of apoplexy. The Sunday staff, during the last four years of the Abell régime, consisted of the Sunday editor (who also wrote some editorials), and two reporters, one male and one female. The former was J. S. M. Hammond, who was later to write many books, and the latter was Helen Forman Kerchner, now the wife of J. Fred Essary, chief of THE SUN's Washington staff and herself well known as a writer.[1] In those days things were still done on a modest scale, and the allowance for contributed copy and art (which last was rationed out to all the free-lance artists of Baltimore) ran to but $100 a week. The first artist regularly employed by THE SUNDAY SUN was Thomas Barclay, who was put to work on March 9, 1908. On the same day his brother, McKee Barclay, who had been cartoonist of the *Evening News* under Grasty, was engaged in the

[1] THE SUN's first woman reporter was Miss May Garrettson Evans, who joined the staff in 1888. She was one of the first, if not the first woman ever to do general assignments on an American newspaper. A graduate of the Peabody Conservatory of Music in Baltimore, Miss Evans resigned from THE SUN in 1894 to found the Peabody Preparatory Department. She served as its head until 1929, when she retired. She is still living in Baltimore. Her successor was Miss Gertrude B. Knipp, who joined the staff in 1897. Miss Knipp is remembered in THE SUN office for a notable news beat — on the resignation of Dr. Daniel C. Gilman as president of the Johns Hopkins University in 1901. She picked it up by overhearing a conversation on a street-car. She left THE SUN in 1905, and after two years on the Baltimore *American*, became editorial assistant in the Maryland State Board of Health, which post she still holds. In 1901 she was joined on THE SUN by Miss Emily Emerson Lantz, who remained a member of the staff until her death on April 22, 1931. Miss Lantz is remembered chiefly for her notable contributions to THE SUNDAY SUN. A series of her articles, dealing with the counties of Maryland, was published as a book, under the title of The Spirit of Maryland, in 1930.

same capacity by THE SUN. One Monday in the Autumn of 1906 the Sunday editor complained to Walter W. Abell that the Circulation Department was neglecting to send him the Sunday circulation figures, and that in consequence he couldn't make out which way he was headed, or at what speed. This was more than a year before the revolutionary resolution of January 29, 1908, and Mr. Abell replied that it was the invariable and immemorial rule of the paper to refuse to reveal its circulation. That rule, it appeared, applied even to responsible members of its own editorial staff. Indeed, it was the general view in the editorial rooms in those days that prying into such matters was not quite sporting. The first duty of a good SUN man was to assume as a cardinal article of faith that the circulation of the paper touched the extreme limits of the desirable, and that there was not a single literate white person in all Maryland who did not read it.[1]

[1] As we have seen in Chapter I, the price of THE SUN was originally 1 cent a copy. Delivered by carrier, it cost six cents a week, and it was mailed to out-of-town subscribers for 25 cents a month. On December 19, 1864, the price on the street was raised to 2 cents, and the paper was served by carriers at a levy (12½ cents) a week, or 25 cents for two weeks. The mail price was simultaneously raised to 75 cents a month, or three months for $1.50. On May 17, 1902, the street price returned to 1 cent, and there it remained until April 18, 1910, the day THE EVENING SUN was begun. THE EVENING SUN, at the start, sold for a cent on the street, but the price of the morning edition once more became 2 cents. On May 19, 1910, THE SUN dropped to a cent again, and it, THE EVENING SUN and THE SUNDAY SUN were delivered by carrier in combination for 10 cents a week — thirteen papers. This rate was changed on January 29, 1917, to 13 cents a week, or two weeks for 25 cents. It was increased three times during 1918 — to 15 cents a week on January 1, to 20 cents on June 10, and to 25 cents on September 1. The price of a single copy of THE SUN was raised to 2 cents on June 10, 1918, and that of THE EVENING SUN to 2 cents on September 1 of the same year. These single-copy prices and the 13-issues-a-week-for-25-cents carrier delivery rate still prevail. On April 18, 1929, the Rural Carrier Delivery Service price was set at 90 cents a month for THE EVENING SUN and THE SUNDAY SUN in combination.

There was no rural free delivery of mail before 1897, and in consequence the country subscribers to The Sun had to go to their local postoffices to get it. Not until 1903 or thereabout did the new rural routes cover the majority of Maryland counties. Most of the country subscribers of The Sun, before that time, took the Weekly Sun rather than the daily edition. It had been established on April 14, 1838, when The Sun itself was but eleven months old, and for sixty-six years it flourished. It was made up in part of news articles lifted from The Sun, and in part of treatises on chicken-raising, tomato-growing, the care of cows, and other subjects of interest to Maryland farmers. It succumbed to the fire of 1904. The last issue came out on February 6, the day before the fire began. Rural free delivery routes were multiplying, and more and more country people were taking the daily edition. Today there are thousands of them on the list. The Sun Almanac, which was founded by George W. Abell in 1876, "to freshen patriotism and treasure up those stirring incidents of the past which illustrate the history of Maryland," survived until 1915. For those thirty-nine years it hung in the kitchen of almost every Baltimore home. It began as a thin pamphlet of thirty-two pages, but in its last years ran to 256. On the cover appeared the words "To the Subscribers of The Sun With the Compliments of the A. S. Abell Company." It was delivered free of charge at the end of every year. It contained all the usual matter that appears in almanacs, but gave special attention, of course, to Maryland affairs. More than once the courts of the State took judicial notice of its accuracy. Printing it had always been one of the proud prerogatives of the Job Printing Office. When the Job Office was finally got rid of in 1914, the Almanac was abandoned, and the issue for 1915, then in press, became the last.[1]

[1] After 1904 the Almanac accepted advertisements, and by 1910, the last year of the Abell régime, it had forty pages of them. Among the

Another old-timer that disappeared in those years was THE SUN Calendar. Printed on a single sheet of paper the full size of a page of THE SUN, it also had a place in every Maryland kitchen, and likewise in many a Maryland business office. It was delivered to subscribers at Christmas every year. At Christmas, 1912, when the issue for 1913 was omitted, there were so many protests that THE SUN was constrained to apologize on January 18, and to promise to sin no more. The Calendar reappeared for 1914, 1915 and 1916, but after that it vanished forever. Down to the end of the century THE SUN occasionally issued handsome lithographed souvenir prints, usually of large size. One of the first, delivered to all subscribers on New Year's Day, 1860, was a portrait of George Washington, lithographed by the Baltimore firm of A. Hoen & Company, still in prosperous existence. It was labeled " This Print is respectfully dedicated by the Carriers of the Baltimore SUN to their patrons." Another, issued on New Year's Day, 1885, showed sketches, at the top, of various kinds of SUN readers enjoying their favorite paper, and, at the bottom, scenes in the Iron Building. A third, issued July 4, 1887, was a lithographed facsimile of the Declaration of Independence. There was an especially elaborate souvenir at the time the cruiser *Baltimore* visited the city in May, 1890: it consisted, for one part, of a lithographed copy of a song called " The *Baltimore*," written by William H. Carpenter, literary editor of THE SUN, and composed by Adam Itzel, Jr., a Baltimore composer, with a cover in colors showing the cruiser, the

---

advertisers were the Johns Hopkins University, the University of Maryland, Bromo Seltzer (a Baltimore product), the North German Lloyd, all the Chesapeake Bay steamship lines, and nearly all the Baltimore banks. The last issue, for 1915, was the only one for which any charge to subscribers was ever made. They were notified in THE SUN of January 12, 1915, that they would have to pay 10 cents for it. The price to non-subscribers was 25 cents. The circulation of the Almanac in its last year was 95,000.

Iron Building and The Sun's Washington building. In the distance was a rising sun with The Sun's motto, "Light For All," in its rays. With this song went a large sheet bearing portraits in colors of Captain (later Rear-Admiral) Winfield Scott Schley, the cruiser's commander; Rear-Admiral Bancroft Gherardi, who used it as his flagship; Lieutenant-Commander Uriel Sebree, and Chief Engineer B. B. H. Wharton, along with a picture of the cruiser, another of a library that The Sun had presented to it, and others of the Baltimore City Hall, the Iron Building, and The Sun's Washington Building. This souvenir went to every subscriber on May 9, 1890. It survived on the wall of many a Baltimore home, fly-specked but still glorious, until the era of the World War.

The Iron Building had not been the property of the A. S. Abell Company, but belonged to the estate of the Founder. The total insurance on the printing equipment and other effects destroyed by the fire of 1904 was $152,800, of which amount, despite the failure of some of the local insurance companies, all save a few thousand dollars was recovered. This was not enough to restore the lost plant, and it was far from enough to buy land and erect a new building, but the prosperity of the company since its incorporation in 1892 had been sufficient to supply what was now needed. As of March 31, 1905, the temporary plant in the Job Printing House at Calvert and Saratoga streets, along with the building itself, but excluding the machinery of the actual job-printing establishment, was carried on the books at a value of $365,000, and in addition there was a surplus in the treasury of nearly $575,000, including interest-bearing securities worth $330,000. Thus the erection of the new Sun office at Baltimore and Charles streets was accomplished without going into debt, though the total cost of the land, building and equipment was about $600,000. On November 28, 1906, a fortnight after the new building was occupied, the president was authorized by the board of directors to borrow $50,000 to settle the few bills outstanding, but he never actually borrowed more than $25,000, and this was quickly repaid. At the stockholders' meeting on April 19, 1907, he was able to report that the whole cost of the building and land had been discharged, saving only a matter of $11,000 that was in dispute. At this same meeting it was resolved to charge off $53,000 from the cost of the land, bringing it down to $150,000, and $100,000 from the cost of the building and equipment, bringing it to $300,000. The contract price for the building alone had been $289,206. It was built by Edward Brady & Sons.

It was ready early in November, 1906, and the issue of THE SUN for November 16 was the last printed in the Job Printing Office. The moment it went to press the onerous business of moving to Baltimore and Charles streets was begun, and so competently was it effected by all departments that the issue of November 17 came out exactly on time. The new home of the paper was in the very heart of Baltimore. It stood at the southwest corner of the two streets which divide the city into four quarters, and at which all street numbers begin. Opposite, directly northward, was the new headquarters building of the Baltimore & Ohio Railroad, and across Charles street to the eastward the banking house of the Savings Bank of Baltimore was soon to rise. Diagonally across the intersection, at the northeast corner, was the Hub department store, since extended to run a full block to Fayette street.

The new building was built on land purchased in part from the Edwin F. Abell estate and in part from other owners. It ran 56¾ feet along Baltimore street, westward from Charles, and 202 feet southward on Charles street to German (now Redwood) street. "Upon this site," said a report of the officers to the stockholders, April 19, 1905, "it is proposed to erect a building that will for all time meet the requirements of the company." It was of four stories, in the French Renaissance style, with high ceilings within, and a row of thirty-foot stone columns fronting the second and third stories without. The architects were Baldwin & Pennington, an old Baltimore firm, and the general effect was massive if not exactly lovely. It was planned at the start to erect " a globe or set-piece " over the Baltimore street front, but this adornment seems to have been discreetly abandoned, for there is nothing there now save an illuminated clock, with another face on the Charles street side.[1] The counting-room, opening on Baltimore street, was a vast chamber, twenty-two feet in height, with a semicircular marble counter and a grand stairway leading to the editorial rooms on the second floor. The marble bill alone ran to $4,800. The composing room was on the third floor, and in it were twenty-four linotypes. The fourth floor, at the start, was vacant, but in a little while the Job Office moved in from the building at Calvert and Saratoga streets that had been used as temporary quarters for the paper after the fire of 1904. In the cellar were four quadruple presses, each capable, under ideal conditions, of producing 24,000 sixteen-page papers an hour.

On November 17 The Sun devoted two whole pages to its new building, which was described in the main headline as " a model Twentieth Century home " for a great newspaper. Unfortunately, it turned out to be something less than a model when the staff settled down. There was no adequate ventilating system, and some one had forgotten to put in a supply of hot water for the ablutions of the editorial staff, though the printers and pressmen had plenty. There was also no passenger elevator. When the Summer of 1908 came on, and the white marble building of the Savings Bank of Baltimore got under way across the street, the afternoon sun, reflected from it, filled the editorial

[1] This clock, according to the original plans, was to have struck the hours, halves and quarters. But it never got its chimes, and remains mute.

rooms with a blinding glare and an almost unbearable heat, and it was discovered that the sixteen massive columns along the east façade were in the way of remedial awnings. This glare and heat pretty well cooked the city editor, telegraph editor, State editor, Sunday editor and other such functionaries, all of whom had offices along the east wall. The reporters, who occupied the inner space, were somewhat more comfortable, but they suffered from bad lighting.

In later years the building had to be extensively revised and enlarged. There is now a large annex to the westward, and two passenger elevators have been put in. The Job Office was disposed of in 1914, and The Sun now has no interest in it, though it continues in business under other management and used the old name until June, 1936, when it was incorporated as The Sun Printing Company. At the start the paper had its own power plant in the cellar, but this was long ago cleared out to make room for more and larger presses, now (1937) consisting of five seven-deck Hoes, each capable of printing papers of as many as fifty-six pages. The battery of linotypes in the composing room has increased to thirty-seven, and it is aided by seven monotype keyboards and twelve monotype casters. Both composing room and pressroom extend into the annex, which was taken over in 1920. The opening of the new building brought throngs of visitors to the office, headed by the Governor of Maryland and the Mayor of Baltimore. Toward the end of the year the following engraved invitation was sent to an almost endless list of Marylanders:

The Publisher of
The Sun
Invites You To An Inspection
Of The
New Building
On Thursday, January Seventeenth, 1907,

When It Will Be Formally Opened
To the Public, Or On Any Day Thereafter At Your Convenience.

SUN Square [1]
Baltimore.

The reception on January 17 was graced by the presence of James Cardinal Gibbons, the much venerated Roman Catholic Archbishop of Baltimore, whose biographer, Allen Sinclair Will, was city editor of THE SUN.[2] His Eminence, then seventy-three years old, walked down Charles street in a snowstorm to felicitate the Abells, who were of his faith. Glancing at the snow outside, and then at the cheer within, he said: " Now is the winter of our discontent made glorious summer by this SUN of Abell." A later visitor was Mark Twain, who came on May 11, 1907. Hundreds of school children from Baltimore and the nearby counties were brought in by their teachers, and permanent arrangements had to be made to conduct them through the building. This duty finally fell upon Henry Edward Warner, then a member of the editorial staff, and he still has it. For years a list of each day's visitors was printed in THE SUN of the next morning under the standing heading of " THE SUN's Friends Call." When they come in organized groups their names are still printed.

---

[1] The crossing of Charles and Baltimore streets, the topographical center of the city, was named SUN Square by an ordinance of the City Council, signed by Mayor E. Clay Timanus, December 12, 1906.

[2] Mr. Will was a Protestant. He was born at Antioch, Va., July 28, 1868, and after several years as a teacher became a reporter on the Baltimore *Herald* in 1888. In 1889 he joined THE SUN, becoming city editor on February 23, 1905, in succession to H. A. Hallett, the city editor of the great fire period, who had resigned on January 25. In 1912 he became associate editor of the Baltimore *News,* in 1914 news editor of the Philadelphia *Public Ledger,* and in 1917 associate editor of the New York *Times*. In 1920 he began to teach journalism at Columbia University, and in 1925 he became head of the department of journalism at Rutgers, where he remained until his death on March 10, 1934. His life of Cardinal Gibbons, first published with the Cardinal's authority in 1911, was reissued in two volumes in 1922, after His Eminence's death.

Of the other Baltimore papers burned out in the great fire, only the *American* rebuilt on its old site. This was at the southwest corner of Baltimore and South streets, opposite the site of the destroyed Iron Building. The new *American* Building was of fourteen stories, and thus overtopped the new SUN Building, but only a small part of it was occupied by the *American*, whereas THE SUN had no tenants, and was in fact in much roomier quarters. The *Herald*, after two years and a half in an old car barn in South Charles street, suspended publication and its Associated Press membership was bought by the other Baltimore papers, including THE SUN.[1] The *News* set its new building at Calvert and Fayette streets, overlooking the Courthouse, the Postoffice and the historic Battle Monument, which is to Baltimore what the Roland before the Rathaus is to Bremen — an emblem of civic pride and glory. The *News* Building was smaller than the new *American* Building, but taller than THE SUN Building. It was torn down and replaced by the present Munsey Building when Frank A. Munsey bought the *News* in 1908. But during the three years after the fire there was yet no thought of Munsey. The *News* was flourishing and if Grasty had been as shrewd a business man as he was bold an editor it might have made very serious inroads on THE SUN's advertising revenue. As it was, he devoted his whole energies to the editorial affairs of his paper, leaving advertising to his business manager, Louis M. Duvall.[2] In the Summer of 1907 he laid plans for what was destined to be the *News's* last great battle. There was an election

[1] THE SUN's share of the purchase price was $3,125, of which $2,500 was paid in cash and $625 in advertising. Who used this advertising does not appear in the record.

[2] Mr. Duvall survived into the Munsey régime, retiring in 1909 to practice law. He had been business manager of the *News* since 1898. After a year at the bar he became secretary to the Public Service Commission of Maryland. During the Grasty régime on THE SUN he was a member of the board of directors of the A. S. Abell Company from February 26, 1912, to his death on December 24 of the same year. He was born in Baltimore in 1855.

for Governor of Maryland coming on in November, and The Sun let it be known that it could not support Henry Williams,[1] the choice of what was left of the old Gorman-Rasin Democratic organization. The organization thereupon turned to Austin L. Crothers, a county judge at Elkton, since become famous as Maryland's Gretna Green. Not much about him was known in Baltimore, but The Sun decided to accept him. Grasty, disliking his political associations and having heard rumors derogatory to his private character, put the *News* behind his Republican opponent, George R. Gaither, a Baltimore lawyer who had been prominent in the reform movement of the 90s, and was, besides, the *News's* counsel and Grasty's personal friend. Thus The Sun and the *News*, which had fought together in 1895, were now arrayed on the two sides of the political fence.

Early in August, taking time by the forelock, Grasty sent a couple of his best reporters [2] to Elkton to look into Crothers's record. They came back with a long series of charges against him, mainly falling under four headings: (a) that he had demanded money for his influence in getting liquor licenses for dubious applicants, (b) that he had used his influence with the county grand jury to squelch prosecutions for violations of the liquor laws, (c) that he had advocated at the State Capitol a local water bill sponsored by the Pennsylvania Railroad and inimical to the interest of the county, and (d) that he had often

[1] There was no objection to Mr. Williams in himself. He was, in fact, a man of the utmost rectitude. But he had allowed the Gorman-Rasin organization to run him for Mayor of Baltimore in 1895 and again in 1897, and The Sun had opposed him so vigorously that it was feared in the office that if he were supported now, the *News* would do execution upon him, and embarrass The Sun, by reprinting some of The Sun's editorials from the two earlier campaigns. Mr. Williams was seventy-two years old in 1912. He died on March 20, 1916.

[2] One of them was John Haslup Adams, who was later to follow Grasty to The Sun and become its editor. He is dealt with at length in Chapter XVI. The other was Raleigh C. Smith, who also became a Sun man later on. Both are now dead.

bought votes in county elections. These charges, dressed in somewhat inflammatory language, were put into type against the time when the campaign should open in earnest, and they could be launched with most effect. Indeed, it appears likely that it was Grasty's plan to hold them until the day before election day, when it would be too late for THE SUN or any of Crothers's other supporters to meet them with anything save vague and futile denials. But proof-sheets of the article, which ran to five columns, were naturally open to all the principal members of the staff of the *News*, and there followed a treason which gave Grasty the shock of his life (at least up to that time), and remains with few parallels in American newspaper history. One of his own men, procuring a set of the proof-sheets, took them to Daniel J. Loden and Max Ways, two Democratic politicians,[1] and offered them for sale at $50. Loden and Ways bought them at once, went through them with great surprise and indignation, and then called in Frank R. Kent, at that time THE SUN's political reporter and later to be its managing editor.[2] Kent took

[1] Mr. Ways had been a newspaper man, and a good one. He had been city editor of the *Herald* at the turn of the century, and president of the Journalists Club in 1890. He and Loden are now both dead.

[2] Mr. Kent was born in Baltimore May 1, 1877. He is a nephew of the late Francis Asbury Richardson, for many years THE SUN's Washington correspondent, whose career was rehearsed in Chapter XII. Mr. Kent's first newspaper experience was gained on the Columbus, Ga. *Enquirer-Sun*. On January 15, 1900, he joined THE SUN, and save for a brief interval when he was secretary and treasurer of the Maryland Agricultural College (now the University of Maryland), he has been a member of its staff ever since. Beginning as a police reporter, he soon became its City Hall reporter, and then began to devote himself to political writing. From 1902 onward he covered the biennial sessions of the Maryland Legislature. He became THE SUN's Washington correspondent in 1910, and a year later was made managing editor of both THE SUN and THE EVENING SUN, which post he held until 1921. In 1921 he became THE SUN's first London correspondent, and at the same time was elected vice-president of the A. S. Abell Company. On his return to Baltimore he began writing a daily article on politics for the

the proofs to The Sun office, and the next day, accompanied by Robert B. Ennis, another member of the staff,[1] went to Elkton to see Crothers and hear his defense. The learned judge delicately evaded the charge that he had bought votes, but offered to provide disproofs of the other accusations. Kent and Ennis spent three days investigating those disproofs, and came to the conclusion that they were sound. They found, indeed, that most of the charges were based upon hearsay, and that some of the leading witnesses to them were far from reliable. They accordingly prepared an elaborate refutation, with affidavits and other documentary evidence, and it was put into type in The Sun office to await Grasty's attack. He was on holiday in the Adirondacks at the time, but he seems to have got wind that there was something afoot, for he presently came back and printed the Adams-Smith story — five columns long. This was on August 29. In those days the *News* printed but one edition a day, coming out at 4 P.M., and the only afternoon train from Baltimore for Elkton left at 5. There was thus no time for The Sun to get men to the judge's stronghold to investigate the charges in time for next morning's paper, but next day its counterblast appeared nevertheless — four columns of it. Each charge that the *News* had made (save the embarrassing charge that the judge had bought votes) was met categorically and in detail, and so

first page of The Sun. It was printed, for a while, under news headings, but on February 4, 1923, the standing heading of The Great Game of Politics was adopted. Mr. Kent's books, all dealing with politics, include: The Story of Maryland Politics, 1911; The Great Game of Politics, 1923; A History of the Democratic Party, 1925, and Political Behavior, 1928. His son, Frank R. Kent Jr., is also a member of The Sun staff.

[1] Mr. Ennis, some years later, transferred to the business office of The Sun, but his stay there was relatively short, and eventually he forsook journalism altogether for politics. He came to considerable prominence in the Democratic organization, and was spoken of as its coming boss when all the old bosses died. But he gradually abated his political activities, and devoted himself mainly to business. He is still living in Baltimore.

the effect that they had produced was destroyed, and Grasty found himself on the defensive, and making very heavy weather of it. THE SUN printed no editorial denunciation of him on August 30: its principal editorials on that day were headed "What the Reclamation of Swamp Lands Would Mean to Maryland," "The Big Stick and the Mob Spirit," "Our Stock of Gold" and "Does New York Need More Police?" But the Kent news story was, in substance and effect, a violent editorial, as its headlines and first paragraph reveal:

CAMPAIGN CHARGES ARE
CALLED A BOOMERANG

Amazement at Attack on Judge Crothers'
Private and Public Record
Discredited Stories are Told Anew
Facts in the Case, as Obtained by Impartial
Investigators, Show the Situation in
a Far Different Light From That
Shed by Partisan Distortion

Indignation and amazement were expressed yesterday by Democrats and many Republicans at the publication by the Baltimore *News*, which is fighting the Democratic ticket in this campaign, of charges against the private character as well as the public record of Judge Austin L. Crothers, nominee for Governor. These charges are nearly all anonymous, the only authorities quoted in direct evidence being two Negroes.

And so on, and so on. The Negro bugaboo has now vanished from Maryland politics, largely because of THE SUN's subsequent efforts to put it down, but in 1907 even THE SUN was not above making discreet use of it. From time to time during the campaign Grasty made fresh attacks upon Judge Crothers, but an inclination to discredit them had been set up in the public mind by Kent's flaming rebuttal of August 30, and so they had little effect. On the afternoon before election day Grasty attempted a last onslaught, but at breakfast next morning voters preparing to go to the polls found a six-column recapitulation of the defense in THE SUN under these headlines in its largest type:

A REFUTATION

The Charges Against Judge Crothers
Disproved in Detail
Are Baseless Slanders
He Did Not Use Influence on the
Liquor License Board

THE SUN, now settled down in its new building, made plans to give out the returns on election night in a manner that, for it, was unprecedented. A huge white screen was hung upon the façade of the Savings Bank of Baltimore across Charles street, a powerful stereopticon was hired, a dozen business office men were recruited to add up figures, and as a final touch some rolls of movie film were procured. This show drew an immense crowd — a much larger crowd, by all accounts, than the one attracted by Grasty's show in Monument Square. Judge Crothers, who was a bachelor of forty-seven and very countrified in his ways, was ill on election day and sought his celibate couch in Elkton before any returns had come in. He snored peacefully until his usual rising hour of 5 A.M., when he got up and read in THE SUN that he had been elected by 10,000 plurality. It should be added that, despite the matter of those boughten votes, he made the best Governor Maryland was to have until the advent of Albert Cabell Ritchie. He established the State road system and the Public Service Commission, reorganized the State's finances, and got through four years in office without the slightest scandal.

Two days after the election THE SUN paid a graceful tribute to his unsuccessful opponent, Gaither. "All through the campaign," it said, "we have never failed to admit his high qualities as a gentleman, a man of honor, and a public-spirited and good citizen." But it had nothing in kindness to say of Mr. Grasty, whose furious onslaught upon Crothers had lost the *News* many supporters, including Roger W. Cull, the chief legal torpedo of the Baltimore Reform League's fight against Gorman and Rasin in 1895. On October 24 THE SUN had printed a long statement by Mr. Cull in which the *News* was mentioned often, and always in blistering terms. But what really dismayed Mr. Grasty was the treason of that member of his staff who had sold his so carefully prepared blast to Loden and Ways. Five years later he told Mr. Kent that this was the consideration that chiefly induced him to sell the *News* to Frank A. Munsey in 1908.

CHAPTER XV

THE ENTRANCE OF CHARLES H. GRASTY

CHARLES HENRY GRASTY was the son of a Presbyterian minister, the Rev. John Marshall Grasty, and was born at Fincastle, Va., on March 3, 1863. When he was a small boy his father moved to Missouri. At 16 he was teaching Latin in the high school at Mexico, a county town of a few thousand people, a hundred miles northwest of St. Louis. His ambition, in those days, was to study law at the University of Missouri, but one Summer day in 1880, Col. J. E. Hutton, proprietor of the Mexico *Intelligencer*, offered him a job as reporter on that paper at $6 a week, and thereafter he thought no more of the law.

In 1882 he was offered a raise of a dollar by William R. Nelson, who had established the Kansas City *Star* six years before, and at once joined the staff of that paper, which remained his model of an independent journal ever afterward, as Mr. Nelson remained his *beau ideal* of a militant and incorruptible editor. After eighteen months on the *Star* he was its managing editor — probably the youngest in the United States. He remained in Kansas City until June, 1890, when he came to Baltimore to become general manager of the *Manufacturers' Record*, a weekly business journal, and to aid E. H. Bouton, also of Kansas City, in interesting certain English investors, through their American representatives, in Roland Park, the first of

Baltimore's more elaborate suburbs. But he could not keep out of daily journalism long, and when, late in 1891, a chance offered to buy the Baltimore *Evening News*, then a struggling six-page sheet owned by James R. Brewer,[1] he made an immediate search for backers who would let him run it according to the principles he had picked up from Mr. Nelson. He found them in Julian LeRoy White, Douglas H. Gordon, Thomas K. Worthington and Gen. Lawrason Riggs, four Baltimoreans of means who fretted under the corruption which then marked the city government of Baltimore, and were eager to see it put down. They gave him brave support during the bitter political battles of the 90s, and all save Mr. Worthington, who had died, were directors of the *Evening News* Publishing Company at the time of the sale of the paper to Frank A. Munsey.[2]

That sale was effected toward the end of February, 1908, and Mr. Grasty's valedictory was published on February 27, under the heading of "The *News* to Pass Into New Ownership." In it he described the paper as "not the least among a group of independent, right-thinking and right-doing newspapers which in the past twenty-five years have put life and hope into the municipal and State politics of America." The next day, under the heading of "16 Years of Square Dealing," there was printed a summary of the *News*' achievements since 1892, somewhat expansive in tone, and perhaps a shade over-optimistic. There was no mention of THE SUN's important share in the political revolution of 1895, but much was made of the *News*' success in putting down gambling in Baltimore in 1893, when it accused some of the principal Democratic politicians of Baltimore of being interested in the policy racket, and they had Mr. Grasty

[1] It had been founded November 4, 1872.

[2] In June, 1899, General Riggs contracted to sell his share of the stock to Mr. Grasty, and the transaction was completed in April, 1903. But General Riggs continued to hold bonds and other obligations of the paper, and remained as a director.

and several of his reporters indicted for criminal libel by a complaisant grand jury. The petit jury returned a verdict of not guilty, and policy went under cover, but it was still prospering in that imperfect concealment, despite the *News'* gloating, in 1908. Indeed, even so late as 1936, under the new name of numbers, it had to be tackled again, and provided months of work for the Baltimore criminal courts.

The price Mr. Munsey paid for the *News* was $1,500,000. Mr. Grasty cleared out for Europe the day after the sale was consummated. He returned in six weeks, and on April 20, 1908, it was announced that he had been made general manager of all the Munsey newspapers, with headquarters in New York. But he and Munsey were temperamentally so dissimilar that it was impossible for them to get on together, and on May 24 he resigned. After a spell of unaccustomed and uncomfortable idleness, he began looking about for a chance to get back to work, and toward the end of 1908 he found it in St. Paul, Minn. There was then, as now, but one morning paper in that city, the *Pioneer Press*, but in the evening field there were three — the *Dispatch*, the *News*, and an afternoon edition of the *Pioneer Press*. Mr. Grasty bought a half interest in the *Dispatch* from George Thompson, who controlled it, and moved to St. Paul to begin operations. For a while he seems to have toyed with the notion of starting a Sunday morning edition of the *Dispatch*, but he presently abandoned that plan. "Personally," he said to an Associated Press reporter on December 31, 1908, "I am not a very strong believer in the Sunday newspaper. I think it has a vogue beyond its merits, and that the impossible Sunday edition, with its multiplicity of pages and its display of stunts and freak specialties, will either disappear or give place to a saner journalism." On January 1, 1909, he reduced the street price of the *Dispatch* from two cents to one, and began delivering it to local subscribers at five cents a week. A little later he bought the *Pioneer Press,* combined its evening edition with the *Dispatch,* and so dominated both the morning and the evening fields in the city. With the *Pioneer Press* he also acquired a Sunday edition, despite his doubts about Sunday papers.

He had a whale of a time during his first six months in St. Paul. "His individuality," said a writer in the *Advertiser's Magazine* for September, 1909, "is the dominating influence in the greatest change in newspaper policy ever known by the Northwest." He made both the *Dispatch* and the *Pioneer Press* genuinely independent, opened their columns to all shades of opinion, and took a strong line with meddling stockholders and advertisers. But St. Paul did not take as kindly to these innovations as he had hoped, and toward the end of 1909, intolerably homesick for the freer air of Baltimore, he sold out to Mr. Thompson. His eye, it appears, was on THE SUN. He must have known that there were differences among the Abells, and he certainly knew that Walter W. Abell had retired as president of the A. S. Abell Company in April, 1909. These differences had been accumulating since the death of Edwin F. Abell in 1904. He had been the surviving trustee of the estate of his brother, Walter R. Abell, and was eventually succeeded, in respect to its shares in THE SUN, by the Safe Deposit & Trust Company of Baltimore. This gave the company the balance of power between the two sons of Edwin F. Abell (Walter W. and Arunah S. 2d) and the son of George W. Abell (Charles S.). It was represented, as we have seen in Chapter XIII, by John J. Nelligan.

During the years from 1904 to 1909 Mr. Nelligan supported Walter W. Abell in the presidency, with Charles S. Abell usually dissenting. There were split votes in the board on all sorts of subjects — the appointment of a city editor, the dispatch of a reporter on a news mission, the increase of a minor functionary's salary, the attitude of the paper toward a new city loan,

CHARLES HENRY GRASTY (1863–1924)

PHOTOGRAPH BY A. AUBREY BODINE

THE SUN BUILDING TODAY

and so on. When, on April 19, 1909, Walter W. Abell announced that he would decline reëlection by the stockholders as a director and by the directors as president, Charles S. Abell was elected vice-president, the presidency remaining vacant, and under the by-laws he began to function as general manager, with Arunah S. 2d as treasurer and Mr. Nelligan as secretary. Charles S. Abell managed the property until January 26, 1910.[1] During the nine months of his administration THE SUN was very prosperous. There were increases in circulation and advertising revenue, and the reorganization and improvement of the paper, in progress since 1904, was carried several steps further. In June, 1909, Walter W. Abell began a leisurely trip around the world. He was in the Eastern Mediterranean when Mr. Grasty returned to Baltimore and paid a fateful visit to Mr. Nelligan's office. Mr. Grasty stated his business briefly. It was to make an offer for control of THE SUN.

---

[1] He was born on June 25, 1876. He entered THE SUN office in 1894 and remained there continuously until 1910. He left when Mr. Grasty took control of the *Sunpapers,* but returned soon afterward at Mr. Grasty's request, and remained a director until October 25, 1911. He then went to Norfolk, Va., and bought the *Landmark* there. At that time, the Norfolk newspapers had no Monday editions. Mr. Abell decided to bring out a Monday *Landmark,* and managed to do so without the rival paper, the *Virginian-Pilot,* getting wind of his plans. A year or so later the two papers were consolidated as the *Virginian-Pilot and Landmark,* with Mr. Abell retaining a large interest in them. He had had long experience in the business office and editorial rooms of the *Sunpapers,* but he knew little about circulation, so he decided to find out something about it on a metropolitan paper. He chose the Philadelphia *Public Ledger,* mainly on the sentimental ground that his grandfather, the first A. S. Abell, had been one of its founders. An interlude in the railroad business followed, but after the World War he returned to the *Virginian-Pilot and Landmark* in the character, as he has said, "of an officer without portfolio." He was later, for a short while, business manager of the Washington *Post.* On his retirement he made a trip around the world, and is now living in Chevy Chase, Md. He has substantial interests in both the *Sunpapers* and the Norfolk paper.

He hadn't money enough to carry out this transaction on his own, but his reputation in Baltimore was such that he had had no difficulty in finding backers. As was the case when he bought the *Evening News* in 1891, he sought the aid of well-to-do Baltimoreans who were notably men of public spirit, and known to be without political entanglements. His associates, he informed Mr. Nelligan, were H. Crawford Black, R. Brent Keyser, Robert Garrett and John Campbell White; and of them we shall hear more anon. Edwin Warfield, who had been Governor of Maryland at the time of the great fire in Baltimore, also offered to subscribe, but Mr. Grasty, though the two were on friendly terms, declined to admit him, in fear that his political interests might compromise The Sun. Mr. Nelligan, on reflection, concluded that his duty to the heirs of Walter R. Abell required him to recommend the acceptance of Mr. Grasty's offer. He was moved by two considerations. The first was that the differences between the Abells, though they had not so far done any harm to the paper, might at any time become serious enough to incommode its operations. The second was that he was convinced that Mr. Grasty was determined to return to Baltimore, and concerned lest a refusal of the offer he had just made might induce him to buy back the *News* from Munsey, or buy the *World* or the *Star* (started as an afternoon edition of the *American* in 1908), or set up an entirely new paper, possibly with a morning edition. So Mr. Nelligan decided, on his own part as agent of the Walter R. Abell estate, that he should accept, and cabled to Walter W. Abell, who was then in Egypt,[1] advising his acquiescence as one of the trustees of the estate of Edwin F. Abell. Mr. Abell was extremely loath to agree, but Mr. Nelligan

[1] He returned from his tour of the world on June 10, 1910, five months after Mr. Grasty took control of The Sun. On April 18, 1910, Governor Crothers of Maryland appointed him one of the members of the State's first Public Service Commission. A place on the commission was also offered to Judge James A. Pearce, a member of the Maryland

was so insistent and even urgent, and presented the possible consequences of non-acceptance in so vigorous a manner, that Mr. Abell's family gave their reluctant consent, and he assented after being advised of their action. The transaction was given formal approval at a meeting of the board of directors on January 28, 1910. At the same meeting Charles S. Abell resigned as vice-president in charge of the paper, and also as a director. On January 28 the following announcement was printed at the top of the second column of the last page of The Sun:

Mr. Grasty Comes to Sun
Joins Present Owners and Becomes President
of A. S. Abell Company

Judge Niles in the Circuit Court yesterday ratified the sale to Mr. Charles H. Grasty of a portion of the interest in The Sun held by the Walter R. Abell estate.

The action of the court completes a transaction by which Mr. Grasty becomes president of the A. S. Abell Company, publishers of The Sun, and the executive head of the paper. All of the present owners retain large interests. No changes are in contemplation.

There was no mention of the matter on the editorial page. Mr. Grasty took charge of the paper at once, but nearly two months were consumed in working out the transfer of control, and it was not until March 24 that the directors met

to consider, and if deemed advisable, determine upon the sale or exchange of all the property and assets of every kind of this company, as an entirety, in consideration for bonds, preferred stock and common stock of the purchasing company and cash, or for a consideration in any one or more of said forms, or for some other considerations.

Court of Appeals, and one of the first members was James M. Ambler, afterward a judge. There was thus no political significance in Mr. Abell's appointment. But on May 18, when he first heard of it, he declined, feeling that men interested in The Sun should refuse all public office.

In order to free the hands of the Abells and Mr. Nelligan, Mr. Grasty resigned as president of the company and also as a director, and Charles S. Abell was reëlected to the board and to his old post of vice-president. Mr. Nelligan then presented "a draft of the contract between the company [*i.e.*, the old A. S. Abell Company of Baltimore City] and The A. S. Abell Company [the name chosen for the new company] for the sale and exchange of all the property of this company," and on motion of Mr. Nelligan, seconded by Arunah S. Abell 2d, it was unanimously resolved,

That this company sell and exchange all of its property in its entirety to The A. S. Abell Company, on the terms and conditions set forth in an agreement submitted to this board, and that said agreement be approved and spread upon the minutes of the meeting as a part of this vote.

This agreement of sale was at once ratified by the stockholders in special meeting. The capital structure of the new company was as follows:

3,000 shares of Class A common stock of a par value of $100	$ 300,000
2,000 shares of Class B common stock of the same par value	200,000
1,000 shares of Class C common stock of the same par value	100,000
6,000 shares of 5% cumulative preferred stock of the same par value	600,000
$1,000,000 of first mortgage 5% bonds, due in 1965[1]	1,000,000
	$2,200,000

Under the agreement of sale all the bonds, all the preferred stock of the new company, all the Class A common stock, 1,980 of the 2,000 shares of Class B common stock, all the Class C

[1] It was provided that $20,000 of these bonds should be redeemed annually, beginning January 1, 1915.

common stock and $2,000 in cash were turned over to the old company in payment for "all its property and assets of every and any kind, and wherever situate," including especially "THE SUN newspaper of Baltimore, THE WEEKLY SUN [1] and THE SUN Job Printing Office; the good-will, trade-marks, copyrights or franchises, membership in the Associated Press or in any other press association, subscription lists and carrier lists used in connection with the publication of said newspapers or in the conduct of said printing office; real estate, buildings, printing presses, machinery, printing material, accounts receivable, shares of stock or other securities, and money." Thus the old company came into possession of all the securities of the new company save twenty shares of its Class B common stock. But by supplemental agreements the old company immediately sold back to Mr. Grasty, acting for himself and his associates, most of the preferred stock, and substantial blocks of the Class B and Class C common stock, and at the same time the remainder of the preferred stock and a part of the Class B common stock were sold to Charles S. Abell. The cash thus received and the securities remaining in the treasury of the old company were divided in accordance with the share holdings in the old company. At the conclusion of the stockholders' meeting of March 24 the following resolution was adopted:

> That the business of the company cease, that its officers and directors cease to discharge their duties, except in so far as may be necessary to wind up the company's affairs, finish unfinished business, and carry out existing contracts.

Thus passed the A. S. Abell Company of Baltimore City, after a corporate existence of twenty-eight years. THE SUN itself was then seventy-three years old.

[1] THE WEEKLY SUN, as we have seen, suspended publication in 1904, but the old company retained the right to resume it at any time, and it was this right that was conveyed. It has never been exercised by the new company.

CHAPTER XVI

THE BIRTH OF THE EVENING SUN

The A. S. Abell Company, the new company, was incorporated on March 24, 1910. To provide the necessary working capital it sold 5,000 shares of its preferred stock in varying amounts, and for $500,000 cash, to H. Crawford Black, Robert Garrett, John Campbell White, and Mr. Grasty himself, acting partly on his own account and partly for R. Brent Keyser. It was not long, however, before more money was needed, and this was raised by authorizing an additional issue of 4,000 shares of Class B common stock, making the total 10,000 shares, worth $1,000,000 at par. Only existing stockholders could subscribe for the new stock. Half of it was taken up at once by Messrs. Black, Garrett, White and Grasty (acting for himself and for Mr. Keyser), and the remaining half was taken up by the same gentlemen on January 25, 1911.

The three different classes of common stock carried widely differing voting rights. The Class A stock, all of it held by the Abells, had one vote a share without any qualification, but the Class B stock, which was held, save for small blocks in the hands of Messrs. Grasty and Charles S. Abell, by Messrs. Black, Garrett, White and Keyser, was severely restricted. So long as there was any Class C stock outstanding, this Class B stock could not vote (*a*) for the amendment or repeal of any by-law providing for the election of the president of the company by the stockholders, (*b*) for the election of the president, or (*c*) for his removal. Class C stock, on the contrary, could vote upon all these questions, and moreover, it was provided that so long as its vote was cast as a whole that vote should count for as much as the combined votes of the Class A and Class B stocks, though there were only 1,000 shares of it outstanding, whereas there were 3,000 shares of Class A and 6,000 of Class B. Inasmuch as Mr. Grasty held all the Class C stock, these somewhat complicated conditions gave him complete control of the company. He could not be ousted as its president without his own consent, nor could any changes be made in the by-laws defining his duties and prerogatives. Those prerogatives were thus set forth in Article III, Section 4 of the by-laws:

> The president shall have full managerial and editorial control of the company. He shall have the right to determine the policy of the company's papers or publications on all matters, to employ and discharge editors, reporters and employés, to determine the contents of the publications, and to enter into any contracts not imposing an obligation in excess of $100,000 for the purchase of presses, machinery, equipment and paper. The board of directors shall have no power to direct, control or reverse any action of the president in the exercise of the powers or discharge of the duties conferred by this section.

Nor was this all. Mr. Grasty had not only made sure that his new associates, in case the inclination should ever seize them, would have no power to interfere with his conduct of THE SUN; he also withheld from them that ordinary familiarity with its affairs which might have been supposed to go with their character as major stockholders in the corporation and financial backers of the whole enterprise. The first directors, elected at his instance, were not chosen from among them; instead, he selected Arunah S. Abell 2d, Charles S. Abell and himself. He was willing to take in the Abells, for they had been trained on the paper and were professional newspaper men, but he kept the others at arm's length, so that even his most important plans were concealed from them. This reluctance to have any unnecessary traffic with the non-professional stockholders in the paper, like his high way with advertisers, was one of the sources of his strength as an editor, but in the long run, as we shall see, both were to bring him into difficulties, and the former was to wreck his career on THE SUN.

How far he was determined to go was revealed almost at once, when he decided without consulting his associates, and even without informing them, to set up an afternoon edition. In the early days of April, 1910, as a first step to that end, he bought the Baltimore *World* for $63,000, and on April 6 THE SUN announced that the new evening paper would appear on April 18, but it was not until April 9 that the purchase of the *World* was laid before the directors and their sanction asked for, and not until April 27 that the stockholders were called in special meeting to be notified officially. They got their first news of THE EVENING SUN when its coming was announced in THE SUN of April 6. They appear to have been somewhat offended by the manner in which the project was carried out, for at the stockholders' meeting of April 27 not enough of them showed up, either in person or by proxy, to make a quorum, and the meeting had to be adjourned to the next day, and then to the next, and then to the next, and finally to May 2. On the latter date Messrs. Grasty, Charles S. Abell and Arunah S. Abell 2d appeared in person, but Messrs. Black, Garrett, White and Keyser were represented only by proxy, and so was the Walter R. Abell estate. The discussion, if there was any, was not recorded. The minute-book of the stockholders simply says that the agreement to buy the *World* was ratified.

The ostensible reason for its purchase was that The Evening Sun would need its United Press franchise, but that was hardly true, for United Press franchises were not exclusive, and could be had by any new paper for the asking. The real reason was that Mr. Grasty had heard a report that William R. Hearst was thinking of buying the *World*. His entry into the Baltimore field at that time would have greatly incommoded the nascent Evening Sun. The *World*, which was in receivership, was sold at a sort of auction, in which a mysterious man from New York, in cahoots with its owners, appeared in the false guise of a Hearst agent. The other bidders were Mr. Grasty and General Felix Agnus, owner of the *American* and the *Evening Star*. Mr. Grasty, on his arrival in Baltimore, had been offered the paper for $25,000, but his plans were not yet formed, and he declined to buy it then. At the auction General Agnus began with a bid of $15,000, but the mysterious stranger jumped at once to $40,000, and soon ran the bids up to $63,000. On a prearranged signal he then retired, and the paper went to Mr. Grasty. Its physical plant consisted of four dilapidated linotype machines, two ancient Potter presses operated by gasoline engines, and a decayed stereotyping outfit. It was worth, at most, $10,000, including editorial equipment, bills receivable, United Press franchise, office cat and good-will.[1]

Mr. Grasty's inclination toward the evening field was partly

---

[1] The *World* had been launched on December 16, 1890, by John S. Sweeney, of Detroit (a leading chain-newspaper magnate of the day); Fred L. Purdy, of Indianapolis, and Herbert C. Cupit, C. M. Purdy and William S. Speed, of Baltimore. It had a capital stock of $20,000. C. M. Purdy became its editor, but he had gone to the *American* two years before the sale to Mr. Grasty. He came to The Evening Sun at its beginning.

sentimental and partly based on his sound knowledge of newspaper trends. All his own experience had been gained on evening papers, and he had a hankering for their rapid turnover of news and ideas. When a notion for an editorial occurred to him, he liked to write it down at once, and print it within a few hours, and see people reading it before the end of the day. And when there was exciting news afoot he liked to see it pass from the reporters' desks to the composing room, the pressroom and the street with all possible speed. Moreover, he was convinced, and with sound reason, that evening papers were destined to go ahead faster in the United States than morning papers, both in circulation and in advertising. The days when they had to put up with meager news reports were past. The press associations were now providing plenty of news for them, and though it was seldom as complete as that provided for the morning papers, it had the advantage of being really new. Most news originated by day, and by 4 P.M. probably a half of what was destined to go into the morning papers next morning was already in hand, if not in much detail, then at least in its main outlines.

On April 6, 1910, scarcely two weeks after the incorporation of the new company, the following brief notice appeared at the top of the first column on the last page of THE SUN, always reserved for the most important local news:

A NEW SUN WILL RISE

Evening Edition of This Paper to
Appear April 18

13 Issues, 10 Cents a Week

Morning and Evening Editions to be
Delivered to All Subscribers
in City and Suburbs

THE SUN will begin the publication of an evening edition on Monday, April 18.

The morning, evening and Sunday editions will be delivered to subscribers of THE SUN in the city and suburbs, all 13 papers for 10 cents a week.

THE EVENING SUN [1] will be similar in make-up to the morning paper. It will be orderly and plain in its presentation of the news, without thrills or frills.

THE SUN has acquired, through the purchase of the *World,* the news franchise of the United Press, which will be supplemented by the service of THE SUN's special correspondents in New York, Washington and elsewhere.

The first issue of the new paper, of twelve pages, came out at 4 P.M. on the afternoon of April 18, with an editorial salutatory headed "Good Evening." Part of that salutatory was as follows:

The evening edition, like the morning, will be orderly in form and reliable in substance. It will be a home paper. It seeks to be interesting to the family circle, and to gain the confidence of the public, in whose interest it will always be on duty.

The headlines of the first issue were moderate in size and blackness, like those of THE SUN itself, and there were four columns of advertisements on the first page — long a hallmark of THE SUN. The body type, slightly larger than was then in customary use, was thus introduced:

The extent to which THE EVENING SUN uses larger print is an experiment, and an interesting one, in metropolitan journalism. The combination of modest headlines with book type is a reversal of the prevalent fashion, which apparently assumes that only headlines are read in a newspaper. Whatever may be the case in other cities, THE SUN has reason to know that Baltimore people read the right kind of newspaper through and through.

---

[1] The first name chosen for the new paper was the *Press.* Mr. Grasty feared that the town wisecrackers would be tempted to call THE EVENING SUN the *Setting Sun.* But at the last minute he throttled these fears, and the ancient family name was chosen.

The editor of the new afternoon paper was John Haslup Adams, who had been managing editor of the *News* under Mr. Grasty, and was destined to die as editor of THE SUN. He was an old-time Liberal of the true Godkin line, and a great admirer of the reformers who had waged the long fight against political corruption in Maryland before the great upheaval of 1895. In the national field he was much interested in William E. Borah, who was just coming to the front in the Senate, and he also had a very friendly eye on Woodrow Wilson, whose battle for the democratization of Princeton University was drawing to a close, and who was to enter history as Governor of New Jersey at the end of 1910.

Mr. Adams was a Baltimorean, born January 31, 1871. His father had been a successful merchant, but had met with reverses, and young Adams left grammar-school to become an office boy in the headquarters of the Baltimore & Ohio Railroad at Baltimore. He mastered stenography while so employed, and was soon making his way in the railroad service. But he had developed meanwhile a great interest in painting — not as a painter, but as a connoisseur — and in his early twenties, having saved up enough money for the purpose, he went to Paris to see the Louvre. He remained there nine months, and by the end of his stay had developed sufficient acquaintance with the Louvre collections to serve American tourists as a guide through them.

On his return to Baltimore, he began writing, chiefly about painting. In 1899 he entered a short-story contest sponsored by the *News*. He won only second prize, but the excellence of his contribution so struck Folger McKinsey, then managing editor of the paper, that he interested Mr. Grasty in the author, and as a result Mr. Adams became a reporter on its staff. By 1904 he was its managing editor, and as such steered it through the difficult days of the great Baltimore fire. In 1906 he gave up this post to write editorials, and he continued at that work until the sale of the *News* to Frank A. Munsey. The first old associate that Mr. Grasty looked up on his return to Baltimore was Mr. Adams. They thought alike on all newspaper essentials.

The editorial page was Mr. Adams's chief concern. Until he became editor of The Sun, he always wrote The Evening Sun's leading editorial himself, and more often than not he also wrote one or two others, for at the start he had but one helper, and that helper had many other duties, including the daily concoction of an editorial page article which sometimes ran to nearly 2,000 words. A department of " Editorials by the People " was set up in the first issue of The Evening Sun, and in a little while it was bristling with contributions from readers, many of them of a ferociously controversial character. Mr. Adams always welcomed these wails and philippics, for he was a complete believer in free speech, and any hint that fair play was being denied to anyone, however unimportant, always brought him galloping to the rescue. After his death in October, 1927, an early Evening Sun associate wrote of him:

> An injustice to Great Britain did not greatly excite him, but the slightest impoliteness to Nicaragua or Honduras set him off. In his last days he raised a dreadful uproar in The Sun office about an obscure subscriber who came to complain that the police were persecuting him. He gave hours to the man, and ordered an inquiry that cost time and money. If President Willard, of the B. & O., had come in with the same complaint I suspect that he would have had a shorter hearing, for Mr. Willard can afford to hire lawyers. But a poor man facing the cops needed help, and he got it instantly. . . .

Mr. Adams saw a great modern newspaper as largely, if not mainly, an engine for rectifying injustice. If it simply printed the news that came in from anywhere and everywhere, it failed in a prime duty. That duty, he believed, obliged it to go behind the news, to find out whence the news had come and by whom it had been set afloat, to detect and expose any falsity that was in it, or any self-interest. To this business he addressed his chief energies all his professional life. He was the most indefatigable of men. No point of view, however grotesque, was too grotesque for him to hear it. . . .

But of all the journalists I have known, he was the only one who never made a visible compromise with his own matured convictions. Such compromises are very common in the profession, as they are in the law, not to mention medicine and the sacred sciences. For journalism is not only a profession, it is also, like the rest, a business — and in business what would be theoretically sweet and nice must always be diluted with what will pay its way. But Adams never seemed to take that fact into his calculations. He had all the virtues of the Puritan — and, at their best, what virtues they are! He could imagine getting beaten for an idea, and even getting beaten by it, but he was quite unable to imagine running away from it.[1]

Mr. Grasty liked to think of himself as a mild and self-effacing man, but the kind of journalism he practiced was really strongly colored by the practices of the old-time personal editors, and he was frequently involved in bitter controversies. When he took over The Sun he found it engaged in a battle precisely to his taste. That battle had to do with a proposal of the Consolidated Gas Electric Light & Power Company, the dominant local utility corporation, to bring natural gas to Baltimore. The Sun opposed this proposal, mainly on the ground that the supply of natural gas was uncertain, and finally brought the company to abandon the scheme by inducing the Maryland Legislature to withdraw some of its franchises.

The Evening Sun was less than a year old when Mr. Grasty

---

[1] Mr. Adams' wife, Lillian Craigen, was a newspaper woman, and from 1910 to 1916 was a member of the staff of The Sun. She was born in Washington, D. C., and spent most of her girlhood in Cumberland, Md., where her father, Dr. William J. Craigen, was in practice as a physician. She came to Baltimore in 1899 and joined the staff of the *News*. She and Mr. Adams were married in 1911. She died on August 20, 1928.

got into a major war of his own. The enemy was James Harry Preston, a Baltimore lawyer of large means who had been Speaker of the Maryland House of Delegates and one of the police commissioners of Baltimore, and was now the Democratic candidate for Mayor. Mr. Preston was a man of considerable ability, and he was destined to serve eight years as Mayor, but he had the misfortune to be on intimate terms with what remained of the old Gorman-Rasin organization, so Grasty and Adams were wary of him, and soon found plenty to object to in his official acts. By the Summer of 1911 war upon him was on in full fury. THE SUN also had some hand in that war, but it was mainly THE EVENING SUN's show. The editorial page bristled with both furious arguments against Mr. Preston and waspish gibes at him.

Himself a man of Berserker disposition, he soon struck back with great energy. He withdrew all the city advertising from both *Sunpapers* — a serious matter to THE EVENING SUN, which was still painfully making its way — and he launched into attacks upon Mr. Grasty's private character, alleging that he had left Kansas City under a cloud. In November, 1911, when the son of the old Maryland boss, Gorman, met defeat as the Democratic candidate for Governor of Maryland, Mr. Preston took columns of advertising space in the *News* to denounce the *Sunpapers* and Mr. Grasty. The *Sunpapers* had supported Mr. Gorman, whose politics were of a much milder variety than his father's, but had opposed most of the lesser candidates on the Democratic ticket, alleging that they were tools of the old Democratic organization, of which Mr. Preston himself was such a shining light. After election it argued that Mr. Gorman had been defeated by the unpopularity of the Preston city administration. This charge made Mr. Preston so indignant that, until toward the end of his eight years in office, the *Sunpapers* were on the municipal black list, and never printed any advertisements of tax sales and city contracts. There were times when the war threatened to include bloodshed. One day, for example, one of Mr. Preston's principal supporters came to THE SUN office, demanded to see Mr. Grasty, and, on being admitted, made obvious preparations for violence. But Mr. Grasty dissuaded him by casually displaying firearms, and he took it out in tall talk.

In a pronunciamento of November 9, 1911, Mr. Preston said: " The Democrats of Maryland do not intend to permit Grasty to become the political dictator of the State or of the Democratic party in this city. He will always injure any cause he espouses." Mr. Grasty, of course, had no yearnings to become a political dictator, whether of the State or of the city, but less than a year later, when the Democratic National Convention of 1912 assembled in Baltimore, he showed that an independent newspaper under vigorous editorship might have tremendous influence. The suggestion that the convention be invited to meet in Baltimore originated with O. P. Baldwin, then managing editor of THE SUN, but the invitation was officially extended by Mr. Preston as Mayor, and when the Democratic National Committee accepted, the arrangements were put into the hands of Robert Crain, legal representative of the United States Brewers Association at Washington and for long a power in Maryland politics.

The Maryland Democratic organization decided to support Champ Clark, of Missouri, for the Presidential nomination, and as the convention approached Mr. Preston began to entertain the hope that he himself might get the second place on the ticket. That hope was not altogether vain, for Mr. Clark was favorable to him — and Mr. Clark came to Baltimore with more votes than any other candidate. Before the end of the first day's balloting, indeed, he had a majority. But in a Democratic National Convention, in those days, two-thirds were necessary to nominate, and Mr. Clark never achieved so much. Thus the dream of Mr. Preston went glimmering, and his animosity to Mr. Grasty was redoubled, for THE SUN, with the convention directly under its guns, had favored Wilson, and most observers on the spot believed that its adroit advocacy had had almost as much to do with his nomination as the support of William Jennings Bryan.[1]

THE SUN and THE EVENING SUN, at the start, did not support Wilson openly and belligerently; instead they devoted themselves to urging him upon the convention by a process of elimination. The Republicans had just held their convention in Chicago, and Theodore Roosevelt had taken his celebrated walk, leaving the Republican party hopelessly split. What was needed, argued the *Sunpapers*, was the nomination of a Democrat capable of holding the Progressive Democrats who would be tempted to follow Roosevelt into schism, thus making uncertain an otherwise easy Democratic victory. Wilson was not mentioned by name, but he was obviously the only aspirant who could meet these specifications. All the other leading Democratic contenders were allied with party machines that were clearly out of step with the Progressive movement of the time.

---

[1] Mr. Clark himself shared this idea. He was embittered to the end of his life over his failure to receive the nomination, and he believed that THE SUN was mainly to blame. A few months after the convention he entertained Mr. Preston at a luncheon at the Capitol in Washington, and one of the guests was J. Fred Essary, head of THE SUN's Washington bureau. In the course of the luncheon he delivered a violent tirade against THE SUN, alleging that it had promised to remain neutral as between the candidates as a condition of getting the convention for Baltimore. Mr. Essary replied that this was not so. He had represented THE SUN at the meeting of the Democratic National Committee called to choose the convention city, and had given no such pledge. But Mr. Clark continued to denounce both THE SUN and Mr. Grasty (whose clerical father had officiated at the marriage of the Clarks) with such vehemence that Mr. Essary finally arose and asked to be excused from hearing more.

Clark was supported by Tammany and its Wall Street allies, and by all the other old-time Democratic organizations in the Eastern States, including an important faction in Maryland. Wilson alone had the confidence of the younger and more hopeful elements in the party, and it seemed a fair assumption that if he were nominated the organizations would be forced to support him also, for opposing him would lose the prospective victory over the divided and demoralized Republicans. On June 25, the day the convention opened, THE SUN printed an editorial headed "What Can the Baltimore Convention Do?" It answered its own question as follows:

> It can make such a nomination and adopt such a platform as will put the Republican party out of business. But if it pursues the course of the Republican convention just adjourned it can and will send an army of Democrats into the ranks of Roosevelt's party.

This editorial was supported by a guest contribution from Col. Henry Watterson, editor of the Louisville *Courier-Journal;* by a blast from Bryan, who charged that a triumvirate consisting of August Belmont, Thomas Fortune Ryan and Charles F. Murphy was intriguing to get control of the convention, and by various other fulminations, all heading toward Wilson without naming him. But the really effective attack upon the Tammany–Wall Street combination took the form of a three-column portrait of Mr. Ryan, printed on the first page of THE SUN. This was the first time the paper had ever printed a picture on its first page, and to every Baltimorean it signified that something sensational was afoot. That feeling, communicating itself to the delegates to the convention, was helped out by a two-column head, also on the first page, reading:

THOMAS F. RYAN, MONEY KING,
HERE TO DIRECT BIG FIGHT

Under it was a news story beginning:

For the first time one of the great money kings of America has appeared in person at a national political convention to carry on the fight for the money interests.

Mr. Ryan, who had arrived in Baltimore in his private car the day before, protested that he was not on hand as a money king, but as an ordinary delegate from Virginia, where he had his legal residence, and his disclaimer, of course, was printed in full by THE SUN, but it continued to allege that he and Mr. Belmont were in a plot with Tammany and the other city machines to nominate a candidate satisfactory to them, on a platform avoiding any taint of Progressivism, and that charge was supported by Mr. Bryan in interviews, at the meetings of the convention's committees, and on the floor. He lost in his fight to make a Progressive the keynoter, and Judge Alton B. Parker (1852–1926), who had been the party's candidate on a sound-money platform in 1904, was chosen, but Bryan's thunderous declamations against the Money Power gradually shook the delegates, and they began to drift away from Clark after the tenth ballot.[1]

The balloting continued without a nomination until Saturday, when the convention adjourned until Monday, July 1, with Clark still ahead, but Wilson gradually catching up with him. On Saturday, still avoiding the advocacy of Wilson by name, THE SUN printed an editorial of one sentence, headed "To the Democratic Convention," and reading: "Roosevelt will catch you if you don't watch out." On Monday, July 1, it came out into the open at last, and under the heading of "Name the Strongest Candidate," argued that Wilson's steady gains showed that he was the real choice of the convention, and that

[1] In an article in the *Saturday Evening Post,* some years later, Samuel G. Blythe, the well-known political commentator, said that THE SUN's first-page portrait of Ryan had even more influence on the convention than Bryan's fulminations.

he alone could stop the threatened flight of Progressive Democrats to Roosevelt. This editorial was supported by new blasts from Bryan, by page after page of cunningly contrived news stories, and by a telegram from Samuel Bowles, editor of the Springfield (Mass.) *Republican*, reading:

> Do urge our Democratic friends to nominate Wilson, whom independents and Progressives can support with some measure of enthusiasm.

Wilson began to poll more votes than Clark on the thirtieth ballot, and on the forty-sixth he got the necessary two-thirds and was nominated. That was late in the afternoon of Tuesday, July 2 — a day of appalling heat. Indeed, the weather had been infernal during the whole of the convention, and many of the delegates had been so tuckered out by the long balloting that they started for home immediately after the nomination of the standard bearer. The choice of a Vice-Presidential candidate was left for the evening. Rather unwisely, Mr. Preston allowed his name to be put before the convention. His chances of being nominated, by that time, were *nil*, for his candidacy had been tied to that of Clark, but he was a dogged fellow, and refused to admit defeat. Unluckily, the friend he chose to present him was a gentleman with a weakness for strong drink, and when this gentleman launched into his prepared speech it was quickly sensed by the audience which packed the huge Fifth Regiment Armory that he was somewhat tight. There were many foes of Preston in that audience, including William H. Anderson, superintendent of the Maryland Anti-Saloon League.[1] These foes made violent whoopee over the speech, and

[1] Anderson, of course, was also a foe of the *Sunpapers*, which had always been doubtful about Prohibition, and were destined to deal it some heavy licks when it came in 1920. It was at least partly because of their campaign against it that the Legislature of Maryland never passed a State enforcement act. Anderson was an Illinoisan, born in

poor Preston went down to the tune of hoots and cat-calls. He received 58 votes on the first ballot, including Maryland's 16. On the second he withdrew his name.

The next day, July 3, THE SUN printed the following telegram from Dr. Wilson:

I want you to know how warmly and deeply I have appreciated the splendid support of THE SUN.

Under this telegram was printed the following letter from his campaign manager, William F. McCombs:

I want to thank THE SUN for its loyal and enthusiastic support of Governor Wilson. It has been one of the most effective agencies in bringing about his nomination for the Presidency. We all appreciate and feel very much indebted to THE SUN for the efforts put forth in the cause of Governor Wilson and in the cause of progressive government. Its work cannot be overestimated.

On December 19, 1912, the Baltimore *American* printed the following dispatch from its Washington bureau:

A report current among Democratic politicians and President-elect Wilson's intimate friends is that Charles H. Grasty, president of The A. S. Abell Company, of Baltimore, will seek the appointment of Ambassador to France under the incoming Democratic administration. Mr. Grasty has not displayed any activity among the members of the Maryland delegation in the Senate and House with a view to securing their aid and coöperation in the gratification of his ambition. At least if he has sought their aid that fact is concealed by them.

According to report here, Mr. Grasty will go direct to President

---

1874. He came to Baltimore in 1907 and remained until 1914, when he was made State superintendent of the Anti-Saloon League of New York. In 1924 or thereabout he was accused of third-degree forgery in connection with the disposition of some contributions to the league, and sent to Sing Sing. At last accounts he was engaged in making propaganda for a constitutional amendment designed to disfranchise Catholic priests.

Wilson in seeking the honor. It is known in the Wilson circles here that the President-elect is anxious to recognize in some manner Mr. Grasty's effort in behalf of his nomination and election as President. How far this recognition will go there has been no development to indicate. From Trenton comes the well-authenticated report that any effort on the part of Mr. Grasty or of W. Cabell Bruce [1] to dictate the Federal appointments for Maryland with a view to building up their own political fortunes will meet with a rebuff. Each, however, according to the same reports from the New Jersey capital, is, in the opinion of Governor Wilson, entitled to any reasonable honor.

If selected as Ambassador, Mr. Grasty's nomination would have to be confirmed by the Senate. If Senators Smith and Jackson, of Maryland, approve, he will be confirmed. If they object the President will have to appoint another Ambassador.

This gross libel naturally distressed Mr. Grasty, and in The Sun of the next morning he printed a denunciation of it under a two-column heading reading:

THE SUN WILL SEND NO BILL TO GOVERNOR WILSON FOR SERVICES RENDERED

Under the heading came the following:

A good many people have a wrong idea about journalistic selfishness. They have the idea that it is worth while to a newspaper to support a man for high office in order that the editor may leave off editing and get an official appointment for himself or his friends or relatives. With the hope of making clear just where a newspaper's self-interest really lies in such matters, The Sun herewith reprints a news article from the Baltimore *American* of yesterday and a letter written six weeks ago by Charles H. Grasty to a brother editor, who had kindly mentioned him for a Cabinet appointment or an Ambassadorship, and which exactly expresses his position now as it did then.

---

[1] Then general counsel to the Public Service Commission of Maryland, and from 1923 to 1929 United States Senator.

The *American's* dispatch followed in facsimile, and after it Mr. Grasty's letter to his "brother editor," who was James M. Thomson, proprietor of the New Orleans *Item*.[1] It was dated November 9, 1912, and read:

My Dear Mr. Thomson — Your letter of November 6 is at hand. I thank you heartily. It is pleasant to think that a man whose newspaper friendship dates back nearly twenty years — to your student days in the Johns Hopkins University — and who has done me the honor to set me up in his own newspaper shop as something of an exemplar, should give me this latest testimony of his regard.

I have had the like suggestions from various quarters. If you will permit me I will make your kind letter the text for some remarks on the reasons upon which all newspaper advocacy should rest and upon the pride, rewards and duties of editorship.

I do not think there is any office that you, or I, or any other earnest and intelligent editor can afford to accept.

This is particularly and preëminently true in a case where an editor has been useful to a cause and his acceptance of an office would put him and his paper in the position of making a sordid swap of his support in return for office.

But aside from that consideration, office means nothing to me. There is one thing in Maryland better worth doing than any other thing. That thing is the piloting of Maryland's great newspaper — THE SUN.

So much for that phase of the matter.

Now as to my reasons for supporting Wilson. If I sought any share in the distribution of patronage as such, or for any other reason than to promote the well being of the Wilson Administration by promoting the interests of the public service, I would be committing an act of disingenuousness. THE SUN began its support of Woodrow Wilson in March, 1910. It gave this support in the most efficient way it knew how up to the time of his nomination and election. But none of this did we do for Woodrow Wilson the man, or Woodrow Wilson the friend. We thought that Mr. Wilson would

[1] Mr. Thomson married Genevieve Clark, daughter of Champ Clark, on June 30, 1915, and so became a son-in-law of Wilson's chief opponent in 1912.

be the best nominee to elect and the best President after he was elected. Mr. Wilson is, therefore, under no obligation whatever to THE SUN or to me. Our purpose was an entirely selfish one, I confess. The only reward for a newspaper that is substantial and enduring is public confidence. To say that the big item on the credit side of our balance sheet is good will is but to state a truism. Public confidence is to be gained by rendering public service, and not otherwise.

We have already had every reward to which we are entitled up to date for our support of Mr. Wilson. He won the nomination brilliantly and splendidly. He came out of that fight without a spot on his armor. He made a magnificent campaign. His victory was a glorious one. THE SUN shares in the public confidence that he has thus earned.

We look for a still bigger reward that will further increase the public good will toward THE SUN. *That reward will come from President Wilson's giving the whole people a fine administration.*

I am simply stating what you well know, for we have talked it all over time and again. You and I enjoy the privilege of doing a work in which the less we bother about direct, personal and material results, the greater will be the real rewards. Our usefulness will grow by leaps and bounds, readers will flock to our papers, merchants will seek our advertising columns in order to have a share in and put to commercial use the confidence inspired by dealing squarely with the public.

And so in the court of public opinion we shall seek our Ambassadorships, you and I! President Wilson can get plenty of men who could perform the duties of the Ambassadorships well enough, but I don't know where New Orleans could look for another Thomson to lead the great fights in the *Item* for civic righteousness. But I thank you with all my heart for a suggestion which has proceeded from an old personal good will very dear to me.

Sincerely yours,
CHARLES H. GRASTY.

On May 8, 1913, after Mr. Bryan had become Secretary of State in the first Wilson Cabinet, Mr. Grasty gave him a dinner at the Belvedere Hotel, Baltimore, to which all the local big-wigs (but not including Mayor Preston) were invited. The Commoner made a speech paying hearty tribute to THE SUN's services to the Progressive movement in the Democratic party, and also had some kind things to say of Mr. Grasty personally. The two, however, hardly saw eye to eye, though they had agreed on Wilson in 1912, and also on the party platform, which advocated an immediate downward revision of the tariff, the enforcement of the anti-trust laws, a revision of the national banking system, the election of Senators by direct vote, Presidential primaries, the revaluation of the railroads and other national utilities, publicity in campaign expenditures, the prohibition of holding companies and stock watering, and State's rights. When the World War came on, and Bryan and Wilson began to differ over grave matters, Mr. Grasty took the side of Wilson.

He became, indeed, one of the most ardent and uncompromising Wilson men ever heard of,[1] and in 1915, after his retirement from the *Sunpapers*, became one of the President's unofficial observers in Europe. In 1919 he went to the length of supporting the Treaty of Versailles, which he described as "a good treaty, a common-sense treaty."[2] He said that it was mainly

[1] His admiration, in fact, went back to Dr. Wilson's battle for the democratization of Princeton. When it was reported, in the Spring of 1910, that Dr. Wilson would resign the presidency of the university at the commencement in June, Mr. Grasty asked him if he would care to become editor of THE SUN. Wilson was apparently tempted, but he decided quickly that politics offered him a better future than journalism, and in September, 1910, he was nominated by the Democrats for Governor of New Jersey. Ten years later, by a curious irony, Herbert Hoover was also considered as a possible editor of THE SUN. He had then just returned from Europe, and was generally thought to be a Democrat. Van-Lear Black, then chairman of the board of the *Sunpapers,* asked Paul Patterson, president of the company, to go to Washington to open negotiations with Mr. Hoover. But Mr. Patterson came back convinced that he would never make a newspaper editor, and so the matter dropped.

[2] In an interview published in THE SUN, July 11, 1919.

the work of Mr. Wilson, who had dominated the peace conference as "the horse and the wagon and the dog under the wagon" and had "made a tremendous impression upon the people he dealt with by his humanity," and also by "the force of his intellect, his reasonableness, his good humor, his readiness to see the other man's point of view, his habit of cracking jokes, his absolute refusal to lose his temper." Eight months later, after the Senate had refused to ratify the treaty and take the United States into the League of Nations, Mr. Grasty described its action as "a calamity." [1] But that was long after he had resigned from The Sun and left Baltimore.

[1] Interview in The Sun, March 23, 1920.

CHAPTER XVII

THE RETIREMENT OF MR. GRASTY

MR. GRASTY sought to launch THE EVENING SUN by forcing it on subscribers to THE SUN at bargain rates. The price of THE SUN had been 1 cent since 1902 and that of THE SUNDAY SUN had been 3 cents since 1908. The two together, delivered by carrier, had been sold at 9 cents a week. On April 17, 1910, the price of THE SUNDAY SUN was dropped to 2 cents and that of THE SUN was raised to 2 cents, and the next day the two were offered in combination, along with the new EVENING SUN, at a carrier rate of 10 cents a week, or only 1 cent more than THE SUN and THE SUNDAY SUN had cost without the evening edition.

This combination rate was not merely offered; it was ordained. No one could have THE SUN delivered by carrier without also taking THE EVENING SUN. The arrangement started off THE EVENING SUN with the whole carrier circulation of THE SUN, and Mr. Grasty hoped to see the new paper firmly established in short order. It apparently never occurred to him that there were thousands of Baltimoreans who, while they preferred THE SUN in the morning, also preferred the *News* in the evening. In a little while he began to hear from these rugged individualists in large numbers, and on May 19 taking THE EVENING SUN became optional.

Its press-run on its first day had been 71,420, but on the day following it had dropped to 60,830, and by July 31, 1910, it was down to 29,100. When, on December 2, both *Sunpapers* began harassing the ghost of Mr. Crummer by printing their daily press-runs at the top of their first pages, THE SUN showed 83,180 and THE EVENING SUN but 33,120. The paid circulation of each paper, of course, was lower than the press-run. The average net paid for the thirty-one days of January, 1911, was 79,795 for THE SUN, and but 28,311 for THE EVENING SUN. THE EVENING SUN did not touch 30,000 until March, 1911, and by May of the same year (May is always a bad month for newspaper sales) it had slipped back to 28,251. Thereafter it began to pick up slowly, and its average for the whole of 1911 was 29,028. In 1912, helped by the Democratic National Convention, it reached 34,077, and in 1914, the last year of Mr. Grasty's administration, it went to 42,978.

The morning and Sunday editions did better. The circulation of THE SUN, under the Abells, had never got above 80,000, but Mr. Grasty lifted it to 81,345 in 1911, to 86,452 in 1912, to 88,242 in 1913, and to 91,652 in 1914. THE SUNDAY SUN had made some progress during the last few years of the Abells, but it still lagged behind THE SUN. Though improved from time to time, it remained small in size, printed relatively few features, and had no comic supplement in color. On November 14, 1910, the directors passed the following resolution:

> That THE SUN publish a larger Sunday paper, including a comic supplement and magazine section and such other features as make up Sunday papers. The president is authorized to make arrangements accordingly.

On December 20, Mr. Grasty reported to the board that he had contracted with the International News Service, a Hearst organization, for four pages of the comics appearing in the New

York *American*, and that he had let the contract for printing them to the World Color Printing Company. At the same time he reported that he had contracted to add the magazine of the Associated Sunday Magazines to the Sunday issue. This was a revolution, indeed, and when the comic supplement duly appeared on January 1, 1911, with Happy Hooligan and the Katzenjammer Kids as its stars, many old subscribers came to The Sun office to protest that the Founder must be turning in his grave. But the majority of readers seemed to like it, and the circulation gradually increased. In 1911 the average net paid sale of The Sunday Sun was 61,882, in 1912 it went to 72,454, in 1913 to 78,463, and in 1914 to 81,999. In 1917 it was destined to overhaul and surpass the circulation of The Sun, and it has maintained that lead ever since.

The slow progress of The Evening Sun during its first few years was due to many factors, but one of the most important of them was the stiff competition of Mr. Grasty's old paper, the *Evening News*. Under his administration the *News* had gained steadily in circulation,[1] but its advertising revenue hardly kept pace. In those days, *c.* 1907, local advertising was developing in Baltimore, but Mr. Grasty apparently made little effort to get his share of it. Instead he had frequent clashes with advertisers, and in 1905 some of them organized a boycott of him.[2] The gross revenues of the *News*, during his last year as its general manager, were but $800,000. When Mr. Munsey took charge there was an immediate increase, for he saw at once the great

---

[1] During his last month its circulation reached 82,661, which was higher than the circulation of The Sun.

[2] This boycott was launched at the beginning of the year. Its ostensible excuse was a raise in advertising rates of 1 cent a line, but in all probability Mr. Grasty's unpopularity with advertisers also had something to do with it. On January 6, 1905, he printed an editorial setting forth his side of the controversy. In the years following he always referred to this editorial as his Declaration of Independence.

possibilities of the paper. Moreover, he found in the office a young managing editor, Stuart Olivier, who had just the capacities needed to execute his plans. Mr. Olivier, who was, like Mr. Grasty himself, a native of the Valley of Virginia,[1] had been on the *News* as reporter and editor since 1898. Mr. Munsey made him general manager, and gave him a free hand. Despite the competition of the *Star*, which was launched in 1908, and of THE EVENING SUN, which followed in 1910, the revenues of the *News* passed $1,000,000 in the latter year, and by 1912 they passed $2,000,000. In 1923, when Mr. Munsey sold the paper to Mr. Hearst, they were well beyond $3,000,000. THE SUN also made steady progress during these years, for its only competitor in the morning field, the *American* (which, on December 1, 1920, followed the *News* into the hands of Munsey), never had much circulation and was of small influence. But in the evening field the *News* under Mr. Olivier took the inside track, and it was a long while before THE EVENING SUN overhauled it. During Mr. Grasty's days in THE SUN office the *News* got all the major afternoon advertising, and THE EVENING SUN had to be content with what was left.

But though his profits from the *News* were thus much larger than those of Mr. Grasty and his associates had ever been, Mr. Munsey regarded Mr. Grasty's return to Baltimore with a bilious eye, and early in November, 1911, war between the two broke out. The overt occasion for it was a series of editorials in THE EVENING SUN on the Taft-Wilson-Roosevelt national

[1] He was born at Staunton on July 2, 1880. He was general manager of the *News* from its purchase by Mr. Munsey to its sale to William R. Hearst in 1923. In 1922 he formed a syndicate in Baltimore which offered Mr. Munsey $3,000,000 cash for the *News* — twice as much as Mr. Munsey had paid for it. On the sale of the property to Mr. Hearst, Mr. Oliver became assistant to Mr. Munsey in New York and publisher of the New York *Telegram*. After leaving the Munsey organization he bought the Springfield (Mo.) *Leader*. He has since retired from the newspaper business and is living in Baltimore.

campaign, then in progress, in one of which Mr. Munsey, who was supporting Roosevelt in the *News*, was denounced as a stand-pat Republican in disguise. Mr. Munsey replied in a two-column signed article in the *News*, very angry in tone. In it he argued that the *Sunpapers'* support of Wilson was support of the old Democratic machine in Baltimore, that Mr. Grasty had come back to Baltimore hoping to repurchase the *News* at a bargain price, and was chagrined because it was doing so well and was not for sale, that he had violated a tacit agreement in putting THE EVENING SUN into competition with it, and that he was, in general, a devious and wicked fellow. Mr. Grasty replied the next day in a long article in THE EVENING SUN. He listed no less than eight misstatements of fact in Mr. Munsey's attack, and answered each of them at length. He denied that he had ever agreed to keep out of the Baltimore field, argued that he had actually set up no new newspaper in the city, for THE SUN was seventy years old, and the *World*, which had been absorbed into THE EVENING SUN, was more than twenty, and ended with the following fling:

> On the whole, Mr. Grasty's return to Baltimore has been helpful to Mr. Munsey's interests by preventing him from transplanting to Baltimore the men and methods that have caused the failure of his newspaper enterprises elsewhere, and certainly the men in the *News* office have no reason to feel otherwise than gratified at the improved conditions since Mr. Grasty has come back into the Baltimore field.

This somewhat unseemly row was scarcely beneficial to THE EVENING SUN, then struggling to reach a circulation of 30,000. It gave the paper the air of an old-time personal organ, and brought down upon it all the animosities that Mr. Grasty had accumulated during his years of violent battle on the *News*. THE SUN suffered too, but not as much, for the war with Munsey, which went on sporadically for a year or more, was carried on in

THE EVENING SUN.[1] It was THE EVENING SUN, again, that bore the brunt of the long combat with Mayor James H. Preston. It was Mr. Grasty's own child and hence his favorite, but when its failure to make an instant success was followed by what promised to be long years of grueling and ill-rewarded effort he gave over his principal energies to the morning edition, which was making better progress.

In the early Spring of 1913 he made the editor of THE EVENING SUN, John Haslup Adams, editor of THE SUN also. It was impossible, of course, for Mr. Adams to give two editorial pages the care they needed, so that of THE EVENING SUN quickly lost force and effect. Beginning May 1, its editorials, reduced to one a day, were transferred to the last page (or, on special occasions, to the first page), and in their old place on the editorial page Mr. Grasty began to print signed articles by various special contributors — for example, Charles J. Bonaparte and Albert C. Ritchie. These gentlemen often had things of moment to say, but they seldom said them with much charm, and so the editorial page tended toward dullness, and was, in fact, mainly given over to short items clipped from other newspapers.[2]

---

[1] Mr. Munsey retained ownership of the *News* until April 1, 1923, when he sold out to Mr. Hearst. On December 1, 1920, he had bought the Baltimore *American*, the oldest newspaper in Baltimore. (See Chapter I.) The *American* went to Mr. Hearst along with the *News*. On March 24, 1934, Mr. Hearst also bought the *Post*, a Scripps-Howard evening paper. It was combined with the *News* as the *News-Post*, which still continues. On March 31, 1928, the week-day issue of the *American*, a morning paper, was abandoned, but it continues as the Sunday issue of the *News-Post*. The present newspaper set-up in Baltimore is thus as follows: THE SUN has no competition in the week-day morning field, but THE SUNDAY SUN faces the *American*. In the evening field THE EVENING SUN's only competitor is the *News-Post*.

[2] With the first issue of THE EVENING SUN, Strickland Gillilan, author of Off Again, On Again, Gone Again, Finnegan, appeared as an editorial page columnist, but he left the paper on October 28, 1910. He was succeeded the next day by

Mr. Grasty set great store by such clipped items, and often argued that they had been largely responsible for the success of the Kansas City *Star*, always his model. But the readers of THE EVENING SUN showed no sign of being inflamed by them.

On November 8, 1913, the paper resumed the printing of editorials on its editorial page, but they were very short, and seldom of any pungency. The rest of the paper, in those hard years, was hardly more exhilarating than the editorial page. It had started out with the sober typographical dress of the old *News*, and had printed but one edition a day, appearing at 4 P.M. The competition of Messrs. Munsey and Olivier, who quickly revised and brightened the dress of the *News* and began to issue multiple editions, forced it to follow suit, but it followed somewhat haltingly. Its headlines, in particular, were badly designed, and it was, in general, somewhat frumpy in aspect.

Its staff, at the start, had been recruited mainly from the staff of THE SUN, but there were also newcomers in the office from other Baltimore papers. Mr. Munsey, in one of his philippics against Mr. Grasty, accused him of raiding the staff of the *News*, but this was hardly true. To be sure, his right-hand editorial man, Mr. Adams, was an old *News* man, but Mr. Adams had actually left the *News* soon after Mr. Grasty did, and was not connected with it when THE EVENING SUN started. Neither

---

Henry Edward Warner, whose daily contribution, under the heading of Sidelights, continued until April 17, 1913. On May 8, 1911, H. L. Mencken began a daily column in the last column of the editorial page under the heading of The Free Lance. It was mainly devoted to belaboring the town reformers and visionaries, though it also made occasional forays into politics. It continued until October 23, 1915. On June 3, 1921, Clark S. Hobbs began a column on the first page entitled Good Evening and signed THE SUN Square Traffic Cop. It later moved to another page, where it continued until September 7, 1935. The next editorial page columnist was F. F. Beirne, who began The Rolling Road under the pseudonym of Christopher Billopp on July 8, 1931. It still continues.

was Dr. Fabian Franklin, for long the chief editor of the *News* under Grasty and later an editorial writer on THE SUN. Dr. Franklin, down to 1895, had been professor of mathematics at the Johns Hopkins University, but he was greatly interested in public questions, and frequently wrote about them in the Baltimore and New York newspapers. His first contributions to THE SUN had been made so long in the past as 1873, when he reported a series of lectures by John Tyndall, delivered at the Peabody Institute, Baltimore. He joined the *News* as chief editorial writer and titular editor in 1895, and continued until the purchase of the paper by Mr. Munsey. He and Mr. Grasty had thought substantially alike in all important matters, but his politics and those of Mr. Munsey were sharply at variance, so he resigned. On September 30, 1908, more than a year before Mr. Grasty's return to Baltimore, Dr. Franklin was engaged by Walter W. Abell to write two editorials a week for THE SUN for the duration of the national campaign of that year, in which THE SUN was supporting Taft against Bryan.[1] After the election he was engaged as a regular editorial writer for three years, but he resigned in 1909 to become associate editor of the New York *Evening Post* under Rollo Ogden. This was a year before Mr. Grasty took over THE SUN.[2] During the campaign

[1] Taft's popular majority in Maryland was 605, but only two of his eight Presidential electors were elected. Thus, in the Electoral College the State voted two for Taft and six for Bryan. If THE SUN had supported Bryan he undoubtedly would have carried the State on the popular vote and won all eight electors.

[2] Dr. Franklin was born at Eger, Hungary, January 18, 1853, but was brought to the United States as a child. Educated at Columbian (now George Washington) University, he practiced from 1869 to 1877 as a civil engineer. He then became a fellow of Johns Hopkins University, and from 1879 to 1895 was professor of mathematics there. He was invited to become editor of the *News* by Mr. Grasty in 1895, and his vigorous editorial writing was largely responsible for the success of the paper. His connection with the New York *Evening Post* lasted until 1917. In 1919, with Harold de Wolf Fuller, he set up a weekly in New York,

of 1912 he wrote some of THE SUN's editorials in support of Woodrow Wilson. Another old *News* man in THE SUN office was McKee Barclay, for many years the *News* cartoonist, but he was engaged in 1908, more than two years before Mr. Grasty's return to Baltimore.[1]

Only a few men came from the *News* at the time THE EVENING SUN was set up. There was a much larger contingent from the *World*, which had some excellent men on the staff, even though its circulation was small and its physical equipment meager. Among these *World* men who came to THE EVENING SUN were Edward Green, who became the first telegraph editor of the latter; Edward McCleavy, the first foreman of its composing room; E. A. Fitzpatrick, later city editor and then assistant managing editor of THE EVENING SUN, and still later promotion manager for all the *Sunpapers;* Charles O. Reville, who is now in charge of their national advertising; and William F. Schmick, now the executive vice-president of The A. S. Abell Company.[2] Other recruits came from the *American* and its eve-

---

the *Review*. It continued until 1922. Dr. Franklin, during the thirteen years of Prohibition, was an ardent opponent of the Eighteenth Amendment, and wrote many articles and three books against it. He is also the author of a life of Daniel Coit Gilman, the first president of the Johns Hopkins, and of various other books, chiefly on economics. He is now living in New York.

[1] The editor of the *News*, at that time, was Charles McHenry Harwood, who had been its managing editor under Mr. Grasty from 1893 to 1900, an associate editor in 1907–8, and continued as its editor from 1908 to 1924. In the latter year he joined the editorial staff of THE SUN, where he remains. Born at Shelbyville, Ky., on April 7, 1864, he got his first newspaper experience on the Kansas City *Times*. He was managing editor of the Kansas City *Evening News* from 1889 to 1891, and of the Syracuse (N. Y.) *Herald* from 1901 to 1907.

[2] Mr. Schmick went to work for the *World* as a boy in the mailing room, and in June, 1903, when but 20 years old, became business manager of the paper. His first post with the *Sunpapers* was in the circulation department, but within a year he was put in charge of classified advertising. He became assistant to the advertising manager in April, 1913, advertising manager in De-

ning edition, the *Star*. One of the newcomers from the *American* was C. M. Purdy, who had been one of the organizers of the *World* and for some years its editor, and was later to be city editor of THE EVENING SUN. He afterward transferred to the staff of THE SUN, and is still there. One of the *Star* men was Philip B. Perlman, who joined THE EVENING SUN as its court reporter and became its city editor in 1913. He had meanwhile studied law, and in 1917 resigned the city editorship to become assistant to Albert C. Ritchie, then Attorney-General of Maryland. As such, he helped to draft much of the war legislation of those days, including the bill creating the Maryland Compulsory Work Bureau, later imitated by many other States. In January, 1920, Mr. Ritchie having become Governor of Maryland, Mr. Perlman became his Secretary of State. After serving for nearly four years, he resigned to become City Solicitor of Baltimore, and has since sat on various committees for the drafting of important legislation. He has been very successful at the bar, and devotes his leisure to the cultivation of the fine arts. He is now a trustee of the Walters Art Gallery, Baltimore; of the Baltimore Museum of Art, of the Baltimore Municipal Museum, and of the Maryland Institute, the chief art school of the city.[1]

On April 11, 1911, there appeared in the office of THE EVENING SUN a man who was destined to reach the top of the whole SUN organization. He was Paul Patterson. He was then only 33 years old, but he already had a wide and varied newspaper

cember of the same year, business manager and secretary of The A. S. Abell Company on November 10, 1919; vice-president of the company on April 28, 1924, and executive vice-president on June 28, 1934. He had a large hand in the rehabilitation of the *Sunpapers*.

[1] Mr. Perlman was born in Baltimore March 5, 1890. He was educated at the Baltimore City College, the University of Maryland and the Johns Hopkins University. He began newspaper work on the Baltimore *American* in 1908, and transferred to the *Star* in 1909.

career behind him. Born at Jacksonville, Ill., in a region that had produced an extraordinarily large number of newspaper executives, on November 18, 1878, he moved with his family, at the age of 10, to the village of Rushville in the same State. He got through the public school there in 1896 and went to Chicago with the determination to take up newspaper work. But he failed to land a job on any newspaper there, so he went to work as a messenger in the wholesale house of Marshall Field & Company, staying there until the Autumn of 1899, by which time he was a salesman. But during the Summer of that year he had been given some Saturday afternoon assignments, covering tennis, golf and other sports, by E. S. Sheridan, sports editor of the Chicago *Tribune*, and later in the year he was offered the post of *Tribune* correspondent at the University of Chicago. This opportunity was accepted eagerly, for it not only offered an introduction to regular newspaper work, but also afforded an opportunity to carry on studies at the university. This Mr. Patterson did, majoring in English and history.

But he never took his degree. The pull of newspaper work was too strong, and he was soon making rapid progress in the craft, and proceeding to better and better jobs. The next ten years were spent in acquiring a varied experience in Chicago, at that time the scene of unparalleled journalistic activity and the work-place of many men who made newspaper history. He worked under many famous editors: on the *Tribune* under the late James Keeley and Edward S. Beck, on the *Journal* under Ralph Booth and John C. Eastman, and on the *Inter-Ocean* when George Wheeler Hinman was its publisher. He became night city editor of the *Inter-Ocean*, and worked directly under City Editor William E. Moore, now managing editor of The Sun. Then he joined the Hearst organization as city editor of the Chicago *Examiner* under a number of managing editors, including Victor Polachek, C. P. J. Mooney and Scott C. Bone.

When Mr. Bone started the Washington *Herald*, Mr. Patterson went there to join the staff, as Capitol and White House correspondent, but shortly afterward was again brought back to desk work as city editor. From there he went to the Washington *Times*, then owned by Frank A. Munsey, and was successively city editor, managing editor and general manager. Differences with Mr. Munsey led him to resign in 1911, and at the suggestion of Frank A. Noyes, president of the company publishing the Washington *Star* and also of the Associated Press, he applied to Mr. Grasty for a post in the office of THE EVENING SUN, then just a year old. Mr. Grasty made him its managing editor in succession to Robert B. Vale, who was appointed, in succession, assistant general manager and business manager.

This transfer of men from the editorial rooms to the business office was a device that Mr. Grasty often resorted to with success, and there have been several instances of its use since his time. Robert B. Ennis, whom we have met as the associate of Frank R. Kent in THE SUN's heroic effort to save Governor Austin L. Crothers from the assault of Grasty and the *News* in 1908, was transmogrified from political reporter to advertising manager in 1913; Henry Edward Warner gave up the post of staff poet to THE EVENING SUN to become circulation manager of all the *Sunpapers* the same year;[1] John E. Cullen, later to become

[1] Mr. Warner had had long newspaper experience when he joined THE EVENING SUN in 1910. Born at Elyria, Ohio, on January 17, 1876, and educated at the University of Southern California, he became a reporter on the Knoxville (Tenn.) *Journal* in 1890. In 1896 he came to Baltimore to join the staff of the *News*, and he was with it off and on until 1904. He also served, at different times, the Denver *Times*, the Binghamton (N. Y.) *Press*, and the St. Paul *Dispatch*. He was the founder and first president of the American Press Humorists. In 1913, Mr. Grasty asked him to write a report, from the editorial standpoint, on the efforts then under way to get circulation for THE EVENING SUN. This report was so searching and convincing that he was soon afterward made circulation manager. It was his theory that prospective readers had to be educated in the merits of the *Sun-*

an important figure in the Hearst and Scripps-Howard organizations, left the managing editorship of THE EVENING SUN in 1914 to become a special assistant in the advertising department;[1] and Emmett P. Kavanaugh left the post of political reporter of THE EVENING SUN in 1927 to become assistant circulation manager and then circulation manager.[2] When Mr. Vale was made business manager, Mr. Patterson, as previously stated, succeeded him as managing editor of THE EVENING SUN, and when Mr. Vale left THE SUN in the Autumn of 1913 Mr. Patterson succeeded him as business manager. Mr. Grasty was then president of The A. S. Abell Company and Arunah S. Abell 2d was secretary and treasurer. In the Summer of 1914, with

---

papers. To that end he established an Educational Division which still goes on under his direction. It publishes brochures describing the making of the *Sunpapers,* conducts parties of visitors (and especially of school children and college students) through THE SUN Building, and is ready to supply illustrated lectures to all interested organizations. Mr. Warner himself has delivered many of these lectures. There is also a four-reel moving-picture.

[1] Mr. Cullen began newspaper work on the Baltimore *World* in 1904. He was later with the Baltimore *Evening Herald* and Baltimore *American,* and joined THE SUN in 1907, under the Abells. He became city editor of THE EVENING SUN in 1913, and soon afterward its managing editor. His tour of duty in the business office lasted until the end of 1914, when he resigned to become advertising and promotion manager of the New York *Evening Mail.* In April, 1917, he became its managing editor. In November, 1922, he joined the Hearst organization as publisher of the Wisconsin *News* and Milwaukee *Sunday Telegram;* in April, 1923, he returned to Baltimore as publisher of the *News* and *American,* which Mr. Hearst had just bought from Frank A. Munsey; in 1924, he joined the Hearst general staff in New York. He left Hearst in 1935, and is now with the Scripps-Howard newspaper chain.

[2] Mr. Kavanaugh was born in Baltimore May 5, 1894, and educated at Calvert Hall College. He joined the staff of THE SUN as a reporter in 1920. He was its political reporter when he left the editorial rooms in 1927 to become assistant circulation manager in charge of street sales. On December 1, 1930, he was made circulation manager of THE SUN, THE EVENING SUN and THE SUNDAY SUN, and on June 28, 1934, he became assistant business manager, remaining in charge of circulation.

Mr. Grasty abroad and Mr. Abell ill, there were no officers at hand to sign checks and other corporation papers. John H. Adams and Frank R. Kent were thereupon elected vice-presidents, and Mr. Patterson was made assistant secretary and treasurer. On the death of Mr. Abell in July, Mr. Patterson became secretary-treasurer.

Mr. Grasty did not favor any compensatory shift of men from the business office to the editorial rooms. He was always the editor first and the publisher only afterward, and he was intensely jealous of every encroachment, however slight and indirect, upon the editorial freedom of his papers. He not only discouraged suggestions as to policy from the staff of the business office; he also frowned upon the intervention of stockholders. Indeed, he kept his associates in control of The A. S. Abell Company at such a distance that most of them never visited THE SUN office, and even matters of first importance, as has been noted (Chapter XVI) in the case of the establishment of THE EVENING SUN, were kept from their knowledge. The largest stockholder in the new company, H. Crawford Black, visited the editorial rooms but once during his eleven years of interest in the *Sunpapers*, and on that occasion he came in search of news, for it was the day in 1918 which saw the false report of an armistice in the World War.

But Mr. Black's younger son, Harry C. Black, was often in the office from the beginning of 1911 onward. He was then but two years out of college, and had developed a great interest in newspaper work — an interest that has never abated. He was an occasional contributor to the editorial page of THE EVENING SUN, and was soon accepted in the office as a newspaper man. He is now chairman of the board, and as such is largely responsible for the direction of the property as a business, but he has retained his essentially editorial point of view, and subscribes to most of the articles of the Grastian code. In the days after Mr.

Grasty's retirement, when both The Sun and The Evening Sun were reorganized and the vigorous policies at the bottom of their subsequent course were formulated, Mr. Black took a leading part in fashioning them, as we shall see hereafter.

One of the Grasty stockholders, John Campbell White, served The Sun as an editorial writer for a short while. He had had previous newspaper experience in St. Paul and was a member of the staff like any other. In 1913 he resigned to enter the diplomatic service, and has been a member of it, as a career man, ever since. He was the son of Henry White, for long secretary to the American embassy at London, and later Ambassador at Rome and Paris, negotiator of the Hay-Pauncefote treaty, and a member of the American delegation at the Versailles Peace Conference. The younger Mr. White's uncle, Julian LeRoy White, had been one of the group of wealthy Baltimoreans who backed Mr. Grasty in the purchase of the *News* in 1891.[1]

Mr. Grasty's reluctance to take his associates into his confidence gave him a free hand with the editorial conduct of the *Sunpapers*, and during his four years in charge of them they certainly did not lack independence of spirit. But he also tried

---

[1] Mr. White was born in Baltimore March 17, 1884. He was private secretary to his father at Rome and Paris. When he decided to enter the diplomatic service himself, he took the usual examination for career men, and passed with very high marks. President Woodrow Wilson at once appointed him third secretary to the legation to Mexico, but before he could proceed to his post he was transferred to Santo Domingo. He has since served in Russia, Germany, Poland, Japan, Greece, Czechoslovakia, Latvia and Venezuela, and has also had tours of duty at the State Department in Washington. At the time of the Russian advance on Warsaw in 1920, he won high praise for his efficient evacuation of 800 Americans from the war area. He is now consul-general at Calcutta. He remains a stockholder in The A. S. Abell Company. The elder Mr. White, who was then in retirement from the diplomatic service, was invited to become a director of the company in 1914, but he declined. The younger was a director from 1911 to 1914.

to run them single-handed as business enterprises, and there he made an error, for he was but an indifferent business man himself, and the aid and counsel of Messrs. Black, Keyser and Garrett, all of them schooled in large affairs, would have been very valuable to him. Indeed, his course presently got him into serious difficulties as an editor, for the property lost money under his management, and he was forced into economies that seriously crippled his editorial enterprises. His amalgamation of the offices of editor and managing editor on the two papers, made in the Spring of 1913, was dictated principally by a desire to cut down expenses, and so were his subsequent changes in the editorial page of The Evening Sun. Both papers had short staffs, and neither had much to spend on special correspondence. Nor were there sufficient funds in hand for promoting the public shows and other stunts which attract attention to newspapers.

On November 7, 1910, The Evening Sun brought Hubert Latham, a French aviator, to Baltimore to fly over the city in his Antoinette monoplane,[1] and in June, 1913, The Sun helped to launch a public loan by selling $993,400 of Baltimore city stock over its counter, but the cost of the former exploit, $5,000, made a big hole in the year's budget, and the latter cost next to nothing. There were plenty of competent men in the business office in those days — most of them are there yet — and they labored valiantly to increase the advertising lineage of all three *Sunpapers*, but their best efforts brought in relatively little revenue. In 1912, the amount of advertising written, set up and illustrated in the office to tempt advertisers ran to hundreds of columns a month, and a large part of it died unsold.

The operating losses for 1910 and 1911 reached large pro-

[1] The flight of an airplane, in those days, was still enough of a novelty to draw crowds. M. Latham was the first aviator ever to fly over Baltimore. To leave open country and its convenient landing fields was then considered hazardous. Ross R. Winans, a rich Baltimorean housebound by illness, paid M. Latham $500 to fly over his house.

portions. Most of them had to be debited to THE EVENING SUN, though the enlargement of THE SUNDAY SUN was also partly responsible.[1] THE SUN itself continued to show a profit, but the total income from circulation and advertising in 1910, with two papers, was less than it had been for 1909, with one. In 1911 and again in 1912 the net loss was larger than in 1910. In 1913, THE SUN and THE SUNDAY SUN showed substantial increases in advertising revenue, and wound up the year with a small profit, but THE EVENING SUN showed a deficit, and made a deficit for the property as a whole.

With such heavy losses recurring, the $400,000 of new capital raised by the issue of additional common stock in 1911 was soon exhausted, and so early as September, 1911, the company was borrowing money from the Baltimore banks. But more was needed, and later in 1911 the directors decided upon an issue of $500,000 worth of 6% four-year coupon notes. These notes were all taken by the stockholders, and chiefly by Messrs. Black, Garrett and Keyser. When the sum they yielded was exhausted, money was raised on demand notes, taken by the same gentlemen. By the end of 1915, when the tide began to turn at last, the accumulated deficits ran to more than $1,100,000.

Mr. Grasty's associates naturally tired of pouring money into the property in such large amounts, especially since they had only the vaguest idea of its operations. They knew that THE SUN, THE SUNDAY SUN and THE EVENING SUN were all increasing in circulation, steadily if somewhat slowly, and they observed with satisfaction that the public influence of all three papers was certainly not diminishing, but the continuing losses had become a heavy burden, and they were all disinclined to make any more loans. On April 27, 1914, they were informed

[1] Altogether, the cost of issuing THE SUNDAY SUN was increased $120,000 a year.

that the deficit for the first months of the year had been more than the deficit for the corresponding months of 1913, and on May 25 they heard that the deficit for April had been more than the deficit for April, 1913. If this kept up they would have to provide fresh money in large sums, with no prospect of a change for the better in the near future.

They met in May, 1914, to discuss the situation realistically. The only way out seemed to be to hand the property back to the Abells under the mortgage covering the $1,000,000 bond issue, and to charge off their own investment to profit and loss. They were extremely reluctant to withdraw, but they were at the limit of their endurance. They decided to ask for the appointment of receivers, and were about to call it a day when Mr. Edwin G. Baetjer, their senior counsel, arose with a suggestion. THE SUN, he pointed out, had been managed successfully for nearly a year by Mr. Charles S. Abell, with Mr. John J. Nelligan keeping a friendly eye upon its finances. Why not try that plan again, with Mr. Grasty remaining as editorial director, and one of the stockholders serving as a sort of business supervisor? Mr. Black was the largest stockholder and, moreover, a man of wide interests and notable capacity for business, so they all looked to him. But he was then 69 years old, and was naturally not eager to take on a new enterprise presenting so many difficulties. He turned to his son, Van-Lear Black, then only 39, but already a very successful financier on his own account. "Would you like to try it?" he asked. The younger Mr. Black hesitated only a moment. He had had no experience of newspapers, but he had been watching the *Sunpapers*, and he believed that, with careful management, they could be rescued from their difficulties. So he agreed to make the attempt to rehabilitate them, and it was so ordered.

Mr. Grasty's peculiar rights under the certificate of incorporation of the company and under its by-laws remained to be disposed of. His $100,000 of Class C common stock, it will be recalled, could outvote all the other stock when it came to elect or remove the president of the company, or to change the by-laws defining his prerogatives, and Article III, Section 4, of the by-laws made him its supreme dictator, with the board of directors forbidden categorically to " direct, control or reverse " any of his acts. But what the board could not accomplish under the by-laws the stockholders could accomplish by cutting off the supply of money, and this was presently done.

On June 30, 1914, it was proposed to Mr. Grasty that he retire from the direction of the business office, and leave its management to Van-Lear Black. He consented at once, and a change in the by-laws was made. It left his autonomy as editor unmodified, but it took away from him his power to spend the funds of the corporation without the consent of the board. He was required instead to keep his expenditures, even for editorial purposes, within " the limit of the appropriations . . . fixed by the board." In order to effect this change there had to be a revision of the stock structure of the company, abolishing the special rights of the Class C common stock, all of which was in his hands. All the three classes of common stock were put upon an equal footing, with one vote for each share and special rights for none. At the same time a new board of directors was elected. It consisted of Van-Lear Black and Harry C. Black (the sons of H. Crawford Black), Robert Garrett, R. Brent Keyser, J. J. Nelligan, James C. Fenhagen and Mr. Grasty himself. Charles S. Abell had resigned from the board in 1911 and Arunah S. Abell 2d, who had held the post of secretary-treasurer, was desperately ill, and died a month later.[1] Mr. Nelligan, who represented

[1] His death occurred on July 28, 1914. He was 49 years old, and had been actively connected with THE SUN since 1892. He was the eldest son of Edwin F. Abell, and was educated at St. Mary's College, Emmitsburg, Md., and at Georgetown University. Mr. Abell was a man of extraordinarily pleasing personality, and was extremely popular in THE

the Safe Deposit & Trust Company, trustee under the will of Walter R. Abell, we have met before in this narrative; he was destined to remain a director in The A. S. Abell Company until his death in 1935. Mr. Fenhagen, then a partner of Mr. Garrett in the banking firm of Robert Garrett and Sons, became a director in September, 1914.[1]

Mr. Grasty, under the new arrangement, remained in complete control of the editorial department of the *Sunpapers*, and continued not only as a director in the company but also as its president. He went abroad immediately after the agreement was arrived at, was caught in Europe by the outbreak of the World War, and did not return until late in the Summer of 1914. For a week or two he resumed his old duties in the editorial rooms, but it was only for a week or two. Early in September he decided suddenly that he didn't want to go on, and on September 12, the following notice appeared on the last page of THE SUN:

MR. GRASTY RETIRES FROM
THE MANAGEMENT OF SUN

Will Continue As Member Of Board
Of Directors Of The A. S.
Abell Company

Charles H. Grasty, who for the last four and a half years has been president and general manager of The A. S. Abell Company, has withdrawn from his active connection with THE SUN.

SUN office. His children still have a stock interest in the paper.

[1] Mr. Fenhagen was born in Baltimore on August 10, 1875, and is a son of Charles D. Fenhagen, who was a prominent banker of the city for many years and served at one time as City Comptroller, the chief financial officer of the municipality. James C. Fenhagen began his business career as a runner for the Merchants National Bank of Baltimore in 1892. He was soon promoted to a clerkship and eventually became an officer of the bank. He left it in 1905 to become cashier of the Maryland National Bank, and in 1907 was elected vice-president of the same bank. In 1911 he became a partner in Robert Garrett and Sons. He retired from the firm in 1931. In 1932 he was called to take part in the reorganization of the Baltimore Trust Company as chair-

Mr. Grasty retains his stock in the Abell Company and will continue to be a member of the board of directors. The other directors are Van-Lear Black, Harry C. Black, Robert Garrett, James C. Fenhagen, J. J. Nelligan and R. Brent Keyser. Van-Lear Black is chairman of the board.

On November 30 Mr. Grasty resigned also as a director in the corporation, and soon afterward he went abroad again. He was succeeded as director on February 22, 1915, by Charles McHenry Howard, of Venable, Baetjer & Howard, counsel to THE SUN.[1] Mr. Howard served until Mr. Patterson was made president in 1919, Mr. Patterson then becoming automatically a member of the board. Mr. Grasty held his stock until September 29, 1919, when he sold it to Van-Lear Black, Harry C. Black, R. Brent Keyser and Walter W. Abell. He spent most of 1915 in Europe. In January, 1916, he joined the New York *Times*, and thereafter, until the end of the war, served as a roving correspondent for it in Europe. Many of his dispatches were also printed in THE SUN. He settled in London after the war, and there he died on January 19, 1924.

The following characterization of him appeared in an editorial in THE SUN on the day following his death:

Mr. Grasty was a fighter, but no bruiser. He was hated cordially and he himself knew how to hate, but few men ever had less rancor

man of its trust committee, and since 1934 he has been a director and chairman of the discount committee of its successor, the Baltimore National Bank. He was one of the organizers of the Commercial Credit Company in 1912 and has been a director of it ever since.

[1] The present members of the firm are Edwin G. Baetjer, Harry N. Baetjer, Joseph France and Mr. Howard. It was founded by Major Richard M. Venable (d. July 10, 1910) in 1900. Major Venable had been counsel to THE SUN since 1893 or thereabout, and Mr. Howard, who had come to the bar in that year, had been associated with him before becoming his partner in 1900. Mr. Baetjer has also had an important part in THE SUN's affairs, though he has never served on the board. He was associated in practice with Major Venable before becoming his partner in 1900.

in them. His campaigns against corrupt politicians, in fact, were always more or less softened and slowed down by his genuine delight in politicians as men, especially in his later years. An extremely social man, he liked to have friends about him, and in him there often showed a wistful hint that he would have liked more than he ever actually had. His associates in journalism will not soon forget him. Every younger man who served under him carried off something of his peculiar philosophy — his ardent belief in a few simple fundamentals, his shrewd and not unkindly cynicism, his unfailing good humor. The messianic delusion never got into him. He believed in his causes and he believed in himself, but there was always room in his faith for a touch of doubt. No man of his extraordinarily high professional skill could have been more tolerant of opposing ideas, however humble their source. No man of his achievements could have been less the oracle and posturer.

He was fond of expounding his professional philosophy, both to his associates in the office and to lay audiences outside. A newspaper, as he saw it, was a sort of public watchman, charged with unearthing and printing all the relevant facts about every matter affecting the well-being of its readers, and especially all such facts as interested parties were trying to conceal or sophisticate. It had to steer clear of all entanglements, however innocent in intent and appearance; in particular, it had to avoid every relationship that might conceivably impede its publication of the whole news. "Every friend," he was fond of saying to young reporters, "is a possible temptation." In an address to the Baltimore Ministerial Union on May 27, 1912 — as the son of a clergyman he was always fond of palavering with the cloth — he amplified this doctrine as follows:

> The man with a sound newspaper heart in him has no friends to help. He has no enemies to hurt. These are two luxuries not permitted by the nature of the journalistic function properly performed. He has no vindictiveness. He hardly allows himself common humanity. If he attacks, it is in the same spirit that the police-

man arrests. He has no feeling against the person attacked, any more than the policeman has for the person arrested, although the person in both cases is apt to have very bitter feeling. Both the journalist and the policeman, if they be the right sort, feel more kindly, rather than less so, toward the individual against whom they perform their duty.

Whenever I have enunciated this doctrine it has usually been received with a sneer. If you think it smacks of demagogy, let me own frankly that it is bottomed on pure business. Right here I want to define newspaper success. Public confidence earned by public service — that is the Alpha and Omega of newspaper success. Let the paper serve its public faithfully enough, a long enough time, and all the rest will take care of itself.

"When I went to Baltimore," he said in an address to the University of Missouri School of Journalism on April 18, 1911, "the opportunity as I saw it was this: The papers had not printed the news about politics. For one reason or another the subject of machines and bosses had been tabooed in the newspaper shops. This seemed to me to constitute an unusual opportunity for a newspaper, because this interesting news had been suppressed so long that it was uncommonly interesting." Interesting it surely was — as Mr. Grasty printed it in the *News*. His influence was felt in THE SUN office long before he ever appeared there in person. Indeed, he changed the whole tone of journalism in Baltimore, and for the better. When he came to the city in 1891 its newspapers were generally feeble, and even THE SUN was in the doldrums; when he left it in 1914 there was a new spirit, and the *Sunpapers* were headed in the direction they have kept to ever since. There was a great deal of missionary zeal in him, no doubt inherited from his Calvinist progenitors, and he revealed it in his relations to his staff as well as in the conduct of his papers. Old SUN men well remember the time — it must have been about 1911 — when he made a belated discovery of Buckle's "History of Civilization," laid in many copies of it, and pressed them upon all his editors. Most of those editors, of course, had read it years before, but he insisted that they read it again. He had many other such enthusiasms, and when he was in the grip of one of them he went about the office with the exhilarated air of a boy who had just learned a new game.

His failure with the *Sunpapers* was due mainly to a defect already mentioned — his incapacity as a man of business. He was, at his best, a really great editor, with a bold imagination, an immense resourcefulness and almost unlimited courage, but his ideas about extending circulation were mainly bad ones, and one of them — the 13-for-10 forced subscription rate, already described — came near ruining THE EVENING SUN in its first year. Neither was he at his best in dealing with advertisers, for his laudable desire to prevent them breaking into the news columns sometimes blinded him to the fact that they had some rights, too, and at worst deserved polite treatment. There were some very competent men in the business office in his day, and more than one of them played an important part in the development of the *Sunpapers* under Van-Lear Black, but he seldom gave them sufficient leeway, and in consequence their best efforts went for little.

He had, to the end, a certain awe of the old SUN, and was slow to change such of its archaic practices as had not succumbed before the younger Abells. He continued to print advertising on the first page of THE SUN, and introduced it on the first page of THE EVENING SUN. He kept on printing want ads on the third, fourth and fifth pages long after all other newspapers had shoved them farther back. He clung to headlines that were ineffective and outmoded, and when the competition of the *News* under Olivier forced him to abandon them at last, he went only half the way toward modern type faces and arrangements. This weakness for the old-fashioned extended, at times, into his handling of news. There was almost as much editorializing in the news columns in his day as there had been in THE SUN of 1895. Indeed, one of the hardest tasks confronting his successors was to make the news printed by the *Sunpapers* as nearly impartial as possible, and to pen up opinion in editorials and special articles.

CHAPTER XVIII

VAN-LEAR BLACK IN COMMAND

THE WITHDRAWAL of Mr. Grasty left the stockholders with much more on their hands than they had bargained for. They had counted on him to go on as editorial director of the *Sunpapers*, and when he departed they left his editorial set-up unchanged, with John Haslup Adams as editor of both THE SUN and THE EVENING SUN, and Frank R. Kent as managing editor of both. Mr. Adams and Mr. Kent thus carried double burdens of duty; they were heavily handicapped, moreover, by the retrenchments that had to be effected during the four expensive years of the World War. But they stuck to their posts, and before Mr. Kent's relinquishment of the managing editorship in 1921 and Mr. Adams's death in 1927 the *Sunpapers* were in a sound and solid condition, and had enough money in the till to pay for any enterprise that suggested itself. The chief figures in the business office at the time of Mr. Grasty's retirement were Paul Patterson, who was then business manager and secretary-treasurer of The A. S. Abell Company; William F. Schmick, who was advertising manager; and Joseph A. Blondell, who came to the office early in 1914 as auditor to reorganize its accounting system, became assistant secretary and treasurer in

1917, and died in 1934 as the chief financial officer of the company.[1]

The commander-in-chief after September, 1914, was Van-Lear Black. He was one of the most extraordinary men that Baltimore has ever produced, and in his fortieth year was at the height of his powers. Born on December 18, 1875, he cut short his schooling after four years at the Belmont School, near Boston, and before he was twenty was hard at work as a clerk in the office of the Fidelity & Deposit Company of Maryland, of which the elder Mr. Black was a director. For five years Van-Lear Black worked hard at his desk, finally becoming a teller in the banking department of the company. In 1900 he was elected assistant secretary and treasurer, and two years later he became a director. Meanwhile, he had become active also in the management of the Black-Sheridan-Wilson Company, a firm of coal operators of which his father was the head, and had begun to venture into business enterprises on his own account.

Most of them were striking successes, and at the time he took charge of the business affairs of the *Sunpapers* his reputation as a financier extended far beyond Baltimore and Maryland. At different times he was a director of the Massachusetts Mutual Life Insurance Company, the American Sugar Refining Company, the Metropolitan Trust Company of New York, and the Chatham-Phenix National Bank & Trust Company of New York. He had a fertile imagination, and was adept at devising bold and novel projects, but there was never anything of the

[1] Mr. Blondell was born in Baltimore on March 19, 1889, and got his education at Calvert Hall College. He studied accounting and became an auditor for the Maryland State Roads Commission, of which O. E. Weller, later a United States Senator, was chairman. He was recommended to The Sun by Mr. Weller, and his remarkable talents quickly advanced him in the business office. On the election of Mr. Patterson to the presidency of the company on November 10, 1919, Mr. Blondell became treasurer and assistant secretary, and on April 28, 1924, he became secretary and treasurer. He died on June 7, 1934.

speculator in him, and his business practices were grounded upon very old-fashioned notions of honor. Once, when a company in which he was an officer and director was wrecked by circumstances far from his control, he stood a loss of $500,000 in order to save from any loss a bank that had lent money to the company.

He was by no means the financier of legend, devoted wholly to business. There was a curious boyishness about him, and he was never more content than when at play. Horses always delighted him, and he was a regular boxholder at the Pimlico race track. In his younger days he owned and drove one of the finest tandem teams in the South, and won many prizes with it. Later he enjoyed horseback riding, and spent much of his scant leisure in the saddle on his farm, Folly Quarters, in Howard county, Maryland, fifteen miles from Baltimore. He also loved swimming and shooting, and was devoted to water sports, including yachting. Some time after the Wright brothers made their first flight in an airplane Mr. Black decided to purchase a plane for himself, but was dissuaded by his father. But in 1927 he chartered a plane from the Royal Dutch Airways, and in it he toured Europe. Later he purchased a Fokker and began a series of long-distance flights which made him known all over the world. This Fokker he named the *Maryland Free State*. He employed two Dutch pilots, G. J. Geysendorffer and J. B. Scholte, and they were in his service until his death. The first trip they made together was from London to Cairo. Mr. Black thereupon projected a westward trip across the North Atlantic by a route hitherto untried, but investigation showed it would not be feasible. Mr. Scholte then suggested going to the Dutch East Indies by way of the Mediterranean, Asia Minor and India. Mr. Black fell in with the idea and the start was made on June 15, 1927. Batavia was reached on June 30, and the plane was back in Amsterdam on July 23. It had made the round trip of 20,000

VAN–LEAR BLACK (1875–1930)

JOSEPH A. BLONDELL
(1889–1934)

JOHN J. NELLIGAN
(1865–1935)

R. BRENT KEYSER
(1859–1927)

miles in 183½ flying hours. The exploit attracted wide attention, Mr. Black was received with enthusiasm in Holland, and Queen Wilhelmina gave him the ribbon of Orange and Nassau.

The next year he set out from London for Cape Town, but his plane got into difficulties over the desert near Khartum and the trip had to be abandoned. Subsequently he started anew and completed the journey. In 1929 he flew from London to Calcutta, where his plane, after landing, was destroyed in a storm. On February 9, 1930, having bought a new Fokker, he started from London around the world. He flew to Tokyo and then took ship for San Francisco. From there he flew to Baltimore. This trip, with his others, rolled up so much mileage that Mr. Black became the champion airship passenger of the world. He never attempted to pilot his own plane. His confidence in Geysendorffer and Scholte was complete, and he often said he would trust them to land safely in any imaginable emergency. He had, curiously enough, little taste for foreign travel, and seldom went anywhere outside the United States save in his plane. What interested him was the possible future of the airship as a means of regular commercial communication. In his own words, his trips were undertaken in an effort to obtain "first-hand information about commercial flying on protracted air routes under varying conditions."

Beside him, in the days which saw the reorganization of the *Sunpapers*, stood his brother, Harry C. Black, who had been gaining newspaper experience in the editorial rooms since 1911,[1]

---

[1] Mr. Black was born in Baltimore in 1887. He was graduated from Princeton in 1909, and went at once to London to enter the London office of the Fidelity & Deposit Company of Maryland. He returned to Baltimore at the end of 1910, and on February 8, 1911, became a director of The A. S. Abell Company. During the World War he served as an assistant paymaster, U. S. N. R., of a ship carrying supplies from various British ports to France. He succeeded his brother as chairman of the board in 1931, and is chairman today.

and behind him were his father, whose confidence in him was always unlimited, and Messrs. Garrett and Keyser. John Campbell White also belonged to this group of trusting stockholders, but he had joined the Diplomatic Corps in 1913, and was no longer a member of the board of directors. The elder Mr. Black was, like his son, a man of forceful and colorful personality. Born May 14, 1845, at Cumberland, Md., he was a boy at school when the Civil War broke out. But in 1863 he enlisted in the Seventeenth Virginia Cavalry, Confederate Army, and was soon seeing hard service. On his first furlough home he was captured by Federal troops, and spent the last eighteen months of the war as a prisoner at Fort Sheridan and Fort Delaware.[1] When he was released in June, 1865, he was still only twenty. Love of adventure sent him to Mexico, where Maximilian was trying to build up an empire. For a while he worked on the construction of the Imperial Mexican Railroad. Then came the downfall and execution of the Austrian Archduke, and with the coming of chaos, Mr. Black drifted back to the United States.

The West was being opened to civilization at that time. It was the day of the pioneer, a rough, hard era. The man who made his way in the Oklahoma and Nebraska of that day, as Mr. Black did, was certain to have his strength and temper tested. Finally, in his late twenties, he returned to Maryland and began his real career in his home town. He got a job in a coal mine at Cumberland, starting as a clerk. Conditions in the Western Maryland mining country were as wild and rough as anything farther West. Those were the days of the Molly Maguires, when strikes were savage and violence almost the rule. On one occasion strikers had piled ties on the track leading from

---

[1] One of his fellow prisoners at Fort Delaware, as we have seen in Chapter XII, was Francis A. Richardson, later to be Washington correspondent of THE SUN. But apparently the two never met, either in prison or afterward.

the mine where Mr. Black was employed. He drove a locomotive down the track, got down from the cab and started to remove the obstructions. A striker stepped out of the crowd and threatened Mr. Black. With one blow of his fist he knocked the striker down, breaking his jaw, and calmly went on lifting the ties out of the way of the locomotive. Then he climbed into the cab and drove on.

During these rough mining days Mr. Black met John Sheridan, an Irishman of great native shrewdness and ability, employed as a conductor of the railroad. One day Mr. Black told Mr. Sheridan that he had located some promising coal land which could be bought cheaply. Mr. Sheridan suggested that they try to get financial backing, saying that perhaps Lloyd Lowndes, a wealthy banker of Cumberland and later Governor of Maryland, might be interested. But Mr. Black and Mr. Lowndes were cousins and the former refused to ask for financial aid from a relative. So the visit to him was made by Mr. Sheridan. Mr. Lowndes agreed to back the pair financially and a coal-mining firm was organized, with Mr. Lowndes as a silent partner. Mr. Sheridan remained in Cumberland to undertake the operation of the mines, Mr. Black moved to Baltimore to manage the business end of the enterprise, and John Wilson, a Scotsman, was taken in to attend to the selling. Later the enterprise was incorporated as the Black-Sheridan-Wilson Company, which became in time the second largest producer of bituminous coal in the Maryland field. Still later, with Senator Clarence W. Watson, of West Virginia, Mr. Black purchased the Consolidation Coal Company, which became, if not the first, then certainly the second largest producer in the whole United States.

The success of this venture made Mr. Black very wealthy, and he became interested in many other enterprises. He was, at different times, a director of the Baltimore & Ohio Railroad, the Union Mining Company, the New York Mining Company, the National Union Bank of Baltimore, the Eutaw Savings Bank of Baltimore, the United Railways of Baltimore and various other corporations. He was one of the founders of the Fidelity & Deposit Company of Maryland, the first of the great national bonding companies.[1] He was also a trustee of the Johns Hopkins Hospital, and a director of the Alliance of Charitable and Social Agencies of Baltimore. Though the partner of two Governors of Maryland, Lowndes and Warfield, he had no political ambitions himself, and always resisted the frequent efforts that were made to thrust him into office. He was, of course, a Democrat, for he had been a Confederate soldier. He was, in his day, one of the most important men of Maryland, but he was not often seen in public, and, as has been recounted, he seldom visited THE SUN office, and came above the first floor only once. It was not until after his death that it became generally known that he had an exceptional faculty for versifying and had written many skillful and amusing pieces. He died on March 22, 1921. By his will he left $100,000 to the Johns Hopkins Hospital for the care of his old friends, the miners of Western Maryland.[2]

[1] It was incorporated February 15, 1890, as the Fidelity Loan & Trust Company, but on April 3, 1900, the name was changed to the Fidelity & Deposit Company of Maryland by an act of the Legislature. There had been two earlier surety companies, but neither covered so wide a scope as the Fidelity. One of them, the Guarantee Company of North America, a Canadian corporation which entered the United States in 1881, confined its business to bonding the officers and employés of banks, railroads and other corporations. The other, the American Surety Company of New York, organized in 1884, furnished bonds for contractors and fiduciaries and in court cases. The Fidelity added public officials, and so covered the whole field. It was organized by Edwin Warfield, later to be Governor of Maryland. At the start it also did a trust, safe deposit and general banking business, but these activities were taken over on July 1, 1905, by a new corporation, the Fidelity Trust Company.

[2] The day after his death the Baltimore *News* printed the following editorial estimate of him: "Strong, steady, generous, H. Crawford Black claimed while living the

Messrs. Garrett and Keyser were both men of wealth, and members of old Maryland families. Mr. Garrett is the grandson of John W. Garrett, the Civil War president of the Baltimore & Ohio Railroad. He was a famous athlete at Princeton, and made history at the first Olympic Games at Athens in 1896. At that time the ancient Greek sport of discus throwing was still unpracticed in America. Mr. Garrett, desiring to engage in it, had a discus made that weighed twenty pounds, but found it impossible to use. When he got to Athens he learned that the standard Greek discus weighed but four and two-fifths pounds. Undaunted, he got one and began to practice, and next day he entered the discus contest against a field of Greeks. He threw the discus ninety-five feet seven inches, and so established a world's record which stood until, on his return to Princeton, he made 110 feet. He was also a star at the broad and high jumps and at putting the shot.

On coming home from college, he founded, with others, the Public Athletic League in Baltimore, and has been its chief

---

rights and privileges of the simple, straight-going, private citizen. He wished neither advertisement nor praise; he needed no publicity to establish his place in this community, and we may believe his desire would be for but restrained, reserved, obituary notice. That feeling is to be respected. He would have disliked, living, being called the premier private citizen of this city and State. But that he was, and wherever he had chanced to live he would have found few rivals able to contend with him for that place in the respect of his community. There have been other men in this State with business sagacity as keen as Mr. Black's. There have been other men able and glad to use their wealth as intelligently. There have been other men of integrity and healthy, reasoned judgment equal to his own. Possibly there have been other men with equal or profounder influence upon the financial life of the city and all that springs from the development of sound business undertakings of wide scope. But back of such a standing as Mr. Black had, lay something far greater than ability, greater than knowledge of human nature. It can appear in no cataloguing of his business career. For all his other assets, his greatest was his personality: vigorous, honest, straight and confidence compelling."

spirit ever since. (It was later combined with the Children's Playground Association, and is now called the Playground Athletic League.) In November, 1920, he was drafted to head a non-partisan Public Improvement Commission appointed to outfit the old Baltimore with extensive additions to its water-supply and sewerage system, improved streets, and new public schools. Down to 1930, when he resigned, he supervised the expenditure of $87,000,000, and a new Baltimore emerged from his hands. Mr. Garrett became a director of The A. S. Abell Company on February 24, 1913, while Mr. Grasty was still president of the company. He served until May 12, 1930, when he retired because of his lack of sympathy with certain of the *Sunpapers'* policies. He has been, for many years, a director of the Baltimore & Ohio Railroad and a trustee of his *alma mater*, Princeton University.

Mr. Keyser became a director on September 8, 1914, and served until his death on March 1, 1927. He was the very *beau ideal* of an old-time Maryland aristocrat. Handsome in person and courtly in manner, he was a descendant on the maternal side of Margaret Brent, kinswoman of Leonard Calvert (*c.* 1582–1647; the first Colonial Governor of Maryland), and famous on her own account for her demand for the right to vote. On the other side Mr. Keyser was descended from Dirck Keyser, who immigrated from Amsterdam to Germantown, Pa., in 1635. His father, William Keyser (d. 1904), was an associate of John W. Garrett in the Baltimore & Ohio Railroad, and was heavily interested in metals.

R. Brent Keyser was born in Baltimore on August 5, 1859, and was educated at St. Paul's School, Concord, N. H. He did not proceed to college, but became a clerk in the office of Keyser Bros. & Company, a steel firm headed by his father, in 1878. When the Baltimore Copper Smelting & Rolling Company was formed in 1883 he transferred to it, becoming its treasurer in

1885 and its president in 1905. In 1910 he negotiated its sale to the Guggenheims. He was also interested in other business enterprises, but in his later years he devoted most of his time to three Baltimore institutions that were very close to his heart — the Johns Hopkins University, the Baltimore & Ohio Railroad, and the *Sunpapers*. He was president of the trustees of the Johns Hopkins from 1903 to 1926, and a trustee afterward to the time of his death. His father had been president, during the political turmoils of the 90s, of the Baltimore Reform League, which was largely responsible for the downfall of the old Democratic machine, and Mr. Keyser himself was always interested in independent movements in politics. But he never sought or accepted office himself.

These were the men who gave Van-Lear Black *carte blanche* to reorganize and revive the *Sunpapers* in the Summer of 1914, with the World War just getting under way and a panic threatening in the United States. He encountered a special problem of great difficulty at the very start. News of the break between Mr. Grasty and his backers had got out in June, and during the month following certain representatives of the *News* had gone about Baltimore saying that the *Sunpapers* were bankrupt and would soon suspend publication. The effect of this gossip on local advertisers was very damaging to the papers. The directors met on August 3 to consider the matter, and decided to instruct their counsel, Edwin G. Baetjer, to take whatever legal action was possible in the premises. But Mr. Black did not wait for the slow processes of the law. He decided to give the advertisers ocular evidence that the *Sunpapers* were still solvent and, in fact, enjoying a new vigor.

That ocular evidence took the form of a special performance of the comedy, " It Pays to Advertise," by Roi Cooper Megrue. The play was then running in New York, and to packed houses. Mr. Black sent John E. Cullen there to see George M. Cohan, who was head of the firm presenting it, and Mr. Cullen induced him to send the whole company, with the necessary scenery and other impedimenta, to Baltimore. The company left New York after the night performance on October 12, breakfasted on its train in the Pennsylvania Railroad's Baltimore yards, moved on to the Academy of Music, and there gave a performance beginning at 10 A.M. Then it returned to New York and was ready for the regular performance there that night. The house in Baltimore was packed with advertisers and their employés, rounded up by Mr. Black and his diligent aides. There was a prologue by THE SUN's staff poet, the Bentztown Bard, and a souvenir program with verse, prose and pictures by members of the staff. The show was a roaring success. The advertisers greatly enjoyed it, and did not fail to be impressed by the moral of the play, which was that advertising always pays. They noted, too, the great amount of publicity that the performance had got in the New York newspapers. Altogether, the venture served its purpose admirably. The tale that the *Sunpapers* were bankrupt began to seem silly. Town report put the cost of the stunt at $10,000 or $12,000. The actual appropriation of the directors, made on September 28, was $2,500.

It was the beginning of a long series of devices whereby Mr. Black attracted attention to the *Sunpapers*, and convinced the Baltimore advertisers that they were very much alive, and would have to be taken seriously. He was, among many other diverse things, a natural showman, and delighted in striking spectacles. Once, for his private amusement, he bought a one-ring circus, and invited half a dozen members of the *Sunpaper* staffs to join him in a two weeks' tour of the country towns of Maryland. Another time, he organized a rodeo at his country place, brought in half a tribe of Indians to give it background, and prepared a barbecue for nearly 500 guests.

But it was not only by such means that he made the advertisers of Baltimore conscious of the *Sunpapers*. He also visited them in person, and tackled them with facts and figures. He believed implicitly in the great future of the papers, and he managed by enormous pertinacity to spread that confidence through the city. At the same time he worked with inexhaustible energy with the staff in effecting economies in operation. He drove home repeatedly his dictum: "An endowed newspaper cannot be made to succeed. We shall never get anywhere until the public, and particularly the advertisers, understand the *Sunpapers* are standing on their own feet." He was handicapped during his first year or so by the fact that Mr. Grasty had sought to bring advertisers into THE EVENING SUN by offering them an extravagant bargain. They could get space in it, along with space in THE SUN, by paying only 2 cents more a line than they would have to pay for space in THE SUN alone. No considerable merchant among them accepted this offer, so the ante was lowered to 1 cent. One of the largest department stores then accepted, and was given a five-year contract. That contract was a dreadful burden to the *Sunpapers* until it expired, for it stood in the way of the advance in advertising rates that was justified by their steady gain in circulation.

THE SUN, which had a net average sale of 91,652 copies a day in 1914, went to 94,715 in 1915, and to 102,404 in 1916. Its price by mail was raised from 1 cent a copy to 2 on June 10, 1918, and on September 1 the city price also went to 2 cents. There was a consequent recession in that year to a net daily average of 99,148. The decline continued into 1919, reaching 94,940. But in 1920 there was a leap forward to 105,157, and in 1921 the circulation was 114,632. THE EVENING SUN did almost as well. Its net paid circulation in 1914, the last year of the Grasty administration, was only 42,978, but it moved forward to 50,543 in 1915, to 60,805 in 1916, to 69,165 in 1917, and to 79,311 in 1918. On July 10, 1918, a month after THE

SUN went to 2 cents, THE EVENING SUN followed suit, and in consequence there was a recession to 71,475 in 1919. In both cases, of course, the end of the World War also had something to do with the decline in paper sales. But in 1920 THE EVENING SUN went to 82,071, and the year following it passed 100,000.

THE SUNDAY SUN did better than either THE SUN or THE EVENING SUN. Beginning with a circulation of 81,999 in 1914, it went to 87,932 in 1915, to 96,212 in 1916, to 102,534 in 1917, to 115,509 in 1918, to 125,164 in 1919, to 137,789 in 1920, and to 150,921 in 1921. It has kept ahead of both THE SUN and THE EVENING SUN ever since, and is now beyond 200,000. THE SUN had joined the Audit Bureau of Circulations (then called the Advertising Audit Association and Bureau of Verified Circulations) as a charter member on April 28, 1914. This organization, consisting of both advertisers and publishers, makes regular audits of the circulation books of all subscribing publications. The circulation figures of THE SUN, THE SUNDAY SUN and THE EVENING SUN are certified by it. W. F. Schmick, executive vice-president of The A. S. Abell Company, has been one of its directors since October, 1932.

Before the performance of "It Pays to Advertise" passed into Baltimore advertising history, Mr. Black was busy with a scheme to charter a steamship to take a party of Baltimore merchants and manufacturers on a tour of South America. The European market, in the last half of 1914, had been cut off by the World War, and business was bad in the United States. This South American project turned out to be beyond the resources of the *Sunpapers* at the time, so Mr. Black quickly shelved it for more feasible enterprises. By November 16, 1914, the circulation department, as he and his aides had reorganized and restimulated it, was doing so well with THE EVENING SUN that the directors were noting with satisfaction that the circulation of the paper was "nearly 50,000," and passing a resolution urging that "steps be taken to get the press-run above the 50,000 mark." Those steps were duly taken, and many others, as the figures just quoted demonstrate. The flow of receipts from both circulation and advertising increased steadily, if (for the first year or two) somewhat slowly. The loss on operations for 1914 was heavy, but in 1915 it was much reduced, and in 1916 it was turned into a profit. There has been a profit every year since, but the deficit accumulated from 1910 to 1915 was not finally wiped out until 1922.

There were no dividends until July, 1924. The money that began to flow in after 1916 was all devoted to four purposes: (*a*) to paying off the accumulated short-term debt of the company, (*b*) to improving the contents and appearance of the papers, (*c*) to increasing the compensation of their employés, and (*d*) to rebuilding and enlarging the physical plant. To all these purposes Mr. Black applied himself assiduously. He might have got rid of the company's debt much sooner than he did if it had not been for two things — the sharp rise in the price of newsprint paper after 1915, and the inescapable need for plant expansions as circulation rose and increasing advertising made it necessary to print larger and larger papers.

In the Abells' day the average cost of paper had been 2 cents a pound, and in Mr. Grasty's day it had been 2¼, but by the close of 1916 it was a cent more, and by 1919 it got to 4 cents. Indeed, the *Sunpapers* had to pay as much as 5 cents for part of their supply, for their regular mills could not furnish all they required, and they were forced to go into the open market for the remainder. All the other publishers of the United States were in the same fix, and some of them, before the return to normal prices in 1921, were mulcted excessively. Mr. Munsey, it was reported at the time, paid as much as 10 cents a pound for a part of his supply. The *Sunpapers*, through the adroit management of Mr. Black and his aides, fared much better, but so late as November, 1920, they were buying paper at 5 cents a pound, or more than double the usual price. What this extra cost amounted to may be figured out from the fact that in 1920 they used 16,884 tons altogether. In 1917 the directors had to borrow $125,000 to buy paper.

The enlargement of the plant was begun as early as September, 1914, when the steam engine and dynamos in the basement of THE SUN Building were taken out to make room for new stereotyping equipment. Before that time the *Sunpapers* had generated their own electricity, but thereafter they bought it from the Consolidated Gas Electric Light & Power Company, thus saving a lot of much needed space. The directors authorized the purchase of new equipment on October 19, 1914, and thereafter for ten years they seldom held a meeting without appropriating money for more. Meanwhile THE SUN Building had to be frequently remodeled. It had been built in 1906 to accommodate one newspaper, and now it was housing two, both of rapidly increasing circulation, and with a huge Sunday edition to be cared for also. Both the business office and the editorial rooms were uncomfortably crowded, and the composing room and pressroom were jammed. There were five presses in the pressroom, all of relatively small size. It was decided to replace them with three large decuples. These monsters had to be installed in a confined space, and the smaller presses had to be kept going all the while. It was an engineering operation of great difficulty, and it took months.

Eventually it became necessary to add two more decuples. There was no room for them in the old cellar, so an annex had to be erected to the westward of THE SUN Building. The large lot at 9 and 11 West Baltimore street was purchased, and a little while later the lot at 4 and 6 West Redwood street, to the rear, was added to it. On this space the present annex was built.[1] It contains a greatly enlarged business office, separate editorial rooms for THE SUN and THE EVENING SUN, an addition of 40,000 square feet to the old composing room, a pressroom of large capacity, and a cafeteria for the use of all employés, capable of seating 200 at a time. The enlarged building accommodates about 1,000 employés, of whom 260 work in the composing room. The building is open day and night the year round. The business office always closes at midnight of Christmas Eve, for THE SUN and THE EVENING SUN never come out on Christmas Day, but its doors are reopened at 2 o'clock on Christmas afternoon. The editorial rooms, of course, are never closed. The job of moving into the annex was almost as onerous as that of installing the three decuples in the old cellar. The floor of the building had to be dropped three or four feet to give the big presses sufficient headroom, and there were other difficulties. The cost of the operation was very heavy, and ran far beyond the first estimates. The new building was not finished until 1927. It still provides adequate space for the editorial and business offices and the mechanical departments, but the circulation department has bulged into two warehouses on Redwood street, a few doors from the annex to the westward. They are six stories in height and occupy a double lot 80 by 80 feet in area. When, as and if any further extension of the *Sunpapers'* premises is necessary they will provide room for it.

During the efforts by Mr. Black and his associates in the office to rehabilitate the *Sunpapers* and put them on a sound financial footing, the extra expenses produced by the World War raised a long series of fresh difficulties. The increase in the cost of newsprint paper has been mentioned. The general cost of living also went up, and it had to be met by increased salaries

[1] The architect was Edward L. Palmer, of Baltimore.

and wages. On February 26, 1917, all employés who had been in the service on September 1, 1916, save only those under union-wage agreements, were raised ten per cent., and a bit later there was another horizontal raise of five per cent. Meanwhile, many much more substantial increases were made in individual salaries, and the general salary scale in the editorial rooms was almost doubled.

Preparations for covering the operations of the Maryland units in the war were undertaken as soon as the first American troops went into camp. In August, 1917, when the Maryland National Guard was ordered to Camp McClellan, Anniston, Ala., for training, Raymond S. Tompkins, of the reportorial staff of The Sun, went along. The Marylanders were presently organized as the Twenty-ninth Division, Major-General Charles J. Morton commanding, along with guardsmen from Virginia, New Jersey and the District of Columbia. As their period of training neared its end, in the Spring of 1918, Mr. Tompkins proceeded to France ahead of them, and when they arrived in July he had already had some experience with other divisions. He followed the Twenty-ninth to the Alsace-Lorraine front, and was with it during the second phase of the Argonne offensive. On October 29, 1918, after three weeks of steady advance against machine-gun resistance, it was relieved by the Seventy-ninth Division. The latter had begun its training at Camp Meade, Md., and included the Three Hundred and Thirteenth Infantry, a regiment made up of Baltimoreans. So Mr. Tompkins remained at the front, and was with the Seventy-ninth when the war ended. Meanwhile, various other members of The Sun staff had covered the training of Maryland units in the camps at home, and especially at Camp Meade, which was but twenty miles from Baltimore.

After the armistice Mr. Tompkins was accredited to the Army of Occupation and attached to the famous Rainbow Division, which began to move into Germany on November 20, 1918. He remained in Germany until the end of the year, when he returned to Paris to join J. Fred Essary, chief of THE SUN's Washington bureau, who had been assigned to the Versailles Peace Conference. Mr. Essary and Mr. Tompkins remained in Paris until the Spring of 1919. In August, 1923, Mr. Tompkins returned to Germany to describe the condition of the country under the great inflation. He reported the Rhineland rebellion, the *Bierhalle Putsch* in Munich which saw the beginnings of Hitler, the passive resistance on the Ruhr, the troubles on the Polish border, and all the other dramatic events of the time. He also crossed to the British Isles, and reported the election which made Ramsay MacDonald Premier for the first time, and the turbulent events in Ireland. He remained in Europe until March, 1924.[1]

The *Sunpapers* gave a great deal of energy and money to the various good causes of the war years. When, in June, 1917, it was found that Maryland was $2,500,000 short of its quota on the First Liberty Loan, The A. S. Abell Company undertook to underwrite the deficit, and the *Sunpapers* sold $1,046,750 of the bonds to 8,748 different persons over their counter. The

---

[1] Mr. Tompkins was born in Nyack, N. Y., October 12, 1890. At fourteen he accompanied his parents to Washington, and was there educated. He studied law at the Georgetown University Law School and was admitted to the bar in 1912. A year later he joined the staff (temporarily, as he thought) of the Frederick (Md.) *Post,* and in 1915 he came to THE SUN. He resigned in 1924, and is now director of information and service for the Baltimore Transit Company. During his days on THE SUN he took special courses in history, political economy, and English and American literature at the Johns Hopkins University, and also taught journalism in its Summer school. He was an excellent reporter, and had a hand in many *Sunpaper* enterprises of the period. Among other things, he organized and operated a Jungle Circle for children, devoted to promoting the improvement of the Baltimore Zoo. It grew to immense proportions, made a great pother in the city for several years, and once actually swung a municipal election.

success of this venture induced them to carry on the sale of all the later loans in the same way, and by May, 1919, they had sold $4,190,750 worth of bonds to 28,499 persons, and $254,993.75 in Thrift and War-Savings stamps to 3,000 more. They also joined in publishing an Overseas edition of THE SUN, issued weekly in tabloid form for the Maryland troops in France. It was one-fourth the size of a page of THE SUN, and contained all the home news in brief. It was sent to the soldiers by letter mail, in sealed envelopes. Beginning on April 22, 1918, it ran for exactly one year. When its accounts were cast up it showed an unexpected profit of $520.50, and this money was donated to the United War Work Campaign. The *Sunpapers* also prepared a 15,000-foot moving picture of home scenes and home people for the Maryland soldiers. In February, 1918, when a bank failed at Odenton, Md., near Camp Meade, Md., to the loss of many of them in training there, it raised $79,825, including its own contribution of $10,000, to make good their loss. Of this sum, only $30,000 was needed, and the rest was returned to the contributors. Eventually, with the rehabilitation of the bank, they were repaid in full. From March 30 to April 28, 1918, the *Sunpapers* presented a huge patriotic spectacle, called "Over There," at the Fifth Regiment Armory, Baltimore, and hundreds of thousands of persons saw it. On the night of the Armistice, November 11, 1918, they arranged a jollification in SUN Square, and among the participants was Mme. Schumann-Heink, the singer, who had had sons on both sides in the war. In May, 1919, when the Maryland soldiers who had been in France began to return, each group was met at Camp Stuart, Newport News, Va., and given a chicken dinner. Altogether, 7,000 men were so entertained. Finally, there was a party for SUN men who had served in the war, at Saunders Range, Md., June 29, 1919.

From this party there were, unhappily, three absentees.

They were Robert Morris Armstrong, a reporter, who was killed in action during the storming of Montfaucon, September 26, 1918; Philip Emil Weigand, a carrier, who was lost in the sinking of the *Tuscania;* and George Seriah Katz, who died in camp at Fort McHenry, Baltimore. There are bronze tablets in memory of all three in the lobby of THE SUN Building. That to Mr. Weigand was erected by his associates of THE SUN Route Owners Association.

During this period from 1914 to 1919 Mr. Black's work as chairman of the board of directors had been devoted exclusively to the business affairs of the *Sunpapers.* He never intervened in their editorial conduct. Mr. Adams was in full control of the editorial pages of both THE SUN and THE EVENING SUN, and Mr. Kent was equally in control of their news departments. Mr. Adams, early in 1915, began to show serious symptoms of the illness that was to take his life twelve years later, and on May 24 he was granted a year's furlough by the directors, but he was back in harness before it ended, and thereafter, until his last year, he kept at his duties, though frequently in intense pain. He looked forward with constant hope, during the first years of the Black régime, to the day when the *Sunpapers* would be out of the woods, financially speaking, and ripe and ready for that large editorial development which he always had in mind for them. He lived to see his dream come true, but until the end of the World War the principal job before him was to do the best possible with the limited means at hand. His was a truly heroic spirit, and he never lost either confidence or energy.

Mr. Kent gave him energetic support, and, despite the lack of funds for ambitious editorial enterprises, greatly extended the scope and variety of the *Sunpapers'* daily supply of news. Discontented with the censored dispatches coming from the scenes of the World War, Mr. Kent went to Europe in the Autumn of 1918, and on his return printed in THE SUN a frank and unadorned account of the momentous events then in progress. It appeared on the first page of The Sun on November 28, 1918, under the heading of "Paris Seethes With International Jealousy and Suspicion." Following the heading was a note:

This article is the first uncensored account of actual conditions in Paris to be printed in this country or abroad. The writer was in Paris at the time the terms of the Armistice were determined upon, and returned to this country on the first ship that left England after it had been signed. It was not possible to have got this article to America either by mail or cable.

All the other newspapers of the United States were full in those days of dispatches describing the Allies as a band of loving brothers, and the United States as the hope and inspiration of them all. But Mr. Kent told the plain truth, and in his customary, vehement way. Parts of his article, which ran to five columns, follow:

For weeks past, under the surface, Paris has been simply seething with international jealousies, friction and feeling, and between us and our noble allies at this time there is a tension and a strain that does not appear on the top, but that is very real none the less. . . . The truth is, and everybody in Paris knows it, that in governmental and political circles they do not love us at all over there, neither the English nor the French. Between individuals of different nations and races warm and sincere friendships are possible and there are plenty of Englishmen and Americans and Frenchmen and Americans between whom there are the strongest personal ties. But there is something about races and nations as a whole that makes the kind of friendships that exist between individuals impossible. Paris these days most beautifully illustrates this.

In the first place, General Pershing is anything but popular over there with the French and British high commands. The distaste for him dates back to the Spring of 1917, when, after having first agreed to permit the American forces to be brigaded with the French and British in platoons, he got cold feet on that proposition and in a memorable conference with Foch and Haig stood up and, in fact, said the American Army was at their disposal to do with what they wanted, but it would have to be used as an army, and there would be no more splitting up of it. The French were furious not only at what Pershing said, but at the way he said it, which was in the most outspoken American language imaginable and not, it is said, entirely free from profanity. Had he been a Frenchman, his friends say, he would probably have had to fight a duel with Foch. But he had his way and subsequent events proved him right. . . .

As to the French, there is believed to be a disposition on their part to reach out for more territory than is exactly just. There is talk of extending France to the Rhine and to the Alps — God's boundary lines, as they call them there — and to look to the acquisition of certain German colonial possessions. In other words, the French statesmen are disposed to feel that the situation rather justifies the "picking of bones" of the enemy, and it is said that Clemenceau, ferocious, forceful and a fighter with a tremendous personality, despite his great age, is sympathetic with the idea of gaining some material advantage to France beyond the items of "indemnity and restoration." Likewise, the French politicians are not averse to England maintaining her sea dominance providing France is permitted to maintain her military machine of several million men. We are expected to sit still, look pleasant, and agree to this programme like a good nation. Some of our representatives over there say emphatically they'll be damned if we do.

You hear, too, in Paris, what will be news in America, of the serious mutiny in the French Army in 1917, and of the difficulty in suppressing it. In this direction the advent of America into the war seems to have saved the situation. Neither England nor France have any use for Italy. They tell you that the Italian troops were a bitter disappointment, that they fight all right when things are going their way, but they cannot be depended upon when they are not, and have to be stiffened by support whenever a real fight is due. And that they were eternally demanding men and money and refusing to carry on unless they got them.

In the month of April alone, of this year, an American official who knows states that the American Red Cross presented to no less than 324,000 Italian families a sum of money ranging from 50 to

150 lire. The money went only to those families whose sons or husbands were fighting in the Italian Army. When she received the money the mother or wife of the Italian soldier received also a letter telling her that it was given by the American Red Cross because her son or husband was at the front fighting valiantly for Italy. She was required to send this letter back to the son or husband at the front. While the Red Cross in this way spent millions of dollars (and they did some of this in France, too) in a way not guessed by the people back home, the statement is flatly made here that the Red Cross disbursements in this way so strengthened the morale of the Italian Army that it prevented Italy from withdrawing from the war.

As for the Portuguese, they are said to be the limit. In April, 1917, the Portuguese were holding a section of the front line with the British. When the Boche launched his attack the entire Portuguese division threw down its arms and streaked for the rear, leaving a gap in the line of 4,000 yards, through which the Boche poured like a current and which nearly gave him the channel ports. The Portuguese scattered in all directions and the only way in which they could be gotten together again at all was by the British refusing to feed them except in one place. This ended their experience as first-line troops.

This sort of stuff, in the complacent days between the Armistice and the Peace Conference, naturally made a tremendous sensation. Today what Mr. Kent wrote is known to everyone as fact, but in November, 1918, it seemed like the worst sort of treason. Letters and telegrams of protest poured into THE SUN office, and there were professional patriots who proposed that Mr. Kent be haled into court. But he stuck to his guns, insisting that he had told only the truth, and gradually his revelations percolated the country, and no doubt had a great deal to do with the growth of American suspicions of the Versailles Conference.

With the war over, Mr. Black redoubled his efforts to pay off the indebtedness of The A. S. Abell Company and put the property on a sound financial basis. It took him ten years to reach the goal that he had set for himself, but he never deviated from his purpose, and in the end he was completely successful. All outstanding notes were paid off, the preferred stock was retired, and there remained in 1924 no obligations save the common stock and such of the mortgage bonds as had not yet come in for redemption. The improvement in the earnings of the *Sunpapers* had been in steady progress since 1915. On February 16, 1919, THE SUNDAY SUN printed its first issue of 100 pages, with 540 columns of paid advertising, each of 300 lines — a record for Baltimore up to that time. On November 14 of the same year 157 columns of advertising had to be omitted from THE EVENING SUN in order to keep it within thirty-two pages — the largest paper that could be printed by the presses then in service. During the whole of that Autumn from twenty-five to 150 columns had to be omitted from THE EVENING SUN every Thursday and Friday. Some of this was national advertising that could be switched to less crowded days, but a large part of it was local advertising that could not be printed at any other time. On March 30, 1920, THE SUN came out with 166 columns of advertising, leaving only forty columns for editorial and news matter. On November 23, 1923, THE EVENING SUN printed an issue of fifty-six pages, with 344 columns of advertising; on April 11, 1924, it printed one of sixty-two pages, with 378 columns of advertising, and on December 14, 1928, it printed one of eighty-six pages with 519 columns of advertising. On December 6, 1925, THE SUNDAY SUN printed 174 pages, with 761 columns of advertising. Beginning in 1919 the *Sunpapers* taken together gained advertising lineage, for a while, at the rate of half a million lines a month. In 1924 they printed altogether 32,786,478 lines of paid advertising, and in 1926 they went to 35,694,751 lines. This last remains a world's record. The onset of the Depression, of course, caused a decline, but the losses of the *Sunpapers* were less than those of most other large American newspapers. In August, 1930, for example, the lineage printed was but 78,000 lines behind August, 1929, whereas the five papers in situations most closely resembling their own lost from 230,000 to 617,000.

Circulation kept pace with the gains in advertising. The carrier system of the *Sunpapers* took them into virtually every home in Baltimore and its vicinity. In 1930 the circulation department was able to make the boast that in the Roland Park-Guilford-Homeland district, the finest residential section of Baltimore, they were served to all save twenty-one of the 1,913 occupied houses and apartments. In Ten Hills, Forest Park, Ashburton and West Arlington, other regions of beautiful homes, it was served to every one of them. In the city proper there were many blocks in which every householder took them. One West Baltimore carrier route included twenty-four such blocks. This record, perhaps unique in the world, has been maintained ever since. The 142 *Sunpaper* carriers, with their large corps of assistants, visit almost every home in Baltimore every day. They are undaunted by weather, and never miss a call. That their work involves perils beyond those of the weather has been shown more than once. On December 6, 1924, crossing a street in the dim light of the early morning, Harry Silverman, a *Sunpaper* carrier, was run down and killed by a hit-and-run driver. The *Sunpapers* offered a reward of $1,000 for the arrest of the culprit, and he was duly taken and punished. On February 14, 1933, Albert Sereboff, another carrier, was shot by a Negro while making collections. A similar reward was offered for the arrest of the guilty man, and he was presently beginning a sentence of twenty years in prison. On November 9, 1934, a *Sunpaper* chauffeur was held up near Upper Marlboro, Md., by four Negro highwaymen, and a man who was riding with him was shot. Again a reward of $1,000 was posted by the *Sunpapers*, and again the offenders were taken and imprisoned.[1]

In the Autumn of 1919, with the World War ended and the rehabilitation of the business organization of the *Sunpapers* well advanced, Mr. Black and the other directors decided that the time had come to center their future efforts on building up the news and editorial departments of the papers. The first step toward that end was to fill the post of president of The A. S. Abell Company, left vacant since Mr. Grasty's resignation in 1914. The man chosen was Paul Patterson, and on November 11, 1919, he was elected by the board of directors.

---

[1] There are 142 *Sunpaper* carrier routes, but only 133 of these belong to the carriers by deeds recorded in the office. Such routes may be bought and sold — of course, with the approval of the *Sunpapers*. The 133 route owners constitute the association, which was organized in 1910, succeeding an earlier SUN Carriers' Association. It is represented, in its dealings with the circulation manager of the *Sunpapers*, by a Carrier Council of seven members. It holds an annual banquet, and is altogether a very prosperous organization. Its president, until his death a few years ago, was Francis J. Wolf, known as the Bishop because of his dignified mien. The present president is A. J. Fritz. There are members who have been serving THE SUN daily for thirty years or more.

CHAPTER XIX

REORGANIZATION AND REJUVENATION

In a way, the election of Mr. Patterson as president of The A. S. Abell Company marked the end of one era and the beginning of another. Under the direction of Van-Lear Black the worst of the company's financial difficulties had been surmounted, and though there were still some ahead it was clear that, barring unforeseen calamities, they could be resolved. But Mr. Black, despite his boldness and resourcefulness in business matters, was curiously modest and retiring when it came to editorial and news policy. Possibly he felt that his own rather brief schooling had left him unfitted for playing a rôle in a realm that always seemed to him mysterious and even Olympian. It is a literal fact that he would sometimes stammer and blush like a boy when confronted by the omniscience of an editorial writer. It was not merely that he refrained from giving orders in the editorial rooms; he completely effaced himself from this end of the papers' concerns.

His brother, Harry C. Black, having seen service in the Navy throughout the War, had returned home, like many others, full of a youthful conviction that the politicians had played the country and the world a scurvy trick and that dull and flatulent newspapers must take their share of the blame. He was delighted with the Kent article described in Chapter XVIII, and was proud to be associated with the paper that had ventured to print it. It started his mind working along similar lines and before long he had persuaded Mr. Adams to let him contribute an occasional article of his own to the editorial page of THE EVENING SUN. Each was an attempt to destroy, by the marshaling of hard facts, some bit of the demagoguery then current. But in the actual business of running a newspaper he too regarded himself as an amateur and it never occurred to him to assume the responsibility of direction in editorial matters. Even today, as chairman of the board, that remains his attitude.

Van-Lear Black, along with his brother and the other members of the board, felt that some sort of centralized professional control over the enterprise in which they were so deeply concerned was essential, but all of them distrusted their ability to choose the needed man. The Blacks accordingly made discreet inquiries over the country and considered several men of already well-established reputation as publishers or editors. But they never found a man with the precise combination of experience and capacity that they were looking for. Finally, the decision was reached to place the responsibility upon Paul Patterson, then the business manager of the *Sunpapers*.

Mr. Patterson's career, before and after his association with the papers, has been described. Since he had become business manager, two other men had grown in stature and importance in association with him. One of these was William F. Schmick and the other was Joseph A. Blondell.[1] Mr. Schmick was obviously qualified to take over the direction of the entire business depart-

[1] There is an account of Mr. Schmick in Chapter XVII and of Mr. Blondell in Chapter XVIII.

ment and Mr. Blondell, though still a very young man, had proved himself adept at handling the somewhat complicated financial affairs of the corporation. Hence it was possible to release Mr. Patterson from the details incident to his position as business manager and, in the words of R. Brent Keyser, to turn him from an executive into an administrator. As a matter of fact, the change was not a revolution but a development. Mr. Patterson was essentially an editorial man, and his news training had been extensive. Though theoretically immersed in the counting-room since 1913, he had so great an interest in news and the problems involved in gathering it that he had never wholly divorced himself from association with the editors and their staffs. He was completely familiar with the set-up of the papers in that department. Van-Lear Black and his brother decided, therefore, that they could best solve their problem by electing him to the vacant presidency, and in September, 1919, they advised him of the impending advancement.

This advance warning gave Mr. Patterson an opportunity to canvass the situation at length with Harry C. Black and with H. L. Mencken, who was called into counsel because he was familiar by thirteen years' experience with the editorial affairs of the two papers, was an eager believer in their future, and yet occupied no executive position, and was notoriously without any desire to take one.[1] Not often in the history of American newspapers have three men approached a new task with more trepidation or greater zest. There was agreement among them

[1] Mr. Patterson and Mr. Mencken were thrown into close contact by the accident that when Mr. Patterson entered the office in 1911 he was given a desk adjoining that of Mr. Mencken in the editorial rooms. The two, becoming friendly, exchanged ideas about the papers, and so, when the time came to undertake their improvement, Mencken's views naturally came into consideration. He had been associated with Harry C. Black in a number of editorial projects before this time, and it was at Mr. Black's suggestion that he had started his Free Lance column in 1911.

that a very considerable development in the news and editorial departments of the two papers was immediately desirable, and that it would hardly be possible for either Mr. Adams or Mr. Kent to carry on much longer under the double burden of duty which still embarrassed them. There was further agreement that any new men who were brought in should be young and promising rather than elderly and established, and that, so far as the finances of the paper made it possible, capable men should be well paid. But especially it was agreed that the days of "personal" journalism were over and that the making of a great newspaper could no longer be the task of any one man, but that it must be the resultant of the work of a group of them; as merchants of ideas they must examine all ideas offered, and permit their own most cherished notions to be subjected to rigorous examination by their associates.

Night after night, when the day's routine was finished, the three met to debate the future of the *Sunpapers*. Mencken, at that time, was one of the editors of the *Smart Set* and spent a part of his time in New York; so it was not always possible for him to be present at these palavers, but few ideas were projected without being subjected at some time in the course of their development to his skeptical analysis. Sometimes Black and Patterson would sit quietly while he walked the floor and demolished some fine plan that they had advanced. At other times he and Black would do the sitting while Patterson paced back and forth, attempting to clarify some problem. Sometimes all three would be on their feet at the same time. Black said afterward that these gyrations cost him a new carpet in his living-room.

After Patterson's election as president the meetings continued. One night Black brought to one of them a document which he had entitled "An Editorial Memorandum" but which is generally referred to in THE SUN office as the White Paper. It ran to twenty-three pages of typescript and embodied a thorough and highly realistic discussion of the position and prospects of the two papers. It was devoted mainly to THE SUN, but its conclusions applied equally well to THE EVENING SUN. It began with an examination of the situation of THE SUN with respect to circulation in Washington and showed that the paper had an unexampled opportunity to attract important and influential readers there and to win their confidence by presenting them with a full report of the world's news, impartially presented and competently interpreted. "Obviously," it went on, "the paper must have a consistent and vigorous

policy to attain any wide influence, and that policy must be free from any suspicion of loyalty to private interest or to rigid formulæ. THE SUN must convince by means of sound information, unquestionable honesty and unshakable common sense. It must be alert to new ideas and hospitable to them. It must be absolutely free, and when I write of freedom I think of the lines of James Russell Lowell:

To honor the man
Who is ready to sink
Half his present repute
For the freedom to think,
And when he has thought,
Be his cause strong or weak,
Will risk t'other half
For the freedom to speak;
Caring not for what vengeance
The mob has in store,
Be that mob the upper
Ten thousand or lower.

All this at once bars out any steady fidelity to either of the great political parties as such. It may, at times, support the policies of either one of them with all of its resources, but THE SUN cannot allow itself to be forced to accept policies ready-made, or to vacillate over them as the two great political parties often vacillate. If it would make its influence felt, it ever must be more vigorous at the precise and very time that politicians are most cautious; and most

JOHN HASLUP ADAMS
(1871–1927)

OLIVER PERRY BALDWIN
(1850–1932)

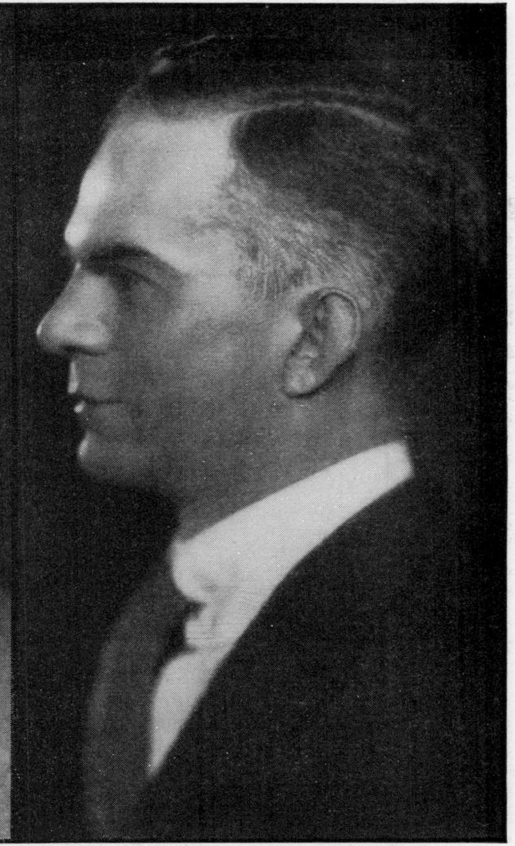

STANLEY MEADE REYNOLDS
(1885–1930)

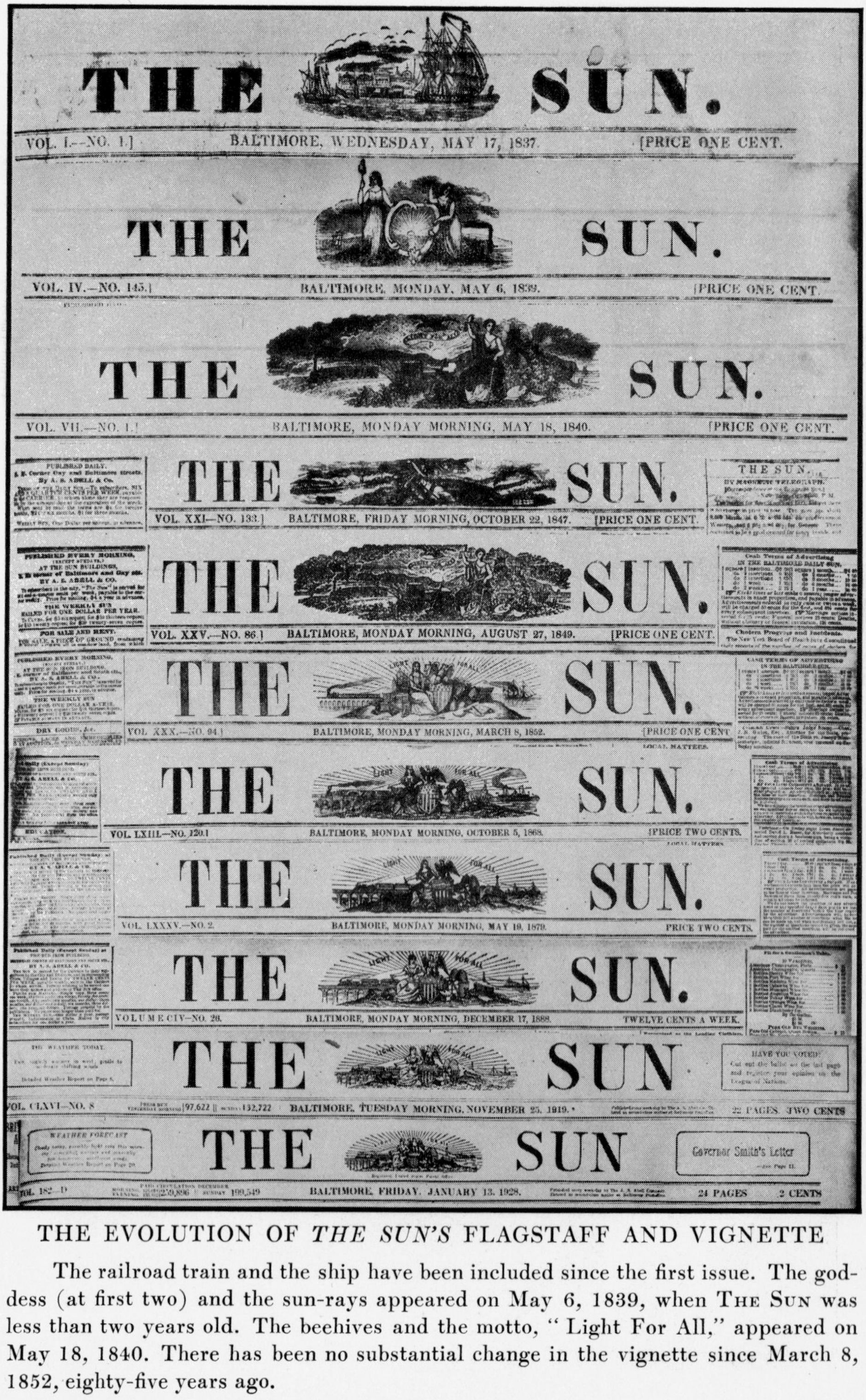

THE SUN.
VOL. I.—NO. 1.] BALTIMORE, WEDNESDAY, MAY 17, 1837. [PRICE ONE CENT.

THE SUN.
VOL. IV.—NO. 145.] BALTIMORE, MONDAY, MAY 6, 1839. [PRICE ONE CENT.

THE SUN.
VOL. VII.—NO. 1.] BALTIMORE, MONDAY MORNING, MAY 18, 1840. [PRICE ONE CENT.

THE SUN.
VOL. XXI—NO. 133.] BALTIMORE, FRIDAY MORNING, OCTOBER 22, 1847. [PRICE ONE CENT.

THE SUN.
VOL. XXV.—NO. 86.] BALTIMORE, MONDAY MORNING, AUGUST 27, 1849. [PRICE ONE CENT.

THE SUN.
VOL. XXX.—NO. 94.] BALTIMORE, MONDAY MORNING, MARCH 8, 1852. [PRICE ONE CENT

THE SUN.
VOL. LXIII.—NO. 120.] BALTIMORE, MONDAY MORNING, OCTOBER 5, 1868. [PRICE TWO CENTS.

THE SUN.
VOL. LXXXV.—NO. 2. BALTIMORE, MONDAY MORNING, MAY 19, 1879. PRICE TWO CENTS.

THE SUN.
VOLUME CIV—NO. 26. BALTIMORE, MONDAY MORNING, DECEMBER 17, 1888. TWELVE CENTS A WEEK.

THE SUN
VOL. CLXVI—NO. 8 BALTIMORE, TUESDAY MORNING, NOVEMBER 25, 1919. 22 PAGES. TWO CENTS

THE SUN
BALTIMORE, FRIDAY, JANUARY 13, 1928. 24 PAGES 2 CENTS

THE EVOLUTION OF *THE SUN'S* FLAGSTAFF AND VIGNETTE

The railroad train and the ship have been included since the first issue. The goddess (at first two) and the sun-rays appeared on May 6, 1839, when THE SUN was less than two years old. The beehives and the motto, "Light For All," appeared on May 18, 1840. There has been no substantial change in the vignette since March 8, 1852, eighty-five years ago.

independent at the precise and very time that politicians are most severely hampered by party loyalties. In other words, THE SUN must march ahead of the thought of the two great political parties and not trail behind either of them. In the long run, so it seems to me, it is safer and better to be wrong on such terms than to be right on the old terms.

The White Paper then proceeded to a clear statement of what has remained fundamental *Sunpaper* doctrine ever since:

What is needed primarily is a careful and unsentimental separation of genuine issues from all merely superficial and transient issues. What is needed secondarily is a prompt and vigorous statement of preferences and a support of them that goes beyond eloquence and enthusiasm — a support which is securely grounded upon complete information, absolute independence of judgment, and a persistent and intelligent concern for the national welfare. To political parties the national welfare must always be less important than the party welfare, and to great popular leaders it must always be less important than their own success. But to a great national newspaper it must be the object of first and sole concern, above and beyond all questions of party personality. To such a newspaper its loyalties are its greatest weaknesses. It must get rid of them in order to acquire something infinitely more valuable and useful, and that is its reputation for having special and early information, for presenting it honestly and fairly, and for interpreting it with the utmost independence that is humanly possible.

These principles, thus hammered out, were, of course, rather too general in their scope to make a working programme. Giving them practical force and effect was a long process, for it was necessary, in the opinion of all three of their protagonists, to subject them to the criticism of many other men. Here entered the question of personnel. Taking stock of their resources under this heading, they saw that the *Sunpapers* already commanded the services of a number of first-class executives. There was, first of all, Mr. Kent, who had struggled along for years getting out a sound newspaper, two of them in fact, under heart-breaking handicaps. There was Mr. Adams, who almost single-handed was writing their editorials. There were Messrs. Schmick and Blondell, already mentioned, and there was a pungent and altogether unique personality, J. Edwin Murphy,[1] on whose shoulders had come to rest many of the burdens incident to the daily production of the papers. As a technician Murphy had displayed unusual ability. His experience was as inclusive as that of any executive in the organization and he had ideas. He was enlisted and made a party to the plans that were forming.

The first public result of all this discussion was the modest one of a change in the typography and make-up of the two papers. In both the morning and evening editions advertising was still being carried on the first pages. The amount of space sold in each had been limited sometime previously to three columns, but even that amount reduced greatly the opportunity for the display of news. There was, naturally, some trepidation over the loss of revenue that would be certain were the first page cleared entirely. As a compromise it was arranged that all advertising should be confined to the lower left-hand corner, thereby making the tops of all columns available for the display of news. With this change as a starter, it was possible gradually to modernize the make-up and bring it more in accord with the practice of newspapers in most of the other large cities.

---

[1] Mr. Murphy was born in Baltimore on April 16, 1876, and was educated at Loyola College (A. B., 1893) and Georgetown University. In 1894 he became a reporter for the Baltimore *News* and remained in its service thereafter (with the exception of three years on the Baltimore *Herald* and six months on the Baltimore *Star*) until 1912. He was its city editor in 1909–10, and its managing editor in 1911–12. Early in 1913 he became managing editor of the New York *Press*, and in 1915 he went to the Washington *Times* in the same capacity. He became news editor of THE EVENING SUN on March 15, 1917, and managing editor on October 11, 1920. He was elected vice-president of The A. S. Abell Company on October 17, 1932.

News enterprise was the prime desideratum of the programme finally formulated. The first opportunity to show its readers that a new spirit had come over THE SUN organization arrived in the Spring of 1920 with the national conventions of the two big political parties. To cover these great shows as they had never been covered by the *Sunpapers* before, a group of men headed by Adams was dispatched to Chicago, where the Republican convention assembled in June. It included J. Fred Essary, chief of THE SUN's Washington bureau;[1] Stanley M. Reynolds, Washington correspondent of THE EVENING SUN;[2] John W. Owens, THE SUN's chief political reporter;[3] and Kent and

[1] Mr. Essary has been its chief since 1912, save for an interval in 1926, when he was London correspondent. He was born at Washburn, Tenn., August 22, 1881, and got his first newspaper experience as a reporter for Norfolk (Va.) papers in 1903. He became financial editor of the Baltimore *Star* in 1908, and in 1910 went to Washington to join the Capitol staff of the Munsey papers as correspondent for the Baltimore *News* and the Boston *Journal*. He is a member and former president of the Gridiron Club, which dines the President of the United States and other notables twice a year, and was the first correspondent to serve both as its president and as that of the National Press Club. In 1932 he received the Chester B. Pugsley Prize for the best Washington correspondence of the year. Mr. Essary has covered every national convention since 1912 and has traveled with every Presidential candidate since 1908, with the exception of La Follette in 1924. He is a frequent contributor of political articles to the leading American magazines and is the author of Maryland in National Politics, A Life of Isidor Rayner (Senator from Maryland, 1904–12), Your War Taxes, Covering Washington, Reverse English, Ships (with B. N. Baker), and Washington Sketch-Book (with his wife, Helen Kerchner Essary).

[2] Mr. Reynolds was a Baltimorean and a graduate of the Johns Hopkins University. He had his first experience in journalism as editor of the Johns Hopkins *News-Letter*. He worked subsequently for the Baltimore *News*, the Washington *Times*, the New York *Tribune*, *Press* and *Sun*, and the International News Service, chiefly in Washington. He moved from THE EVENING SUN to THE SUN in 1922, becoming its managing editor. He died on January 19, 1930.

[3] John Whitefield Owens was born in Anne Arundel county, Maryland, on November 2, 1884. He was educated in the public schools and at the Johns Hopkins

Mencken. Two newcomers accompanied them, an indication of the spirit of expansion that was in the air. The first was Stephen Bonsal, an experienced newspaper man who had an intimate acquaintance with many political figures, national as well as local.[1] The second was Henry M. Hyde. Mr. Hyde had been for many years on the staff of the Chicago *Tribune*. He had in fact been a star reporter, albeit a very young one, in the days of the World's Fair of 1893. But he had managed to fulfill the dream cherished by most newspaper men by retiring to a farm in Albemarle county, Virginia, near Monticello. Early in 1920 he had been persuaded to give up the bucolic life and come to the staff of THE EVENING SUN as a special writer. He was fascinated by the Baltimore scene, and a series of articles dealing with the quaint and picturesque aspects of the old city speedily endeared him to THE EVENING SUN's readers.[2]

Mr. Patterson accompanied the group of *Sunpaper* men to

University, where he took Summer and night courses. He began newspaper work on THE EVENING SUN in 1911, and became THE SUN's political reporter in 1913. In 1920 he joined the Washington bureau, and in 1924 became London correspondent. After his return from London in 1926, he became an editorial writer, and since 1927 he has been editor of THE SUN.

[1] Mr. Bonsal was a Baltimorean, born in 1865. He had had many years of foreign service for the New York *Herald* and *Times* and had covered wars in Serbia, Morocco, Macedonia, China, Mexico, Cuba, Manchuria and Venezuela. He entered the American diplomatic service in 1893, and ten years later became secretary to the Governor-General of the Philippines. He was attached to the American delegation to the Peace Conference in 1919. He is the author of Morocco As It Is, 1892; The Real Condition of Cuba, 1897; The Fight for Santiago, 1899; The Golden Horseshoe, 1900, and The American Mediterranean, 1912.

[2] Mr. Hyde was born at Freeport, Ill., October 6, 1866, and was educated at Beloit College. After serving as editor of the *Technical World*, he joined the staff of the Chicago *Tribune*. He was London correspondent of the *Tribune* in 1919. He is the author of Animal Alphabet (a book of verse for children), 1900; One Forty Two, 1901; Through the Stage Door, 1903; The Buccaneers, 1904, and The Upstart, 1906, and has contributed often to the leading American magazines.

Chicago, serving as a sort of general editor. Some of them, after the Republican National Convention was over, proceeded to San Francisco, where the Democrats met. Since that time all national conventions have been covered in the same way. Kent, Essary, Hyde and Mencken have been to all of them, always accompanied by other members of the Washington and Baltimore staffs, and with Patterson superintending the job. On occasion as many as a dozen men and women have been engaged upon one convention. At the long-drawn-out Democratic convention in New York in 1924 the reports in the *Sunpapers* were so unbiased and so comprehensive that many of the delegates read both papers daily, and they had a large circulation in New York among other persons. Until he left THE SUN, the chief of its telegraph service at national conventions and other such affairs was always Robert E. L. Russell, who was famous for his speed and accuracy.[1]

As soon as the election was over in the Autumn of 1920 the real reorganization of the *Sunpapers* was begun. It was not the sort of reorganization that some of the members of the staff may have feared. No one was fired. The plan was, primarily, to separate the two papers, morning and evening, and give each of them a complete and independent staff, from managing editor and editor down to copy-boys, and so encourage them to friendly rivalry. The news of the separation was broken to the evening

[1] Mr. Russell came to THE SUN on April 11, 1899, to receive the report sent by a Postal Telegraph wire from New York. He continued in that post until 1914, when he left to work for a firm of stock brokers. Returning in November, 1918, he did valiant service for the *Sunpapers* until 1929. On the night of the *Titanic* disaster he took 1,900 words in 35 minutes, or at the rate of 54 words a minute, or 3,300 an hour. At the Republican National Convention in Cleveland, in 1924, he sent 22,000 words in one night. He was born at Harpers Ferry, W. Va., and went to work as a messenger for the Valley Railroad of Virginia at Harrisonburg, Va., in his teens. Two years later he became a telegraph operator at Staunton, Va.

crew at a dinner attended by all the men of its news and editorial staff. The members of the board were present and heartily seconded the plans that were outlined by Mr. Patterson. Messrs. Adams and Kent were likewise there, and they gave the new baby their blessing. A few days later, the members of the morning staff received a similar invitation, turned over their work temporarily to their evening colleagues, and heard the story of the change told again. The two "divorce dinners," as they have been called ever since, may have been somewhat dramatically conceived and carried out, but the effect was immediate and good. The two staffs, while friendly, have been seriously competitive ever since.

Under the reorganization, Mr. Kent remained managing editor of THE SUN and Mr. Adams its editor. Mr. Murphy was made managing editor of THE EVENING SUN and Mr. Reynolds was intrusted with the task of creating for it an editorial page. All four were encouraged to seek new blood, to find men capable of accepting and using responsibility and of growing with the paper.

How all these changes worked out and the sort of newspapers which developed when they were put into effect will be told in the last two chapters. Their first effect, so far as the board of directors was concerned, was to remove from its members the necessity of continuous worry about the progress of a property with whose preservation and development they had been intrusted. As the new régime gradually gathered momentum, and the heads of the various departments began to grow into their new positions and take over their new responsibilities, more and more of the detail and even of the policy of the whole organization was intrusted to them.

One of the most important and effective developments on the operating side of the rapidly growing papers was the initiation, under the leadership of Mr. Blondell, of a thorough-going budget system. A budget committee was formed. It consisted, and still consists, of the chief executives of the papers — the president, the two editors, the two managing editors, the editor of THE SUNDAY SUN, the business manager, the treasurer, and the circulation manager. Each is called upon to submit annually a budget made up on a monthly basis, with all the expenditures set down thereon which his experience and his expectations lead him to believe will be needed during the year. With full knowledge of the income that may be expected, each departmental budget is dissected and pruned, rejected or passed as the case may be, by a vote of the members of the committee. The general budget thus made is laid before the board for final action, but once passed by the committee it is seldom altered. The effect of this procedure is to make the managerial staff aware at all times of the financial position of the company and conscious of the part each department plays in the general scheme.

Another innovation, based upon the conviction that it was important to maintain in the organization a feeling that each contributed to the common welfare not in his own department alone but in all other departments, was the institution of daily editorial conferences. Every afternoon, after the rush of THE EVENING SUN's day is over and before that of THE SUN begins, the editors and managing editors meet with the president, sometimes jointly but more often at different hours, for the discussion of undertakings projected and in process. Other members of the organization come to these meetings from time to time, as they are needed, to criticize or add to the general store of information. The business manager and his assistants, and likewise the circulation manager and his, are expected to make their special knowledge available as the need arises.

Mr. Mencken's enjoyment of the bizarre aspects of the American scene helped to give a special tone to the editorial page of THE EVENING SUN in the 1920s. He wrote an article for it once a week, as, indeed, he does to this day. His articles were often devoted to an appreciative exposure of some current aberration of his Bible Belt or his Cow States. His essay, "The Sahara of the Bozart," an excoriation of the South for its indifference to the fine arts, was published in its first form in THE EVENING SUN. Later expanded for the *Smart Set* and still later expanded again for his book, "Prejudices: Second Series" (1920), it made an uproar below the Potomac, and even launched a boycott of Baltimore by Southern merchants. But the more intelligent Southerners were inspired to a realistic examination of its charges, and out of that examination flowed a considerable improvement. On May 15, 1922, Mr. Mencken discussed the new æsthetic enterprise of the South in an article in THE EVENING SUN entitled "Violets in the Sahara."

It was their peculiar interest in the so-called cultural lag which led the two *Sunpapers*, in 1925, to take the Scopes trial in Tennessee seriously, and to cover it somewhat elaborately. Essary and Kent were dispatched to Dayton by THE SUN, and Hyde and Mencken by THE EVENING SUN. Edmund Duffy, who had become cartoonist for THE SUN, went along to study at first hand the gyrations of William Jennings Bryan. Hyde and Mencken improved the opportunity to investigate the Holy Roller cult in the mountains behind Dayton, and Mencken sent to THE EVENING SUN two articles, "The Hills of Zion" and "In Memoriam: W. J. B.," that were later republished in his book, "Prejudices: Fifth Series" (1926). The people of Baltimore were left in no doubt on which side of the Evolution controversy the *Sunpapers* stood, but in case there should be any the two provided Scopes' bond and when he was found guilty paid his $100 fine.[1]

---

1 The money was later returned. It turned out that the trial judge had set the fine beyond the amount fixed by the statutes, and the Tennessee Supreme Court vacated it.

While such enterprises were occupying the staffs of the two papers changes were taking place in the make-up of the board of directors. R. Brent Keyser, one of the best-loved members of the board as well as one of the most useful, died in March, 1927, and Robert Garrett resigned in May, 1930. Since this left two vacancies, the by-laws of the company were changed, reducing the board from seven to five.

On August 18, 1930, the *Sunpapers* received a blow which genuinely shook them. It was the death of Van-Lear Black, the dominant figure in their rehabilitation, and a man of such amiable spirit that the devotion of all his associates to him was endless. He had been absent from the office a great deal during the two years before his death, and had given much of his time to the long voyages by air that have been described in Chapter XVIII, but he was still chairman of the board, and his interest in the papers remained as keen as his counsel was valuable. On the morning of August 18 he flew from New York to Newport, R. I., to visit one of his daughters, the wife of a young naval officer stationed there. She had just presented him with twin grandchildren, and he was so delighted by the news that he must see them. In a happy mood, he returned to New York later in the day, and toward evening set sail for Baltimore on his yacht *Sabalo,* on which he made many voyages up and down the coast, often with his old friend, Franklin D. Roosevelt, by now become Governor of New York, as his companion. After dinner, while the yacht was proceeding down the Jersey coast, he went on deck to smoke and take the air, and, as was his frequent habit, climbed upon the taffrail sailor-fashion, and there anchored himself. The members of the crew, having seen him sit thus many an evening before, paid no heed to him. Suddenly one of them noted that he had disappeared. An alarm was sounded and the yacht was searched, but he could not be found. There was a heavy swell running, and the craft had been pitching in a way that would have been uncomfortable to a less experienced sailor. Unseen by anyone, he had been thrown from his place and washed away. A search was begun by Coast Guard and Navy ships that continued for three days. Many other craft joined it, and Governor Roosevelt ordered airplanes sent out from New York. Mr. Black was a powerful swimmer, and it was hoped that he might have managed to keep afloat. But no trace of him was ever found.

Mr. Black's place was filled, on February 22, 1932, by the election of John E. Semmes,[1] and on November 14, 1934, after it had been decided to go back to a board of seven members, Edwin F. Abell Morgan was elected. Mr. Morgan is the son of the late Dr. James Dudley Morgan and of Mrs. Mary Abell Morgan, the only daughter of Edwin F. Abell. He is thus a great-grandson of the Founder. He has been engaged in the practice of the law in Baltimore since his graduation from the Harvard Law School in 1920, and is now a member of the firm of Semmes, Bowen and Semmes, of which his colleague on The A. S. Abell Company board, John E. Semmes, is the head.[2] H.

---

[1] Mr. Semmes is the son of John E. Semmes, a distinguished lawyer of the last generation, whom we have encountered as a leading spirit in the Baltimore Reform League. The younger Semmes is a grand-nephew of both Raphael Semmes, commander of the famous Confederate cruiser *Alabama* and of Commodore John Guest, U. S. N., who in 1854 fought the Chinese at Shanghai and in 1864–5 commanded the *Lehigh* and *Itasca* at the storming of Fort Fisher. Mr. Semmes was born in Baltimore April 15, 1881, and was educated at Princeton and the University of Maryland. In 1902 he entered the United States Forestry Service, but soon abandoned it for the law. In 1905 he forsook the law in turn to become an officer in the United States Marine Corps. As such he served in Cuba during the American occupation of 1906. He resigned in 1908 and returned to the law.

[2] Mr. Morgan was born in Washington, D. C., on September 28, 1892, and took an A. B. degree at Harvard before proceeding to the law school. In April, 1917, he suspended his studies to join the Army and thereafter served in the Three Hundred and Thirteenth Field Artillery, Eightieth Division, until the end of the World War. Trained at

L. Mencken, who had been a member of the staff of the *Sunpapers* since 1906, was also elected a director on the day Mr. Morgan became a member of the board,[1] and on February 24, 1936, George C. Cutler was chosen to take the place of John J. Nelligan, who had died on October 14, 1935.[2]

Fort Myer, Va., he was commissioned a second lieutenant and then promoted to first lieutenant and captain. He served at the front during the entire Meuse-Argonne offensive. In the great advance of September 26, 1918, his battery was the first to cross the Rau des Forges into territory that the Germans had held for four years. In the pursuit of early November it crossed the Meuse in advance of the infantry it was supporting. After the war Mr. Morgan served in the Officers' Reserve Corps and was promoted to major and then to lieutenant-colonel. On the repeal of Prohibition in 1933 he was appointed chief counsel to the newly created Federal Alcohol Administration at Washington, of which Joseph H. Choate, Jr., was director. He was for ten years associate editor of *American Maritime Cases,* a legal publication.

[1] Six other members of the staff of the *Sunpapers* are officers of The A. S. Abell Company. William F. Schmick is executive vice-president, Frank R. Kent and J. Edwin Murphy are vice-presidents. John W. Owens is secretary, E. P. Flaherty is treasurer and assistant secretary, and W. L. Fitzell is assistant treasurer.

[2] Mr. Cutler was born at Brookline, Mass., in 1891 and is a graduate of Harvard University and the Harvard Law School. On the outbreak of the World War he went into training at the Naval Academy, Annapolis, and was commissioned an officer on a destroyer engaged in Atlantic patrol duty. After the war he joined the law firm of Herrick, Smith, Donald and Farley and was soon made a partner. In 1925 he moved to New York and entered the investment banking business. In 1935 he was a vice-president of the Guaranty Trust Company. On the death of Joseph B. Kirby in that year he was invited to come to Baltimore as president of the Safe Deposit and Trust Company, of which Mr. Nelligan was chairman of the board. The company has been trustee of the Walter R. Abell estate for many years and is also trustee for other stockholders in The A. S. Abell Company.

CHAPTER XX

THE EVENING SUN AND ITS MEN

It was in The Evening Sun, perhaps, that the effects of the "divorce" described in the preceding chapter were first apparent. Although it was already producing more revenue than its parent, its status in the family had been hardly higher than that of a stepchild. Ever since Mr. Grasty had attempted to abolish its editorial columns and fill their space with contributed articles, it had suffered from an unmistakable anæmia. The new blood gave it both strength and direction and not a little speed.

Mr. Reynolds, the new editor, had served under Mr. Murphy on the Baltimore *News* as well as on The Evening Sun and each knew intimately the other's mind and point of view. Mr. Reynolds' relation with Mr. Adams was likewise a long-established one and on most fundamentals they were in close agreement. Hence, it was possible for them to avoid the somewhat embarrassing spectacle which might have ensued had one of them insisted upon arguing for a low tariff, for instance, and the other for a high.

But Reynolds had also another quality which proved intensely valuable. He was a man of high spirits. He loved a joke and he especially loved to make them at the expense of the buffoons who frequent the political scene. Nothing pleased him more than to make a politician look ridiculous and his work on the editorial page gave him many opportunities. The Democratic politicians of the State, since the exit of Mr. Grasty, had come to regard the *Sunpapers* as more or less " safe." They soon learned that they had been cherishing a delusion, for the new staff of THE EVENING SUN was soon devoting itself *con amore* to exposing the weaknesses and shortcomings of self-satisfied public officials.

Against Prohibition, then newly afflicting the country, the paper fought vigorously from the start. Its editors refused to admit that the issue was out of politics, as the professional vote-snarers hoped and declared. They seized upon every manifestation of its failure and gave them all prominent space. They lit upon the Ku Klux Klan with all arms, and lambasted it day after day. They jeered against the anti-Red campaigns, and when Postmaster-General Burleson barred the New York *Call*, a Socialist newspaper, from the mails, they sent the editors of the *Call* a check for $500 to help it fight its case in the courts.[1]

After a year of hard and valuable service, Mr. Reynolds shifted from THE EVENING SUN to THE SUN. His place was vacant for several months, Mr. Murphy acting as both editor and managing editor. Finally, early in 1922, Hamilton Owens, who had been associated with Mr. Murphy in both Baltimore and New York, was appointed to fill it. Mr. Owens has been editor of THE EVENING SUN ever since.[2]

---

[1] Said the *Nation* on July 13, 1931: " No more gratifying episode has occurred in American journalism in recent years."

[2] He was born in Baltimore August 8, 1888. He was graduated from the Johns Hopkins University in 1909, and had his first newspaper experience on the Baltimore *American* during Summer vacations. He joined the staff of the Baltimore *News* in September, 1909, working under Mr. Murphy, then its city editor. In 1913 he moved to the New York *Press*, becoming its Sunday editor and dramatic critic. In 1916 he went to the New York *Evening Mail* as assistant to S. S. McClure, then its editor. When the United States entered the World

This change in character of the paper did not go unnoticed in the country and there was not a little comment in other papers about it. But so little emphasis had previously been laid upon the difference between THE SUN and THE EVENING SUN that editors were constantly confusing one with the other. Whenever, as a result of that confusion, a newspaper reprinted something from THE EVENING SUN and credited it to THE SUN, Mr. Murphy would solemnly dictate a letter of explanation and remonstrance. He let it be known in editorial rooms throughout the country, and also abroad, that THE EVENING SUN was no longer under the tutelage of THE SUN, but had become a completely independent newspaper, with qualities all its own and even policies of its own. That separation of the two papers is still in effect, but there is, of course, constant coöperation between them, and they pursue many enterprises in common. In 1934 a sort of intermediate body was set up to bridge the gap between them. Its staff, so far, consists of but two men — Miles H. Wolff, who is assistant to the president,[1] and Mr. Mencken, who remained on the staff of THE EVENING SUN until January 1, 1936, but

War he became managing editor of the Foreign Press Bureau of the Committee on Public Information, under George Creel. At the conclusion of the war he joined the publicity staff of the Guaranty Trust Company of New York, serving a year in New York and two years in London. It was from London that he came to THE EVENING SUN. He and John W. Owens, editor of THE SUN, are both Marylanders, but they are related only very remotely.

[1] Mr. Wolff was born in Dallas, N. C., on August 4, 1899. He received an A. B. degree from Roanoke College, at Salem, Va., and an M. A. from the University of North Carolina, 1922. After teaching two years, he started work on the Concord *Daily Tribune* in 1924. In February, 1926, he joined the Charlotte (N. C.) *Observer* as a reporter and remained there until November, 1928, when he went with the Associated Press in Columbia, S. C., as night editor. He was transferred to Charlotte and then back to Columbia, and in 1930 was put in charge of the bureau. On June 1, 1932, he was transferred to Baltimore to take charge of the Associated Press bureau there. On Auugst 1, 1934, he joined THE SUN.

had always been at the service of THE SUN and THE SUNDAY SUN for occasional special duties.

During all this time Mr. Murphy and Mr. Reynolds and later Mr. Owens were working as rapidly as possible to augment the staff with promising young men, and to organize a corps of special correspondents covering the United States and especially the South. The correspondents they assembled included a great many writers who have since come to nation-wide notice — for example, Grover C. Hall, of Montgomery, Ala., a Pulitzer prize winner; David Warren Ryder, of San Francisco; Duncan Aikman, formerly of El Paso, Texas, and now a Washington correspondent; R. Charlton Wright, formerly of Columbia, S. C., and another Pulitzer prize winner; W. G. Clugston, of Topeka, Kan.; Ralph Coghlan, of St. Louis; Will Campbell, of Helena, Mont.; Louis Graves, of Chapel Hill, N. C.; Robert Lathan, of Asheville; Malcolm B. Ronald, of Mitchell, S. D.; Wayne Gard, of Dallas, Texas; Virginius Dabney, of Richmond, Va.; Louis I. Jaffé, of Norfolk — the list lengthens, but it is not nearly complete.

Two results flowed from this activity. The first and more obvious was a constant stream of lively material for both news columns and editorial page. The second was not less important. It is found in the fact that one of the correspondents thus recruited — Gerald W. Johnson, of Greensboro, N. C.,[1] was taken

[1] He was born at Riverton, N. C., August 6, 1890. After taking his A. B. at Wake Forest College, he established a paper in Thomasville, N. C., at the age of twenty. In 1911 he went to the Lexington *Dispatch* and two years later to the Greensboro *Daily News*. In August, 1918, he landed in France with the Three Hundred and Twenty-first Infantry, and after service in the Vosges, was sent to the officers' training school at Langres. He was commissioned on November 9, 1918, but when the armistice followed two days later his commission was canceled on a cabled order from Washington, "to save expenses." He thus had the curious experience of serving as an officer something less than 48 hours out of 29 months in the Army. After the armistice he was

on the editorial staff in 1926. His editorials had already made the Greensboro *Daily News* a noteworthy paper in its region and his presence in Baltimore not only added vigor to THE EVENING SUN but gave it ground for speaking authoritatively on matters affecting the South.

There was a constant flow of young men to the paper. Once, at the close of the collegiate year at Princeton, a half-dozen graduates were taken on to see what they could do. Several turned into first-rate newspaper men, and one of them, Alfred S. Dashiell, later became editor of *Scribner's Magazine*.[1] But their presence in the office for the Summer period only did not make it any easier for the rest of the staff to work, and this experiment was not repeated. For a time some of the readers of the paper may have thought that it was concerned only with giving a show, with amusing its readers by performing intellectual acrobatics, but those who cherished such notions were not allowed to hold them very long. Actually, what Owens and Murphy were about was something that to them and to the whole organization was important and, therefore, serious. They were seek-

---

sent to the University of Toulouse, remaining there until July, 1919. On his return to the United States he rejoined the staff of the Greensboro *News*. In 1924 he became professor of journalism at the University of North Carolina, and it was from that post that he came to THE EVENING SUN. He has written many books, including The Story of Man's Work (with W. R. Hayward), 1925; The Undefeated, What Is News?, 1926; Andrew Jackson: An Epic in Homespun, 1927; Randolph of Roanoke: A Political Fantastic, 1929; By Reason of Strength, 1930; Number Thirty-Six, 1933; and The Secession of the Southern States, 1933. He is a frequent contributor to the magazines and reviews.

[1] He is now (1937) one of the editors of the *Readers' Digest*. Another magazine editor who got his first journalistic experience in the *Sunpaper* office is Paul Palmer, editor of the *American Mercury*. He came to THE SUN, not THE EVENING SUN, on his graduation from Harvard in 1922. In 1924 he went to St. Louis as Sunday editor of the *Post-Dispatch* and in 1926 to New York as Sunday editor of the *World*. He became editor of the *American Mercury* in 1935.

ing to undermine as far as possible the many complacent but palpably false and dangerous assumptions that underlay much of the political activity of the time. Ridicule was a convenient weapon and one which was sharply different from the heavier armament of THE SUN. They were seeking, in short, to carry on the same fight in a different manner and on a new front. Shady politicians and other enemies of the general good who thought they could ignore the pin-prickings of the paper soon found that pin-pricks, continued day after day, week in and week out, could be exceedingly painful. They discovered, too, that the hand which jabbed the pin could also, on occasion, throw a brick or swing a bludgeon. After such an affray, the man or the movement attacked never had any doubt about the seriousness of purpose of THE EVENING SUN.

In 1925, Francis F. Beirne, who had become a member of the editorial staff in 1924, described the general outlook of the paper in these terms:

Observers sometimes make the mistake of speaking of THE EVENING SUN as Liberal. This the editors emphatically deny, for, according to their definition, " a Liberal is one who stands for more laws, more jobholders, higher taxes, and, in consequence, less liberty." They maintain rather that THE EVENING SUN is an old-fashioned Conservative, in that it believes in personal liberty, freedom of speech, and the other privileges listed under the first ten amendments to the Constitution. In line with this Conservative policy it howls against " spies, snoopers and agents provocateurs," and deplores the Paul-Pryism of income tax publicity, the invitation to blackmail presented by the Mann Act, modern uses of the injunction, and the advent of educational experts, urging a return in the schools to the teaching of the three R's in preference to courses in basket-weaving. . . . It throws its weight against goose-stepping and standardization, and clamors for State's Rights as against Federal bureaucracy and Federal aid, making frequent reference to its own province as the Maryland Free State. Politicians, according to THE EVENING SUN, are men whose one aim is to hold their own jobs and create jobs for others through the making of more laws and subsequent increase of taxes. It has discovered the almost inevitable truth that a reduction of the tax-rate is accompanied by an increased assessment, and, in the face of all encouraging announcements of economy on the part of politicians, it warns the citizen to hold his applause until he has looked at the right-hand corner of his tax bill.[1]

One of the early inventions (1924) of the ingenious fellows who made THE EVENING SUN's editorial page was the More Laws Association, which still flourishes. In it "any politician is entitled to life, active or associate membership according to his zeal in the proposing of new laws." Most of the more eminent politicians of the country, regardless of party, are members, and so are most of the reformers. A smaller sodality is THE EVENING SUN *Bloc*, organized in 1922 — an involuntary association of public men who have, in one way or another, supported THE EVENING SUN's concept of the good, the true or the beautiful. Its grand master is George Washington, and at various times figures as diverse as Thomas Jefferson, Bismarck and former Senator James A. Reed, of Missouri, have been nominated for the honor of membership. William M. Jardine, later to be Mr. Hoover's Secretary of Agriculture, was put up on May 14, 1925, for saying that "the only way in which the farmer can be helped is for him to help himself"; F. W. Besley, State Forester of Maryland, on June 21, 1926, for suggesting that trees be planted along the Maryland roads to hide unsightly billboards; Congressman Melvin O. McLaughlin, of Nebraska, on March 12, 1924, for proposing that the Interstate Commerce Commission be abolished; and Congressman Otis Wingo, of Arkansas, on December 20, 1929, for advocating the repeal of 40,000 Federal laws.

[1] The Paper That Won't Grow Old, *The Quill,* December, 1925.

The Maryland Free State is the invention of Hamilton Owens. Some time in 1923, at the height of the debate over Prohibition, Congressman William D. Upshaw, of Georgia, a fierce dry, denounced Maryland as a traitor to the Union because it had refused (largely through the urging of THE EVENING SUN) to pass a State enforcement act. Mr. Owens thereupon wrote a mock-serious editorial headed " The Maryland Free State," arguing that Maryland should really secede from the Union and go it alone. The irony in this editorial was somewhat finely spun, and on second thought Mr. Owens decided not to print it, but the idea embodied in the title stuck in his mind, and in a little while he began to use it in other editorials. It caught on quickly, and the Maryland Free State is now heard of almost as often as Maryland. One of its great apostles was the late Governor Albert C. Ritchie, who was a candidate for the Democratic Presidential nomination in 1924, 1928 and 1932 on a platform including all the cardinal articles of sound EVENING SUN philosophy. THE EVENING SUN seldom advocates any cause save the general cause of liberty. Whenever it condescends to support a given man or measure, that man or measure commonly comes to grief, and at frequent intervals it rehearses these defeats sadly, and sheds a few crocodile tears over them. This summing-up of forensic disaster is usually done on its birthday, April 18. On the same day it sometimes invites its principal enemies to express their opinion of it on its editorial page, and more than once it has been reviled with great violence. In 1923, for example, it drew forth the following from James H. Preston, the Baltimore Mayor who fought both *Sunpapers* tooth and nail from 1911 to 1919:

What I dislike most about THE EVENING SUN is its congenital insincerity — an inborn defect of character which is unfortunately inherited from its morning progenitor. As a modern newspaper from the standpoint of publishing the news, THE EVENING SUN, like the morning SUN, leaves little to be desired. Editorially, however, I think that even you will agree that the force and power with which THE SUN was endowed by the Abells is now but the fine tradition of an earlier day in Baltimore journalism. What I dislike about THE EVENING SUN, also, is its lack of independent thought — its easy submission to the hypocrisy and cant and humbug of the disgruntled and defeated political editors of the morning SUN. Why don't you try to write editorials that will "animate the conduct and mold the destiny" of Baltimore?

In the same issue the president of the Anti-Saloon League of Maryland denounced the editorial page as favoring "evil-minded men" and crying down the heroes "fighting the stubbornly contested battles of reform," and Governor Ritchie protested that the paper "should stop asking candidates for public office, 'How many jobholders will you fire?'" Many other Maryland notables added their criticism. Most of them, it should be added, were much more friendly than Mr. Preston's. THE EVENING SUN, on the same day, printed an editorial reciting its chief articles of faith. The substance of it follows:

The most important things in this country are the men who make it up. Experience has taught — the Founding Fathers knew it better than we know it today — that men grow best when they are treated as men and not as children. The important thing for the conservative is to conserve the opportunity for men to grow to their full stature. Hence THE EVENING SUN opposes all those measures, all those organizations, all those movements which seek to encroach upon the right of men to be men.

Of all the evils threatening this country today the greatest is the constant inflation of government. We Americans have more government to start with than most peoples. We have our local governments, our State governments and on top of them the Federal government. This last is the most dangerous because it is the furthest removed from the people over whom it rules.

And it is swelling enormously. Nearly every law which Congress passes clips a little off the edge of the citizen's independence. And the same law takes a little more out of his earnings. The lawmakers get us coming and going. If they keep on, we shall soon have little of either left. THE EVENING SUN proposes to try to conserve that liberty which we still have and get as much back of what we have lost as it is possible to get.

In addition to this vastly bloated legal government, there are a whole host of extra-legal governments which are striving with might and main to do their bit toward taking away from the citizen his few remaining rights. The Anti-Saloon League is the arch example of this kind of extra-legal government. The Ku Klux Klan is one of its absurder manifestations. One is run by shrewd fanatics, the other by avaricious clowns. But the spirit which animates both of them, and all the other leagues and associations of those who want to make the other fellow do it their way, is precisely the same. Consistent with our "live-and-let-live" policy, we are against the lot of them.

If we have a rule about these things, it is this — let them talk. That goes also for the Bolsheviki, the Babbitts, the uplifters-in-general. When they talk, they are fulfilling their God-given right. When they strive to do more, they are to be scotched.

THE EVENING SUN, finally, is a firm believer in old-fashioned economics. It has an abiding faith in the law of supply and demand, and it resents any interference by the Government with that law.

Herein, we believe, are contained the most important of the articles of faith to which this paper has subscribed.[1]

THE EVENING SUN's skeptical view of professional politicians, regardless of party, inspired it in April, 1924, to offer a prize of $100 to the reader furnishing the best answer to the question, What is the difference between a Republican and a Democrat? The prize winner was Mrs. Esther M. Hollander, of Baltimore, who sent in this:

[1] This editorial was reprinted on July 28, 1936, with a resounding reaffirmation of its principles.

A Republican is a person who thinks a Democratic administration is bad for business. A Democrat is a person who thinks a Republican administration is bad for business. Both are right.

On May 8, 1928, with Prohibition still afflicting the politicians, THE EVENING SUN offered a similar prize for a model platform plank " which would seem like a wet plank to the wets and like a dry plank to the drys." The money went to Mrs. Emily Stone Whiteley, of Baltimore, for the following:

On the subject of law enforcement we desire to make our position perfectly clear. We believe that our precious heritage of liberty can be secured only by the strict enforcement of laws which are the concrete expression of the will of the people. We stand for the sanctity of the home. It is the poor man's castle, and it is the cradle of the future of our nation. We hereby solemnly rededicate ourselves to the maintenance of the Constitution as a great charter of freedom established by our fathers which guarantees to the American people liberty in the highest sense under the sacred protection of law.

The editorial staff of THE EVENING SUN, as at present constituted, consists, in addition to Mr. Owens, of Philip Wagner,[1] Gerald W. Johnson, Clark S. Hobbs,[2] Francis F. Beirne,[3] Gilbert Kanour [4] and R. P. Harriss.[5]

[1] Now (1937) loaned to THE SUN and serving as its London correspondent. Mr. Wagner was born in New Haven, Conn., in 1904, but grew up in Ann Arbor, Mich., where his father is professor of Romance languages at the University of Michigan. He himself was graduated from the university in 1925. In his undergraduate days he was managing editor of the Michigan *Daily*. He came to THE EVENING SUN in 1932. He is an enthusiastic winegrower, maintains an experimental vineyard, and has written two books on the subject.

[2] Mr. Hobbs is a Baltimorean, born July 1, 1888. After graduating from the Baltimore City College in 1907, he joined the staff of the Baltimore *American*. In 1910 he went to the Baltimore *News* and in 1919 he came to THE EVENING SUN. After two years as a reporter he transferred to the editorial staff in 1921. He is a trustee of Goucher College, Baltimore.

[3] Mr. Beirne was born at Ashland, Va., August 20, 1890. On his graduation from the University of Virginia in 1911 he went to Oxford as a Rhodes scholar, taking his mas-

An editorial page, however important it may be, is only one page in the many that make up the present-day newspaper. And Mr. Murphy had been charged by Mr. Patterson not only to find men who could run an editorial page but also to build up the news department of THE EVENING SUN. This, while less spectacular and dramatic, was a longer and more difficult task, made more exacting by the fact that the paper faced rigorous and resourceful competition.

Mr. Murphy took over the managing editorship of THE EVENING SUN when it had only a skeleton staff. He found he had no assistant managing editor to take charge while he was out of the

---

ter's degree in 1919. He joined THE SUN staff in 1914, but resigned in 1917 to enter the Army. He served until 1919. After the war he put in two years in the tobacco business in Richmond, Va., but in 1921 he returned to newspaper work on the Baltimore *News*. He became an editorial writer on THE EVENING SUN in 1923, and since 1931 has been writing an editorial page column over the pen name of Christopher Billopp.

[4] Mr. Kanour was born at Spruce Creek, Pa., on November 30, 1893. He was graduated from the Tyrone (Pa.) High School in 1911, and after special courses in mechanical engineering became chief draftsman at the Tyrone plant of the West Virginia Pulp & Paper Co. In 1916–17 he was a member of the Sheridan Troop, First Pennsylvania Cavalry, on duty on the Mexican border. He served with the One Hundred and Third Trench Mortar Battery, Twenty-eighth Division, in France, and participated in the second battle of the Marne and the Meuse-Argonne offensive. Graduated from the Saumur Artillery School, he was commissioned a second lieutenant and served for five years as a member of the C. A. C. Officers' Reserve. He went back to work for the paper company after the war, and later became a designer of cranes in the offices of the Morgan Engineering Company, at Alliance, Ohio. He joined the staff of the Covington (Va.) *Virginian* in 1921, and in 1922 became a member of the staff of THE EVENING SUN. He is its theater and motion-picture critic.

[5] Mr. Harriss was born at Fayetteville, N. C., in 1903, and was graduated from Duke University. While working on North Carolina papers he began to contribute to the editorial page of THE EVENING SUN, and in 1927 he joined its staff. He left in 1930 to work for the Paris edition of the New York *Herald*, but returned in 1934. He published a novel, The Foxes, in 1936, and it was a best-seller.

office for any cause. There was no developed financial department, no real sports department, no society editor, no one specifically charged with handling existing features and finding new ones. The copy desk was sadly undermanned and the reportorial staff had obvious weaknesses. Incidentally, the last had obvious strength, too, for on it were H. S. Sherwood,[1] then, as now, one of the best reporters in Baltimore; Henry M. Hyde,[2] mentioned in Chapter XIX, and several other competent men. One of them was Roger S. Williamson, who had come to the *Sunpapers* back in 1912, served in the war, and came back to the staff of THE EVENING SUN thereafter. He knew the craft, he knew the city, and especially he knew the municipal government and its vagaries, a phase of reporting which Murphy, himself an old City Hall man, had always considered of primary importance.

---

[1] Harry Sheffield Sherwood was born in Baltimore in 1879. His formal education was brief, for he was working in an office at the age of 13. In 1897 he became secretary to Mr. Grasty, then in charge of the Baltimore *News*, and in 1900 began reporting. He came to THE SUN first in 1905. Soon after he moved to Philadelphia, but he came back to Baltimore in 1910 when Mr. Grasty took over THE SUN. He knows everyone in Baltimore of any consequence, produces a prodigious amount of copy, and has never been known to misquote anyone.

[2] Mr. Hyde began to go to Washington for THE EVENING SUN in 1928, and since 1929 he has lived there, devoting himself largely to the onerous work of covering the hearings of Congressional investigating committees and other such bodies. His colleague in the Washington bureau of THE EVENING SUN is Frederick R. Barkley. Mr. Barkley was born in Watertown, N. Y., in 1892, and spent his youth there. He was graduated from the local high school and worked as a newsboy, an elevator operator, a bellhop, an aluminum salesman, a time clerk and a harvest hand, and even, for four years, as an undertaker's assistant, before finding his *métier* in journalism. He served various up-State New York and New England papers before joining the staff of THE EVENING SUN. His speciality is the Western Progressive movement, and in 1932, in collaboration with Ray Tucker, he described it in a book called Sons of the Wild Jackass. He is a frequent contributor to the magazines.

Since it had been decided that it was not wise to go out and bid for established men, Mr. Murphy took the slower course of keeping his eyes open and drawing upon the knowledge of the newspaper field possessed by the others. Mr. Mencken, for instance, was engaged in that period in a correspondence with hundreds of hopeful young writers all over the country. Here was a valuable source of new men, and it was tapped often and produced results on more than one occasion. Whenever possible, men were promoted from minor positions to those of larger responsibility. Even copy-boys profited by this policy and today on the staff of THE EVENING SUN there are perhaps a dozen men — including one assistant city editor — who started as copy-boys.

Building up a staff was a matter of years, but using the existing staff to the best advantage was a day-to-day job. Mr. Murphy was a man of explosive ideas. Always there was something germinating in his head which might break forth in some special effort that would arrest attention. Mr. Black, also, was fecund in such ideas. A characteristic enterprise was launched early in 1922. The bonus agitation was at its height. Veterans, come back to find Prohibition fastened upon the country, were organizing to get what they could out of Congress. THE EVENING SUN polled them, not to discover whether they wanted a bonus or not, but on this question:

> Do you favor a tax on beer and light wines to help pay the soldiers' bonus?

Thousands of the returned soldiers got the point, and 4,280 out of 4,320 voted for beer. The percentage, solemnly tabulated and published, was 99.07 for the affirmative and 0.93 for the negative. The professional drys denounced this "diabolical propaganda" and demanded to know how much THE EVENING SUN was getting from the "liquor gang" for promoting it.

Out of this poll there emerged a farcical scheme of more than merely humorous significance. John Philip Hill, a young Baltimore lawyer who emerged from the war with the rank of colonel, had gone in for politics and cast his lot with the Republican party. The Evening Sun was calling upon all Maryland politicians to express themselves on the Prohibition issue. Most of them refused at first, but Colonel Hill, who had managed to squeeze into Congress from a Democratic district largely inhabited by working people, had the wit to see that whooping for beer was good politics, so he answered The Evening Sun's question, " Are you wet or are you dry? ", which was laid before every candidate, with an emphatic " I am wet! " One of the paper's chief arguments was that the Volstead Act was unfair in that it allowed farmers to make homemade wine, but denied the city man his beer. To give graphic proof of this point, Colonel Hill called his house in Baltimore " Franklin Farms " (it is an old house in downtown Franklin street), planted some apple saplings and baby grape vines in his backyard, hung fruit on the fence, collected the fruit, pressed it, and let nature do the rest. As fermentation increased the alcoholic content of the concoctions, he called — through The Evening Sun — for Federal advice. His cider and wine, not himself, he claimed, were breaking the law. What should he do? Thus put to the test, the Federal agents arrested him and he was duly tried in the awful solemnity of the United States District Court. The jury tasted his products and although his wine contained more than 12% of alcohol, decided gravely that it was not " intoxicating in fact." He was, therefore, released, and soon afterward he was reëlected triumphantly to Congress. Thereafter the local candidates, in order to be sure of a hearing, had to claim to be as wet or wetter than John Philip Hill. The Evening Sun, of course, had made its point clear: the farmer could get 12% cider or wine, but the city man couldn't even get 2.75% beer.

Such enlivening enterprises called attention to the paper and gave point to its editorial objectives. They made news, but they alone did not make a rounded newspaper. The basic theory remained that the primary aim of a newspaper should be to print the news. THE EVENING SUN had started off with the dispatches of the United Press. They were adequate, but THE SUN was an Associated Press paper and so early as May, 1914, Mr. Grasty made an effort to obtain membership for THE EVENING SUN also. The Associated Press, however, is a coöperative, non-profit organization, and the admission of a new member is subject to veto by the existing members in its city. Mr. Grasty quickly came to an agreement with General Felix Agnus, then publisher of both the *American* (morning) and the *Star* (evening), whereby THE SUN and the *American*, both members, would waive their vetoes, and so permit both THE EVENING SUN and the *Star* to be admitted. But this arrangement needed the consent of Frank A. Munsey, then publisher of the *News*, and he refused it. Ten years later, in 1924, THE EVENING SUN sought to take advantage of an Associated Press by-law whereby a local veto may be overridden by a four-fifths vote of the whole membership. Of the fifteen directors of the Associated Press, fourteen were in favor of admitting THE EVENING SUN to membership, but when the proposal was put to a vote of all the members the necessary four-fifths majority was not obtained. The *News*, by that time, was owned by William R. Hearst, but it continued to maintain the Munsey veto. The matter remained in abeyance until the early part of 1928, when negotiations were opened with Colonel Frank Knox, then general manager of all the Hearst newspapers. On his recommendation Mr. Hearst finally waived the veto, and on March 31, 1928, THE EVENING SUN became a member of the Associated Press.

On the day that the AP membership was acquired, another spectacular enterprise was carried out. Billy Barton, Howard

Bruce's famous gelding, had been taken to England to run in the Grand National Steeplechase. Baltimore is a horse-loving town and Mr. Bruce is a Baltimorean. Thus everyone was anxious to know as quickly as possible how the race would come out. Transatlantic telephony was a novelty in those days, so Mr. Murphy arranged to have direct communication between the track at Aintree and THE SUN office. Graham McNamee was persuaded to come to Baltimore, put earphones on his head, listen to a description of the race from a man who was watching it in the press stand on the other side of the Atlantic and reannounce it, through loud speakers, to the huge crowd gathered in Sun Square.

A full list of the contests sponsored by THE EVENING SUN would be almost endless. In the field of amateur sports it has offered so many cups, statuettes and medals that one of the Baltimore sculptors, Jack Lambert, has spent a good part of his time designing them. There have been prizes for proficiency in tennis, basket ball, coasting, work-boat racing on the Chesapeake, model-yacht racing, bowling, football, swimming and quoit pitching. There have been contests to determine the best country fiddler in Maryland, the bravest policeman and fireman in Baltimore, the politest street car conductor, the best caddie, the most meritorious mut dog and alley cat, and the wettest wet. Annual prizes have been awarded since 1911 for the best gardens in Baltimore and its vicinity, and since 1922 for the best sketches of Baltimore scenes submitted by local artists. In 1925 an anonymous donor offered, through THE EVENING SUN, an annual gold medal to " that citizen of Baltimore who, during the calendar year, puts up the most pleasing building or group of buildings in the city." The donor thus set forth the terms of his offer:

This medal is not offered to architects or to builders, but to owners. There are no conditions regarding the character of the building erected. It may be a church or a garage, a dwelling-house or a factory. It may cost much or little. The one aim is to pay a small tribute to the man (or organization) who does most during the year to make Baltimore a more beautiful city.

The winner the first year was the Baltimore branch of the Pittsburgh Glass Company, which had erected an office and warehouse building of modest cost but very charming design. Another year the prize went to the pastor of a new Polish Catholic Church down near the water front. A third year it was awarded to the Mayor and City Council of Baltimore for a new City College building — the erection of which, incidentally, The Evening Sun had denounced as an extravagant use of the taxpayers' money. A fourth year it was given to the owner of a filling-station. The prize was awarded annually until, in 1933, the Depression reduced the number of likely candidates to next to none.

One of the great prides of The Evening Sun, for ten years, was its Newsboys Band, organized on May 29, 1922. This band, at the start, was composed entirely of newsboys, but in a few years many of them graduated into other work, and the rules had to be revised from time to time to prevent too many older boys hanging on. Not a few of the alumni became professional musicians. The band played often in public, and once or twice a year it made a tour of Maryland, and was heard by immense crowds. It always gave its services gratis, and never played anywhere where admission fees were charged. On July 4, 1924, it met with a lamentable catastrophe on its way home from the annual workboat races at Crisfield, Md., on Chesapeake Bay. Fifty-nine members of the band, in charge of their director, Frank Morse, were passengers on the steamer *Three Rivers*. Toward midnight, when the boat was off the mouth of the Patuxent river, fire was discovered aboard, and in a few minutes the whole craft was in flames. The newsboys conducted themselves heroically. They went about the boat waking sleeping passengers, and gave what aid they could in getting the women and children into lifeboats. When rescue ships came up and the last survivor was mustered Mr. Morse found that five of his young musicians were missing. They were Nelson A. Miles, Alfred Lester Seligman, Thomas A. Pilker, Vernon E. Jefferson and Walter C. Millikin. Miles, the oldest of the five, was seventeen years old, Jefferson and Seligman were fifteen, and Millikin and Pilker were thirteen. The bodies were all recovered, and the boys were buried together in Loudon Park Cemetery, Baltimore, where a monument to them was unveiled in 1925. Twelve members of the band were pallbearers, and the other members acted as a guard of honor. There was an investigation of the disaster by the United States Steamboat Inspection Service. It reported on August 1, 1924, that the captain and crew of the *Three Rivers* had fought the fire and carried on efforts to save the passengers with courage and good judgment. The Newsboys Band continued to flourish until 1932, when it was disbanded.

THE EVENING SUN made newspaper history on September 1, 1920, by putting into service the first airship ever owned and staffed by a newspaper on this earth. The craft was a Canadian Curtiss biplane, and its commander was Lieut. (now Lieut.-Col.) W. D. Tipton, a flight commander in the Seventeenth Flight Squadron during the World War, with four enemy planes to his account. It made but seventy-five miles an hour, but it was fast for those days, and it was soon bringing in news and photographs at a speed far beyond anything possible on the ground. On its first day in service it covered a railroad wreck at Back River, Md., and on its third day it flew out to sea and located the U. S. Submarine *S*-5, in trouble off the Delaware Capes. On February 3, 1921, when a wreck made it impossible to deliver EVENING SUNS in the regular way to the Eastern Shore of

Maryland, it carried them across the Chesapeake Bay and got them to readers ahead of time. Airships are now used by many American newspapers in the collection of news and photographs, and also by the press associations. When the development of commercial aviation made fast planes available at all hours, THE EVENING SUN retired its Canadian Curtiss. But Colonel Tipton still frequently flies its reporters and photographers. He is also a contributor to its editorial page, always on the subject of aviation.

The 1920s, as all newspaper men know, were a time of great ferment in newspaper offices. The attention which had come to both *Sunpapers* and the wide acquaintanceship which was developing, kept attracting to Baltimore a steady stream of ambitious young men, usually from the South or Middle West. Many of these have since gone on to other papers and some of them have achieved high positions. In every case, the man given a responsible position in THE EVENING SUN news-room was chosen not only because it was believed he could fill it, but also because it was believed that he would outgrow it. Sometimes these hopes were disappointed, but gradually, by a constant winnowing and shifting, a stable organization was created in the news-room. Edwin A. Fitzpatrick, long with THE SUN, was the first man selected by Mr. Murphy as city editor. Later he was advanced to assistant managing editor, and then went to the business office as promotion manager. In 1935 he left the *Sunpapers* to operate a business of his own. When he was made assistant managing editor, his first assistant on the city desk, C. Bruce Earnest [1] was promoted to head that desk and still holds it, with

[1] Mr. Earnest was born in Williamsport, Pa., in 1894. He finished high school there, became a bank clerk, went to the war, and came back to begin newspaper work on the Williamsport *Grit*. He moved on to Harrisburg, where he served on the *Patriot* and finally, in 1920, came to Baltimore and landed on the sports page of THE SUN. He later became assistant city editor.

William B. Thomas as his first assistant. Mr. Thomas is one of that considerable body of *Sunpaper* men who started as copy-boys. Save for one brief interval he has been on THE EVENING SUN since 1910. Another ex-copy-boy of its staff is Walter W. Ward, who devotes himself to police news.

The news editor, when Mr. Murphy took charge of THE EVENING SUN, was Clark Keefer. He died in 1923 and Harold T. Lutz [1] was promoted to the post of news editor and still occupies it. The building up of the copy-desk was a matter of years, for good copy-readers show a tendency to be rovers; their skill is a special one and they are always in demand. For the last few years, however, the copy-desk of THE EVENING SUN has been an unusually stable one. It is headed by Keen Rafferty.[2]

In 1927, having lost his assistant managing editor to the business office, Mr. Murphy cast about for a man to take his place. His choice fell upon Paul J. Banker, who was then managing the news department of a paper in Middletown, Ohio, and managing it very well. Mr. Banker came to Baltimore, accepted the position, filled it for more than two years, and then moved over to THE SUN. His shift meant that an important place in the evening paper was again vacant. Mr. Murphy had been watching the work of a young man in Pittsburgh who was showing exceptional ability as a news editor, supplementing a record previously established in Minneapolis. The decision was made in

[1] Mr. Lutz was born in Maysville, W. Va., in 1899, went through the public school there, and spent two years at Lebanon Valley College and two years at the Johns Hopkins University. He was a reporter for and then city editor of the Chambersburg (Pa.) *Public Opinion* before coming to THE EVENING SUN in 1921.

[2] Mr. Rafferty is the son of a country doctor in Robinson, Ill., where he was born in 1902. He attended the University of Illinois for two years and then began newspaper work on the Terre Haute *Star*. He worked on the Evansville *Courier* and the Evansville *Press* before coming to Baltimore in 1927.

July, 1931, and Neil H. Swanson [1] was made assistant managing editor of THE EVENING SUN, and is still functioning.

On the local staff a number of unusually competent men had developed. Back in 1922, word had come of a Virginia columnist who had outraged a small town by criticizing the architecture of one of its favorite landmarks. He was Gilbert E. Kanour and he came to Baltimore in 1922. The expert of the staff at that time in dealing with the arts was J. O. Lambdin, known to all Baltimoreans as J. O. L. His daily column was a feature of the paper and his dramatic criticism, especially, had given him a place in the community. He was taken with pneumonia in 1923 and it carried him off speedily. Because J. O. L. had been much beloved by Baltimoreans, to fill his place with the young iconoclast from Virginia seemed a doubtful venture, but it worked, and first as G. E. K. and later as Gilbert Kanour, he gained his own following, especially as a critic of the drama and of motion pictures. Thomas M. O'Neill is the paper's expert on local and State politics and politicians; T. Denton Miller, who is himself a member of the bar, directs the covering of proceedings in the courts, and Donald K. Miller holds the post, so beloved of dram-

---

[1] Mr. Swanson was born in Minneapolis on June 30, 1896, spent most of his boyhood on a Minnesota farm, attended the State University, edited the college paper there, and flunked his English but got a job on the Minneapolis *Journal*. With two years out for the war, he was on the staff of that paper for fourteen years, becoming finally its managing editor. He moved to the Pittsburgh *Post* in 1929 and to THE EVENING SUN in 1931. He has written three historical novels — The Judas Tree, 1932; The Phantom Emperor, 1933; and The Temporary Gentleman, 1937; a story for boys — The Flag Is Still There, 1932; and a biography — The First Rebel, the story of one James Smith, who led an insurrection against the British ten years before the Battle of Lexington. In 1917 Mr. Swanson was commissioned a first lieutenant of infantry. He saw action in France as commander of a company on detached service with the Alpine Chasseurs — the Blue Devils — of the French Army.

atists and writers of romance, of police headquarters man. In THE EVENING SUN sports department the chief is Paul Menton,[1] whose special interests are basket ball and football, and who has served as an official of various associations devoted to their promotion. Horse racing, the traditional sport of Maryland, is the special province of Russell Oakes, who has developed into an expert of more than local standing.

With editions ever coming out more frequently and reporting done more and more by telephone, the presence of a capable group of rewrite men, so called, is essential to a modern newspaper. It is their function to listen by telephone to the report of the man on the scene and rewrite his account for publication. For several years past THE EVENING SUN's main battery has consisted of James P. Connolly, Lee McCardell and Stephen A. Fitzgerald, with a group of young men coming along.

When the *Sunpapers* subscribed to the new Wirephoto service of the Associated Press, they found it even more useful and stimulating than they had expected. THE EVENING SUN began the publication of a full page of news pictures every day, and soon found that it was printing, in all, as many half-tones as the picture tabloids. Selecting these pictures and writing captions for them became a special undertaking. The man chosen for the task was Vernon C. Sherwin, an experienced newspaper man already well known to the *Sunpapers*. He came to Baltimore from Florida in 1933.

On April 18, 1935, THE EVENING SUN celebrated the completion of its first quarter of a century. Looking back over the ups-

[1] Mr. Menton was born at Sparrows Point, Md., October 23, 1900. He was graduated from Loyola College, Baltimore, in 1922. He covered sports for THE EVENING SUN while still in college, but after graduation he went to work for the Baltimore *American*. Later he joined THE SUN and then the Baltimore *Post*. In 1923 he became a member of the sports staff of THE EVENING SUN, and in 1925 sports editor.

and-downs it had endured, the editors grew lyrical and printed the following:

Today is the twenty-fifth birthday of THE EVENING SUN. On earlier birthdays it was our custom to say that this date was the anniversary of two other noteworthy events. It was on April 18, 1739, that Dick Turpin, the famous highwayman, was hanged in London and it was on April 18, 1775, that Paul Revere rode through the suburbs of Boston shouting that the British were coming. There must be some point to this coincidence, but no one has ever explained just what the point was.

Today we make no celebration but merely note the obvious: that the paper is still here, that it is still losing most of its battles, and that it still manages to irritate its friends as well as its enemies. No longer young, it cannot blame its mistakes on inexperience. Dodging brickbats has kept its joints supple, but there are, alas, just as many to dodge.

The town has been so good-humored through all the years of our fault-finding and so tolerant of our errors and shortcomings that instead of praising ourselves for enduring we should better be praising Baltimore for enduring us.

CHAPTER XXI

☼

THE SUN SINCE 1920

On November 22, 1920, the board of directors of The A. S. Abell Company passed a resolution authorizing "the improvement of all three editions of The Sun from the editorial standpoint." The directors present at that meeting were Van-Lear Black, Harry C. Black, Paul Patterson, Robert Garrett, J. J. Nelligan, R. Brent Keyser and James C. Fenhagen. With The Sun and The Evening Sun now separated, and The Evening Sun launched upon what promised to be a very prosperous course, the time was at hand to undertake the editorial reorganization and rejuvenation of The Sun.

The "divorce" of the two papers had provided an opportunity for both Mr. Kent and Mr. Adams to rid themselves at least in part of the exhausting grind that getting out a newspaper always involves. Mr. Kent had already revealed, in the trip he took to Europe in 1918 and in ensuing undertakings, that he had great skill at the sort of writing which attracts national attention. He was at work on an unusual book, "The Great Game of Politics," which showed such an intimate and detailed knowledge of the technique of practical politics that it later became a textbook in many colleges. It seemed a pity that his abilities should be stifled by the routine of administration work. Mr. Adams, at the time, was far from a well man, but the illness which sapped his strength spared his mind and spirit. The White Paper described in Chapter XIX had his full support because it coincided with his own ideals of newspaper integrity and seemed a natural development of the liberal and humanitarian principles which made up the bulk of his social philosophy. He had proved, in the trip to the national conventions in the Summer of 1920 that he could still stand the strain of daily work; indeed, the jaunt seemed to rejuvenate him and he came home filled with new ideas and avid for action.

His enthusiasm, and Mr. Patterson's keenness for news enterprise, led to an undertaking which still stands out, in the recent history of The Sun, as an event of the first importance. When the Harding Naval Disarmament Conference was called to meet in December, 1921, Mr. Adams saw in it a splendid opportunity for The Sun. He felt that if the paper undertook to report it in a manner and on a scale hitherto never attempted by an American newspaper, it would make a marked gain in prestige and influence. Its situation was peculiarly favorable for the project. It could get into Washington by breakfast time with editions printed late in the night, and containing complete news reports. The New York papers would either have to send earlier editions, or content themselves with late deliveries. The Sun already had a large circulation in Washington. It was, in fact, delivered there by carrier, as it was delivered to subscribers in Baltimore, and most of the principal officers of the Federal government read it daily. It was served at the White House, at the State Department, and at many of the foreign embassies and legations.

It was Mr. Patterson's idea that, in covering such things as the coming conference, American newspapers were commonly content with very superficial reports of what was going on. They reported every overt happening fully enough, and they gave a great deal of space to official statements and explanations, but they seldom undertook to explain clearly the forces underlying and determining events. He believed that if such a gloss upon the conference were attempted, with the aid of well-informed men, THE SUN's reports of the proceedings would be read with unusual attention, and might be of great value to the American delegates. He accordingly reported to the directors of the *Sunpapers*, in the early Summer of 1921, that he and Mr. Adams, who was in complete accord with his ideas, proposed to go to Europe to unearth experts who really knew what the conference would be about, and had intimate first-hand acquaintance with its leading personalities, and with the national aspirations lying behind it. The directors were unanimously in favor of the plan, and Messrs. Patterson and Adams sailed from New York on August 26. They carried with them a long list of men they wanted to see — most of them European journalists specializing in foreign affairs, but along with them a number of publicists and politicians. Above all, they wanted to see C. P. Scott, the famous editor of the Manchester *Guardian*. Mr. Adams, as an old Liberal, was a great admirer of Mr. Scott, and THE SUN, in association with the New York *World*, was already receiving, by cable every day, the *Guardian's* dispatches from the chief news centers of Europe.

The two pilgrims did not wait until they got to England to begin operations. On the ship they met a French Colonial newspaper proprietor who gave them a great deal of information about the political situation in France, and the affiliations of the more prominent French journalists, and that information turned out to be very useful later on. Arriving in England, they proceeded to London and there began a series of conferences with all sorts of persons, ranging from officials of the Foreign Office to the editors of the chief London newspapers, and including such distinguished English political writers as H. W. Nevinson, H. N. Brailsford and S. K. Ratcliffe. These conferences clarified their ideas, and they began to see the solution of the problem confronting them. It was to give the delegates to the conference, at breakfast every morning, an accurate account of the reactions of world opinion to their deliberations. It would not suffice to print American views of the proceedings; it would also be necessary to print an accurate report of foreign views. The way to obtain those views, obviously, was to enter upon arrangements with the foreign newspapers that would be represented, so that the dispatches sent home by their correspondents would appear also in THE SUN. This service would not only be enlightening to the American delegates, who would otherwise have to be content with brief summaries cabled back to Washington; it would also be enlightening to the British, French and Japanese delegates, who would thus learn what the people of their own countries were reading about their work.

On September 4 Messrs. Patterson and Adams went to Manchester and saw Mr. Scott. The famous editor was at first somewhat cool to the proposals of his visitors, though his welcome had been polite enough. He had heard of THE SUN, but knew nothing about it. It was, to him, simply a provincial newspaper in a far country. Gradually, however, he thawed, and when the interview ended there was effected a friendly understanding which was to have important future consequences. But let Mr. Adams' diary tell the story:

Patterson put our proposition up to Scott, very skillfully, I thought. The old gentleman was very cordial, very sympathetic, but it was evident that he was examining the proposal in his mind from all standpoints. During the recital his keen eyes roved from Patterson's face to mine and back again. Sizing us up very carefully, he first brought up the *Guardian's* connection with the New York *World* and said that that might prevent any special arrangement. Patterson told him that we took the *World's* service and would do anything that was necessary to secure the *World's* approval. He next began to talk on the assumption that what we wanted from him was a special appeal to American readers. "That wouldn't do at all," he said, "I cannot interfere in American politics." Patterson said that wasn't the idea at all. What we wanted was for him and the *Guardian* to appeal through THE SUN to the British delegation at Washington. "Ah," he said, "that puts a new phase on the matter," and he showed a renewed interest in the proposition; had Patterson repeat some of the details again and seemed genuinely impressed. When Patterson said that this was not an ordinary business proposition with us, but rather an idealistic one, born of the idea that we had a duty resting on us to be of service at the conference, he said, "Yes, yes, I understand. That is what appeals to me about it."

Returning to London, Messrs. Patterson and Adams continued their conferences with journalists, publicists and politicians, including Sir Campbell Stuart, of the *Times;* Robert Hield, of the *Morning Post;* Hall Richardson, of the *Daily Telegraph;* Stuart Hodgson and L. J. Cadbury, of the *Daily News;* J. St. Loe Strachey, of the *Spectator;* Sir Arthur Willert and Stephen Gazelee, of the permanent staff of the Foreign Office; Major (now Sir) Evelyn Wrench, founder of the English-Speaking Union; Sir Joseph Ward, former Premier of New Zealand; Sir Harry Brittain, M. P.; Chang-Min Lin, former Minister of Justice of China; J. M. Keynes, author of "The Economic Consequences of the Peace"; [1] H. M. Tomlinson and George Bernard Shaw.[2] They were given friendly aid by Ed

[1] From Mr. Adams' diary: "Keynes has a crisp way of talking and his fame has made him confident, not to say dogmatic. He does not hesitate to make flat assertions about matters which are, after all, matters of opinion. As for instance: 'Lloyd George will not go to the Washington conference. He cannot possibly get away.' As for instance: 'England will never get a cent of reparations payments and everybody here knows it.' As for instance: 'The Allied war debts to America will never be paid and all intelligent men in America know it.'" Events proved that Mr. Keynes was right all three times.

[2] They called on Shaw at 10 Adelphi Terrace. From Mr. Adams'

Keen, chief correspondent of the United Press in London, and by J. W. Grigg, head of the New York *World* bureau. Between two rounds of English calls they proceeded to Paris, where they saw Stephen Lausanne, editor of *Le Matin*, and various other persons, including the Irish-American expatriate, Vincent O'Sullivan, who gave them a long and very useful dissertation on the inner workings of French journalism.

On their return to Baltimore at the end of September their plans for covering the approaching Disarmament Conference were completed. They had arranged in London for some preliminary articles by H. N. Brailsford, and when the conference opened on November 12 THE SUN was represented at Washington by a truly remarkable body of correspondents. There was, to begin with, its own Washington staff, headed by J. Fred Essary and reinforced from the home office. Then there were the Englishmen — Mr. Brailsford, a spokesman for the more radical sort of English opinion; Mr. Strachey, editor of the London *Spectator* and an exponent of conservative ideas; H. W. Nevinson, the veteran war correspondent; H. W. Massingham, of the London *Nation;* Hector C. Bywater, author of "Sea Power in the Pacific" and the foremost English naval expert,

---

diary: "Shaw came in, tall, erect, vigorous. His attire as neat as his library. Wore a well-fitting, well-pressed suit of brown tweeds. His white, silky hair neatly brushed; his white beard, less silky, neatly parted. A disillusioning pattern of elegance and form. Shows his teeth in talking in a manner strikingly reminiscent of Charles Evans Hughes. I began by regretting that he was tied up with Hearst on Disarmament Conference matter. 'Well,' he said, 'Mr. Hearst pays me very well for my stuff and he gives a wide circulation to what I have to say. Therefore I have the utmost respect for him. Some of my friends have told me that I ought to have nothing to do with him. I tell them that the fact that he seems eager to print my compositions proves him a connoisseur and a gentleman. And the circulation of his papers is so large that to reflect upon its quality is to reflect upon the character of the American people, which is the last thing in the world that I should care to do.'"

and Wilson Harris, an authority on the League of Nations. Then came the Frenchmen — George Lechartier, of the *Journal des Débats*, and Jean Longuet, the Socialist leader; the Japanese — Adachi Konnosuki, K. Ishikawa and Midori Komatsu, and the Chinese — Jabin Hsu. Finally, there were a number of American specialists in matters before the conference — Dr. John Dewey, of Columbia University, who had just returned from a long visit to China; Dr. John H. Latané, professor of American history and head of the department of history at the Johns Hopkins, and Rear Admiral Walter McLean, U. S. N. (retired); and a group of guest contributors from other American newspapers — among them J. G. Hamilton, of the New York *Times;* James E. Touhy and Heywood Broun, of the *World*, and Arthur Sears Henning, of the Chicago *Tribune*. Frank R. Kent, whose dramatic European news-hunt in 1918 has been described in Chapter XVIII, went to London to send home a daily summary of English opinion. Going far beyond the terms of this commission, he undertook inquiries which, among other things, enabled him to beat even the London *Times* on the news of Lloyd George's plans for the Cannes conference of January 6–13, 1922. His dispatches to THE SUN were cabled back to London every day by the American correspondents of the chief London newspapers. Boardman Robinson, now one of the most distinguished of American painters, served THE SUN as cartoonist at this time, and Hendrik Willem Van Loon became a columnist of its staff soon afterward.[1] The star of THE EVE-

[1] Mr. Robinson was followed in 1924 by Edmund Duffy, who is still THE SUN's chief cartoonist. Born at Jersey City on March 1, 1899, Mr. Duffy studied at the Art Students' League in New York with Mr. Robinson, John Sloan and George Bridgman. He went to Paris for further studies in 1920. Before coming to THE SUN he had contributed to the New York *Herald Tribune, Evening Post* and *Leader,* the Brooklyn *Eagle,* the London *Evening News, Scribner's* and the *Century*. He was awarded the Pulitzer Prize for his cartoons in THE

NING SUN's corps of guest contributors was H. G. Wells, who had come to the United States to do the conference for a syndicate of American and English papers.[1]

The success of the enterprise was even greater than Mr. Patterson had anticipated. The Disarmament Conference itself accomplished little of permanent value, but the handling of it by the *Sunpapers*, and especially by THE SUN, got them much favorable notice, both at home and abroad.[2] In this country newspaper men began to be aware that a pair of enterprising and lively dailies, of a strongly Liberal tendency, had come into the field, and across the two oceans they began to be read and heeded in quarters where they had not been so much as heard of before.

One of the most important by-products of this venture did not flower for two years more. Both Patterson and Adams had returned from Europe with their admiration for the Manchester *Guardian* confirmed and strengthened. But by some curious chance they did not on this trip meet one of its outstanding personalities, James Bone, its London editor. However, Bone was a friend of Hamilton Owens, who became editor of THE EVENING SUN while the conference was in session. In 1924 the New York *World* and the *Guardian* agreed to discontinue their news exchange arrangement and Bone cabled Owens suggesting that it might be possible to work out an agreement with THE SUN. The

SUN in 1931 and again in 1933. Dr. Van Loon joined THE SUN on May 10, 1922, and remained until April 29, 1923. His column was headed H. V. L., was devoted to all sorts of matters, and was frequently illustrated by the author.

[1] On November 20, 1921, Mr. Van-Lear Black entertained the journalists in attendance on the conference at his country place, Folly Quarters, in Howard county, Maryland. Nearly 500 guests came from Washington for the day. There was an immense barbecue and a Western rodeo, with a troupe of Indians.

[2] See, for example, the chapter entitled The Baltimore SUNS: a Notable Journalistic Resurrection, in Oswald Garrison Villard's Some Newspapers and Newspapermen, New York, 1923.

suggestion was accepted with alacrity and since that time there has been a close alliance between the two papers, under which THE SUN has the exclusive right in the United States to all the special correspondence and other valuable material published in the *Guardian*.

This connection was seized upon as an opportunity to expand the paper's news service. It was decided to open a London bureau. John W. Owens was selected as the first London correspondent and he sailed for his post in November, 1924. It was not intended that his stay should be permanent and ever since there has been a sort of rotation in office in the matter of the London assignment. For this there are two reasons. The first is that it is regarded as desirable to give as many members of the staff as possible the advantage of foreign experience, and the second is that it is thought even more desirable to prevent any of them losing contact with American ideas and the American scene — a common fate among foreign correspondents, some of whom, domiciled abroad for years, lose their American point of view entirely, and become almost natives. THE SUN's London correspondents have all enjoyed intimate contact with the staff of the *Guardian*, and especially with Mr. Bone. He has taken each in succession under his wing, and all of them have returned home his undying friends and admirers. During the Summer of 1936, when he came to the United States to cover the two national conventions for the *Guardian* (and to write some pungent and amusing comments on them for THE EVENING SUN), there was a reunion of his alumni in Baltimore. When Mr. Owens returned from London in 1926, he was succeeded by Mr. Essary; later, W. A. S. Douglas, M. Farmer Murphy, Dewey L. Fleming, A. D. Emmart, Frederic C. Nelson, Newton Aiken and Philip Wagner have served in the post. The London office of THE SUN, at 40 Fleet street, adjoins the London bureau of the *Guardian*.

Another valuable by-product of the Disarmament Conference (one which had, indeed, been anticipated) was the knowledge it gave THE SUN's executives of European journalists and their abilities. Through the connections formed during those busy weeks, the paper was able to select and appoint an extraordinarily competent group of correspondents in the principal foreign news-centers. In Paris its representative is André Geraud, whose dispatches appear under the pen name of Pertinax. M. Geraud is the chief political writer for *L'Écho de Paris*, and has access to many sources of information that are closed to other correspondents. He writes, incidentally, very excellent English. In Berlin, for a number of years, THE SUN had two correspondents. One of them, an American by birth, was a strong partisan of Hitler, then slowly struggling to power, and the other, a German, was an ardent advocate of the Weimar constitution. They wrote against each other, and between the two of them THE SUN was able to present a comprehensive picture of the battle of ideas in Germany. When Hitler became Chancellor the German went over to him and the American turned against him — and soon had to leave the country. In July, 1936, another SUN correspondent, Wilbur Burton, of Shanghai, ran afoul of the Japanese, and was turned back when he sought to visit Japan. THE SUN allows all such foreign correspondents the utmost leeway. They are chosen with care, but once they are in the service they are free to write whatever seems to them to be the truth. Among the more conspicuous of them are H. M. Brailsford, whose articles on international politics supplement the dispatches of the London bureau; C. R. Bradish, who writes from Australia; J. A. Stevenson, who deals with Canadian affairs; Louis Fisher, whose post is Moscow but who occasionally goes elsewhere; and Mrs. Paula Arnold, who formerly represented THE SUN in Vienna and is now its correspondent in Palestine.

One of the problems confronting Messrs. Patterson and Adams in the days of reorganization was to find a man capable of taking over the administrative work of Frank R. Kent, so as to allow him free exercise of the extraordinary talents for political reporting and interpretation which he had displayed on both his European trips and, especially, in his book, "The Great Game of Politics." That work had been printed as a serial in THE SUN before its publication as a book and attracted an unusual amount of attention, for it told in simple and forthright language just how the practical politician gets and holds his power and how he uses it. It was not a philosophical treatise but a case record based upon long years of observation. Its success suggested that Mr. Kent might use a somewhat similar technique in the news columns and, accordingly, he started a column which ran every day on the first page of THE SUN. At first it was printed under a news head, but as it gained momentum and began to attract national attention, it began to appear under a standing heading. The title chosen, naturally enough, was the same as that of his book.[1]

His diversion to this new field of work left, however, a big gap in the organization of THE SUN. Fortunately, there was a man at hand. Although Stanley M. Reynolds, who was acting as editor of THE EVENING SUN, was enjoying himself hugely in that post and obviously doing a good job, he had been trained mainly as a gatherer of news. He had had experience also in the management of men. Moreover, he himself preferred news itself to the ensuing comment upon it. He was accordingly transferred from the editor's office of the evening paper to the managing

[1] So many papers asked permission to reprint the column that finally it was agreed, in 1934, to break a long-standing rule of the *Sunpapers* and allow it to be syndicated. Concerning his work, Mr. Kent said, in an address to the American Society of Newspaper Editors in 1931: "I am free as a bird and should like to say it seems to me the best job in the world."

editor's desk of the morning edition, and went to work upon the task of building up his news staff. He was fortunate in several respects. Mr. Kent had selected an assistant some time before, a young man named Mark S. Watson,[1] whose experience was such that the routine of the paper was safe in his hands. Reynolds was at home in both Baltimore and Washington, and hence knew not only the local scene, but also the importance, from The Sun's point of view, of a competent news service from the Capital. He grasped the fact that an opportunity was being given him to build up a paper of some distinction.

He seemed to be everywhere at once. At one moment he was with Mr. Watson or his city editor directing the handling of some local story. In another minute he would be found in Mr. Adams' office arguing over some point of relationship between news and editorial policy. He had a real, not a perfunctory, interest in sports, and he labored for months to bring the sports pages to the standard he had set up in his mind. He tried, in fact, to do much more than his far from robust physique could stand. He was a perfectionist and no detail was too small for his attention. The net result was that he burned himself out all too soon. Recurring illnesses kept him away from the office for periods that grew longer and longer, until finally he could no longer keep his hands upon the work. He died in 1930.

But he had, in the meantime, gathered together a capable

---

[1] Mr. Watson was born at Plattsburgh June 24, 1887, and is a graduate of Union College. He got his first newspaper experience on the Plattsburgh *Press* and later served the Chicago *Tribune* as reporter, traveling correspondent and member of the Washington and New York bureaus. He enlisted in the Field Artillery, went overseas in August, 1917, and when he returned to civil life in July, 1919, was a major. He was made officer-in-charge of the soldiers' newspaper, the *Stars and Stripes,* a week after the Armistice. On returning to the United States he became managing editor of the *Ladies' Home Journal.* He joined the staff of The Sun as assistant managing editor in 1920 and became editor of The Sunday Sun in 1927.

staff. Luck played some part in this achievement, for it was only by chance that, late in 1922, Mr. Patterson discovered that William E. Moore, an experienced newspaper-maker, with whom he had long been associated in Chicago and with whose capacities he was thoroughly familiar, could be persuaded to come to Baltimore. Mr. Moore was so persuaded and, as it turned out, this discovery was as important for THE SUN as that of J. Edwin Murphy had been for THE EVENING SUN a few years previously.[1] Mr. Reynolds assigned Mr. Watson to the post of day assistant managing editor and appointed Mr. Moore to the night side. When it seemed desirable that THE SUNDAY SUN should be brought to a higher standard, and especially that a first-rate magazine section should be added to it (1927), he yielded up Mr. Watson to do the job of managing the undertaking.

Mr. Moore succeeded Mr. Reynolds when illness finally forced him to relinquish his post, and Paul J. Banker, who had been trained in the methods of the office on THE EVENING SUN, was shifted to the assistant's chair which Moore himself had just vacated.[2] At the same time Burwell C. Snyder was given charge

[1] Mr. Moore was born at La Grange, Mo., June 30, 1878, and was educated at the University of Missouri. He got his first newspaper experience on the Quincy (Ill.) *Herald and Journal* in 1899. In 1901 he joined the staff of the Chicago *American* and in 1904 became city editor of the Chicago *Inter-Ocean.* After two years in New York on the *Herald* he returned to the *Inter-Ocean* as its night editor in 1909 and three years later became its managing editor. He went to the Chicago *Daily News* as an editorial writer in 1914 and then to the New York *Tribune* as city editor, becoming managing editor in 1917. He was a captain in the Signal Corps during the World War and was attached to General Pershing's headquarters as director of the pictorial history of the A. E. F. He served in the Aisne-Marne, Marne-Vesle and St. Mihiel campaigns. He prepared the official volume of pictures of the war and wrote the Democratic Campaign Textbook of 1920. He joined THE SUN in 1922.

[2] Mr. Banker was born in 1893 near Middletown, Ohio, and after graduation from Yale College in 1915 returned to resume work he had begun during previous summer

of the gradually growing copy desk and encouraged to put young men on its rim.[1] As the paper grew in influence and reputation, newspaper men in many parts of the country learned about it and, as in the case of THE EVENING SUN, sought to join its staff. The present city editor, H. K. Fleming, offers a case in point. He is an Englishman who came to the United States on a visit, liked it so much here that he decided to stay — and then got himself a job in Washington so that he would be at hand should THE SUN decide to give him an opportunity.[2] That opportunity came quickly.

---

vacations as a reporter on the Middletown *News-Signal*. Late in 1915 he became associate editor of *Commerce and Finance*, New York City, leaving this position in 1917 to attend the Officers' Training Camp at Plattsburgh, N. Y., where he was commissioned a first lieutenant of infantry. He served with the Three Hundred and Fourteenth Infantry, Seventy-ninth Division, at Camp Meade and in France, also with the press section of the second section of the general staff as photographic censor in Paris. Returning to the United States after the peace treaty was signed, he was offered the managing editorship of the Middletown *News-Signal* and remained there until he came to THE EVENING SUN in Baltimore in August, 1927. He served as assistant managing editor of THE EVENING SUN until October, 1929, and since then has held the same position on THE SUN.

[1] Mr. Snyder was born in Jefferson county, West Virginia, on September 26, 1883, and was educated at Shepherd College, the State Normal School at Shepherdstown, and Randolph-Macon College. He taught school for several years and then entered the ministry of the Methodist Episcopal Church South, but he retired before ordination and joined the staff of the Baltimore *Evening Herald* in the Summer of 1905. He continued with it until it suspended in 1906. He returned to newspaper work on the Baltimore *American* in 1909 and transferred to THE SUN in April, 1910. He has served it as reporter, State editor, night editor and news editor.

[2] Mr. Fleming was born in Cheshire in 1901. He spent three years (1918–1920) at the London School of Economics, and thereafter served with the Friends Relief Mission in Poland and Galicia. He was in Lvoff during the drive of Budenny's Cossacks on that city in 1922. On his return to England he became assistant to the editor of the *North Eastern Daily Gazette*. In 1923 he went to London as assistant to the editor of the London *Daily Herald*, organ of the Labor party. He came to THE SUN in October, 1924, and after serving as editorial

It has always been the rule in THE SUN office to promote men on the staff to the higher positions whenever it is possible to do so. William H. Y. Knighton, Jr., the present cable editor, started as a cub reporter. So did Donald Kirkley, theater and motion picture critic. So did Frank R. Kent, Jr., assistant city editor; Louis J. O'Donnell, political reporter; Jesse A. Linthicum,[1] sports editor, and many others in posts of responsibility. Every man in the Washington bureau has served his time in the city room.

When John W. Owens came back from London, he was installed as assistant to Mr. Adams. Charles McHenry Harwood, who had been with Mr. Grasty on the Baltimore *News* and was editor of that paper during the Munsey régime, was invited to join the editorial staff of THE SUN in 1924, that his vast knowledge of local affairs might be utilized. Felix Morley, who was a Baltimorean born, but whose comparatively brief career had given him large opportunities for learning about foreign affairs, was brought in that he might follow in editorials the day-to-day developments abroad.[2] A. D. Emmart,[3] who had shown

---

writer, copy reader, New York correspondent and in the Washington bureau, was appointed city editor in 1933. He became a citizen of the United States in 1936.

[1] Mr. Linthicum joined the *Sunpapers* in 1912, first served as assistant sports editor of THE EVENING SUN, and was transferred to THE SUN after the outbreak of the World War. He was night editor and make-up editor of THE SUN for five years, city editor for two and served as news editor before returning to sports. Before joining the *Sunpapers* he had been a member of the staffs of the Baltimore *News* and Baltimore *Star*. He was born in Baltimore October 27, 1891.

[2] Mr. Morley is now editor of the Washington *Post*. He is a son of Dr. Frank Morley, professor emeritus of mathematics at the Johns Hopkins University, and a brother to Christopher Morley. He joined the editorial staff of THE SUN in 1922 and served until 1929. In 1925 he went to the Far East for THE SUN and in 1928 he was its correspondent at Geneva.

[3] Mr. Emmart is a Baltimorean, born in 1902. He is a graduate of the Johns Hopkins University. He had a brief period on the *News* and

a great interest in the fine arts, was made keeper of the paper's æsthetic conscience. An economist was needed, and he was found in Dexter M. Keezer, who joined the editorial staff in 1929, and remained until 1933, when he was drafted by General Hugh S. Johnson, then head of the NRA, to serve as executive director of the Consumers' Advisory Board.[1] He was succeeded by Mauritz A. Hallgren,[2] whose reputation had been made largely on the *Nation*. Meantime, Frederic C. Nelson, writing for the Hartford *Times*, had made such an impression that he was persuaded to come to Baltimore and join up,[3] and Newton Aiken had been transferred to the editorial staff from the Washington bureau.[4]

---

came to THE SUN in January, 1923. He has been reporter, copy reader, art critic and editorial writer in addition to his tour of duty in London (1932–1934). He contributes frequently to the weeklies both here and in England.

[1] Dr. Keezer came to THE SUN from Dartmouth. He was born at Acton, Mass., August 24, 1895, and educated at Amherst and Cornell. He taught economics at Cornell, the University of Colorado, the University of North Carolina and Dartmouth. He is now president of Reed College at Portland, Ore.

[2] Mr. Hallgren was born in Chicago in 1899 and is a graduate of the University of Chicago. He began work as a reporter on the Chicago *Daily News* in 1920. He was made State Department correspondent for the United Press in 1926 and was sent by that organization to Berlin, where he served for two years. For three years, from 1930 to 1933, he was associate editor of the *Nation*. He is a frequent contributor to the reviews, both at home and abroad, and has published two political works, Seeds of Revolt, 1933, and The Gay Reformer, 1935.

[3] Mr. Nelson was born at Windsor, Conn., on November 17, 1893, and was graduated from Harvard in 1916. His first newspaper job was with the Hartford *Times* during summer vacations. After graduation, he joined the city staff of the Boston *Post* for a few months. He was instructor in English at Dartmouth in 1916 and 1917. Later he was a reporter on the Hartford *Courant*, from which he returned to the *Times* as editorial writer in 1920. He remained on that paper until the Spring of 1929, when he came to THE SUN. In 1931 he was sent to the London bureau, remaining a year.

[4] Mr. Aiken is a Tennesseean, born at Cleveland in that State on February 21, 1892. He took his B. A. at Trinity College in North Carolina, now Duke University. He got his first newspaper experience on the Durham (N. C.) *Sun* in 1912. Later he went to the

Following the policy established by the Founder, local matters have always been of intense concern to THE SUN. How much money shall be spent on an airport, for instance, or indeed shall the taxpayers' money be spent on an airport at all? Should the city build and subsidize an art gallery? Shall the schools be permitted, unchallenged, to adopt all the fads and fancies of progressive education? Is Mr. A likely to make a better Mayor than Mr. B? What is needed in a budget system to make it work? What proportion of the municipal income shall come from taxes on real estate? Are voting machines a good investment? What about the Continental Sunday? Where the choice between two courses is clear, it is not difficult for the paper to make the proper decision and support it. But only a few local issues, or national ones either, are as simple as the choice between black and white. Sometimes, in attempting such judgments, THE SUN has been proven wrong by later events. Watchful readers never fail to point out such errors when they occur and it is the settled course of THE SUN, and of THE EVENING SUN as well, to admit them publicly and promptly.

Equally important in the viewpoint of the paper is the larger one of trying to keep open the channels of public discussion. In Baltimore, Miss Elisabeth Gilman, who is the daughter of the first president of the Johns Hopkins University and a Socialist of pronounced opinions, runs an open forum where ideas ranging as far to the Left as those of the extreme Communists are frequently given voice. It is more important to the community, in the long run, in the opinion of THE SUN, that Miss Gilman be allowed to proceed unmolested, than that a few thousand dollars

Richmond *Times-Dispatch,* the Norfolk *Ledger-Dispatch* and the Norfolk *Virginia-Pilot*. He joined the Washington bureau of THE SUN in 1929. During 1935–1936 he served as London correspondent. He went to the Mexican border with the Tennessee National Guard in 1916, and during the World War was a captain in the Three Hundred and Sixth Ammunition Train.

be saved on a paving contract. It is more important that the followers of some strange sect in Southern Maryland be protected in their sincere belief that it is wrong to salute the flag than it is to take violent sides in some controversy over the location of a new road in the same county. THE SUN probably insisted more vehemently that Governor Ritchie take active steps to punish the mob which lynched a Negro on the Eastern Shore of Maryland than that he punish thieves found operating in his State roads office.

All sorts of minorities, some of them advocating painfully absurd theories, have been given space to express their ideas in the columns of the paper, and have been defended vigorously when it appeared that their rights were being infringed upon. Once, indeed, the editors got so wrought up over what appeared to them to be an injustice, that they went out of character so far as to send a telegram to Governor Alvan T. Fuller of Massachusetts, urging him to ask the president of the American Bar Association to appoint a committee of impartial lawyers to study the case of Sacco and Vanzetti. It was perhaps characteristic that there was no reply to this telegram, which was dated August 20, 1927, and that the two prisoners were duly executed three days later.

That was one of the few times that the editors of the paper departed from the rule of the office that they must engage only in purely journalistic enterprises. For the rest, they are expected to eschew all outside connections, save those of a purely social nature. Following the tradition established by the Abells, they serve on no boards or committees, sign no memorials, and avoid membership in organizations which have business or political ends to serve. They take no part in politics except through the columns of the paper.

There is one peculiarity of the *Sunpapers* which seems odd to the newspaper men of other cities. In the old days, when all the

Baltimore papers filled the first page as far as possible with advertisements, it was convenient to print important local news on the back page. THE SUN adhered to that custom and still believes in it, for it gives, as Baltimoreans say, " two first pages." But it lays a special burden upon the city editor and his staff, for he must find news every day that is worth this special display.

In Mr. Black's White Paper, mentioned in Chapter XIX, emphasis was laid upon the proximity of Baltimore to Washington and the opportunity thereby created for an expansion of THE SUN's circulation and prestige. That expansion required, of course, a development of the Washington staff, which had always been a special care of the editors. Some of the early Washington correspondents are listed in Chapter XII in the notice of Francis A. Richardson, who held the post from 1866 to 1901. Among his predecessors not listed there were W. W. Warden, O. K. Harris and James Lawrenson, the latter a clerk in the Postoffice Department who contributed Washington " letters " to THE SUN from its first years to the opening of the Civil War. Mr. Richardson began as an occasional contributor, but after 1872 he devoted his whole time to THE SUN. In 1876 he opened its new building at 1314 F street, N. W. — the first building to be put up in Washington by an out-of-town newspaper and the city's first skyscraper. It was ten stories in height and from its spire glowed THE SUN's insignia, a golden sunburst. It was, during the late 70s and 80s, one of the sights of the town, just as the Iron Building was one of the sights of Baltimore. The first floor was occupied by the Washington staff of THE SUN, with room for a counting room which booked subscriptions and advertisements. Upstairs there were tenants. During the years preceding the World War all the upper floors were occupied by the Interstate Commerce Commission. The building was sold in 1907 and THE SUN's Washington bureau began a series of migrations which ended on September 1, 1927, with the lease of a suite of offices in the National Press Building, which also houses the Washington bureaus of nearly 500 other publications, including many daily newspapers. The bureau is connected with the home office by leased telegraph and telephone wires.

On Mr. Richardson's retirement in 1901 he was succeeded by John Pierce Miller, who had been the chief political writer of the Washington *Star*. Mr. Miller was followed in 1910 by Frank R. Kent, and Mr. Kent after a year by McKee Barclay, who had been THE SUN's cartoonist but was also a good reporter. Mr. Barclay was succeeded in 1912 by Mr. Essary, who has been in charge ever since, save for the interval when he was London correspondent. On his staff in the ensuing years have been a number of interesting figures. One of them was John W. Owens, later to become editor of THE SUN; others were M. Farmer Murphy, one of the ablest reporters in the country, and Drew Pearson, who now runs a syndicated column with Robert J. Allen. The present group consists, in addition to Mr. Essary, of C. P. Trussell,[1] Dewey L. Fleming,[2] Paul W. Ward,[3] George

[1] Mr. Trussell comes from old newspaper stock. He was born in Chicago in 1892, and early in life migrated to the Eastern Shore of Maryland with his widowed mother. In 1916 he started as a reporter on the Baltimore *American*. He came to THE SUN the next year and was moved to the city editor's post in 1925. He has been with the Washington bureau since 1932. He is a brother of Percy L. Trussell, of the New York *Evening Post*.

[2] Mr. Fleming, who covers the Senate for THE SUN, was born in Whitmer, W. Va., in 1898. He was graduated from Davis and Elkins College, at Elkins, in 1918. His first newspaper work was in Elkins, but he came to Baltimore in 1922 to work on the *American*. Since joining THE SUN in 1923 he has served in New York, Chicago and London as well as in Washington.

[3] Mr. Ward was born in Lorain, Ohio, in 1905. He got his A. B. at Middlebury College in 1925. Before that he had been a professional singer and a professional baseball player, with interludes of drug-clerking, selling automobile accessories, rubber working and teaching school. His first newspaper work was on the New Bedford (Mass.) *Standard*. While there he began contributing to the editorial page of

W. Combs [1] and Gerald Griffin, formerly a member of the staff of THE SUNDAY SUN.

THE SUN's Washington bureau was the first to permit any of its members save its chief to sign their articles. Its example is now followed by the bureaus of nearly all the metropolitan papers. In the late 1920s bureaus were also established in New York and Chicago and the same system of rotation was used in manning them that had become the rule in the London office. In New York THE SUN acquired rights to news gathered by the New York *World* and later to the news service of the *Herald Tribune.* In Chicago it maintained for a long time a similar relationship with the *Tribune* of that city.

From time to time, as occasion arose, it showed its continuing interest in foreign affairs. It organized a special group to cover the Pan-American Conference held at Havana in 1928, leasing a special cable and sending along Messrs. John W. Owens, Reynolds and Mencken, with Mr. Patterson acting as bureau chief. In 1930, when a second Naval Conference met at London, the London correspondent, then Dewey L. Fleming, was reinforced by Messrs. Owens, Geraud (Pertinax) and Pearson and, after a little while, by Mr. Mencken, who had been traveling on the Continent. Hector C. Bywater, the British naval expert who had written for THE SUN during the first Naval Conference at Washington and had later become a regular contributor to the paper, was also present. At the Economic Conference of 1933

THE EVENING SUN. He became a member of the staff of THE SUN in 1930 and was assigned to the Washington bureau in 1933. He specializes in farm, labor and social legislation.

[1] Mr. Combs was born in Clay county, Kentucky, in 1877, and was educated at what is now the University of Kentucky. After some experience as a school teacher and in business, he joined the Washington bureau of THE SUN in 1908. At the start he represented the business office and was in charge of Washington circulation and advertising, but in 1927 he transferred to the news staff. He was elected chairman of the board of governors of the National Press Club in 1936.

the chief representative of THE SUN was Dr. Keezer, and M. Geraud moved over from Paris to describe its deliberations from the French point of view. At various other times members of the staff have made foreign journeys for the paper.

When the national campaign of 1936 was getting under way THE SUN ventured upon an enterprise that was new to it, and indeed to American journalism. It proposed to take a poll of *all* the registered voters in Maryland — not of a sample, large or small, but of the whole number. The poll would be an unusually significant one, it was believed, because on only one occasion in fifty years had the voters of Maryland failed to give a popular plurality to the winning Presidential candidate. " As Maryland goes, so goes the nation " was therefore a more nearly truthful adage than the old one about Maine. There were at that time about 770,000 voters registered in the State, and conducting a poll of all of them was a task requiring a large emergency staff and a considerable expenditure. Nevertheless, an envelope containing a letter of instructions and a ballot was addressed to every voter registered in the State, and the whole mass, weighing many tons, was dispatched by mail. As the returns came in they were tabulated by machinery and published in both papers from day to day.

It was the irony of fate that, at the very time the first returns from the poll were showing that the sentiment of the State was overwhelmingly in favor of Mr. Roosevelt, the editors reached the conclusion that the *Sunpapers* could not support him for reëlection. They had supported him gladly in 1932, and were whole-heartedly in favor of the platform on which he ran — a platform embodying many cardinal articles of traditional SUN doctrine. He had been long known to many men in the office, and they all admired his courage and resourcefulness; he had been, furthermore, an intimate friend of Van-Lear Black. But as the platform of 1932 began to disappear plank by plank and the

New Deal to unfold itself, the *Sunpapers* were constrained to register a long series of dissents. They flew the Blue Eagle, but they were in doubt about the NRA from the beginning, and later on they were in doubt about various other salient New Deal devices. In the end, about the only Administration enterprise to which they could give complete approval was the effort by the Secretary of State, Cordell Hull, to reopen the channels of international trade. The rest of the platform of 1932 seemed to have disappeared, and with it most of the Democratic principles that THE SUN had been advocating for nearly a hundred years.

On September 11 the position of the paper (in which, of course, THE EVENING SUN concurred) was stated in an editorial, the essential parts of which follow:

> Within sixty days the people must make their choice in the Presidential election. It is, therefore, incumbent upon those who undertake to address themselves to public opinion to give expression to their views. THE SUN now states that in this campaign it is unable to advocate the reëlection of President Roosevelt.
>
> This statement is made with regret. We remember Mr. Roosevelt's courage in the black days of March, 1933. We respect his devotion to the cause of the unfortunate. We believe he has created in many citizens a new sense of civic duty. We admire him for the enemies he has made among pirates of high finance. Standing at the crossroads and looking back over three years, memories of gallantry arise in the mind and make criticism an unpleasant task. But we cannot close our eyes to what we conceive to have been fundamental errors in Mr. Roosevelt's policies.
>
> In April, 1933, Mr. Roosevelt began to turn away from the spirit, and to a large extent the letter, of his platform and from the spirit of his first acts as President. He inaugurated the New Deal and he based it upon vaguely formed and superficially considered ideas of planned economy. These ideas were directed toward nationalistic limitation of economic life and toward overriding Federal control of economic life within this nation. THE SUN was definitely opposed to the concept and to the details. . . .

The Sun stands for competitive capitalism. It is the system which most effectively uproots the unfit, the unworthy, the lazy. It is the system which gives place to the vigorous, the competent, the purposeful. It is the system which constantly provides room for originality and thereby constantly enlarges achievement. It is the system which carries technological advance to its rational conclusion of lower prices and increased mass consumption. Even as distorted in recent periods, it has produced in this country a degree of well-being which has never been equaled, and in that well-being all classes of men have shared. In the worst of depressions, our store of resources has been such that we have been able to extend relief on a scale probably without precedent.

This system is not inconsistent with social responsibility. On the contrary, we have set the pace for the world in public education and in philanthropy. Within this system modern instruments for the relief of the unfortunate and the handicapped have been established and can be expanded. Within this system labor may organize and exercise its rights to bargain collectively. Progressively wise distribution of wealth need not be an insoluble problem, if we but persist in the policy which produces an abundant store of wealth to distribute among the people.

This system of competition is, moreover, the protection of political liberty. It is the best protection for the ordinary citizen, the working man. In 1933 The Sun contended that planned economy could not be effectual without such control over individuals as would negative liberty. It was not long before NRA made that fact apparent. Further proof is piled up each day in the planned economies, of the Right and of the Left, in Europe. When government controls one's property, government controls one's vote. It is the economic freedom of competition which guards political freedom. It is the economic freedom of competition which gives the ordinary man his best defense against coercion. . . .

But the *Sunpapers'* inability to support Mr. Roosevelt was by no means a sign, of course, that it was in accord with Mr. Landon. At the time the editorial was printed, in fact, he had not yet disclosed his main ideas, and there was little in his party platform to indicate which way he would go. Hamilton Owens, editor of THE EVENING SUN, had gone to Topeka in July to ascertain his position on the principal questions at issue in the campaign, and John W. Owens, editor of THE SUN, had joined him on one of his speaking tours for the same purpose, but he had not yet set forth his programme in anything approaching fullness. "Where," asked THE SUN on September 11, "does he stand? Does he propose merely to take over what is left of the New Deal and to administer it more economically? Does he propose to revert to Hooverism? Or does he stand for genuinely free competition?" In the absence of categorical answers, the *Sunpapers* could only announce a policy of watchful waiting. THE SUN's editorial concluded:

If Governor Landon speaks in clear and bold terms, facing specific problems and taking his stand unequivocally on the side of this true economic liberalism, THE SUN will support him, no matter what his prospects may be. If he does not speak in clear terms, THE SUN intends to continue to fight for ideas that it believes to be sound and in the interest of the people, and will make the best of a situation in which it cannot advocate the election of either candidate.

As the campaign developed, it became increasingly evident that THE SUN would have to take the second of the two courses here outlined. Governor Landon made so many compromises with the New Deal theory that in the end he seemed to be supporting it far more than he was opposing it. On October 30 THE SUN announced that it could no more advocate his election than it could advocate the reëlection of President Roosevelt. Thus it was forced by events to close the campaign as a sort of neutral. But it continued, and continues, to argue for all the ideas that have been fundamental articles of its credo for almost a century.

INDEX

A NOTE ON THE TYPE IN WHICH THIS BOOK IS SET

This book is composed (on the linotype), in Scotch. There is a divergence of opinion regarding the exact origin of this face, some authorities holding that it was first cut by Alexander Wilson & Son, of Glasgow, in 1837; others trace it back to a modernized Caslon old style brought out by Mrs. Henry Caslon in 1796 to meet the demand for modern faces resulting from the popularity of the Bodoni types. Whatever its origin, it is certain that the face was widely used in Scotland, where it was called Modern Roman, and since its introduction into America it has been known as Scotch. The essential characteristics of the Scotch face are its sturdy capitals, its full rounded lower case, the graceful fillet of its serifs, and the general effect of crispness.

THIS BOOK HAS BEEN DESIGNED BY
W. A. DWIGGINS AND MANUFAC-
TURED BY THE PLIMPTON
PRESS, NORWOOD, MASS.
PAPER MADE BY S. D.
WARREN CO.,
BOSTON